The Princeton Review®

D0756804

AP® ENGLISH LITERATURE & COMPOSITION PREP

2023 Edition

The Staff of The Princeton Review

PrincetonReview.com

Penguin
Random
House

The Princeton Review
110 East 42nd St, 7th Floor
New York, NY 10017

Copyright © 2022 by TPR Education IP Holdings, LLC. All rights reserved.

Published in the United States by Penguin Random House LLC, New York, and in Canada by Random House of Canada, a division of Penguin Random House Ltd., Toronto.

Terms of Service: The Princeton Review Online Companion Tools ("Student Tools") for retail books are available for only the two most recent editions of that book. Student Tools may be activated only once per eligible book purchased for a total of 24 months of access. Activation of Student Tools more than once per book is in direct violation of these Terms of Service and may result in discontinuation of access to Student Tools Services.

ISBN: 978-0-593-45077-2
eBook ISBN: 978-0-593-45110-6
ISSN: 2690-5388

AP is a trademark registered and owned by the College Board, which is not affiliated with, and does not endorse, this product.

The Princeton Review is not affiliated with Princeton University.

The material in this book is up-to-date at the time of publication. However, changes may have been instituted by the testing body in the test after this book was published.

If there are any important late-breaking developments, changes, or corrections to the materials in this book, we will post that information online in the Student Tools. Register your book and check your Student Tools to see if there are any updates posted there.

Editor: Selena Coppock
Production Editors: Lee Elder, Nina Mozes
Production Artist: Tanya Chernyak
Content Developer: Tracey Starin

Printed in the United States of America.

10 9 8 7 6 5 4 3 2 1

2023 Edition

The Princeton Review Publishing Team

Rob Franek, Editor-in-Chief
David Soto, Senior Director, Data Operations
Stephen Koch, Senior Manager, Data Operations
Deborah Weber, Director of Production
Jason Ullmeyer, Production Design Manager
Jennifer Chapman, Senior Production Artist
Selena Coppock, Director of Editorial
Aaron Riccio, Senior Editor
Meave Shelton, Senior Editor
Chris Chimera, Editor
Orion McBean, Editor
Patricia Murphy, Editor
Laura Rose, Editor
Alexa Schmitt Bugler, Editorial Assistant

Penguin Random House Publishing Team

Tom Russell, VP, Publisher
Alison Stoltzfus, Senior Director, Publishing
Brett Wright, Senior Editor
Emily Hoffman, Assistant Managing Editor
Ellen Reed, Production Manager
Suzanne Lee, Designer
Eugenia Lo, Publishing Assistant

For customer service, please contact **editorialsupport@review.com**, and be sure to include:

- full title of the book
- ISBN
- page number

Acknowledgments

The Editor of this book would like to thank content developer Tracey Starin for her fantastic work on the revision of this book. Her hard work and care in creating the newest practice test has improved this book immeasurably.

Permissions

Permission has been granted to reprint portions of the following:

–Excerpt(s) from THE NIGHT CIRCUS by Erin Morgenstern, Copyright © 2011 by Night Circus, LLC. Used by permission of Doubleday, an imprint of the Knopf Doubleday Publishing Group, a division of Penguin Random House LLC. All rights reserved.

–"In My Craft or Sullen Art" from The Poems of Dylan Thomas by Dylan Thomas. Copyright © 1952 by Dylan Thomas. Used by permission of David Higham Associates, London, as agents for the Trustees of Copyrights of Dylan Thomas.

–"February" from Morning In The Burned House by Margaret Atwood. Copyright © 1995 by Margaret Atwood. Reprinted by permission of Houghton Mifflin Harcourt Publishing Company. All rights reserved.

–"Advice to a Prophet" from Collected Poems 1943-2004 by Richard Wilbur. Copyright © 2004 by Richard Wilbur. Reprinted by permission of Houghton Mifflin Harcourt Publishing Company. All rights reserved.

–Excerpt from Libra by Don DeLillo. Copyright © 1988 by Don DeLillo. Used by permission of Viking Books, an imprint of Penguin Publishing Group, a division of Penguin Random House LLC; Penguin Canada, a division of Penguin Random House Canada Limited; and Penguin Books Ltd., a division of Penguin UK.

–Excerpt(s) from White Teeth: A Novel by Zadie Smith, Copyright © 2000 by Zadie Smith. Used by permission of Random House, an imprint and division of Penguin Random House LLC. All rights reserved.

–Excerpt from Ultramarine by Malcolm Lowry. Copyright © 1962 by Margerie Bonner Lowry. Published in 2005 by The Overlook Press, Peter Mayer Publishers, Inc. New York, NY. www.overlookpress.com. All rights reserved.

–"Paterson" by William Carlos Williams, from PATERSON, Copyright © 1946, 1948,1949,1951,1958 by William Carlos Williams. Reprinted by permission of New Directions Publishing Corp.

–"The White Lilies" by Louise Gluck from The Wild Iris (1992, Ecco). Reprinted with kind permission of HarperCollins and Carcanet Press, Manchester, UK.

Contents

Once you've registered, you can...

- Access your 5th AP English Literature & Composition practice test (there are 4 right here in your book and 1 online), plus an answer key and complete answers and explanations

- Find any late-breaking information released about the AP English Literature and Composition Exam

- Take a full-length practice SAT and ACT

- Gel valuable advice about the college application process, including tips for writing a great essay and where to apply for financial aid

- Access comprehensive study guides and a variety of printable resources, including bubble sheets for the practice tests in the book, AP Score Conversion charts, and a glossary of need-to-know literary terms

- Check to see whether there have been any corrections or updates to this edition

Need to report a potential **content** issue?

Contact **EditorialSupport@review.com** and include:

- full title of the book
- ISBN
- page number

Need to report a **technical** issue?

Contact **TPRStudentTech@review.com** and provide:

- your full name
- email address used to register the book
- full book title and ISBN
- Operating system (Mac/PC) and browser (Chrome, Firefox, Safari, etc.)

Look For These Icons Throughout The Book

 ONLINE ARTICLES

 GOING DEEPER

 PROVEN TECHNIQUES

 APPLIED STRATEGIES

 TIME-SAVING TIP

 STUDY BREAK

 OTHER REFERENCES

CONSIDERING AN AP PREP COURSE?

Pick the Option That's Right For You

AP 5 GUARANTEE TUTORING

OUR MOST POPULAR!

Score a 5 on your AP exam, guaranteed, or your money back.*

- 24 hours of 1:1 LiveOnline instruction
- Elite AP instructors
- Practice questions, practice tests, score report by category

AP 4 GUARANTEE COURSE

Score a 4 on your AP exam, guaranteed, or your money back.*

- 24 hours of LiveOnline classroom instruction
- Elite AP instructors
- Practice questions, practice tests, score report by category

CRAM COURSES

SHORT ON TIME?

- 6 hours of LiveOnline classroom instruction
- Elite AP instructors
- #1 Best Selling AP book

www.PrincetonReview.com | 1-800-2-REVIEW

* For full details, please visit princetonreview.com/legal/guarantee.

Part I
Using This
Book to Improve
Your AP Score

- Preview: Your Knowledge, Your Expectations
- Your Guide to Using This Book
- How to Begin

PREVIEW: YOUR KNOWLEDGE, YOUR EXPECTATIONS

Your route to a high score on the AP English Literature and Composition Exam depends a lot on how you plan to use this book. Respond to the following questions.

1. Rate your level of confidence about your knowledge of the content tested by the AP English Literature and Composition Exam:

    A. Very confident—I know it all
    B. I'm pretty confident, but there are topics for which I could use help
    C. Not confident—I need quite a bit of support
    D. I'm not sure

2. Circle your goal score for the Exam:

    5   4   3   2   1   I'm not sure yet

3. What do you expect to learn from this book? Circle all that apply to you.

    A. A general overview of the test and what to expect
    B. Strategies for how to approach the test
    C. The content tested by this exam
    D. I'm not sure yet

YOUR GUIDE TO USING THIS BOOK

This book is organized to provide as much—or as little—support as you need, so you can use this book in whatever way will be most helpful to improving your score on the AP English Literature and Composition Exam.

*   The remainder of **Part I** will provide guidance on how to use this book and help you determine your strengths and weaknesses.

*   **Part II** of this book contains Practice Test 1, along with its answers and explanations. (Bubble sheets can be found in the very back of the book for easy tear-out.) We strongly recommend that you take this test before going any further, in order to realistically determine
    o   your starting point right now
    o   which question types you're ready for and which you might need to practice
    o   which content topics you are familiar with and which you should carefully review

    Once you have nailed down your strengths and weaknesses with regard to this exam, you can focus your preparation, build a study plan, and be efficient with your time.

Need Another Bubble Sheet?

Bubble sheets can be found in the back of this book for easy tear-out, but if for some reason you need more, you can print them from your online Student Tools.

- **Part III** of this book will
  - provide information about the structure, scoring, and content of the exam, including the latest updates that were recently announced by the College Board
  - help you to make a study plan
  - point you toward additional resources

- **Part IV** of this book will explore various strategies, such as
  - how to attack multiple-choice questions
  - how to write effective essays
  - how to manage your time to maximize the number of points available to you

- **Part V** of this book covers the content you need to review and practice for the AP English Literature and Composition Exam.

- **Part VI** of this book contains Practice Tests 2, 3, and 4 and their respective answers and explanations. We recommend that you take advantage of all 5 Practice Tests (one lives online). But don't take them all in a row—take them as you progress through your prep. Take Practice Test 1 (in the front of this book) first—before you even start any review—and see where you are and what areas you should focus on. Consider it a diagnostic. Then dive into prep and after a few weeks (or days, depending on your timeline), take Practice Test 2. See what subjects and test areas are still challenging for you. Take Practice Tests 3 and 4 in a similar way, after a few more weeks. Then close to your real test day, take Practice Test 5.

- The final section of the book, **Part VII,** is a glossary covering all the literary terms you need to know for the exam.

You may choose to use some parts of this book over others, or you may work through the entire book. Your approach will depend on your needs and how much time you have. Let's take a look at how you will make this determination.

Room to Write
On the actual test, you will be given space along with the bubble sheet to record your answers for each free-response question. You should use scrap paper for the free-responses on the practice tests found within this book and online. After you've gotten a hang of the timing, be aware of how much space each response is taking up, in case you need to write in smaller print or use fewer words on the test.

HOW TO BEGIN

1. **Take Practice Test 1**
   Before you can decide how to use this book, you need to take a practice test. Doing so will give you insight into your strengths and weaknesses, and the test will also help you make an effective study plan. If you're feeling test-phobic, remind yourself that a practice test is a tool for diagnosing yourself—it's not how well you do that matters, but how you use the information gleaned from your performance to guide your preparation.

   So, before you read further, take Practice Test 1, which is found in Part II of this book. Be sure to do so in one sitting, following the instructions that appear before the test.

2. **Check Your Answers**
   Using the answer key on page 26 count the number of multiple-choice questions you got right and the number you missed. Don't worry about the explanations for now, and don't worry about why you missed questions. We'll get to that soon.

3. **Reflect on the Test**
   Now that you've taken your first test, respond to the following questions:

   - How much time did you spend on the multiple-choice questions?

   - How much time did you spend on each essay?

   - How many multiple-choice questions did you miss?

   - Do you feel you had the knowledge to address the subject matter of the essays?

   - Do you feel you wrote well-organized, thoughtful essays?

4. **Read Part III of this Book and Complete the Self-Evaluation**
   Part III provides information on test content areas, structure, and scoring.

   As you read Part III, reevaluate your answers to the questions above. At the end of Part III, you will revisit and refine the questions. You will then be able to make a study plan, based on your needs and time available, that allows you to use this book most effectively.

5. **Engage with Parts IV and V as Needed**
   Notice the word *engage*. You'll get more out of this book if you use it intentionally than if you read it passively and hope for an improved score through osmosis.

The strategy chapters in Part IV will help you think about your approach to the question types on this exam. This part opens with a reminder to think about how you approach questions now and closes with a reflection section asking you to think about how/whether you will change your approach in the future.

The content chapters in Part V provide a review of the content tested on the AP English Literature and Composition Test, including the level of detail you need to know and how the content is tested.

6. **Take Practice Tests 2, 3, 4 and later, 5, and Assess Your Performance**
Once you feel you have developed the strategies you need and gained the knowledge you lacked, you should take Practice Test 2, which is found in Part VI of this book. You should do so in one sitting, following the instructions at the beginning of the test.

When you are done, check your answers to the multiple-choice questions. See whether a teacher will read your responses to the free-response questions and provide feedback.

Once you have taken the test, reflect on what areas you still need to work on, and revisit the chapters in this book that address those deficiencies. Through this type of reflection and engagement, you will continue to improve.

Repeat this for Practice Tests 3, 4, and 5.

7. **Keep Working**
There are other resources available to you, including a wealth of information on APStudents.org. You can continue to explore areas that can stand to improve and engage in those areas right up to the day of the test. Visit the following page for exam practice and information: https://apstudents.collegeboard.org/courscs/ap-english-literature-and-composition

Looking to Guarantee a 4 or 5?
We now offer one-on-one tutoring for a guaranteed 5 or an online course for a guaranteed 4 on the AP English Lit and Comp exam. For information on rates, availability, and to learn more about the guarantee, visit PrincetonReview. com/college/ap-test-prep

Part II
Practice Test 1

Practice Test 1

The Exam

AP® English Literature and Composition Exam

SECTION I: Multiple-Choice Questions

DO NOT OPEN THIS BOOKLET UNTIL YOU ARE TOLD TO DO SO.

At a Glance

Total Time
1 hour
Number of Questions
55
Percent of Total Grade
45%
Writing Instrument
Pencil required

Instructions

Section I of this examination contains 55 multiple-choice questions. Fill in only the ovals for numbers 1 through 55 on your answer sheet.

Indicate all of your answers to the multiple-choice questions on the answer sheet. No credit will be given for anything written in this exam booklet, but you may use the booklet for notes or scratch work. After you have decided which of the suggested answers is best, completely fill in the corresponding oval on the answer sheet. Give only one answer to each question. If you change an answer, be sure that the previous mark is erased completely. Here is a sample question and answer.

Sample Question   Sample Answer

Chicago is a   Ⓐ ● Ⓒ Ⓓ Ⓔ
(A) state
(B) city
(C) country
(D) continent
(E) village

Use your time effectively, working as quickly as you can without losing accuracy. Do not spend too much time on any one question. Go on to other questions and come back to the ones you have not answered if you have time. It is not expected that everyone will know the answers to all the multiple-choice questions.

About Guessing

Many candidates wonder whether or not to guess the answers to questions about which they are not certain. Multiple-choice scores are based on the number of questions answered correctly. Points are not deducted for incorrect answers, and no points are awarded for unanswered questions. Because points are not deducted for incorrect answers, you are encouraged to answer all multiple-choice questions. On any questions you do not know the answer to, you should eliminate as many choices as you can, and then select the best answer among the remaining choices.

GO ON TO THE NEXT PAGE.

ENGLISH LITERATURE AND COMPOSITION

SECTION I

Time—1 hour

<u>Directions:</u> This section consists of selections from literary works and questions on their content, form, and style. After reading each passage or poem, choose the best answer to each question and then completely fill in the corresponding oval on the answer sheet.

<u>Questions 1–13.</u> Choose your answers to questions 1–13 based on a careful reading of the following poem by Phillis Wheatley.

On Imagination

Thy various works, imperial queen, we see,
　How bright their forms! how deck'd with pomp by thee!
Thy wond'rous acts in beauteous order stand,
And all attest how potent is thine hand.
Line
(5)　From Helicon's refulgent heights attend,
Ye sacred choir, and my attempts befriend:
To tell her glories with a faithful tongue,
Ye blooming graces, triumph in my song.

　Now here, now there, the roving Fancy flies,
(10)　Till some lov'd object strikes her wand'ring eyes,
Whose silken fetters all the senses bind,
And soft captivity involves the mind.

　Imagination! who can sing thy force?
Or who describe the swiftness of thy course?
(15)　Soaring through air to find the bright abode,
Th' empyreal palace of the thund'ring God,
We on thy pinions can surpass the wind,
And leave the rolling universe behind:
From star to star the mental optics rove,
(20)　Measure the skies, and range the realms above.
There in one view we grasp the mighty whole,
Or with new worlds amaze th' unbounded soul.

　Though Winter frowns to Fancy's raptur'd eyes
The fields may flourish, and gay scenes arise;
(25)　The frozen deeps may break their iron bands,
And bid their waters murmur o'er the sands.
Fair Flora may resume her fragrant reign,
And with her flow'ry riches deck the plain;
Sylvanus may diffuse his honours round,
(30)　And all the forest may with leaves be crown'd:
Show'rs may descend, and dews their gems disclose,
And nectar sparkle on the blooming rose.

　Such is thy pow'r, nor are thine orders vain,
O thou the leader of the mental train:
(35)　In full perfection all thy works are wrought,
And thine the sceptre o'er the realms of thought.
Before thy throne the subject-passions bow,

Of subject-passions sov'reign ruler thou;
At thy command joy rushes on the heart,
(40)　And through the glowing veins the spirits dart.

　Fancy might now her silken pinions try
To rise from earth, and sweep th' expanse on high:
From Tithon's bed now might Aurora rise,
Her cheeks all glowing with celestial dies,
(45)　While a pure stream of light o'erflows the skies.
The monarch of the day I might behold,
And all the mountains tipt with radiant gold,
But I reluctant leave the pleasing views,
Which Fancy dresses to delight the Muse;
(50)　Winter austere forbids me to aspire,
And northern tempests damp the rising fire;
They chill the tides of Fancy's flowing sea,
Cease then, my song, cease the unequal lay.

1. Who does "thy" refer to in line 1 ("Thy various works, imperial queen, we see,")?

　(A)　Imagination
　(B)　Winter
　(C)　Aurora
　(D)　the reader
　(E)　Fancy

2. Line 13 ("Imagination! who can sing thy force?") is an example of

　(A)　synecdoche
　(B)　simile
　(C)　personification
　(D)　imagery
　(E)　hyperbole

3. What is the speaker trying to convey with lines 17–22 ("We on they pinions...we grasp...the unbounded soul.")?

　(A)　Reality is more valuable than Imagination.
　(B)　Imagination lets us leave unhappiness behind.
　(C)　Imagination prevents us from being reasonable.
　(D)　Imagination allows us to grasp possibilities outside the self.
　(E)　Imagination is limited to what's in our view.

GO ON TO THE NEXT PAGE.

4. In line 26, "murmur" is an example of

   (A) onomatopoeia
   (B) euphemism
   (C) alliteration
   (D) anaphora
   (E) oxymoron

5. What is the tone of the poem as a whole?

   (A) Curious then regretful
   (B) Whimsical then melancholy
   (C) Skeptical then frightened
   (D) Delighted then exasperated
   (E) Grateful then angry

6. What change occurs from stanza 4 to stanza 7?

   (A) Imagination, yearning to grasp possibilities beyond
       the self, is set free.
   (B) Imagination, uncertain, retreats back to reality.
   (C) Imagination joins Winter to celebrate the rising sun
       and the golden mountains.
   (D) Imagination is grounded by reality, no longer free
       to wander.
   (E) Imagination battles winter for mastery over the
       realms of passion and thought.

7. What can the reader infer from lines 52–53 ("They chill
   the tides of Fancy's flowing sea, Cease then, my song,
   cease the unequal lay.")?

   (A) Imagination is Fancy's most powerful tool.
   (B) Reality is ultimately more powerful than
       imagination.
   (C) The fight between imagination and reality is eternal
   (D) Reality is unjust.
   (E) The speaker no longer has faith in Imagination.

8. What can the reader infer Winter is doing to the speaker?

   (A) Setting her free
   (B) Raising her to the mountain top
   (C) Grounding her
   (D) Punishing her
   (E) Celebrating her

9. In what style is *On Imagination* written?

   (A) Free verse
   (B) Rhyming couplets
   (C) Haiku
   (D) Elegy
   (E) Ballad

10. In lines 11–12, what does "Whose silken feathers...
    involves the mind" imply in context?

    (A) Love only exists in Fancy's imagination
    (B) Falling in love is painful
    (C) Fancy is lost without love
    (D) Without Imagination love is not possible
    (E) Fancy is bound by love

11. The speaker's primary purpose is most nearly to

    (A) contemplate creativity
    (B) express fear
    (C) declare love
    (D) celebrate freedom
    (E) question reality

12. What can the reader infer from lines 34-36 ("O thou
    the leader...And thine the sceptre o'er the realms of
    thought.")?

    (A) Imagination controls the mind.
    (B) Imagination demands perfection.
    (C) Imagination fosters creativity and free thought.
    (D) Imagination hampers creativity.
    (E) Imagination is mythical.

13. The poem as a whole can be understood as

    (A) a pastoral about an artist
    (B) a sonnet about the strength of the mind
    (C) a ballad the importance of creativity
    (D) free verse about the power of love
    (E) an allegory about enslaved people

GO ON TO THE NEXT PAGE.

Questions 14–25. Read the following passage carefully before choosing your answers. The selection is an excerpt from the short story *Drenched in Light* by Zora Neale Hurston.

Isis saw no longer any reason to die. She came up out of the water, holding up the dripping fringe of the tablecloth.

"Naw indeedy. You go to Maitlan' by the shell road — it
Line goes by mah house — an' turn off at Lake Sebelia to the clay
(5) road that takes you right to the do'."

"Well," went on the driver, smiling furtively, "Could you quit dying long enough to go with us?"

"Yessuh," she said thoughtfully, "Ah wanta go wid you."
The door of the car swung open. She was invited to a
(10) seat beside the driver. She had often dreamed of riding in one of these heavenly chariots but never thought she would, actually.

"Jump in then, Madame Tagedy, and show us. We lost ourselves after we left your barbecue."
(15) During the drive Isis explained to the nice lady who smelt faintly of violets and to the indifferent men that she was really a princess. She told them about her trips to the horizon, about the trailing gowns, the gold shoes with blue bottoms — she insisted on the blue bottoms — the white charger,
(20) the time when she was Hercules and had slain numerous dragons and sundry giants. At last the car approached her gate over which stood the umbrella China-berry tree. The car was abreast of the gate and had all but passed when Grandma spied her glorious tablecloth lying back against the
(25) upholstery of the Packard.

"You Isie - e!" she bawled. "You lil' wretch you! come heah dis instant."

"That's me," the child confessed, mortified, to the lady on the rear seat.
(30) "Oh, Sewell, stop the car. This is where the child lives. I hate to give her up though."

"Do you wanta keep me?" Isis brightened.

"Oh, I wish I could, you shining little morsel. Wait, I'll try to save you a whipping this time."
(35) She dismounted with the gaudy lemon flavored culprit and advanced to the gate where Grandma stood glowering, switches in hand.

"You're gointuh ketchit f'um yo' haid to yo' heels m'lady. Jes' come in heah."
(40) "Why, good afteroon," she accosted the furious grandparent. "You're not going to whip this poor little thing, are you?" the lady asked in conciliatory tones.

"Yes, Ma'am. She's de wustest lil' limb dat ever drawed bref. Jes' look at mah new table cloth, dat ain't never been
(45) washed. She done traipsed all over de woods, uh dancin' an' uh' prancin' in it. She done took a razor to me t'day an' Lawd knows whut mo'."

Isis clung to the white hand fearfully.

"Ah wuzn't gointer hurt Gran'ma, miss — Ah wuz jus'
(50) gointer shave her whiskers fuh huh 'cause she's old an' can't."

The white hand closed tightly over the little brown one that was quite soiled. She could understand a voluntary act of love even though it miscarried.
(55) "Now, Mrs. er—er— I didn't get the name— how much did your tablecloth cost?"

"One whole big silvah dollar down at O'landah — ain't had it a week yit."

"Now here's five dollars to get another one. The little
(60) thing loves laughter. I want her to go on to the hotel and dance in that tablecloth for me. I can stand a little light today —"

"Oh, yessum, yessum," Grandma cut in, "Everything's alright, sho' she kin go, yessum."
(65) The lady went on: "I want brightness and this Isis is joy itself, why she's drenched in light!"

Isis for the first time in her life, felt herself appreciated and danced up and down in an ecstasy of joy for a minute.

"Now, behave yo'seff, Isie, ovah at de hotel wid de folks,"
(70) Grandma cautioned, pride in her voice, though she strove to hide it. "Lawd, ma'am, dat gal keeps me so frackshus, Ah doan know mah haid from mah feet. I orter comb huh haid, too, befo' she go wid you all."

"No, no, don't bother. I like her as she is. I don't think
(75) she'd like it either, being combed and scrubbed. Come on, Isis."

Feeling that Grandma had been somewhat squelched did not detract from Isis' spirit at all. She pranced over to the waiting motor and this time seated herself on the rear seat
(80) between the sweet, smiling lady and the rather aloof man in gray.

"Ah'm gointer stay wid you all," she said with a great deal of warmth, and snuggled up to her benefactress. "Want me tuh sing a song fuh you?"
(85) "There, Hen, you've been adopted," said the man with a short, harsh laugh.

"Oh, I hope so, Harry." She put her arm about the red draped figure at her side and drew it closer until she felt the warm puffs of the child's breath against her side. She looked
(90) hungrily ahead of her and spoke into space rather than to anyone in the car. "I want a little of her sunshine to soak into my soul. I need it."

14. How is the character of Helen, the white woman, portrayed?

   (A) Generous and caring
   (B) Self-centered and greedy
   (C) Underhanded and devious
   (D) Apathetic and unmoved
   (E) Clueless and gleeful

GO ON TO THE NEXT PAGE.

15. How would you characterize the relationship between Isis and Helen, the white woman?

    (A) Parent and child
    (B) Teacher and student
    (C) Benefactor and artist
    (D) Savior and pauper
    (E) Regent and subject

16. The tone of the passage as a whole can best be described as

    (A) comedic
    (B) foreboding
    (C) sad
    (D) hopeful
    (E) threatening

17. What is the reader to infer the horizon represents from lines 17–19, "She told them about her trips to the horizon, about the trailing gowns, the gold shoes with the blue bottoms..."?

    (A) The setting sun
    (B) Places Isis has traveled
    (C) Isis' desire to explore
    (D) Isis' future
    (E) The hotel Isis is going to visit with the white people

18. In line 71, what does "frackshus" most nearly mean in context?

    (A) Exhausted
    (B) Angry
    (C) Happy
    (D) Breathless
    (E) Irritable

19. What is the author trying to convey in lines 65–66, "I want brightness and this Isis is joy itself, why she's drenched in light!"?

    (A) Wealthy people do not have happy lives
    (B) Happiness is not relative to wealth
    (C) Money buys happiness
    (D) Isis had supernatural powers
    (E) Helen was very self-centered

20. "Isis is joy itself" is an example of

    (A) simile
    (B) synecdoche
    (C) metaphor
    (D) hyperbole
    (E) imagery

21. What is the author most nearly trying to convey in lines 60–61, "I want her to go on to the hotel and dance in that tablecloth for me. I can stand a little light today —" ?

    (A) Poverty is a pitiable condition, and charity is necessary to remedy it
    (B) Wealth and social status are very important to artistic expression
    (C) Artistic expression is dependent upon having an appreciative audience
    (D) Black cultural expression is as valuable as more regimented forms of art practiced by white society
    (E) The upper class decides what forms of artistic expression are most valuable

22. How would you describe the change in Grandma's character after her encounter with Helen?

    (A) Belligerent then placated
    (B) Suspicious then fearful
    (C) Frustrated then concerned
    (D) Disgruntled then apathetic
    (E) Caustic then proud

23. What is the author most nearly conveying by having Grandma & Isis speak in the Black vernacular?

    (A) To illustrate the difference between written language and spoken language
    (B) To highlight moments of excitement or enthusiasm
    (C) That what Grandma and Isis say is of little value
    (D) That Isis could learn a lot from Helen
    (E) That the South has a rich and nuanced culture of its own

24. Why does Helen give Grandma $5?

    (A) So she can buy 5 tablecloths to replace her ruined tablecloth
    (B) For giving her directions
    (C) To mollify her rage so she would allow Isis accompany Helen to the hotel
    (D) To impress her, and gain her admiration
    (E) As an act of charity because Grandma lives in poverty

25. The passage as a whole can best be understood as a(n)

    (A) commentary on race relations in the South
    (B) allegory about the Harlem renaissance
    (C) fable about friendship
    (D) story about self-confidence
    (E) anecdote about creativity

GO ON TO THE NEXT PAGE.

Questions 26–33. Choose your answers to each of the following questions based on careful reading of the following poem by Alice Walker.

Wherever You Are Grieving

It does not matter to me:

wherever you are grieving
whether Paris, Damascus, Jerusalem, Bamako
Line   Mexico or Beirut or New York City
(5)   my heart, too, is bruised
and dragging,
There used to be such a thing
as melodrama
when feelings could be
(10)   made up,
but now there is bare pain
and sorrow,
a sense of endlessly missed
opportunities
(15)   to smile and embrace
"The other."
We mourn the loss
of goodness
that was so divinely
(20)   ordinary:
babyhood
youth
the blessings of maturity
and of old age.
(25)   All sacrificed now
almost predictably
to the same Greed
our histories
—every one of them—
(30)   could have warned us against
if only we knew them.

26. How does the speaker feel about grief?

    (A)   sad then hopeful
    (B)   vengeful then calm
    (C)   angry then reflective
    (D)   hopeless then contemplative
    (E)   curious then angry

27. What is the author most nearly trying to convey in lines 3–4, "whether Paris, Damascus…or New York City"?

    (A)   Grieving is universal; we have all lost something
    (B)   There is unrest in those places that make them dangerous
    (C)   Those are places she has been, and grieved over something lost
    (D)   You cannot escape tragedy
    (E)   The world is a sad place

28. In lines 5–6, "My heart, too, is bruised and dragging" is an example of

    (A)   simile
    (B)   metaphor
    (C)   synecdoche
    (D)   hyperbole
    (E)   metonym

29. The poem as a whole can best be understood as

    (A)   a rhapsody about morality
    (B)   a ballad about lost love
    (C)   a sonnet about heartbreak
    (D)   an elegy about suffering
    (E)   an ode to travel

30. In lines 30–31, "Our histories—every one of them— could have warned us against if only we knew them" is an example of

    (A)   alliteration
    (B)   paradox
    (C)   euphemism
    (D)   allusion
    (E)   personification

GO ON TO THE NEXT PAGE.

31. What can the reader infer from lines 25–27, "All sacrificed now almost predictably to the same Greed"?

    (A) Money is responsible for grief
    (B) The relentless pursuit of wealth has consequences that routinely cause suffering
    (C) We know in advance when we will have to sacrifice
    (D) We have suffered the losses of many because of the actions of a few
    (E) Sacrifice has become routine and mundane

32. What was the author conveying in lines 28–31, "Our histories...if only we knew them"?

    (A) We are helpless in our suffering
    (B) We are lost in our grief, overwhelmed by our suffering
    (C) Because we do not process past suffering, the past is destined to repeat itself
    (D) Our grief keeps us from understanding our own histories
    (E) If we knew our histories, we would not have to suffer

33. The author's purpose with this poem is most nearly to

    (A) vent anger
    (B) express bitterness
    (C) mourn many losses
    (D) provide support to the suffering
    (E) bid farewell to the world

GO ON TO THE NEXT PAGE.

Questions 34–45. Choose your answers to each of the following questions based on careful reading of the following excerpt from a short story by Edgar Allan Poe.

The "Red Death" had long devastated the country. No pestilence had ever been so fatal, or so hideous. Blood was its Avatar and its seal - the redness and the horror of blood.
Line There were sharp pains, and sudden dizziness, and then
(5) profuse bleeding at the pores, with dissolution. The scarlet stains upon the body and especially upon the face of the victim, were the pest ban which shut him out from the aid and from the sympathy of his fellow-men. And the whole seizure, progress and termination of the disease, were the
(10) incidents of half an hour.

But the Prince Prospero was happy and dauntless and sagacious. When his dominions were half depopulated, he summoned to his presence a thousand hale and light-hearted friends from among the knights and dames of his court,
(15) and with these retired to the deep seclusion of one of his castellated abbeys. This was an extensive and magnificent structure, the creation of the prince's own eccentric yet august taste. A strong and lofty wall girdled it in. This wall had gates of iron. The courtiers, having entered, brought
(20) furnaces and massy hammers and welded the bolts. They resolved to leave means neither of ingress or egress to the sudden impulses of despair or of frenzy from within. The abbey was amply provisioned. With such precautions the courtiers might bid defiance to contagion. The external world
(25) could take care of itself. In the meantime it was folly to grieve, or to think. The prince had provided all the appliances of pleasure. There were buffoons, there were improvisatori, there were ballet-dancers, there were musicians, there was Beauty, there was wine. All these and security were within.
(30) Without was the "Red Death."

It was toward the close of the fifth or sixth month of his seclusion, and while the pestilence raged most furiously abroad, that the Prince Prospero entertained his thousand friends at a masked ball of the most unusual magnificence.
(35) It was a voluptuous scene, that masquerade. But first let me tell of the rooms in which it was held. There were seven - an imperial suite. In many palaces, however, such suites form a long and straight vista, while the folding doors slide back nearly to the walls on either hand, so that the view of
(40) the whole extent is scarcely impeded. Here the case was very different; as might have been expected from the duke's love of the bizarre. The apartments were so irregularly disposed that the vision embraced but little more than one at a time. There was a sharp turn at every twenty or thirty yards, and at
(45) each turn a novel effect. To the right and left, in the middle of each wall, a tall and narrow Gothic window looked out upon a closed corridor which pursued the windings of the suite. These windows were of stained glass whose colour varied in accordance with the prevailing hue of the decorations
(50) of the chamber into which it opened. That at the eastern

extremity was hung, for example, in blue - and vividly blue were its windows. The second chamber was purple in its ornaments and tapestries, and here the panes were purple. The third was green throughout, and so were the casements.
(55) The fourth was furnished and lighted with orange - the fifth with white - the sixth with violet. The seventh apartment was closely shrouded in black velvet tapestries that hung all over the ceiling and down the walls, falling in heavy folds upon a carpet of the same material and hue. But in this chamber
(60) only, the colour of the windows failed to correspond with the decorations. The panes here were scarlet - a deep blood colour. Now in no one of the seven apartments was there any lamp or candelabrum, amid the profusion of golden ornaments that lay scattered to and fro or depended from the
(65) roof. There was no light of any kind emanating from lamp or candle within the suite of chambers. But in the corridors that followed the suite, there stood, opposite to each window, a heavy tripod, bearing a brazier of fire that protected its rays through the tinted glass and so glaringly illumined the room.
(70) And thus were produced a multitude of gaudy and fantastic appearances. But in the western or black chamber the effect of the fire-light that streamed upon the dark hangings through the blood-tinted panes, was ghastly in the extreme, and produced so wild a look upon the countenances of those who
(75) entered, that there were few of the company bold enough to set foot within its precincts at all.

It was in this apartment, also, that there stood against the western wall, a gigantic clock of ebony.

34. In lines 32–34, "the pestilence raged most furiously abroad," is an example of

(A) hyperbole
(B) simile
(C) personification
(D) alliteration
(E) imagery

35. What was the author trying to convey in lines 12–16, "When his dominions were half depopulated, ... castellated abbeys."?

(A) The good health of the aristocracy
(B) The inequality inherent in social stratification
(C) The Prince's strong ties to his court
(D) The security of the castle
(E) The Prince's propensity for problem solving

GO ON TO THE NEXT PAGE.

36. What can the reader infer from lines 24–25, "The external world can take care of itself" in context?

(A) That the Prince and his guests do not care about the rest of the country
(B) That the rest of the country has plenty of resources to care for themselves
(C) The outside world is welcome to join the party in the abbey
(D) Prospero is anxious to help the outside world
(E) The Red Death is not a problem for the outside world

37. What is the tone of the passage as a whole?

(A) Hopeful
(B) Ironic
(C) Satirical
(D) Ominous
(E) Regretful

38. What is the author trying to convey by putting the clock on the western wall of the seventh chamber?

(A) The passage of time in life is inevitable
(B) The guests would not be concerned with the time during the party
(C) Time is precious
(D) Time is not important
(E) Hide your clocks when you throw a party

39. What is the author's purpose in describing The Red Death in detail first, and introducing Prince Prospero second?

(A) To engender sympathy for the victims of The Red Death
(B) To instill fear in the audience
(C) To establish The Red Death as the driving force of the story
(D) To establish Prince Prospero as the driving force of the story
(E) To establish the Red Death as the main character of the story

40. "There were sharp pains…which shut him out from the sympathy of his fellow man" (lines 4–5) is an example of

(A) simile
(B) imagery
(C) metaphor
(D) oxymoron
(E) synecdoche

41. How is the character of Prince Prospero portrayed?

(A) Self-centered and uncaring
(B) Regal and responsible
(C) Stalwart and stable
(D) Generous and charitable
(E) Brave and bold

42. Why do guests avoid the seventh room?

(A) It is a stark reminder of the disease that rages on beyond the castle walls
(B) It is too dark to socialize with other guests
(C) The guests want to avoid seeing the clock
(D) It is too far removed from the rest of the party
(E) The mood of the room did not match the mood of the party

43. If the seventh room, draped in black, is a metaphor for death, what can the reader infer the author was trying to convey about the seven different colored rooms?

(A) They represented the seven days of the week
(B) They represented the seven continents on Earth
(C) They represented the seven colors of the rainbow
(D) They represented the seven deadly sins
(E) They represented the seven stages of life

44. Why is the decor of the seven apartments paradoxical to the purpose of the party?

(A) The rooms were specifically ordered and decorated, while the party was wild and untamed
(B) The ebony clock kept strict time while the guests revel unconcerned
(C) The different color rooms are separated, the diverse guests are celebrating together
(D) The party is to forget mortality. The rooms remind guests of their mortality
(E) The rooms represent the entire color spectrum, while the guests only represent one class of people

45. What is the author trying to convey in lines 61–62, "a deep blood color. Now in no one of the seven apartments…"?

(A) That the room is very dark
(B) The Prince did not want guests in the seventh apartment
(C) Death is inevitable
(D) The Red Death is beyond the castle walls
(E) The lush decor of the room mirrored the extravagance of the guests

GO ON TO THE NEXT PAGE.

Questions 46–55. Choose your answers to each of the following questions based on a careful reading of the following excerpt from a novel by writer Erin Morgenstern.

"Ha!" Hector exclaims, "Then you are willing to play."

The man in the gray suit hesitates only a moment before he nods. "Something a bit more complex than last time, and
Line yes, I may be interested," he says. "Possibly."
(5) "Of course it will be more complex," Hector says. "I have a natural talent to play with. I'm not wagering that for anything simple."

"Natural talent is a questionable phenomenon, inclination perhaps, but innate ability is extremely rare."

(10) "She's my own child, of course she has innate ability."

"You admit she has had lessons," the man in the gray suit says. "How can you be certain?"

"Celia, when did you start your lessons?" Hector asks without looking at her.

(15) "March," she answers.

"What year, dearest?" Hector adds.

"This year," she says, as though this is a particularly stupid question.

"Eight months of lessons," Hector clarifies. "At barely
(20) six years of age. If I recall correctly you sometimes start your own students a bit younger than that. Celia is clearly more advanced than she would be if she did not have natural ability. She could levitate that watch on her first try."

The man in the gray suit turns his attention to Celia.

(25) "You broke that by accident, did you not?" He asks, nodding at the watch, sitting on the table. Celia frowns and gives him the tiniest of nods.

"She has remarkable control for one so young," he remarks to Hector. "But such a temper is always an
(30) unfortunate variable. It can lead to impulsive behavior."

"She'll either grow out of it or learn to control it. It's a minor issue."

The man in the gray suit keeps his eyes on the girl but addresses Hector when he speaks. To Celia's ears, the sounds
(35) no longer resolve into words, and she frowns as her father's responses take on the same muddled quality.

"You would wager your own child?"

"She won't lose," Hector says.

"I suggest you find a student you can tolerate parting with
(40) if you do not already have one to spare."

"I assumed her mother has no opinion on the matter."

"You assume correctly."

The man in the gray suit considers the girl for some time before he speaks again, and still, she does not comprehend
(45) the words.

"I understand your confidence in her ability though I encourage you to at least consider the possibility that she could be lost should the competition not play out in her favor. I will find a player to truly challenge her. Otherwise there is
(50) no reason for me to agree to participate. Her victory cannot be guaranteed."

"That is a risk I am willing to take," Hector says without even glancing at his daughter. "If you would like to make it official here, now go right ahead."

(55) The man in the gray suit looks back at Celia, and when he speaks she understands the words once more. "Very well," he says with a nod.

"He made me not hear right," Celia whispers when her father turns to her.

(60) "I know, dearest, and it wasn't very polite," Hector says as he guides her closer to the chair, where the man scrutinizes her with eyes that are almost as light and gray as his suit. "Have you always been able to do such things?" He asks her looking back at the watch again.

(65) Celia nods.

"My, my mamma said I was the devil's child," she says quietly.

The man in the gray suit leans forward and whispers something in her ear too low for her father to overhear. A
(70) small smile brightens her face.

"Hold out your right hand," he says, leaning back in his chair. Celia immediately puts out her hand palm up unsure of what to expect. But the man in the gray suit does not place anything in her open palm. Instead he turns her hand over
(75) and removes a silver ring from his pinky. He slides it onto her ring finger. Though it is too loose for her slim fingers, keeping his other hand around her wrist. She is opening her mouth to state the obvious fact, that the ring, though very pretty, does not fit, when she realizes that it is shrinking on
(80) her hand. Her momentary glee at the adjustment is crushed by the pain that follows as the ring continues to close around her finger, the metal burning into her skin. She tries to pull away but the man in the gray suit keeps his hand firmly around her wrist. The ring thins and fades, leaving only a
(85) bright red scar around Celia's finger. The man in the gray suit releases her wrist and she steps back, retreating into a corner, and staring at her hand.

"Good girl," her father says.

46. What can the reader infer from the line ""That is a risk I am willing to take," Hector says without even glancing at his daughter" (lines 52–53)?

(A) Hector has faith in Celia's abilities
(B) Hector values Celia's skill more than he values her life
(C) Hector is embarrassed to look Celia in the eye
(D) Hector is trying to impress the man in the gray suit
(E) Celia's lessons will prepare her for the challenge

GO ON TO THE NEXT PAGE.

47. How would you characterize the relationship between Hector and the man in the gray suit?

    (A) Student and teacher
    (B) Old friends
    (C) Rivals
    (D) Colleagues
    (E) Mentor and protégé

48. What can the reader infer from lines 23–26, "She could levitate that watch…nodding at the watch, sitting on the table."?

    (A) Hector was proud of his daughter for her natural ability
    (B) The man in the gray suit was concerned about Celia's lack of control
    (C) Celia's skills were still undeveloped
    (D) Time is a construct of man, and unimportant
    (E) Celia's skills are more powerful than Hector thought

49. What is the author trying to convey in lines 75–82, "He slides it onto her ring finger... the metal burning into her skin."?

    (A) Celia has just been permanently committed to the challenge
    (B) The man in the gray suit is now Celia's instructor
    (C) Celia was being punished for her lack of control
    (D) Celia's magic skills affect anything that touches her
    (E) Celia's magic skills were not as developed as she thought

50. The tone of the passage as a whole can best be described as

    (A) whimsical
    (B) romantic
    (C) melancholy
    (D) foreboding
    (E) nostalgic

51. How is the competition characterized based on lines 29–32, "But such a temper is always an unfortunate variable. It can lead to impulsive behavior." "She'll either grow out of it or learn to control it. It's a minor issue."?

    (A) Order vs chaos
    (B) Power vs love
    (C) Anger vs indifference
    (D) Fear vs confidence
    (E) Concern vs pride

52. What can the reader infer from the contrasting references to the challenge in lines 28–30, "She has remarkable control for one so young" and "It can lead to impulsive behavior"?

    (A) Hector and the man in the gray suit do not understand each other
    (B) Hector and the man in the gray suit do not mean any harm to Celia
    (C) Hector and the man in the gray suit have a callous disregard for the lives of others
    (D) Celia's welfare is of utmost concern to both Hector and the man in the gray suit
    (E) The man in the gray suit is intimidated by Celia's skills

53. Lines 33–34, "The man in the gray suit keeps his eyes on the girl but addresses Hector when he speaks" is an example of

    (A) hyperbole
    (B) synecdoche
    (C) metonymy
    (D) simile
    (E) metaphor

54. What is the author trying to convey in lines 34–36, "To Celia's ears, the sounds no longer resolve into words, and she frowns as her father's responses take on the same muddled quality."?

    (A) Celia was too young to understand what her father and the man in the gray suit were saying
    (B) Hector and the man in the gray suit did not want to scare Celia
    (C) Celia was afraid of her father and the man in the gray suit
    (D) Celia is sad that she does not understand her father and the man in the gray suit
    (E) Celia should not trust Hector and the man in the gray suit

55. What is the narrator's attitude toward Hector?

    (A) Pitying
    (B) Admiring
    (C) Duplicitous
    (D) Condescending
    (E) Apathetic

STOP
END OF SECTION I
IF YOU FINISH BEFORE TIME IS CALLED, YOU MAY CHECK YOUR WORK ON THIS SECTION.
DO NOT GO ON TO SECTION II UNTIL YOU ARE TOLD TO DO SO.

ENGLISH LITERATURE AND COMPOSITION

SECTION II

Total Time—2 hours

Question 1

(Suggested time—40 minutes. This question counts as one-third of the total essay score.)

In the following poem by Margaret Atwood (published in 2019), the narrator guides us, cryptically, through a mysterious photograph. Read the poem carefully. Then, in a well-written essay, analyze how Atwood uses poetic elements and techniques to convey its haunting and mysterious theme.

In your response you should do the following:

- Respond to the prompt with a thesis that presents an interpretation and may establish a line of reasoning.
- Select and use evidence to develop and support your line of reasoning.
- Explain the relationship between the evidence and your thesis.
- Use appropriate grammar and punctuation in communicating your argument.

This Is A Photograph of Me

It was taken some time ago.
At first it seems to be
a smeared
Line print: blurred lines and grey flecks
(5) blended with the paper;
then, as you scan
it, you see in the left-hand corner
a thing that is like a branch: part of a tree
(balsam or spruce) emerging
(10) and, to the right, halfway up
what ought to be a gentle
slope, a small frame house.
In the background there is a lake,
and beyond that, some low hills.
(15) (The photograph was taken
the day after I drowned.
I am in the lake, in the center
of the picture, just under the surface.
It is difficult to say where
(20) precisely, or to say
how large or small I am:
the effect of water
on light is a distortion
but if you look long enough,
(25) eventually
you will be able to see me.)

Question 2

(Suggested time—40 minutes. This question counts as one-third of the total essay score.)

The following excerpt is from the novel *The Poisonwood Bible* (1998) by Barbara Kingsolver. This passage is narrated by Orleanna Price, the matriarch of an American missionary family in the Belgian Congo during a politically turbulent era of the 1960s. Despite the family's best intentions, they suffer many tragedies during their ill-fated mission. Read the passage carefully. Then, in a well-written essay, analyze how Kingsolver uses literary elements and techniques such as imagery and point of view to convey guilt, pride, shame, and responsibility.

In your response you should do the following:

- Respond to the prompt with a thesis that presents an interpretation and may establish a line of reasoning.
- Select and use evidence to develop and support your line of reasoning.
- Explain the relationship between the evidence and your thesis.
- Use appropriate grammar and punctuation in communicating your argument.

The Poisonwood Bible
By Barbara Kingsolver

I know how people are, with their habits of mind. Most
will sail through from cradle to grave with a conscience
clean as snow. It's easy to point at other men, conveniently
Line dead, starting with the ones who first scooped up mud
(5) from riverbanks to catch the scent of a source. Why, Dr,
Livingston, I presume, wasn't he the rascal! He and all the
profiteers who've since walked out on Africa as a husband
quits a wife, leaving her with her naked body curled
around the emptied-out mine of her womb. I know people.
(10) Most have no earthly notion of the price of a snow white
conscience.
I would be no different from the next one, if I hadn't
paid my own little part in blood. I trod on Africa without
a thought, straight from our family's divinely inspired
(15) beginning to our terrible end. In between, in the midst of all
those steaming nights and days darkly colored, smelling of
earth, I believe there lay some marrow of honest instruction.
Sometimes I can nearly say what it was. If I could, I would
fling it at others, I'm afraid, at risk to their ease. I'd slide
(20) this awful story off my shoulders, flatten it, sketch out our
crimes like a failed battle plan and shake it in the faces of
my neighbors, who are wary of me already. But Africa shifts
under my hands, refusing to be party to failed relations.
Refusing to be any place at all, or anything but itself: the
(25) animal kingdom making hay in the kingdom of glory. So
there it is, take your place. Leave nothing for a haunted old
bat to use for disturbing the peace. Nothing, save for this life
of her own.

We aimed for no more than to have dominion over every
(30) creature that moved upon the earth. And so it came to pass
that we stepped down there on a place we believed unformed,
where only darkness moved on the face of the waters. Now
you laugh, day and night, while you gnaw on my bones.
But what else could we have thought? Only that it began
(35) and ended with us. What do we know, even now? Ask the
children. Look at what they grew up to be. We can only
speak of the things we carried with us, and the things we
took away.

GO ON TO THE NEXT PAGE.

Question 3

(Suggested time—40 minutes. This question counts as one-third of the total essay score.)

Food, and eating, is often depicted in literature. Food can be symbolic of wealth, culture, family, tradition, and locale. It can be used as reward, punishment, community, hope, and love. Either from your own reading, or from the list below choose a work of fiction in which characters are affected by food.

In your response you should do the following:

- Respond to the prompt with a thesis that presents an interpretation and may establish a line of reasoning.
- Select and use evidence to develop and support your line of reasoning.
- Explain the relationship between the evidence and your thesis.
- Use appropriate grammar and punctuation in communicating your argument.

Like Water for Chocolate
Babette's Feast
Heartburn
To the Lighthouse
Crazy Rich Asians
Fried Green Tomatoes
Middlesex
Gravity's Rainbow
The Lion, The Witch, and the Wardrobe
The Great Gatsby
Moby Dick
Oliver Twist
Charlie and the Chocolate Factory

STOP
END OF EXAM
IF YOU FINISH BEFORE TIME IS CALLED, YOU MAY CHECK YOUR WORK ON THIS SECTION.

Practice Test 1:
Answers and
Explanations

PRACTICE TEST 1 ANSWER KEY

1.	A	21.	D	41.	A
2.	C	22.	A	42.	A
3.	D	23.	E	43.	E
4.	A	24.	C	44.	D
5.	B	25.	B	45.	C
6.	D	26.	C	46.	B
7.	B	27.	A	47.	C
8.	C	28.	D	48.	D
9.	B	29.	D	49.	A
10.	E	30.	E	50.	D
11.	D	31.	B	51.	A
12.	C	32.	C	52.	E
13.	E	33.	D	53.	B
14.	A	34.	C	54.	E
15.	C	35.	B	55.	C
16.	D	36.	A		
17.	C	37.	D		
18.	E	38.	A		
19.	B	39.	C		
20.	C	40.	B		

PRACTICE TEST EXPLANATIONS

Questions 1–13

Phillis Wheatley spent much of her life enslaved. She was the first African American and second woman (after Anne Bradstreet) to publish a book of poems. Born around 1753 in Gambia, Africa, Wheatley was captured by slave traders and brought to America in 1761. This poem, "On Imagination," was published in Poems on Various Subjects Religious and Moral (1773).

1. **A** "Thy" refers to the personified Imagination. The answer is (A) and not (D). Choices (B), (C), and (E) are not introduced until later in the poem.

2. **C** The answer is (C), personification. Presenting Imagination as a being who possesses force is a great example of personification. Choice (A) is not correct because synecdoche is a figure of speech where a part represents the whole, so synecdoche is not correct. Choice (B), simile, is a comparison, so that is not correct. Imagery is language that is visually descriptive. As for (E), do not be confused by hyperbole, which is an exaggerated word or phrase not meant to be taken seriously. Hyperbole is not correct here.

3. **D** The answer is (D), Imagination allows us to grasp possibilities outside the self. "We can surpass the mind" means Imagination allows us to go beyond ourselves. Do not be confused by (B) because it is not as accurate as (D). Always read all the options before making a choice! Choice (C) is not true because Imagination is not shown to prevent or hinder us, only to inspire, and facilitate aspiration. Choices (A) and (E) are the opposite of what is being conveyed.

4. **A** The answer is (A), onomatopoeia, a word formed from a sound associated from what is being named. Be careful not to fall for (C), alliteration, because of the double "m" sound in murmur. Choice (D) is not correct because anaphora is the repetition of a word at the beginning of successive phrases. Choices (B) and (E) do not occur here.

5. **B** The answer is (B) because the poem is fanciful and even playful, until the end when it takes on a sad tone, as Winter limits Imagination. Choice (A) is not correct because at the end the poem is more sad than regretful. Do not be tempted by (D) because the tone at the end of the poem is not exasperation, which is intense irritation. It is sad, or melancholy. Choices (C) and (E) are not evident here at all.

6. **D** The answer is (D), "Winter grounds Imagination, limiting her ability to rise, to breathe, to soar." Choice (A) is not correct because Winter forbids Imagination to aspire. You can eliminate (B) because Imagination is not uncertain, and does not retreat, but is fettered by Winter. Choice (C) is not correct because Winter and Imagination are opposed to each other. Finally, you can eliminate (E) because Imagination does not battle, but is limited by Winter.

7. **B** The answer is Choice (B). "Cease the unequal lay" acknowledges the unequal relationship between imagination and reality, because Winter imposes itself on Fancy, limiting her. That is why (A) is not correct. Choice (C) is not correct because reality imposes limits that even Imagination cannot surpass. Choice (D) is not correct—reality is not presented as unfair, but more powerful than

Imagination. Finally, eliminate (E) because the speaker implores the inequality between reality and Imagination to cease.

8. **C** Within the poem, the line "Winter forbids me to aspire" answers this question. The speaker seems unable to rise, to breathe, to imagine—Winter grounds her. Thus, the correct answer is (C), grounding her. Choice (D) is not correct—she is not being punished, but returned to reality. Choices (A), (B), and (E) are the opposite of what is happening.

9. **B** The answer is (B), rhyming couplets. The first three stanzas have four lines each, and the rhyme scheme for these stanzas is AABB. The final four stanzas have variable line lengths, mostly maintaining the rhyming couplets. In the final stanza, in lines 43-45, there is a rhyming triplet. Choice (A) is not correct because free verse poetry does not rhyme. Choice (C) is not correct because Haiku has a very specific structure of 3 lines of 5, 7, and 5 syllables per line. You can eliminate (D) because an elegy is usually a lament for the dead. And last, (E) is not correct because a ballad traditionally tells a story.

10. **E** The answer is (E), as "silken fetters" and "soft captivity" refer to the hold love has on Fancy. Choice (A) is not correct as Imagination is what makes love possible. While love is likened to imprisonment, the descriptors "silken" fetters and "soft" captivity are meant to redeem the idea of love, so cross out (B). Choice (C) is not correct because Imagination provides inspiration for Fancy to reach beyond the self. The answer is not (D) because this does not answer the question as accurately as (E). Remember, the most precise option that completely, accurately answers the question is always a stronger pick than the choice that somewhat or vaguely answers the question. Choice (E) it is!

11. **D** Don't be fooled into picking (A) because the language of the poem is more celebratory than contemplative, with lines like "How bright their forms!" Choice (C) is not correct because the poem celebrates the freedom of the mind that makes love possible. Choice (E) is not correct because the poem does not question reality, as much as it acknowledges reality, which, in the poem, is Winter. Choice (B) is not evident in the poem and can be eliminated straight away. The answer is (D) Celebrate freedom—the freedom of the mind—which is symbolic of personal freedom.

12. **C** The answer is (C) Imagination fosters creativity and free thought. Note that the quotation in the question stem ("O thou the leader…And thine the sceptre o'er the realms of thought") includes the word "thought" in particular. Because of that, (C) should jump out at you. Be careful about (A), as Imagination inspires free thought but does not have control of the mind. Choice (B) is not correct because Imagination does not demand perfection, but offers the opportunity for perfection. Finally, (D) and (E) are the opposite of what is being conveyed.

13. **E** Phillis Wheatley constructs a liberated world outside the confines of slavery. Imagination is ultimately topped by Winter's control. Phillis Wheatley lived much of her life as an enslaved person, and she uses the imagination as a vehicle to free the mind and soul, even when the body is fettered. Choice (A) is not correct because a pastoral is about land, (B) is not correct because it does not conform to the length of a sonnet. Choice (C) is not correct because a ballad tells a story. Choice (D) is not correct because free verse poetry does not rhyme. The poem is indeed an allegory about enslaved people, so (E) is the correct answer.

Questions 14–25

Zora Neale Hurston (1891–1960) was a writer, anthropologist, and ethnographer who wrote the masterwork *Their Eyes Were Watching God.* She was a folklorist who recorded cultural history, and was a fixture in New York City's Harlem Renaissance. This passage is an excerpt from Hurston's first published work, the short story *Drenched in Light*, set in 1920's Florida.

14. **A** Helen's concern for and interest in Isis was genuine, so the answer is (A), and not (C). Helen only wanted the company of Isis, so (B) is not correct. Choice (D) is the opposite, so it is not correct. And (E) does not apply here.

15. **C** Helen wants access to genuine cultural folk art, Isis' dancing. She pays Grandma $5 to get permission to take Isis with her to the hotel. She provides the way and the means for Isis to engage in artistic expression. That is why (C) is more accurate than (A) or (B). Don't be confused by (D)—she is not providing salvation for Isis. She, in fact, is in awe of Isis' spirit. Choice (E) does not describe them at all.

16. **D** The tone of a piece is how it makes you feel. Hopeful means inspiring optimism about a future event. Choices (B) and (E) might be tempting, because of Isis and Helen's confrontation with Grandma, but the passage overall is hopeful. Choice (C) is also not correct. And (A) does not apply here.

17. **C** The horizon represents Isis' desire to explore. Don't be confused by (D). While it is partially correct, it is not as specifically correct as (C) and remember, specificity wins the day! Isis has not been anywhere yet, so (B) is not correct. Choices (E) and (A) are not correct.

18. **E** Frackshus is Black vernacular for fractious, which means irritable. Don't be tempted by (A) or (B), either of which would describe Grandma's mood. Choices (C) and (D) are not accurate here.

19. **B** The wealthy woman seemed to lack joy in her life, a joy that she found in Isis, who lived in poverty. Choice (A) does not entirely capture the sentiment of the line. Always read all the options before making your choice. Choice (C) is the opposite of what the line is conveying, so it can be eliminated straight away. Choice (E) is not correct because she has genuine admiration for Isis and (D) does not occur here.

20. **C** The answer is (C), metaphor. A metaphor is a direct comparison and "Isis is joy itself" is a perfect example of a solid metaphor. A simile is a comparison that uses "like" or "as," so (A) is not correct. Don't be confused by (D)—hyperbole is an exaggerated claim not meant to be taken seriously. When Helen says that Isis is joy itself, she does mean it literally—Isis brings her joy. Choices (B) and (E) do not apply here.

21. **D** Isis' dancing is an example of Black folk art. That the wealthy white woman wants to facilitate Isis' artistic expression is Hurston's (a folklorist) way of equating it with forms of art usually enjoyed by white society. Don't be confused by (C), as the Helen admires Isis for her inner light, which is not dependent on appreciation. Choice (E) might seem tempting but this option does not capture the sentiment of the cultural exchange between Helen and Isis. Choice (B) is the opposite of the sentiment of the line and there is no evidence for (A) in this line.

22. **A**   When Helen and Isis first get to Grandma's, she's very quarrelsome. After Helen gives her $5 and explains she would like Isis to come to the hotel with her, Grandma is mollified. That is why (A), belligerent then placated, is correct. Choice (B) is not correct because she does not exhibit signs of being suspicious of Helen, nor fearful of her. Don't be fooled by (C), as Grandma does express some frustration with Isis, but that does not encapsulate Grandma's behavior entirely, nor does concerned. Choice (D) is not correct because Grandma is never apathetic (disinterested, indifferent). And (E) is not correct because caustic means sarcastic, and that is not an accurate way to describe Grandma.

23. **E**   Zora Neale Hurston was a folklorist from the south, and she used the Black vernacular to offer a compelling perspective on Black southern culture. Choices (A) and (B) are not as correct as (E). Hurston showcased Black southern culture as rich and nuanced. Choice (C) is not correct because Hurston used the Black vernacular to draw attention to her characters, not to hide them. And (D) is not correct because the passage was about Helen, wealthy and educated, admiring Isis.

24. **C**   Helen told Isis she wanted to save her from getting a beating. One of the things Grandma was so angry about was her ruined tablecloth. So Helen gave her money to pay for the tablecloth and more to mollify her, and to get her to allow Isis to accompany Helen to the hotel. To mollify is to appease the anger or anxiety of someone—it's a great word to know. Choice (B) is not correct because Grandma did not give Helen directions—Isis did. Choice (A) is not correct because it's beyond the scope of this passage—it is never stated that Grandma wants or needs five tablecloths, or would use the extra money for more tablecloths. Choice (D) is not correct because Helen was not concerned with Grandma's admiration, her concern was saving Isis a beating. Finally, eliminate (E) as this does not accurately encapsulate the exchange between Helen and Grandma.

25. **B**   The answer is (B). This requires a close reading of the text, as (A) and (B) both might seem like strong options. Hurston was a major figure in the Harlem Renaissance, and this story is representative of elements of the Harlem Renaissance, with Isis representing the artists, Helen representing wealthy white patrons who supported artists, and Grandma representing the older conservative establishment, like Booker T. Washington, who believed African-Americans should concentrate on vocational and agricultural training.

Questions 26–33

Alice Walker (b. 1944) is an American writer whose novels, short stories, and poems are noted for their insightful treatment of African-Americans. Her novels, most notably, *The Color Purple,* focus particularly on women. This poem, "Wherever You Are Grieving" was published in 2015 in the collection *Taking the Arrow Out of the Heart.*

26. **C**   The answer is (C) angry then reflective. The poem galvanizes suffering into frustration and anger, and ultimately reveals the need to examine our own histories to mitigate our own suffering. Don't be tempted by (A) or (D) because, though the poem is about grieving, the author does not convey herself as sad or hopeless. Choices (B) and (E) do not occur here.

27.   **A**   Grieving is universal; we have all lost something, regardless of where you are (A). The places mentioned are examples of anywhere in the world where one could experience loss, not examples of specific places where the author has experienced loss, or where suffering is expected. That is why (B) and (C) are not correct. Choices (D) and (E) are not correct because the line is to share grief, to let the grieving know that their grief does not go unnoticed, rather than as a warning about impending tragedy.

28.   **D**   Hyperbole is an exaggerated word or phrase not meant to be taken literally—Walker's heart isn't literally covered in bruises and dragging across the floor (that imagery, though!), so (D) is correct. A simile is a comparison (with "like" or "as") and there is no comparison here, so eliminate (A). A metaphor is a term applied to a subject for which it is not literally applicable so (B) may seem correct but be careful! Walker is using exaggerated words to describe a broken heart, to describe suffering and hyperbole (D) is more accurate than metaphor (B) here. Choice (C) is not correct because synecdoche is when a part is substituted for a whole. Choice (E) Metonym is a word substituted for something else with which it is associated.

29.   **D**   Choice (A) is not correct because a rhapsody is highly emotional with irregular form. While the poem reflects on highly emotional things like grief, loss, and suffering, the poem itself is not highly emotional—it is reflective. Choices (B) and (C) can be eliminated because a ballad tells a story and a sonnet has a formal rhyme structure. Choice (E) is not correct because an ode is a poem written in an elevated manner. The correct answer is (D)—this poem is an elegy, a poem of serious reflection, typically a lament for the dead.

30.   **E**   The answer is (E), personification; our histories are being portrayed as beings that could warn us. Choice (A) is not correct because alliteration is the occurrence of the same sound at the beginning of adjacent or closely connected words. Choice (B) is not correct because paradox is a statement that appears to be contradictory, but upon reflection makes sense. Choice (C) is not correct because euphemism is a figure of speech used to replace impolite or unpleasant words and (D) is incorrect because allusion is a reference to unrelated material.

31.   **B**   The answer is (B). The pursuit of wealth has continuously devastating consequences. Choice (A) is not correct because money itself is not responsible for grief. Choice (C) is not correct because while there may be predictable patterns with consequences, we don't know when we will experience loss. Choice (D) does not answer the question as completely as (B) in context. Choice (E) is not correct because the poem talks about how devastating loss continues to be, even as it continues to happen.

32.   **C**   Starting from the top, (A) is not correct because the poem says if we knew our histories they would warn us—that is, we have choices. Choice (B) is not correct because we do not grieve alone, in silence. The poem touches on community ("we") and shared experiences of suffering and pain. Our suffering is not unacknowledged—that is what this poem is for. Choice (D) is just the converse of the original statement. Choice (E) is not correct because, while knowing our own stories could prepare us for future loss, relief of all suffering is not possible. The correct answer is (C) because we are too distracted to process our pain, the past is destined to repeat itself.

33.   **D**   The answer is (D) to provide support. Don't be confused by (A) or (C), while there are both expressions of anger and mourning within the poem, the purpose of the poem is to let those who grieve know they are not alone—to provide support and community. Choices (B) and (E) do not occur here.

Questions 34–45

Edgar Allan Poe (1809–1849), one of the best-known and most widely anthologized U.S. authors, wrote short stories, poetry, and criticism. His "The Murders in the Rue Morgue" is considered the first detective story. This passage is an excerpt from "The Masque of the Red Death," which exemplifies nineteenth-century horror and the macabre. It was published in 1842.

34.   **C**   This makes the disease seem like an angry person full of hatred, so the correct answer is (C), personification. Be careful of (A), hyperbole: exaggerated statements not meant to be taken literally. Make sure to read all options before making your choice as there may be an option that more accurately answers the question and as we have gone over, specificity and accuracy are the name of the game. Similarly, don't be tempted by (E), imagery, which is also not as accurate as personification. Choices (B) simile and (D) alliteration do not occur here.

35.   **B**   The answer is (B). The Prince chose a thousand friends from the aristocracy to safely sequester in his castle, with no concern for anyone with lower status. The healthy members of the aristocracy were handpicked by the Prince, and then sequestered in his castle. That is why the answer is not (A). Don't be tempted by (D), because, while the castle was secure, that was not the point of the passage. Choices (C) and (E) are the opposite of what the passage is conveying.

36.   **A**   The answer is (A), the Prince and his guests do not care about the rest of the country because they decided that the rest of the world was not worth worrying about, literally. They were taking care of themselves—everyone else was on their own. The scene brings to mind the quotation supposedly from Marie-Antoinette during the French Revolution: "let them eat cake." That is, like the Prince's attitude, selfish and tone-deaf. We already know that the country has lost half its population to the Red Death, so the answer is not (B). The gates around the castle are welded shut, to keep the guests in and the Red Death and the rest of the world out. So the answer is not (C). The Prince had no concern for the world outside his castle, so the answer is not (D). Half the population had already died from the Red Death, so the answer is not (E).

37.   **D**   The tone of a passage is the author's feelings about a subject. "Ominous" means giving the impression that something unfortunate is going to happen. Poe creates a feeling of uneasiness that something terrible is waiting ahead, so (D) is your best bet. The answer is not (B) or (C) because the tone of the story is gravely serious, not humorous, ironic, or satirical. The answer is not (A) because the author never relents from the feeling of uneasiness—we do not see any hope. And the answer is not (E) because the passage seems to be alluding to an unfortunate event yet to happen—it's looking forward, not backward with regret. Choice (D), ominous, it is.

38. **A** The answer is (A), The passage of time in life is inevitable. Time is a metaphor for mortality. The seven rooms represent the seven stages of life, with the seventh chamber—the one cloaked in black—representing death. The clock was on the western wall, symbolically where the sun sets. Choice (B) is not correct because the guests are very concerned about their mortality—that's why they are sequestered in the castle. Choice (C) might seem appealing, but don't fall for that one—it does not answer the question as accurately as (A). Choice (D) is not correct because time represents mortality, and is very important. Choice (E) isn't supported by the passage at all.

39. **C** The answer is (C) because this establishes the Red Death as the driving force of the story. When reading, be sure to notice the order in which elements are presented and also, the amount of text or space given to certain items—they can reveal clues about importance. Here, everything in the story happens because of the Red Death. The Prince is the main character, but the Red Death is the driving force behind the story. Do not be fooled by (A) or (B) because neither of them answers the question as accurately as (C) and accuracy and specificity are crucial. Choices (D) and (E) are not correct because Prince Prospero is the main character and the Red Death is the driving force of the story.

40. **B** The answer is (B): Imagery is language that invokes a visual or other kind of sense impression. A metaphor is when a word is applied to a subject to which it is not literally applicable—(C) is not correct. Simile is a comparison, so (A) is not correct. Choices (D) and (E) do not occur here.

41. **A** Each answer choice has 2 adjectives and both must apply to this character (half wrong is all wrong, as we say). Choices (B) through (E) are all positive traits. But after reading the passage, we know that Prince Prospero was mostly concerned with his own well-being and that of very few of his court, so we don't think of him in a positive light. Choice (A), self-centered and uncaring, is the only choice that aligns with what we have read, so it's correct.

42. **A** The seventh room, draped in black, with scarlet windows that created "ghastly" effects on the guests who entered reminded guests of the Red Death, so (A) should call to you as the correct answer. It is not (C) or (E) because neither of those answers the question as accurately and precisely as (A). Choices (B) and (D) are not implied in context.

43. **E** The answer is (E). Choices (A) and (B) are not correct because the party and the rooms are metaphors for mortality. Choice (C) is not correct because the seven colors of the rainbow (commonly referred to as ROYGBIV) are not all represented here. Choice (D) is not correct because the character traits such as greed, gluttony, and vanity are evident in the revelers, rather than in the rooms. The only answer it could be is (E). The seven stages of life with the colored rooms representing, going east to west, birth (blue), childhood (purple), adolescence (green), adulthood (orange), old-age (white), imminent death (violet), and death (black).

44. **D** The answer is (D). The purpose of the party is to forget the fatal disease raging beyond the castle walls. The clock was a constant reminder that time waits for no one. It was a constant reminder of mortality. Choice (A) is not correct because the guests at the party were carefully selected from a specific group of people by the Prince, much as the rooms were carefully ordered and decorated. Choice (B) is not correct because the guests were not unconcerned—the party is to distract

them from the looming threat of death. Eliminate (C) because we don't know how the guests have ordered themselves within the rooms. Choice (E) does not answer the question as accurately as (D) and as we know, specificity is key. Go with (D).

45.   C   The answer is (C): Death is inevitable. The last room is representative of the final stage of a person's life—death. And the scarlet windows in the room produce an effect on the face not unlike the Red Death itself, the very threat the party guests are sequestering themselves from. The message here is that all their efforts are futile; death is inevitable. Choices (A) and (B) do not answer the question as accurately as (C). Make sure to read all the options before making your choice. Choice (D) is not correct because the author is warning that death might be within the castle walls and while (E) isn't incorrect, it's not the strongest option that you have. Go with (C).

Questions 46–55

Erin Morgenstern (b. 1978) is an American multimedia artist and the author of two novels. This passage is an excerpt from *The Night Circus*, which was published in 2011 and won the Locus Award for Best First Novel.

46.   B   The answer is (B), Hector values Celia's skill more than he values her life. He exhibits a blatant disregard for her life, as he is willing to risk it. You may be tempted to choose (C) or (D), but those do not accurately encapsulate the sentiment of the line. Choices (A) and (E) do not apply here.

47.   C   The answer is (C), rivals. This entire encounter sets up a new challenge between them. Though (B) and (C) may also seem tempting, they are not as accurate. In this passage, there is no evidence that (A) and (E) are accurate.

48.   D   This requires an interpretive reading of the lines. The idea that Celia can so easily manipulate a timepiece, even shatter it, symbolizes the manipulation of time (D). While (B) and (C) are partially true, neither accurately sum up these lines. Choices (A) and (E) are not accurate.

49.   A   The answer is (A), Celia has now been permanently committed to the challenge. The metal burning into her skin is almost like a form of branding. You may have been tempted by (B), but that is not correct as it would be a few steps ahead of what is happening here—it's not what is happening in this moment. And (D) is also not correct because it was not Celia's magic that affected the ring. Finally, (C) and (E) do not apply here.

50.   D   The tone of this passage is (D), foreboding. The tone of a piece is the mood it evokes or the way it makes you feel. Foreboding means a strong sense of future misfortune. Melancholy (C) does not accurately describe this encounter as a whole. Nor does (E), nostalgic, though both describe isolated parts of this passage. We want the tone of the passage as a whole, remember. Choices (A) and (B) are not evident here—there is nothing light, fun, or romantic about this passage.

51.   A   The answer is (A), order vs chaos. This theme is evident in how concerned each of them is with the idea of impulsive behavior and then control. Don't be confused by (B) and (E), as neither pride nor love accurately describe Hector's feelings towards Celia. Choice (D) is not correct because the man in the gray suit is not afraid. And (C) does not describe either man's attitude correctly.

52. **E** The man is impressed by Celia's control at her very young age, but then expresses concern that her temper could result in impulsiveness—so he is aware that with years and lessons, she will only get more powerful, and harder to control. Choice (A) is not correct because Hector and the man in the gray suit certainly do both understand the seriousness of what they are talking about. Choices (B) and (D) are not correct because neither man is concerned if harm comes to Celia. Choice (C) does not answer this question as accurately as (E) and we always go for accuracy. Read and consider all the options before making your choice.

53. **B** Synecdoche (B) is when the part is made to represent the whole, which is what we see here ("suit" stands for business executive). Metonymy is a lot like synecdoche but slightly different—it is the substitution of the name of the attribute for that of the thing meant (for example, referring to the President and their administration as "the White House") which isn't happening here, so (C) is not correct. Hyperbole is an exaggeration, not meant to be taken literally, and that does not accurately describe this sentence, so (A) is out. Finally, (D) and (E) do not occur here.

54. **E** Hector and the man in the gray suit are concealing their words, and Celia should be wary (E). While Celia is very young, and not yet able to understand the ramifications of this challenge, that is not why she cannot understand them, so (A) is not correct. There may be some truth to (B), but that does not encapsulate the entire meaning of these lines. Though it says "Celia frowns," that is not to imply that she is sad, but to illustrate her consternation at not being able to understand their words, so (D) is not correct. There is no evidence here that Celia is afraid, so (C) is not correct.

55. **C** Hector is shown being solicitous towards Celia, while at the same time offering to risk her life to win the challenge. That is why (C), duplicitous (treacherous, deceitful) is correct. You may read some condescension in the passage with regards to Hector's parenting, but (D) is not wholly accurate, nor is (A) pitying. Choices (B) and (E) are not accurate here.

Part III
About the AP English Literature and Composition Exam

- The Structure of the AP English Literature and Composition Exam
- How the AP English Literature and Composition Exam Is Scored
- Overview of Content Topics
- How AP Exams Are Used
- Other Resources
- Designing Your Study Plan

THE STRUCTURE OF THE AP ENGLISH LITERATURE AND COMPOSITION EXAM

Test Date: Early May
Total Time: 3 hours (usually administered at 8:00 A.M.)

Section I: Multiple Choice (60 minutes)—45% of your grade
Total number of questions: 55
You will see 5 passages and/or poems and between 8–13 questions per passage/poem, for a total of 55 multiple-choice questions.

Section II: Free Response (120 minutes)—55% of your grade
Three Essays:
1. Poetry Analysis (40-minute essay on a single poem or comparison of two poems, which will be provided to you)
2. Prose Fiction Analysis (40-minute essay on a story, novel excerpt, or essay that is provided to you)
3. Literary Argument (40-minute essay on a given literary topic, supported by the reading)

The Big Six and You

The AP English Literature and Composition course description content reflects content from the AP course, including the big ideas that undergird the questions you ask of all the literature you study. We're going to call the six big ideas the Big Six. The Big Six are concepts that enable you to study and understand literature—and to write about it. Five of the Big Six are elements of literature. The sixth is how you take the five elements and analyze literature yourself.

Let's review the Big Six. They are:

Character—Characters in literature show a wide range of values, beliefs, assumptions, biases, and cultural norms, and provide an opportunity to study and explore what the characters represent.

Setting—A setting and the details associated with it represent a time and place, but also convey values associated with the setting.

Structure—Structure refers to the arrangements of sections and parts of a text, the relationship of the parts to each other, and the sequence in which the text reveals information. These are all choices made by a writer that allow you to interpret a text.

Narration—Any narrator's or speaker's perspective controls the details and emphases that readers encounter; therefore, narration affects how readers experience and interpret a text.

Figurative language—Comparisons, representations, and associations shift meaning from the literal to the figurative. Figurative language can include word choice, imagery, and symbols. Simile, metaphor, personification, and allusions are all examples of figurative language.

Literary argumentation—How do you write about literature yourself? You develop your interpretation (using the first five of the Big Six!) and then communicate it. You need to develop a thesis—a defensible claim—and support it with textual evidence.

The multiple-choice section of the AP English Literature and Composition exam will be testing your knowledge of the Big Six. Each one is weighted a certain amount in the multiple-choice questions.

You are evaluated on your knowledge of the Big Six throughout the Exam. For the multiple-choice section, for example, you are evaluated on seven skill categories that map very closely to the Big Six. (Two of the skill categories, 5 and 6, are covered under Figurative Language, one of the Big Six.) The weighting is shown below.

Skill Category	Exam Weighting
1: Explain the function of character	16–20%
2: Explain the function of setting	3–6%
3: Explain the function of plot and structure	16–20%
4: Explain the function of narrator or speaker	21–26%
5: Explain the function of word choice, imagery, and symbols	10–13%
6: Explain the function of comparison	10–13%
7: Develop textually substantiated arguments about interpretations of part or all of a text	10–13%

Stay Up to Date!
For late-breaking information about test dates, exam formats, and any other changes pertaining to AP English Literature and Composition, make sure to check the College Board's website at apstudents. collegeboard.org/courses/ ap-english-literature-and- composition

Who Writes the Exam?

The initial content for the exam is generally gathered by an AP Development Committee that is equally made up of high school and college teachers. This ensures that the material presented on the test falls within the range of topics associated with the course itself. Once those topics and questions have been written, however, they are often fine-tuned by professional test designers who work to keep the test, especially the multiple-choice section, similar to previous administrations. This is actually an asset to you, since that stability also adds a degree of predictability to the ways in which questions are shaped and wrong answers are selected. On multiple-choice tests, knowing how the wrong answers are written and how they can be eliminated is key. We'll discuss this topic in detail in Part IV, Chapter 4.

HOW THE AP ENGLISH LITERATURE AND COMPOSITION EXAM IS SCORED

What Your Final Score Means

After taking the test in early May, you will receive your scores sometime around the first week of July, which is right about when you've just started to forget about the whole experience. Your score will be, simply enough, a single number from 1 to 5. Here is what those numbers mean:

Looking to Guarantee a 5 or Your Money Back?

We now offer one-on-one tutoring for a guaranteed 5 on the AP English Literature and Composition exam. For information on rates and availability, visit www.princetonreview.com/college/ap-test-prep

Score	2021 Percentage	Credit Recommendation	College Grade Equivalent
5	4.9%	Extremely Well Qualified	A
4	12.0%	Well qualified	A–, B+, B
3	26.9%	Qualified	B–, C+, C
2	37.3%	Possibly Qualified	N/A
1	18.8%	No Recommendation	N/A

Scores from May 2021 AP Exam administration. Data taken from the College Board website.

Your Multiple-Choice Score

In the multiple-choice section of the test, you receive one point for each question you answer correctly. You receive no points for a question you leave blank or answer incorrectly. That is, the famous "guessing penalty" on some standardized tests does not exist here. So, if you are completely unsure, guess. However, it is always best to use Process of Elimination (POE, as discussed in Chapter 4) to narrow down your choices and make an educated guess.

Your Essay Score

As of September 2019, each AP essay in the Free-Response section will be scored on a scale from 0 to 6, with 6 being the highest score. Each AP Reader (a high school or college-level English teacher) is given a precise rubric to guide their grading of the essay. Gone are the days of vague, "holistic" scoring—we're using scoring rubrics now!

The rubrics can be downloaded from the College Board's website, but here is a summary of how all 3 essay question types will be graded using this 6-point scale:

Thesis: 0–1 point

Evidence and Commentary: 0–4 points

Sophistication: 0–1 point

In essence, your essays must include a clear thesis, evidence to buttress your thesis (and commentary about that evidence). In addition, they must possess sophistication, which essentially means that you develop a complex literary argument. We will explore this in depth in Chapter 5.

Your Final Score

Your final 1 to 5 score is a combination of your section scores. Remember that the multiple-choice section counts for 45 percent of the total and the essays count for 55 percent. While this proportion makes them almost equal, they are not entirely equal. A somewhat convoluted mathematical formula is applied to arrive at your score.

Neither you nor the colleges you apply to will ever know your individual section scores on your AP Exam—the College Board doesn't share that information. You get a final AP exam score between 1 and 5, and that's it. In the immortal words of elementary school teachers everywhere, "you get what you get and you don't get upset." (Because you're going to crush this exam, dear reader!)

Does this mean you don't need to think about how your multiple-choice and essay scores combine? No. You should get a feel for how your multiple-choice score affects your final, total score.

Look at the overall test as two separate assessments:

> Multiple Choice: 55 questions; 45% of the overall score
>
> Free Response: 3 essays, each scored on a 0 to 6 scale; 55% of the overall score

Bonus Tips and Tricks…
Check us out on YouTube for additional test taking tips and must-know strategies at www.youtube.com/ThePrincetonReview

Updates Online
Be sure to visit your online
Student Tools and/or the
College Board's website
for any additional rubrics
or updated rubrics.

The cutoff point for each grade varies from year to year and is set only after all the multiple-choice sections and essays have been scored. Regardless, a good bottom-line goal is to get at least 30 questions right on the multiple-choice sections and to earn at least 12 points on the essays. These two scores will net you a final passing grade of 3. Increases in either category can increase your final scores. The grading scale for the AP English Literature and Composition Exam looks something like this:

Essay Points	12	14	16	18
MC Points				
20	3	3	4	5
25	3	4	4	5
30	4	4	5	5
35	4	4	5	5
40	4	5	5	5
45	5	5	5	5
50	5	5	5	5
55	5	5	5	5

Conclusions

1. The bottom-line goal on the multiple-choice section is 30, or a little more than half. The bottom-line goal on the essays is the minimum passing score on each essay, 4 (3 × 4 = 12).
2. Set realistic goals for yourself. Look what happens if your multiple-choice score stays at 25 while you raise your essays one point each (from a 12 to a 14): You go from a 3 to a 4!

The average score is a 3, but earning a 5 is possible, even if you scored only within the 20 to 35 range on the multiple-choice section.

Now let's start practicing ways for you to get your best possible score.

Pacing Chart for AP English Literature and Composition Exam				
My Score on Practice	Shooting for Minimum of	Time Spent	Must Get Right	Guess
————	30 of 55	60 mins	30	25

The AP English Literature and Composition Exam is unlike other AP Exams in one other factor: time. The multiple-choice section is always one hour long. Be sure to visit your online Student Tools and/or the College Board's website for any additional or updated rubrics.

While you are getting the feel of the passages and the kinds of questions, take all the time you need. Your purpose, after all, is different at this stage, as you are familiarizing yourself with the process. Later, when you are practicing for the real experience, limit your time to precisely one hour.

Remember—you can guess. Look at it this way:

Time: 1 hour
Practice Test of 55 questions

Passage/Poem	Number of Questions	Number to Get Right	Number to Guess On
1	8	6	25 (from any section)
2	13	6	
3	10	6	
4	13	6	
5	13	6	

30 total (from any section)

This Is An Example
The chart right here (well, left here—heyo!) is just an example of what you might see on test day. We know there will be 5 passages/poems and between 8-13 questions per passage/poem.

Use a chart like this one to evaluate your performance when practicing:

The Time Factor			
Time Evenly Divided	Time I Spent	Time Shooting For	Number to Get Right
_____	_____	_____	_____

OVERVIEW OF CONTENT TOPICS

There is not a required reading list for the AP English Literature and Composition Exam, but the College Board provides a list of authors and poets with whom you should be familiar and whose work is of the caliber and density that you are expected to understand. They can be works written in, or translated into, English. Their list includes many of the following, plus we have included our recommended writers, as well.

Poetry

- John Ashbery
- W. H. Auden
- Amiri Baraka
- John Berryman
- Elizabeth Bishop
- William Blake
- Anne Bradstreet
- Edward Kamau Brathwaite
- Gwendolyn Brooks
- Robert Browning
- George Gordon, Lord Byron
- Lorna Dee Cervantes
- Geoffrey Chaucer
- Lucille Clifton
- Samuel Taylor Coleridge
- Billy Collins
- Gregory Corso
- Robert Creeley
- Countee Cullen
- E.E. Cummings
- H. D. (Hilda Doolittle)
- Emily Dickinson
- John Donne
- Rita Dove
- John Dryden
- Paul Laurence Dunbar
- T. S. Eliot
- Lawrence Ferlinghetti
- Robert Frost
- Allen Ginsberg
- Barbara Guest
- Joy Harjo
- Seamus Heaney
- George Herbert
- Garrett Hongo
- Gerard Manley Hopkins
- Langston Hughes
- Ben Jonson
- John Keats
- Kenneth Koch
- Philip Larkin
- Denise Levertov
- Robert Lowell
- Andrew Marvell
- Claude McKay
- John Milton
- Marianne Moore
- Frank O'Hara
- Charles Olson
- Sylvia Plath
- Edgar Allan Poe
- Alexander Pope
- Ezra Pound
- Adrienne Rich
- Sonia Sanchez
- Anne Sexton
- William Shakespeare
- Ntozake Shange
- Percy Bysshe Shelley
- Leslie Marmon Silko
- Gary Snyder
- Cathy Song
- Wallace Stevens
- Alfred, Lord Tennyson
- Derek Walcott
- Walt Whitman
- Richard Wilbur
- William Carlos Williams
- William Wordsworth
- William Butler Yeats

Drama

- Aeschylus
- Edward Albee
- Amiri Baraka
- Samuel Beckett
- Anton Chekhov
- Caryl Churchill
- William Congreve
- Athol Fugard
- Lorraine Hansberry
- Lillian Hellman
- David Henry Hwang
- Henrik Ibsen
- Ben Jonson
- David Mamet
- Arthur Miller
- Molière
- Marsha Norman
- Sean O'Casey
- Eugene O'Neill
- Suzan-Lori Parks
- Harold Pinter
- Luigi Pirandello
- William Shakespeare
- George Bernard Shaw
- Sam Shepard
- Neil Simon
- Sophocles
- Tom Stoppard
- Luis Valdez
- Oscar Wilde
- Tennessee Williams
- August Wilson

Fiction (Novel and Short Story)

- Chinua Achebe
- Chimamanda Ngozi Adichie
- Sherman Alexie
- Isabel Allende
- Rudolfo Anaya
- Margaret Atwood
- Jane Austen
- James Baldwin
- Saul Bellow
- Charlotte Brontë
- Emily Brontë
- William S. Burroughs
- Octavia E. Butler
- Raymond Carver
- Willa Cather
- John Cheever
- Kate Chopin
- Sandra Cisneros
- Joseph Conrad
- Edwidge Danticat
- Daniel Defoe
- Anita Desai
- Charles Dickens
- Fyodor Dostoevsky
- George Eliot
- Ralph Ellison
- Louise Erdrich
- William Faulkner
- Henry Fielding
- F. Scott Fitzgerald
- E. M. Forster
- Charles Frazier
- John Gay
- Yaa Gyasi
- Mohsin Hamid
- Thomas Hardy
- Nathaniel Hawthorne
- Ernest Hemingway
- Oscar Hijuelos
- Brandon Hobson
- Khaled Hosseini
- Victor Hugo
- Zora Neale Hurston
- Kazuo Ishiguro
- Henry James
- Ha Jin
- Edward P. Jones
- James Joyce
- Jack Kerouac
- Porochista Khakpour
- Barbara Kingsolver
- Maxine Hong Kingston
- Joy Kogawa
- Jhumpa Lahiri
- Nella Larsen
- Margaret Laurence
- D. H. Lawrence
- Chang-rae Lee

Fiction (Novel and Short Story) (continued)

- Bernard Malamud
- Gabriel García Márquez
- Cormac McCarthy
- Ian McEwan
- Herman Melville
- Toni Morrison
- Bharati Mukherjee
- Vladimir Nabokov
- Flannery O'Connor
- Orhan Pamuk
- Katherine Anne Porter
- Marilynne Robinson
- Sir Walter Scott
- Samuel Selvon
- Leslie Marmon Silko
- Jonathan Swift
- Amy Tan
- Mark Twain
- John Updike
- Luis Alberto Urrea
- Alice Walker
- Evelyn Waugh
- Eudora Welty
- Edith Wharton
- John Edgar Wideman
- Virginia Woolf
- Richard Wright

Expository Prose

- Joseph Addison
- Gloria Anzaldua
- Matthew Arnold
- James Baldwin
- James Boswell
- Jesús Colón
- Joan Didion
- Frederick Douglass
- W. E. B. Du Bois
- Ralph Waldo Emerson
- William Hazlitt
- bell hooks
- Samuel Johnson
- Charles Lamb
- Thomas Macaulay
- Mary McCarthy
- John Stuart Mill
- George Orwell
- Michael Pollan
- Richard Rodriguez
- Edward Said
- Lewis Thomas
- Henry David Thoreau
- E. B. White
- Virginia Woolf

More Great Books
For more information on colleges, you might want to check out some of our guide books, which include *The Best 388 Colleges*, *The Complete Book of Colleges*, *Paying for College*, and many more!

HOW AP EXAMS ARE USED

Different colleges use AP Exam scores in different ways, so it is important that you go to a particular college's website to determine how it uses AP Exam scores. The three items below represent the main ways in which AP Exam scores can be used.

- **College Credit**. Some colleges will give you college credit if you score well on an AP Exam. These credits count toward your graduation requirements, meaning that you can take fewer courses while in college. Given the cost of college, this could be quite a benefit.
- **Satisfy Requirements**. Some colleges will allow you to "place out" of certain requirements if you do well on an AP Exam, even if they do not give you actual college credits. For example, you might not need to take an introductory-level course, or perhaps you might not need to take a class in a certain discipline at all.

- **Admissions Plus**. Even if your AP Exam will not result in college credit or even allow you to place out of certain courses, most colleges will respect your decision to push yourself by taking an AP course or even an AP Exam outside of a course. A high score on an AP Exam shows a mastery of more difficult content than is taught in many high school courses, and colleges may take that into account during the admissions process.

OTHER RESOURCES

There are many resources available to help you improve your score on the AP English Literature and Composition Exam, not the least of which are your **teachers**. If you are taking an AP class, you may be able to get extra attention from your teacher, such as obtaining feedback on your essays. If you are not in an AP course, reach out to a teacher who teaches AP English Literature and Composition and ask whether the teacher will review your essays or otherwise help you with content.

Another wonderful resource is **AP Students**, the official site of the AP Exams. The scope of the information at this site is quite broad and includes the following:

- course descriptions, which include details on what content is covered and sample questions
- reading and writing study skills tips
- essay prompts from previous years
- information about exam fees and reductions
- tons of practice content: multiple choice, passages, and more

The AP Students home page address is http://apstudent.collegeboard.org

The page where you can find gobs of information about AP English Literature and Composition is https://apstudent.collegeboard.org/apcourse/ap-english-literature-and-composition

Finally, The Princeton Review offers tutoring for the AP English Literature and Composition Exam. Our expert instructors can help you refine your strategic approach and add to your content knowledge. For more information, call 1-800-2REVIEW.

Go Online!
If you're looking for additional resources to prepare for the AP Exam, remember to visit the course home page on AP Students. Here you can find more information about the exam, including sample questions and scoring details.

Time Well Spent
If you're not sure how to best spend your time, register this book and log into your online Student Tools so that you can download our helpful, free study guide for this book.

DESIGNING YOUR STUDY PLAN

In Part I, you identified some areas of potential improvement. Let's now delve further into your performance on Practice Test 1, with the goal of developing a study plan appropriate to your needs and time commitment.

Read the answers and explanations associated with the multiple-choice questions (starting at page 27). After you have done so, respond to the following questions:

- How many days/weeks/months away is your AP English Literature and Composition Exam?

- What time of day is your best, most focused study time?

- How much time per day/week/month will you devote to preparing for your AP English Literature and Composition Exam?

- When will you do this preparation? (Be as specific as possible: Mondays and Wednesdays from 3:00 to 4:00 P.M., for example.)

- Based on the answers above, will you focus on strategy or content or both?

- What are your overall goals in using this book?

Part IV
Test-Taking Strategies for the AP English Literature and Composition Exam

PREVIEW

Review your responses to the questions in "Reflect on the Test" on page 4, and then respond to the following questions:

- How many multiple-choice questions did you miss even though you knew the answer?

- On how many multiple-choice questions did you guess blindly?

- How many multiple-choice questions did you miss after eliminating some answers and guessing based on the remaining answers?

- Did you find any of the essays easier/harder than the others—and if so, why?

HOW TO USE THE CHAPTERS IN THIS PART

For the following Strategy chapters, think about what you are doing now before you read the chapters. As you read and engage in the directed practice, be sure to appreciate the ways you can change your approach. At the end of Part IV, you will have the opportunity to reflect on how you will change your approach.

Chapter 1
Basic Principles of the Multiple-Choice Section

Books are a uniquely portable magic.

—Stephen King

WHAT ARE THE BASIC PRINCIPLES OF CRACKING THE EXAM?

As with any multiple-choice test, there will come a time when the studying is over, and you are as prepared as you are ever going to be. You will be sitting at your desk with a sealed exam booklet and an answer sheet in front of you. The proctor, droning on at the front of the room, will finally finish reading the instructions and say, "You may break the seal and begin the test."

At that moment, what you know isn't going to change. Your head will be crammed with knowledge, and you might wish you knew even more, but your score will depend on getting what you know onto that answer sheet.

Imagine your exact double sitting at the next desk. In terms of English literature, your double knows exactly what you know. Will you and your double's scores be the same? *Well, if you know how to beat the test, your score will be better.* You will squeeze every possible drop of what you know onto that answer sheet while your double will struggle to bring all his or her knowledge to the table. The scores will reflect the difference.

The multiple-choice section of the AP English Literature and Composition Exam is just like any other standardized test in that you should have three serious considerations:

1) Time management is crucial.
2) Process of Elimination is necessary for narrowing answers to more viable options.
3) You must answer EVERY question. Leave NOTHING blank.

Have a Plan

In order to do your best on the AP Exam, you need a plan. Stop worrying about doing things the "right way" and start concentrating on answering every question most efficiently. Unanswered questions have no chance, but even randomly answered questions have hope. Go into test day with a plan for answering questions you don't know and a plan for managing your time.

The Plan

Here's an outline of what you should do on the multiple-choice section:

1. Note the Time and Number of Passages or Poems

When the test begins, make note of the time. The proctor might put the start time on the board; most rooms have a clock, but don't count on either. Your best bet is to take a wrist watch and set it to 12:00. It's easy to read how much time you have left if you have everything in even increments. This is a good trick for taking any timed test.

Because you'll be faced with five passages or poems, you can bet on about 12 minutes per passage or poem, with questions. Keep track of time. Don't rush, but try not to dedicate too much time to any one passage or question.

2. Pick a Passage or Poem to Complete First

Some passages/poems may be a bit easier than others. There is no order of difficulty on the test, but you know yourself and your skills best. If you see 20th-century literature and 17th-century poetry, choose the one that makes you most comfortable. Reading the text that is easiest for you will help you to start the test confidently and efficiently. Then you reserve time for harder passages or poems to come.

3. Pick a Passage or Poem to Complete Last

Scan the 5 texts for one that looks harder (to you) than the others. Save this one for the end so that you can use any extra time on it. If you complete the other items in under 12 minutes, you can dedicate the remaining time to the reading and questions that will be most difficult. Remember, this passage or poem is one on which you may have to guess because you don't know the answers or you're running out of time, but that's okay. If you answered the easier texts with more consideration, it won't hurt you as badly to miss a few here.

4. Work the Passage/Poem

Note our verb choice: *work*, not *read*. You'll see what we mean when we get to the next chapter.

5. Answer the Questions Using Planned-Ahead Strategies

All texts are not created equal. Because you can't count on easier texts first and more difficult texts later, you have to rely on your instinct and prior knowledge to assess the situation and go confidently in the direction of the test.

No Order of Difficulty
Unlike some other exams, questions on the AP English Literature and Composition Exam are not arranged in order of difficulty. Passages deemed "easy" or "difficult" by the test-writers could appear earlier or later.

Letter of the Day (LOTD)

One such automatic strategy is to pick a "Letter of the Day" (LOTD) from A to E in advance. If you run into a situation in which you can't eliminate any answers or simply don't have time to look at the remaining questions, you can just bubble in that letter. (Remember, you are not penalized for wrong answers!)

This is a quick and easy way to make sure that you've answered every question. And theoretically, if the questions are evenly distributed across all five choices, being consistent in your guesses should help to pick up a couple of freebie points.

TIME MANAGEMENT

A key factor on standardized tests is time management. You have to answer 55 questions in 60 minutes, and that means there's no time to waste. The more questions you answer, the better chance you have of correct answers—LEAVE NOTHING BLANK.

Analyze yourself as a test-taker and determine how to tackle the test in the best way for you. We can present general guidelines to get you going, but you have to come up with your own personal plan for test day.

Do It Your Way

Don't listen to other kids say how "easy" that test was or how "it was so hard I didn't even get to everything!" If you worry about how others are testing, you won't be confident in your own abilities. Remember that the first thing you should do is look over the passages to determine your approach.

If you can get to all the passages and poems and answer all the questions with five minutes left over, great, but don't count on it. Plan ahead. There's no law that says you have to do the passages in order. Don't.

As we've already mentioned, the first thing you should do as soon as the multiple-choice section begins is look over the passages and poems—this is definitely allowed. Decide which text to tackle first, but much more important—decide which text to do last.

The object is to find the most difficult passage/poem and put off doing it until the end. There are a couple of reasons for doing this. First, if you're going to run out of time, why not run out of time on the passage/poem on which you might miss a lot of questions anyway? Second, a more difficult passage/poem is undoubtedly going to take the most time. You don't want to get into a situation in which you have to rush just to finish four out of the five texts. This is such a simple technique. All you have to do is remember to use it.

A Word of Advice
We recommend that you save the passage/poem (and questions) you find most challenging for last. This strategy ensures that you answer all of the questions you know before moving on to the ones you may not know and which, therefore, might cost you valuable time.

You Can Skip a Text and Still Get a Good Score

It's true. It is completely possible to get a final score of 5 without doing all the passages/poems. No, it isn't easy. It calls for excellent essays and accurate answers on the passages you do attempt. If you'd be satisfied with a final score of 4 (and you should be; it's an excellent score), and if you know that reading comprehension questions are tough for you, then you should definitely consider skipping one passage or poem. Of course, skipping one text does not mean leaving questions blank. When you get to questions that are too time-consuming or that you don't know the answer to (and you can't eliminate any options), use your Letter of the Day (LOTD).

ACTIVE READING

With five prose fiction and poetry analysis passages and 55 questions to do in an hour, you need a strategy to make the most of your reading time. It's called active reading, and it will help you wring information from the passage quickly.

Steps in active reading

Spacing Out?
If you feel your eyes glazing over at any point during the test, stop, take a deep breath, and get yourself to refocus. We know it's easier said than done, but sharp concentration is a key to test success!

1. Preview the questions—just the stems, not the answer choices. In this way, you'll have an idea of what information to watch for as you read the passage. This technique works well for some people and not for others. The passages in this book give you plenty of opportunity to try it a couple of times. If it works for you—if you can retain most or even some of the information you'll need to find in order to answer the questions—then you'll be one step ahead when you start reading the passage.

2. Identify the main point of each paragraph or stanza *before* you allow yourself to move on to the next one. This will force you to concentrate intensely and will avoid that lost, "what did I just read?" feeling that comes from skimming through a passage. It might help you to make a quick note of a key word or two for each part of the passage. Don't let this step slow you down, though. If a sentence or stanza really doesn't make sense to you, stop and close your eyes for a couple of seconds, look at it again, and, if necessary, just move on. It might make sense later in the context of one of the questions.

3. Ask questions constantly as you read. Why is the author talking so much about snowflakes? Why doesn't John want to go to the beach with his family? What is the red truck supposed to symbolize? Why does the author use "despondent" instead of "sad"? Why is this dream sequence here? Tear the prose fiction selection or poem apart instead of simply letting it flow into you as written. This step forces you to engage with the passage instead of letting it slip past you.

4. Identify the main point of the whole passage. There—you've got the theme and the author's purpose.

Once you master active reading techniques, you'll probably find them useful far beyond the exam.

Types of Answer Choices

1. All True But One Word or Phrase

If part of the answer is wrong, then the whole thing is wrong. Read the entire answer choice to determine whether the answer is appropriate for what the question is asking.

2. Distractor/Absolute Wrong Answer

This is the answer that just cannot be the answer based on what you read in the passage. Through Process of Elimination (POE), you should be able to spot this answer pretty quickly.

3. Key/Right or Best Answer

This is the answer that is most suitable in response to the question. The Key may be similar to other answer choices; however, all parts of this answer fulfill the question and align with the passage.

4. Irrelevant Details/Information

Sometimes you'll see details and think, "ooh! I read that," but you have to be careful that this doesn't throw you from the true focus of the question. Some answer choices will include some relevant details but will also include speculative details or things that just aren't in the passage. Read the entire answer choice before making an incorrect choice based on one small detail.

Why Is This Wrong?
Half Wrong = All Wrong

The key is to take each answer a word at a time. Don't fixate on what's right about the answer; if any part of the answer is wrong, then eliminate the answer. **Half wrong equals all wrong**. In fact, one-tenth bad equals all bad. Read the following excerpt from Zadie Smith's *White Teeth* and the question that follows.

> Early in the morning, late in the century, Cricklewood Broadway. At 0627 hours on January 1, 1975, Alfred
> *Line* Archibald Jones was dressed in cor-
> (5) duroy and sat in a fume-filled Cavalier Musketeer Estate facedown on the steering wheel, hoping the judgment would not be too heavy upon him. He lay in a prostrate cross, jaw slack, arms
> (10) splayed on cither side like some fallen angel; scrunched up in each fist he held his army service medals (left) and his marriage license (right), for he had decided to take his mistakes with him.
> (15) A little green light flashed in his eye, signaling a right turn he had resolved never to make. He was resigned to it. He was prepared for it. He had flipped a coin and stood staunchly by the results.
> (20) This was a decided-upon suicide. In fact, it was a New Year's resolution.
>
> ....
>
> While he slipped in and out of consciousness, the position of the planets, the music of the spheres, the
> (25) flap of a tiger moth's diaphanous wings in Central Africa, and a whole bunch of other stuff that Makes Shit Happen had decided it was second-chance time for Archie. Somewhere, somehow, by
> (30) somebody, it had been decided that he would live.

1. Lines 3–21 of the passage best describe the author's portrayal of Alfred Archibald Jones as

    (A) a harshly condemnatory treatment of a coward
    (B) a sympathetic portrayal of a man who regrets his life
    (C) a farcical portrayal of an attempted suicide
    (D) a mock heroic portrait of a vintage car enthusiast
    (E) a darkly ironic treatment of an overly sensitive man

(A) You see "harsh" and "coward" and those items strongly imply he has failed in life because he means to take "mistakes" with him, and the mistakes are both military service and marriage, major events in the lives of many men. He is not described as cowardly, though, but as someone who "stood staunchly" by coin-toss results. If one part of the question is wrong, then the choice is wrong. Eliminate this answer.

(B) While the tone is somewhat arch, the description of him as "like some fallen angel" and lying "in a prostrate cross" indicates some sympathy for him. It is certainly not *un*sympathetic. Hold on to this one.

(C) We are told that he plans to commit suicide in the passage, so the last part of this answer is correct. But is the tone farcical? While there is some irony involved in saying that a "bunch of other stuff that Makes Shit Happen" decides his fate, "farcical" is too strong a word. Half wrong is all wrong, so eliminate this one.

(D) Is the passage mock heroic? Again, he "stood staunchly" by his decision and his "army service medals" indicate military service, which may lead you to associate him with heroism. But there's no indication he's particularly heroic in the passage. As for vintage car enthusiasm, you don't have an indication of whether his car—the "Cavalier Musketeer Estate" of lines 5–6—is an old classic or not. Don't be distracted by a detail that may appear in the passage but does not provide the information needed to answer the question.

(E) There seems to be some irony in the passage, and an attempted suicide may lead you to conclude that it's dark. But you cannot be sure whether he's overly sensitive.

Eliminate the Obvious and Come Back
That leaves choices (B) and (E).

Ask yourself if the portrait is sympathetic. The author doesn't exactly seem to be shedding tears for him, so you're not sure. But neither is he condemned. You are also not clear about what the word "ironic" means. What should you do? Be brave.

Process of Elimination (POE)
Pick (B). You couldn't find anything wrong with (B).

Don't be afraid to pick answers you aren't sure are right. Sometimes that's necessary. Just make sure you don't pick answers that you think are probably wrong. We know that sounds obvious, but students do pick weak answers and they know they're doing it. Why? Because one answer was kind-of-but-not-really-right while the other was totally unfamiliar. The student thinks the unfamiliar answer might be right but then again, it might be embarrassingly wrong. The student picks the kind-of-but-not-really-right answer and loses points but thinks that's okay because at least it wasn't the embarrassing answer. Relax! You can't embarrass yourself on this exam. The multiple-choice questions are scored by a machine. No one—not

POE = BFF
Process of Elimination (POE) is your friend when it comes to multiple-choice questions. Instead of trying to pinpoint the right answer, focus instead on getting rid of the ones that are wrong.

your AP teacher, not your classmates, not the AP Essay Readers—knows or cares which answer you pick. Be fearless. If POE leaves you with two or three answers you aren't sure about—*pick one*. In the example above, (B) was correct. Don't let uncertainty on the definition of "ironic" mislead you into thinking material is darkly ironic when another answer might be more appropriate for the passage. Often irony takes the form of a subtle kind of humor when what is said is different from what is meant. **Irony** is an important term, both for the test and for the study of literature in general. We give it a full treatment in the glossary at the back of this book. But this is just one example, and irony comes in dozens of colors and flavors.

POE Summary

- When in doubt, narrow down the choices by looking for wrong answers.
- Eliminate what you can and then look more closely at what's left.
- Half wrong = all wrong.
- Don't leave any question blank, ever.

A PREVIEW OF COMING ATTRACTIONS

There's one more time management technique that you absolutely have to know. It's called the "Art of the Seven-Minute Passage." We'd like to tell you about it now, but unfortunately the full technique won't make sense until we've outlined the general principles of reading prose fiction or poetry analysis passages and shown you examples of the kinds of questions you'll see on the AP English Literature and Composition Exam. You'll find our explanation of the Art of the Seven-Minute Passage in Chapter 8.

Summary

Have a Plan

o   Note the time and number of texts to read: there will always be a total of 5 items and it will be a mix of poems and passages.

o   Pick a passage/poem to do first.

o   Pick a passage/poem to do last.

o   Work the text. Use active reading techniques.

o   Answer *all* the questions on the text, using our techniques.

Time Management

o   Guess aggressively.

o   Pick a text to do last based on what you consider your greatest weakness.

o   Skip a text, guess, or use your Letter of the Day (LOTD) on *all* the questions in that text, and still get a good score.

POE

o   Guess aggressively.

o   Use POE (Process of Elimination).

o   The best way to use POE is to look closely at the wording of each answer choice for what is wrong, and eliminate.

o   Bubble an answer for *all* questions, even if it's just your LOTD.

Chapter 2
Using Time Effectively to Maximize Points

> My alma mater was books, a good library.... I could spend the rest of my life reading, just satisfying my curiosity.
>
> —Malcolm X

BECOMING A BETTER TEST-TAKER

Very few students stop to think about how to improve their test-taking skills. Most assume that if they study hard, they will test well, and if they do not study, they will do poorly. Most students continue to believe this even after experience teaches them otherwise. Have you ever studied really hard for an exam and then blown it on test day? Have you ever aced an exam for which you thought you weren't well prepared? Most students have had one, if not both, of these experiences. The lesson should be clear: factors other than your level of preparation influence your final test score. This chapter will provide you with some insights that will help you perform better on the AP English Literature and Composition Exam and on other exams as well.

PACING AND TIMING

A big part of scoring well on an exam is working at a consistent pace. The worst mistake made by inexperienced or unsavvy test-takers is that they come to a question that stumps them and rather than just skip it, they panic and stall. Time stands still when you're working on a question you cannot answer, and it is not unusual for students to waste five minutes on a single question (especially a question involving the word *except*) because they are too stubborn to cut their losses. It is important to be aware of how much time you have spent on a given question and on the section you are working. There are several ways to improve your pacing and timing for the test:

- **Know your average pace.** While you prepare for your test, try to gauge how long you take on 5, 10, or 20 questions. Knowing how long you spend on average per question will help you identify how many questions you can answer effectively and how best to pace yourself for the test.
- **Have a watch or clock nearby.** You are permitted to have a watch or clock nearby to help you keep track of time. However, it's important to remember that constantly checking the clock is in itself a waste of time and can be distracting. Devise a plan. Try checking the clock every 15 or 30 questions to see whether you are keeping the correct pace or whether you need to speed up. This will ensure that you're cognizant of the time but will not permit you to fall into the trap of dwelling on it.
- **Know when to move on.** Since all questions are scored equally, investing appreciable amounts of time on a single question is inefficient and can potentially deprive you of the chance to answer easier ones later on. You should eliminate answer choices if you are able to, but don't worry about picking a random answer and moving on if you cannot find the correct answer. Remember, tests are like marathons; you do best when you work through them at a steady

pace. You can always come back to a question you don't know. When you do, very often you will find that your previous mental block is gone and you will wonder why the question perplexed you the first time around (as you gleefully move on to the next question). Even if you still don't know the answer, you will not have wasted valuable time you could have spent on questions that come easier to you.

- **Be selective.** You don't have to do any of the questions in a given section in order. If you are stumped by an essay or multiple-choice question, skip it or choose a different one and come back. Also, you probably do not have to answer every question correctly to achieve your desired score. Select the questions or essays that you can answer and work on them first. This will make you more efficient and give you the greatest chance of getting the most questions correct.

- **Use Process of Elimination (POE) on multiple-choice questions.** Many times, one or more answer choices can be eliminated. Every answer choice that can be eliminated increases the odds that you will answer the question correctly.

Remember, when all the questions on a test are of equal value, no one question is that important and your overall goal for pacing is to get the most questions correct. Finally, you should set a realistic goal for your final score. In the next section, we will break down how to achieve your desired score and how to pace yourself to do so.

GETTING THE SCORE YOU WANT

Depending on the score you need, it may be in your best interest not to try to work through every question. Check with the schools to which you are applying to determine your needed score.

AP Exams in all subjects no longer include a "guessing penalty" of a quarter of a point for every incorrect answer. Instead, students are assessed only on the total number of correct answers. A lot of AP materials, even those you receive in your AP class, may not include this information. It's really important to remember that if you are running out of time, you should fill in all the bubbles before the time for the multiple-choice section is up. Even if you don't plan to spend a lot of time on every question or even if you have no idea what the correct answer is, you need to fill something in. Use your LOTD, as we discussed earlier.

Go Online!
Check out us out on YouTube for test taking tips and techniques to help you ace your next exam at www.youtube.com/ThePrincetonReview

TEST ANXIETY

Everybody experiences anxiety before and during an exam. To a certain extent, test anxiety can be helpful. Some people find that they perform more quickly and efficiently under stress. If you've ever pulled an all-nighter to write a paper and ended up doing good work, you know the feeling.

However, too much stress is definitely a bad thing. Hyperventilating during the test, for example, almost always leads to a lower score. If you find that you stress out during exams, here are a few preemptive actions you can take.

Looking for More Help with Your APs?
We now offer specialized AP tutoring and course packages that guarantee a 4 or 5 on the AP. To see which courses are offered and available, and to learn more about the guarantee, visit PrincetonReview.com/college/ap-test-prep

- **Take a reality check.** Evaluate your situation before the test begins. If you have studied hard, remind yourself that you are well prepared. Remember that many others taking the test are not as well prepared, and (in your classes, at least) you are being graded against them, so you have an advantage. If you didn't study, accept the fact that you will probably not ace the test. Make sure you get to every question you know something about. In either scenario, it's best to think of a test as if it were a game. How can you get the most points in the time allotted to you? Always begin with questions you can answer easily and quickly before tackling those that will take more time.
- **Focus on what you can control.** Don't stress out or fixate on what you don't know. Even if you've underprepared (which shouldn't be the case since you're using this book), you can still improve your score by maximizing the benefits of what you do know.
- **Try to relax.** Slow, deep breathing works for almost everyone. Close your eyes, take a few slow, deep breaths, and concentrate on nothing but your inhalation and exhalation for a few seconds. This is a basic form of meditation that should help you to clear your mind of stress and, as a result, concentrate better on the test. If you have ever taken yoga classes, you probably know some other good relaxation techniques. Use them when you can (obviously, anything that requires leaving your seat and, say, assuming a handstand position won't be allowed by any but the most free-spirited proctors).
- **Eliminate as many surprises as you can.** Make sure you know where the test will be given, when it starts, what type of questions are going to be asked, and how long the test will take. You don't want to be worrying about any of these things on test day or, even worse, after the test has already begun.

The best way to avoid stress is to study both the test material and the test itself. Congratulations! By using this book, you are taking a major step toward a stress-free AP English Literature and Composition Exam.

REFLECT

Respond to the following questions:

- How long will you spend on multiple-choice questions?

- How will you change your approach to multiple-choice questions?

- What is your multiple-choice guessing strategy?

- How much time will you spend on the first essay? The second? The third?

- What will you do before you begin writing your essays?

- How will you change your approach to the essays?

- Will you seek further help, outside of this book (such as from a teacher, tutor, or AP Students), on how to approach multiple-choice questions, the essays, or a pacing strategy?

Chapter 3
Advanced Principles: Reading the Multiple-Choice Passages

> That's the thing about books. They let you travel without moving your feet.
>
> —Jhumpa Lahiri

READING THE PASSAGES IN THE MULTIPLE-CHOICE SECTION

Because of the time constraints, you should make sure that you go about reading the passages in the most efficient way possible. You might also want to use a slightly different approach depending on whether the passage is prose fiction or poetry analysis, but there are a few things you should keep in mind regarding both types of passages.

- You are reading in order to answer questions, not for enjoyment or appreciation. As you read, ask yourself, "Do I understand this well enough to answer a multiple-choice question about what it means?"
- You can come back to the passage anytime you want, and you *should* go back to the passage in order to answer the questions.

Both of these points address the same issue. The passages are on a test, but you don't do most of your reading on tests. Generally when you study for an English test, you read the works your teacher assigned and have to answer questions from memory; however, on the AP English Literature and Composition Exam, the passages will likely be unfamiliar, which can be a tad daunting. The test-writers deliberately select works that aren't typically taught in schools. The writers are great, familiar authors, but the works are more obscure.

The good news is that it's unlikely anyone else taking the test has seen the work before either; therefore, you're all starting with a similar level of knowledge. The best news is that this is an open-book test. You don't have to read the passage in the same way you read for English class. You're not looking to memorize information —you can use the passage to your advantage while answering the questions. Soak up the basic structure of the passage, but don't stress over remembering every little detail. Focus your attention only on what the questions are asking you, and find the parts of the passages that will help you answer appropriately.

Reading Prose Fiction Passages

The right way to read prose fiction passages in the multiple-choice section is simple. It's the method that works for YOU. Bear in mind that this is a timed test, so while we stand by the Active Reading tools provided in Chapter 1, you may want to modify or supplement those skills with the following. As you work through the practice drills and tests, make a point of trying different methods so that you can identify the one that's most efficient for you. It does you little good to fully understand a passage if that means you only have time to read and answer half the questions.

1. Preview the Questions

For some students, a quick reading of the questions provides *context*. For others, it's a total waste of time. When you're practicing on passages, try it each way and see what works best for you. Then, stick to that strategy. What you should do is read each question and only the question. Don't read the answer choices. Don't try to memorize the questions. Just get a sense of what they're asking you about—questions about literary devices or a certain character, for example. This can provide clues that will make your reading more active.

2a. Skim the Passage

There are two stances on active reading; one is to identify the main idea of each paragraph before moving on. The other expands upon the idea of previewing questions and suggests that you skim only the first and last sentences of the paragraphs to get an overall sense of what the passage is about. When you go back, either guided by questions or, time permitting, to read the passage (as outlined in the next step), you'll be less likely to trip up on context. The trade-off is the time you spend doing this.

2b. Read the Passage

Just read, without fixating on details, without getting stuck or going blank. When you hit a sentence you don't understand in a book, you don't panic, do you? You don't assume: "I might as well throw this book away...without that sentence it's just a useless collection of incomplete alphabetical symbols." When you read normally, you read for the *main idea*. You read to understand what's going on. When you hit a tricky sentence, you figure that you'll be able to make sense of it from what comes later, or that one missing piece of the puzzle isn't going to keep you from getting the outline of the overall picture. This is exactly how you want to read an AP English Literature and Composition Exam passage.

What Is the Main Idea?

For the AP English Literature and Composition Exam, main idea means the general point. It is the 10-words-or-fewer summary of the passage. The main idea is the gist, or the big picture. For example, suppose there's a passage about all the different ways a man is stingy, how he cheats his best friend out of an inheritance, and scrimps on food around the house so badly that his kids go to bed crying from hunger every night. The passage goes on for 50 or 60 lines describing this guy. The main idea is that this guy is an evil, greedy miser. If the passage gives a reason for the miser's obsession with money, you might include that in your mental picture of the main idea: This guy is an evil, greedy miser because he grew up poor. No doubt the passage tells you exactly how he grew up and where (in an orphanage, let's say), and exactly what kind of leftover beans he eats (lima) and exactly how many cold leftover lima beans he serves to his starving kids each night (three apiece), but those are details, not the big picture. Use the details to build up to the big picture.

The Magic Topic Sentence Has Vanished

We don't want you to think that the main idea can be found in some magic "topic sentence." The writers on the AP Exam are sophisticated; they often don't use any obvious clues like topic sentences. With poetry analysis passages especially, looking for topic sentences is a waste of time; however, use context clues to make inferences regarding theme and main idea.

Don't Be Afraid to Skim!
The idea of "skimming" might inspire panic in some students who want to read every single word. But when done correctly, skimming is a great way to get a sense of the passage before diving into the questions.

Summary—How Do You Read an AP Multiple-Choice Prose Fiction Passage?

- Preview the questions (optional).
- Skim the passage.
- Read for the main idea.

Reading Poetry Analysis Passages

Ideally, you read a poem several times, ponder, scratch your head, and read some more. Then again, ideally you have your favorite poem by your favorite poet, and all afternoon to read—not 12 minutes with some poem you couldn't care less about and between 8 and 13 multiple-choice questions staring you in the face.

It's a test, so you've got to read the poem efficiently, and the key to the process is keeping your mind open, especially the first time through.

It might help to be clear about the difference between a narrative and the kind of poetry you'll see on the AP Exam. A narrative unfolds and builds on itself. Although one's understanding of what came earlier in the narrative is deepened and changed by later developments, by and large the work makes sense as it flows; it is meant to be understood "on the run."

Verse is different. Yes, the way it unfolds is important, but one often doesn't even grasp that unfolding until the second or third (or ninetieth) read. A poem is like a sculpture; it is meant to be wandered around, looked at from all sides, and finally taken in as a whole. You wouldn't try to understand a sculpture until you'd seen the whole thing. In the same way, think of your first reading of a poem as a walk around an interesting sculpture. You aren't trying to interpret. You are just trying to look at the whole thing. Once you've seen it and taken in its dimensions, then you can go back and puzzle it out.

What we've just said applies to poetry in general. But how can you apply that to the AP Exam? Here's the answer: *when you approach a poem on the AP Exam, always read it at least twice before you go to the questions.*

Poem Preview
Leave analysis out of your first read of a poem. Instead, look at it as a whole and get a general feel for it.

Skim

The first read is to get all the words in your head. Go from top to bottom. Don't stop at individual lines to figure them out. If everything makes sense, great. If it doesn't, no problem. The main thing you want is a basic sense of what's going on. The main thing to avoid is getting a fixed impression of the poem before you've even finished it.

Then Focus

The second read should be phrase by phrase. Focus on understanding what you read in the simplest way possible. This is when you should look for the main idea.

Don't worry about symbols. Don't worry about deeper meanings. The questions will direct you toward those aspects of the poem. You will need to go back and read parts of it, perhaps the entire thing, several more times, but only as is necessary to answer individual questions. To prepare yourself for the questions, all you need is a general sense of what the poem says and to get that understanding you need only the literal sense of the lines. We can't emphasize this point enough: *keep it simple.*

Panic and Obsession

Don't panic if you can't seem to grasp the meaning of a poem. Many people are probably struggling and completely baffled by the same poem. Don't skip the passage. Look for questions that take you to specific line item details ("In lines 56–60...") and attempt to answer those questions using the specific lines of poetry. POE is your friend here! Don't obsess over the poem or the answers. Do your best to provide an answer using POE, but if you really get stuck, don't dwell. Choose an answer (maybe your LOTD) and move on.

The Difficulties of Poetry Analysis

Good poetry makes conscious use of all language's resources. By pushing the limits of language, poetry creates a heightened awareness in the reader. Poets sometimes use uncommon vocabulary, odd figures of speech, and unusual combinations of words in strange orders; they play with time and stretch the connections we see between ideas. All of these essential resources can make poetry analysis seem difficult, but it's not impossible. One important thing to remember is that many poems are open to a myriad of valid interpretations. It's not your job to have a meaningful experience when reading poetry on a test; it's your job to read for language resources and main ideas that will help you to answer the questions correctly.

Reading Poetry Resourcefully

You can connect to a poem in many ways, but you aren't reading for a nice, meditative experience on the AP Exam: you're reading to answer the questions correctly. The following things are what you're looking to identify and analyze as you read:

- Punctuation use
- Diction (word choice)
- Imagery
- Theme/main idea
- Figurative language (metaphors, similes, synecdoche)
- Character
- Setting
- Structure
- Narrator

A Word by Any Other Name Would Still Smell As Neat
You won't necessarily have to define words like "synecdoche" or use them in a sentence, but you should be aware of the different varieties of figurative language, the better to be on the lookout for them. Be sure to read through the Glossary beginning on page 333.

The Pros Read Poetry for Prose

The secret to understanding AP poetry analysis passages quickly and fully is to simply ignore the "poetry parts." Ignore the rhythm, ignore the music of the language, and above all, ignore the form. This means you should do the following:

- Ignore line breaks.
- Read in sentences, not in lines. Emphasize punctuation.
- Ignore rhyme and rhyme scheme.
- Be prepared for "long" thoughts—ideas that develop over several lines.

When approaching poetry, many students tend to do the opposite of what we suggest here: they emphasize lines and line breaks and totally ignore sentence punctuation.

True, sometimes there's no problem: when lines break at natural pauses and each line has a packet of meaning complete in itself (these are termed *end-stopped* lines), the poem becomes easier to read.

Challenging Poetry

Consider the next selection. It's the first 13 or so lines of "My Last Duchess" by Robert Browning. This is the kind of poetry you can expect to find on the AP Exam, but it is unlikely that you would see a poem that is this well known.

The poem is a monologue spoken by a nobleman, the Duke of Ferrara, to a representative of the Count of Tyrol. Ferrara seeks to take the wealthy count's daughter for his bride and is in the midst of discussing the arrangement with the count's representative. When Ferrara speaks of his "last duchess," he refers to his first wife, who has quite recently died at the age of 17 under mysterious circumstances. The implication is that Ferrara has had his first wife murdered, an implication the poem brings home with understated menace.

You won't be given this kind of information on the test, but with practice, you should be able to figure out many of the aspects of the poem by yourself. For example, the first two lines of the poem (which is printed below in sections) give a careful reader some important information. The speaker of the poem is a duke, who is talking about his "last duchess." He is standing in front of a painting of this woman who is no longer alive. All of this information, if assimilated readily and with an eye toward tone and the big picture, will help you answer questions, even if the questions don't ask specifically who the speaker is or whether the duchess is alive.

My Last Duchess
FERRARA

That's my last duchess painted on the wall,
Looking as if she were alive. I call
That piece a wonder, now: Frà Pandolf's hands
Line   Worked busily a day, and there she stands.
(5)   Will't please you sit and look at her? I said
"Frà Pandolf" by design, for never read
Strangers like you that pictured countenance,
The depth and passion of its earnest glance,
But to myself they turned (since none puts by
(10)   The curtain I have drawn for you, but I)
And seemed as they would ask me, if they durst,
how such a glance came there; so, not the first
Are you to turn and ask thus…

This poem is challenging, but it's not impossible with the right reading strategies. Remember: you're supposed to come into the test with a plan! The first few lines are relatively straightforward: the duke points to the painting, remarks on its lifelike quality, mentions the artist (Frà Pandolf), and invites his listener to sit and contemplate the portrait for a moment. Although lines 3–4, "Frà Pandolf's hands/ Worked busily a day" consist of distinctly unmodern speech and might give some folks a moment's pause, there are signposts to help guide readers. Even if you don't know that "Frà" is used as a title of address to an Italian monk (and who does?), you can still figure out the big picture of this poem.

Then comes the remainder of the passage, beginning from line 5, "I said/'Frà Pandolf' by design, for never read," and the trouble begins. Now, the truth is that what is written there is easy enough that if you can break the habit of placing too much emphasis on line breaks, you can read it as prose. Browning has deliberately written his verse so that the lines break against the flow of the punctuation. If you expect little parcels of complete meaning at every break, you'll end up lost. Let's consider the troubling part written as prose:

"I said 'Frà Pandolf' by design, for never read strangers like you that pictured countenance, the depth and passion of its earnest glance, but to myself they turned (since none puts by the curtain I have drawn for you, but I) and seemed as they would ask me, if they durst, how such a glance came there."

Poem Woes
If the way lines break in a poem is completely confusing for you, read the poem as if it were prose. This strategy will help you crack even notoriously challenging poems by poets such as Robert Browning.

This is just one long sentence, broken by parenthetical asides, in which the duke says, "I said 'Frà Pandolf' on purpose because strangers never see that portrait (or its expression of depth and passion) without turning to me (because nobody sees the portrait unless I'm here to pull aside the curtain) and looking at me as though they want to ask, if they dare, 'How did that expression get there?'"

Read the poem as prose and you'll see it's pretty easy. If you have trouble doing this, try putting brackets around each sentence.

Now if you're really alert, you'll notice that the duke still hasn't exactly explained why he mentioned Frà Pandolf on purpose. He eventually does (in his sideways fashion), but if you read poetry without being ready for long thoughts that develop over several lines, you're going to read "I said, 'Frà Pandolf' by design, for never…" and expect the explanation—pronto. When it doesn't come you think you're lost, and once you think you're lost, you are. How is "that pictured countenance" an explanation of why he said "Frà Pandolf?" It isn't, and it never will be, but you can spend hours trying to come up with reasons why it is.

Don't get the wrong impression. Browning isn't easy reading. But you'll find that if you follow our suggestions for reading poetry, you can cut to the heart of what Browning and poets like him are saying. Ignore line breaks and instead pay close attention to punctuation and sentence structure. Be ready for "long" thoughts that develop over several lines or even stanzas. You'll still find the poems on the AP Exam challenging for a variety of reasons: because of their vocabulary, because of their compression of a great deal of information into just a few lines, and because of their often complicated and unusual sentence structure.

If you read poetry the way we suggest, however, you'll find that you can still use the context of what you do understand to answer questions.

Here's Browning's "My Last Duchess" in complete form. Read it according to our advice and see what you can get from it. (Many discussions of this famous poem exist online, and you can read a few in order to compare what you've figured out with what others have said about it.)

Prose Pros

Reading poetry effectively boils down to one simple concept: before you read a poem as poetry, read it as prose.

Ferrara

That's my last duchess painted on the wall,
Looking as if she were alive. I call
That piece a wonder, now: Frà Pandolf's hands
Line   Worked busily a day, and there she stands.
(5)   Will't please you sit and look at her? I said
"Frà Pandolf" by design, for never read
Strangers like you that pictured countenance,
The depth and passion of its earnest glance,
But to myself they turned (since none puts by
(10)   The curtain I have drawn for you, but I)
And seemed as they would ask me, if they durst,
how such a glance came there; so, not the first

Are you to turn and ask thus. Sir, 'twas not
Line   Her husband's presence only, called that spot
(15)   Of joy into the Duchess' cheek: perhaps
Frà Pandolf chanced to say, "Her mantle laps
"Over my lady's wrist too much," or "Paint
"Must never hope to reproduce the faint
"Half-flush that dies along her throat": such stuff
(20)   Was courtesy, she thought, and cause enough
For calling up that spot of joy. She had
A heart—how shall I say?—too soon made glad,
Too easily impressed; she liked whate'er
She looked on, and her looks went everywhere.
(25)   Sir, 'twas all one! My favor at her breast,
The dropping of the daylight in the West,
The bough of cherries some officious fool
Broke in the orchard for her, the white mule
She rode with round the terrace—all and each
(30)   Would draw from her alike the approving speech,
Or blush, at least. She thanked men—good! but thanked
Somehow—I know not how—as if she ranked
My gift of a nine-hundred-years-old name
With anybody's gift. Who'd stoop to blame
(35)   This sort of trifling? Even had you skill
In speech—which I have not—to make your will
Quite clear to such an one, and say, "Just this
"Or that in you disgusts me; here you miss,
"Or there exceed the mark"—and if she let
(40)   Herself be lessoned so, nor plainly set
Her wits to yours, forsooth, and made excuse,
—E'en then would be some stooping; and I choose
Never to stoop. Oh sir, she smiled, no doubt,
Whene'er I passed her; but who passed without
(45)   Much the same smile? This grew; I gave commands;
Then all smiles stopped together. There she stands
As if alive. Will't please you rise? We'll meet
The company below, then. I repeat,
The Count your master's known munificence
(50)   Is ample warrant that no just pretense
Of mine for dowry will be disallowed;
Though his fair daughter's self, as I avowed
At starting, is my object. Nay, we'll go
Together down, sir. Notice Neptune, though,
(55)   Taming a sea-horse, thought a rarity,
Which Claus of Innsbrück cast in bronze for me!

Easier Poetry

Look at these lines from Thomas Gray's "Elegy Written in a Country Churchyard":

> Now fades the glimmering landscape on the sight,
> And all the air a solemn stillness holds,
> Save where the beetle wheels his droning flight,
> And drowsy tinklings lull the distant folds.

Read this passage aloud, and you can't help but stop on the line endings even if there were no commas. The lines build, one upon the next, shaping a picture as they combine to form a mildly complex sentence. The ease with which these lines can be read stems from the fact that each line contains only complete thoughts; there are no loose ends trailing from line to line. This is "nice" poetry; that is, it's nice to you. Each line ends on a natural pause that lets you gather your thoughts. Each line holds something like a complete thought with very little runover into the next line. Although the stanza is written in one sentence, it easily could have been written in four separate sentences:

> The landscape fades.
> The air is still.
> The beetle wheels and drones.
> The tinklings [of bells worn by livestock] lull the folds.*

*Folds are enclosures where sheep graze, or the flocks of sheep themselves.

This paraphrase is lousy poetry, but it gets the main idea across. If the poetry you see on the AP Exam reads like the example above, great. But if you think every poem should be like that stanza or if you try to make every poem read like that one, you're headed for trouble. The poetry on the AP Exam is likely to be more challenging.

Summary

Basics of Reading Passages

o   You are reading in order to answer the questions—that's the whole point.

o   Reading for a test is different from normal reading. You have limited time, and you have to approach the passages in a way that takes that restriction into account.

o   You can reread the passage (or parts of it) anytime you want, and you should go back to the passage in order to answer the questions.

Reading Prose Fiction Passages

o   Preview the questions if it helps you.

o   Skim the passage.

o   Skimming should never take more than a minute.

o   Read for the main idea.

Reading Poetry Analysis Passages

o   Preview the questions if it helps you.

o   On the exam, read the poem twice before you answer the questions.

o   The first read is to get all the words in your head.
   •   The main thing you want is a basic sense of what's going on.
   •   Try not to get a fixed impression of the poem before you've even finished it.

o   The second read should be done phrase by phrase. Focus on understanding what you read in the simplest way possible. Don't worry about symbols. Don't worry about deeper meanings. Try to visualize what you're reading as you follow the narration of the poem. Also try reading the poem as you would read prose. (See "Poetry into Prose" below.)

o   You will need to go back and read parts of the poem—perhaps the entire poem—several more times, but only as necessary for your work on individual questions.

Poetry into Prose

o   Find the spine—the prose meaning—of the poem.
   •   Ignore line breaks.
   •   Emphasize punctuation. Read in sentences, not in lines.
   •   Be prepared for "long" thoughts: ideas that develop over several lines.

o   Before you read a poem as poetry, read it as prose.

Chapter 4
Cracking the System: Multiple-Choice Questions

"

Education is not preparation for life;
education is life itself.

—John Dewey

"

QUESTION TYPES AND FORMATS

Once you've finished working a passage using active reading techniques, you need to answer the questions. If you've paid attention so far, you already know you're going to answer *all* of the questions, using your Letter of the Day to guess when you aren't sure of the answer. You should also know by now that you must approach the test efficiently, making the most of your time in order to get the best possible score.

In order to answer the questions efficiently, you'll need to be able to recognize two main types of questions:

- general comprehension questions that concern the prose fiction selection or poem as a whole
- detail questions that focus on one part of the passage

and two question formats:

- Standard
- EXCEPT/LEAST/NOT

Answer all of the questions. Use your Letter of the Day to guess if you don't know the answer.

General Comprehension Questions

General comprehension questions ask about the overall passage. These questions don't send you back to any specific line(s) or paragraph(s) in the passage.

Here are some examples of general comprehension questions.

- The passage is primarily concerned with…
- Which one of the following choices best describes the tone of the passage?
- Which one of the following choices best describes the narrator's relationship to her mother?
- How does the author's use of irony contribute to the effect of the poem?
- To whom does the speaker of the poem address his speech?
- It is evident in the passage that the author feels her home town is…

As these examples show, a general comprehension question can target either the passage as a whole, as the first question about theme (main point) does, or it can focus on one aspect of the entire passage, as the second question about tone does. In either case, the scope of the question covers the whole passage from beginning to end. If (in the third question) the narrator's relationship to her mother sounds harmonious in the first couple of lines but is revealed as adversarial throughout the rest of the passage, then "adversarial" is the answer that "best describes" the relationship. You need to consider the overall impression given by the whole passage.

General comprehension questions will often ask about the following:

- **The theme (main point) or author's purpose.** What is the author writing about? Why? What does the author intend for readers to think or feel or believe or do after they finish reading?

- **The tone.** What is the author's (or the narrator's) overall attitude toward the subject of the passage? Is he or she critical? Approving? Neutral? Is the author being humorous, satirical, ironic or deadly serious? Is he or she skeptical or a believer? And—very important—how do you know what the author's attitude is?

- **The style.** Here you're looking for diction (word choice), syntax (sentence choice) and literary devices—in other words, how the author conveys the theme and purpose. Is the vocabulary sophisticated or something that almost all readers could understand? Are the sentence structures varied (a mix of simple and complex, loose and periodic)? Does the author rely on literary devices (such as allusions, repetition, and symbols) to convey the theme, or is the delivery straightforward?

- **The structure.** How does the narrative progress? Do events occur in chronological order? Is the progression interrupted by flashbacks or flashforwards or dream sequences? When are the main characters introduced? When do major points in the plot occur? Are two similar plots being developed in parallel? Is there a sudden change (perhaps in emphasis or tone) part of the way through? Why? How are the different pieces connected and— very important—why did the author choose to connect them in this way?

- **The narrator's point of view.** Does the author use a first-person narrator ("I") whose personality, background, and biases act as a filter through which events are described? Or is the narrator an objective, camera-type recorder of events? What impact does the type of narrator have on the passage? Is there more than one narrator?

- **The development.** How does the plot develop? What techniques does the author use in order to develop a character? How does the author develop the main point?

- **The character(s).** Who are the characters? How are they described? What qualities or attributes do they have? What do they indicate about the author's values, beliefs, or assumptions? Do they reveal any biases or assumptions of a time or place? Do the characters change? Stay the same?

- **The setting.** What, if anything, are you told about the setting? Where are the characters physically? What time period are they in? What do aspects of the setting reveal about the theme, the plot, or the characters? What effect do aspects of the setting have on the passage?

Detail Questions

Detail questions almost always send you back to specific places in the passage. They tell you where to look and ask something about a particular segment or even a specific word.

> Always read at least one sentence or line before and after the place indicated in the question, so you'll have the correct context.

Here are some examples of detail questions.

- What significant change occurs in the speaker's attitude toward the countryside in lines 5–9?
- How do the final words of the third paragraph, "but then, I should have known better than to trust him," alter the remainder of the passage?
- In lines 1–5, the phrase "This loaf's big" is used as a metaphor for
- The poet's use of the word "sublime" (line 21) suggests that
- What does the pond in the first paragraph symbolize?
- Which of the following is the best paraphrase for the sentence that begins at line 9?

If you're having trouble grasping the overall theme of a passage or the author's purpose, the specific questions are a good place to start. You'll learn more about the passage with each one you answer, and the whole passage just might fall into place.

QUESTION FORMATS

Standard

The most common question format on the exam, standard format questions have a straightforward question stem, followed by five answer choices. Here are some examples of standard format question stems:

- The metaphor "fountain of delight" in paragraph 2 has the effect of
- The dream described in lines 30–32 suggests that
- The author's attitude toward his subject could be characterized as

EXCEPT/LEAST/NOT

Even though the test-writers put EXCEPT, LEAST or NOT in capital letters, you could still miss those crucial words if you're just racing through the question stems instead of reading them carefully, word for word. In essence, these three qualifiers invert the answer you'd normally be looking for in a standard format question. Consider these examples:

- Ludwig seems to value all of the following characteristics in a business partner EXCEPT
- Which of the following characteristics does Ludwig consider the LEAST important in a business partner?
- Ludwig is NOT looking for which of these characteristics in a business partner?

Which four characteristics does the passage say Ludwig wants to see in a business partner? Those four will be in the answer choices. But those aren't what you're looking for. You want the one characteristic he does NOT consider important, or considers the LEAST important, or is the EXCEPTion to what he thinks is important.

To tackle these tricky questions, disregard the EXCEPT, LEAST or NOT; cross them out. You'll be left with a standard format question:

- Ludwig seems to value [which of] the following characteristics in a business partner ~~EXCEPT~~
- Which of the following characteristics does Ludwig consider ~~the LEAST~~ important in a business partner?
- Ludwig is ~~NOT~~ looking for which of these characteristics in a business partner?

Now eliminate any choice that would be a correct answer for your new, standard format question. The remaining choice will be the correct answer for the EXCEPT/LEAST/NOT version of the question.

How Much Grammar Do You Need to Know for the AP English Lit Exam?

There are usually three or four questions on basic grammar. That's one grammar question or fewer per passage, so grammar is not a big deal on the multiple-choice section. The samples we provide in Chapters 7 and 8 should give you a good idea of what the grammar questions are like. Because there are so few grammar questions, we don't recommend you spend a lot of time studying grammar. You'd be far better off working on writing timed essays or reading poetry.

Model Sentence I

Here's a great simple sentence to memorize for basic grammatical relations:

Sam threw the orange to Irene.

It isn't poetry, but this sentence clearly shows the basic grammatical relationships you need to concern yourself with on the AP Exam.

- *Sam* is the subject.
- *The orange* is the direct object.
- *Irene* is the indirect object.
- *Threw* is the verb.

Notice that in this sentence, the direct object is in fact an object (an orange). The orange is thrown to Irene, the indirect object. In other words, the indirect object receives the direct object. The concept is pretty simple.

Model Sentence II

There are two more sentence elements you should understand: the phrase and the clause. Here's a model sentence that should help you keep clear on their definitions.

Feeling generous, Sam threw the orange to Irene, who tried to catch it.

The heart of the sentence is still *Sam threw the orange to Irene*, as subject, verb, direct object, and indirect object all remain the same. But we've added a phrase to the beginning of the sentence and a dependent (also called *subordinate*) clause to the end. Both phrases and dependent clauses function as modifiers. *Feeling generous* (a phrase) modifies *Sam*; and *who tried to catch it* (a clause) modifies *Irene*.

The difference between clauses and phrases is simple:

> A **clause** has both a subject and a verb.
>
> A **phrase** does not have both a subject and a verb.

Because a clause has both a subject and verb, a clause is always close to being a sentence of its own. The dependent clause, *who tried to catch it,* could be turned into a complete sentence by replacing *who* with *Irene* or *she,* or adding a question mark at the end.

The hallmark of a phrase is its lack of a subject or verb (or both). Phrases obviously cannot stand alone. *Feeling generous* needs the addition of both a subject (*Sam*) and a verb (*was*) in order to become the sentence *Sam was feeling generous.*

Our model sentence contains another clause besides the dependent clause we've already mentioned. The other clause is *Sam threw the orange to Irene*. Because it has both a subject and a verb, it must be a clause. Notice that it doesn't need any changes in order to stand alone as a complete sentence: that makes it an *independent* clause.

Terms of Disservice

Grammar is one of those things that helps with just about everything else, from comprehension of a tricky sentence to linking up parallel ideas and identifying structure. But specific questions about grammar basically boil down to things like whether you know what an antecedent is. Because there are so few grammar questions on this test, it's better to focus on the active reading and POE skills that will help you get through the other questions.

ORDERING THE QUESTIONS

You can complete the questions in any order you like, but that doesn't mean you should jump around and do them in any old order. After you finish reading a passage, but before you begin answering the questions, ask yourself, "Do I feel confident about this passage? Would I be able to explain this to a friend? Could I explain its main idea?"

The answer to this question determines the order in which you should tackle the test questions.

- If you feel confident about your comprehension of the passage, complete the questions in the order they are given to you. Don't worry about the order of the questions; you're in good shape.
- If you don't feel confident about the main idea, do the detail questions first.

The reasoning behind this ordering method is simple. The main idea is the crucial thing to get from a reading passage, whether prose fiction or poetry. When you have the main idea nailed down, you aren't likely to miss more than a few questions on the passage. Knowing the main idea will help you answer all of the other general questions and many of the specific questions as well.

When you don't feel confident about the main idea (which usually means the passage is pretty confusing), start with the specific questions because they tell you exactly where to go and also give you something on which to focus.

As you reread the lines toward which the specific questions point you, you should become more and more familiar with the passage. Often after doing a specific question or two, the meaning of the passage "clicks" for you, and you will get what's going on. Don't answer the general questions until you have a firm sense of the main idea. If, after answering all the specific questions, you still don't really know what the point of the passage is, give the general questions your best shot and move on.

Bonus Tips and Tricks…
Check us out on YouTube for additional test taking tips and must-know strategies at www.youtube.com/ThePrincetonReview

CONSISTENCY OF ANSWERS #1

The main idea should be your guiding rule for most of the questions on any passage. We call this principle *Consistency of Answers*. As you work on a passage or poem, you will find that the best answer on several of the questions has to do with the main idea. Here's the rule: **when in doubt, pick an answer that agrees with the main idea.**

CONSISTENCY OF ANSWERS #2

Pick answers that agree with each other. You'll also find that correct answers tend to be consistent. It's a simple idea that comes in very handy. For example, if you're sure the correct answer to question 9 is (B), and (B) says that Mr. Buffalo is extremely hairy, you can be sure that question 10's Mr. Buffalo isn't bald. Correct answers agree with each other.

Consistency Is Key
When in doubt, choose an answer that agrees with the main idea of the passage.

The best way to understand how to use this very effective technique is to see it at work. You'll see plenty of examples in Chapters 7 and 8; we'll discuss this technique in detail when we work on actual questions.

GUESSING AGGRESSIVELY WITH POE

First things first: don't leave any questions blank! There is no guessing penalty: worst-case scenario, guess blindly. But guessing smartly is much better! POE is an acronym for Process of Elimination. You are probably already acquainted with POE in its simplest form: cross out the answers that you know are wrong.

There are always two ways to answer a multiple-choice question correctly. The first is to have the answer in mind right from the moment you read the question. If you understand the passage and the question, you'll often see the best answer among the choices. Far more often, however, you'll be slightly (or not-so-slightly) unsure. The test-writers are pretty good at spotting places in a text where students are likely to have trouble, and they tend to write questions about these spots. The test-writers are also pretty good at writing wrong answers that are quite appealing. Before you doubt yourself, however, make sure you have read the question carefully. It's possible to understand the passage but misread a question. The extra second or two you devote to reading the question may increase the number of questions you answer correctly. Still, no matter how strong a reader you are, some questions will cause you to have doubts about the answer. That's when you use The Princeton Review–style POE. What does that mean? It means: *Stop looking for the right answer—look for wrong answers and eliminate them.* Let's look at the same example we used on page 56, from Zadie Smith's *White Teeth*:

Early in the morning, late in the century,
Cricklewood Broadway. At 0627 hours on January
1, 1975, Alfred Archibald Jones was dressed in
Line corduroy and sat in a fume-filled Cavalier Muske-
(5) teer Estate facedown on the steering wheel, hoping
the judgment would not be too heavy upon him.
He lay in a prostrate cross, jaw slack, arms splayed
on either side like some fallen angel; scrunched up
in each fist he held his army service medals (left)
(10) and his marriage license (right), for he had decided
to take his mistakes with him. A little green light
flashed in his eye, signaling a right turn he had
resolved never to make. He was resigned to it. He
was prepared for it. He had flipped a coin and stood
(15) staunchly by the results. This was a decided-upon
suicide. In fact, it was a New Year's resolution.

....

While he slipped in and out of consciousness, the
position of the planets, the music of the spheres, the
flap of a tiger moth's diaphanous wings in Central
(20) Africa, and a whole bunch of other stuff that Makes
Shit Happen had decided it was second-chance time
for Archie. Somewhere, somehow, by somebody, it
had been decided that he would live.

1. Lines 3–16 of the passage best describe the author's portrayal
   of Alfred Archibald Jones as

   (A) a harshly condemnatory treatment of a coward
   (B) a sympathetic portrayal of a man who regrets his life
   (C) a farcical portrayal of an attempted suicide
   (D) a mock heroic portrait of a vintage car enthusiast
   (E) a darkly ironic treatment of an overly sensitive man

This is a typical AP English Lit question. It asks for an evaluation of a passage for comprehension. The majority of the questions take this form. In the example above, you've been asked, essentially, "What's going on in lines 3–16?" The actual passage would have been longer (usually around 55 lines), and the rest of the passage would certainly help you understand this section by putting it in context, but nevertheless, there is enough here to answer the question.

If you don't immediately spot the best answer, use POE. Go to each choice and say, "Why is this wrong?" You can look back at the explanations on pages 56–57 to check your thinking.

Summary

- o Recognize the basic categories of questions.
  - General Comprehension
  - Detail

- o Don't worry about grammar for the AP English Literature and Composition Exam. It isn't worth enough points to cause perspiration.

- o Do it your way.
  - If you know the main idea, answer the questions in order.
  - If you're uncomfortable with the main idea, answer detail and factual questions first.

- o Use Consistency of Answers.
  - When in doubt, pick an answer that agrees with the main idea.
  - Pick answers that agree with each other.

- o Guess aggressively as needed using POE.

Chapter 5
Basic Principles of the Essay Section

> Fill your paper with the breathings of your heart.
>
> —William Wadsworth

FORMAT AND CONTENT OF THE ESSAY SECTION

Section II of the AP English Literature and Composition Exam is the Free-Response, or essay, section. While the College Board officially refers to this section of the exam as "Free Response," in this book we will often refer to it as the "essay" section, and your responses as "essays," for the sake of brevity. The format of this section has been consistent for years. Here's what to expect.

- You will be asked to write a response, in essay form, to each of the following subjects:
  1. A passage of poetry or a comparison of two thematically related poems
  2. A passage of prose fiction
  3. A literary argument: an essay on a literary concept or idea supported by evidence from your own reading or a provided list
- You'll be given all the paper you need (including scratch paper), and you'll be instructed to write in pen (blue or black ink only).
- You'll have two hours to complete this section, which works out to be 40 minutes per essay.

Remember the Big Six!
The AP exam expects you to make use of the Big Six during the essay section. Remember, that's character, setting, structure, narration, figurative language like metaphor and personification, plus using the skills of literary argumentation (developing a thesis supported by textual evidence). In fact, the essays are all exercises in literary argumentation! So while you may be reading a 20th-century novelist or an English Renaissance poet, don't forget the Big Six. As you read each passage for the essay, thinking about how character, setting, structure, and narration can help you develop what you want to say, and how any figurative language you see in the passage works.

What Will You Be Writing About?

When ETS considers the mix of literary periods and styles on the test, it includes the essay section in that mix. If you see two passages on 18th-century poetry in the multiple-choice section, you won't see any 18th-century poetry in the essay section. ETS also tries to give male and female authors (roughly) equal representation and aims to include at least one author who identifies as African American, Native American, Latino, or Asian.

What Are The Directions?

The College Board will give you a bit of text to orient you to the work (they will likely map out the work's themes and date of publication), then they will ask that you do 4 things, which they put in a handy bulleted list that we will print right here.

In your response you should do the following:

- Respond to the prompt with a thesis that presents an interpretation and may establish a line of reasoning.
- Select and use evidence to develop and support your line of reasoning.
- Explain the relationship between the evidence and your thesis.
- Use appropriate grammar and punctuation in communicating your argument.

If you have written essays for classes, you probably see that this is standard stuff that they want:

Thesis—Your take on exactly what they are asking. You're confident and eager to show them that you understand both the essay prompt and the work itself!

Evidence—You definitely get it and now we're diving into your reasoning. Here are your examples that back up your thesis.

More Evidence—Would they like some MORE examples with those examples? You're happy to oblige!

Finally, remember to use some solid vocabulary, correct punctuation, grammar, and spelling throughout. The word "throughout" makes us think about how much time you have to crank out this spectacular essay. It's time to talk pacing.

Pacing

On each individual essay, you can take as much or as little time as you like as long as you don't go over the two-hour limit for all three essays. Each essay is worth the same number of points, so it's a good idea to pace yourself and allot 40 minutes for each, give or take a few minutes. If you spend an hour and a half on your first essay, you're not going to finish the other two. Remember to take a watch so that you don't lose track of time.

The Importance of the Essay Section to Your Score

The essay section of the AP English Literature and Composition Exam counts for 55 percent of your total score. It is only slightly more important than the multiple-choice section of the test. It's obvious, but let's say it anyway: both sections are important to your score.

Which section *feels* more important is another issue. For most students, the essay section feels like the whole test. The multiple-choice section seems like a bunch of hoops you have to jump through before getting to the part that matters. Students tend to look at the essay section with quite a bit of anxiety. However, we're going to take the anxiety out of this process and replace it with knowledge and confidence.

Here's the interesting part: while it is true that the multiple-choice and essay sections are nearly equal in respect to determining your score, there is a world of difference between the two sections when it comes to score improvement.

More Great Titles from The Princeton Review
Are you a king or queen of composition? Are you also taking the AP English Language and Composition course? Check out *AP English Language & Composition Prep,* our comprehensive prep guide for the test.

When It Comes to Improving Your Score, the Essays Are King

If you're the kind of student who gets A's in class and then bombs on standardized tests, using our multiple-choice techniques will make a huge difference. If you are already a natural test-taker, that's great—our techniques will help you take your skills to the next level. You probably fall somewhere in between (the vast majority of students do), and so using our techniques for the multiple-choice section squeezes out a half-dozen or so extra points to ensure that you get your best possible score. Why settle for anything less? But when you work on improving your score (and your skills), the essays are different.

These Essays Are Different

Essay points add up fast. If we can show you a way to improve your essays by just 1 point—*bam*—then that means 3 extra essay points just like that, 1 for each essay. And there are only 18 total essay points available. And now that the College Board has made the essay grading "analytical" (no longer "holistic") and released detailed grading rubrics, you can know precisely how you can rack up points on the 3 essays.

Think about this: unlike the old, familiar multiple-choice questions, the essays are completely new. You've never done anything like them before, so you may as well learn to do them in a way that will get you the most points. "What!?" you're thinking, "It's the multiple-choice that's weird; I write essays *all the time* in school."

Sorry, but you're mistaken. You write essays, true—but not AP Exam essays.

Your Teacher Knows You

You usually write essays for teachers who know you and (we hope) care about you. They know what your writing looked like at the beginning of the semester, they know whether you do your homework, they know whether you spend most of class daydreaming, they know you occasionally make brilliant comments in class, and they know your real passion is for track or violin or painting or science or maybe even writing.

When your teachers see your name at the top of the page, they already know a thousand things about you, and all of it goes into their reading of what you write. The AP Reader, on the other hand, doesn't know you at all.

You Know Your Teacher

Second, and just as important, you don't know anything about the Reader of your AP essays. Who is she or he? In school, you know your teachers. You probably know what they want to hear. You may know that they detest misspellings, or that they love it when you use humor, or that they give extra credit for artistic originality. The AP essays are written to someone who is completely anonymous. When was the last time you wrote an essay to a total stranger for a grade?

Read It—Write It—Go!

AP essays are written under intense time restraints. You've probably never seen the excerpt or the prompt, but that's okay. You have the reading and writing strategies to tackle anything at this point. Your teachers have probably told you that good writing is rewriting; however, you don't have time to write and revise on the AP Exam. In a test setting, your draft is your final submission, and that means you have to be extra attentive to the structural and content quality of your writing. The type of writing you'll complete for the AP Exam is kind of the opposite of how you should approach a writing task. In short, the "ready, set, write" approach of the AP Exam feels a little unnatural, but you can do it.

Your AP teacher should be drilling you with this style of essay for the duration of the course because it is the closest thing to writing for the AP Exam that you'll experience before test day. Most in-class tests are administered over materials you've studied and know well, but AP Exam prompts are most likely unfamiliar to you and the rest of the test-takers. We call this a cold reading and writing—that just means this is a passage you're seeing and writing on for the first time. You will be graded on quality of writing and content, but remember that comprehension and originality are also important. Address the prompts directly; don't talk around the questions, and be sure to stay on top of the Conventions of Standard English (CSE). If you write clearly and on topic, you should be just fine.

It may be a little nerve wracking to write this way, but remember that everyone else is in the same boat. This chapter is designed to give you the tools you need to understand how the essays are scored so that you can tailor your writing to fit the rubrics. We aren't necessarily teaching you how to write well: we're trying to teach you how to write a high-scoring AP essay. AP essays are different beasts, but they can be tackled!

Need More Help on Essays?
We've got just the book for that! *How to Write Essays for Standardized Tests* contains advice and examples of best practices on an assortment of AP exams, plus ACT, and others!

Any Changes? Go Online
Download the detailed grading rubrics directly from the College Board's website for even more information.

ALL ABOUT AP ESSAY SCORING

The 0 to 6 Scale

Each of your 3 essays will be graded according to a 6-point scale. Zero is the worst you can get and 6 is the best. Students' scores are not spread out evenly over that range.

After the College Board released its revised AP English Literature and Composition Course and Exam Description in May 2019, it decided to change things again and released updates to that in September 2019. Never a dull moment in the world of AP test prep!

The September 2019 update included major updates to the Free-Response Section, as we mentioned earlier. These essays are now scored on a scale of 0–6 (no more 0–9) and holistic scoring has been replaced by analytical scoring.

"Analytic" Scoring

The essays are scored "analytically" now. They used to be scored "holistically" which was somewhat vague and subjective, so we are thrilled at the release of a clear scoring rubric and point-by-point guidelines. Let's look at the scoring rubrics by question type and remember that each question could earn 6 points maximum.

Question 1: Poetry Analysis

Thesis	0–1 point available	• You will get 1 point if the essay responds to the prompt with a thesis (can be a single sentence or more and anywhere within the response) that presents a defensible interpretation of the poem. If your thesis is more than one sentence, the sentences need to be in close proximity. • You will get 0 points if there is no defensible thesis, no coherent claims are made, or the thesis only restates the prompt and does not respond to it.
Evidence and Commentary	0–4 points available	• You will get 4 points if your essay provides specific evidence to support all claims in a line of reasoning, consistently explains how evidence supports that line of reasoning, and explains how multiple literary elements/techniques in a poem contribute to its meaning. Note that writing that suffers from grammatical and/or mechanical errors that interfere with communication cannot get 4 points total. • You will get 0 points if the essay is simply a repetition of provided information or offers information irrelevant to the prompt. • You will get 1 point if your essay provides evidence that is mostly general and summarizes without explaining evidence. • You will get 2 points if your essay provides some specific, relevant evidence, but no line of reasoning is established or your line of reasoning is faulty. • You will get 3 points if your essay provides specific evidence in support of all claims in your line of reasoning, explains how some of the evidence supports the line of reasoning, and explains how at least 1 literary element/technique contributes to the meaning of the poem.
Sophistication	0–1 point available	• You will get 1 point if your essay demonstrates sophistication of thought and/or develops a complex literary argument. • You will get 0 points if your essay oversimplifies the poem, uses ineffective language, only hints at interpretations of the poem, or makes sweeping generalizations about the content of the poem.

Question 2: Prose Fiction Analysis

Thesis	0–1 point available	• You will get 1 point if your essay responds to the prompt with a thesis (can be a single sentence or more and anywhere within the response) that presents a defensible interpretation of the passage. If your thesis is more than one sentence, the sentences need to be in close proximity. • You will get 0 points if there is no defensible thesis, no coherent claims are made, or the thesis only restates the prompt and does not respond to it.
Evidence and Commentary	0–4 points available	• You will get 4 points if your essay provides specific evidence to support all claims in a line of reasoning and consistently explains how evidence supports that line of reasoning, explains how multiple literary elements/techniques in the passage contribute to its meaning. Note that writing that suffers from grammatical and/or mechanical errors that interfere with communication cannot get 4 points total. • You will get 0 points if the essay is simply a repetition of provided information or offers information irrelevant to the prompt. • You will get 1 point if your essay provides evidence that is mostly general and summarizes without explaining evidence. • You will get 2 points if your essay provides some specific, relevant evidence, but no line of reasoning is established or your line of reasoning is faulty. • You will get 3 points if your essay provides specific evidence in support of all claims in your line of reasoning and explains how some of the evidence supports that line of reasoning, and explains how at least 1 literary element/technique contributes to the meaning of the passage.
Sophistication	0–1 point available	• You will get 1 point if your essay demonstrates sophistication of thought and/or develops a complex literary argument. • You will get 0 points if your essay oversimplifies the passage, uses ineffective language, only hints at interpretations of the passage, or makes sweeping generalizations about the interpretation of the passage.

Question 3: Literary Argument

Thesis	0–1 point available	• You will get 1 point if your essay responds to the prompt with a thesis (can be a single sentence or more and anywhere within the response) that presents a defensible interpretation of the selected work. If your thesis is more than one sentence, the sentences need to be in close proximity. • You will get 0 points if there is no defensible thesis, no coherent claims are made, or the thesis only restates the prompt and does not respond to it.
Evidence and Commentary	0–4 points available	• You will get 4 points if your essay provides specific evidence to support all claims in a line of reasoning and consistently explains how evidence supports that line of reasoning. • You will get 0 points if the essay is simply a repetition of provided information or offers information irrelevant to the prompt. • You will get 1 point if your essay provides evidence that is mostly general and summarizes without explaining evidence. • You will get 2 points if your essay provides some specific, relevant evidence, but no line of reasoning is established or your line of reasoning is faulty. • You will get 3 points if your essay provides specific evidence in support of all claims in your line of reasoning and explains how some of the evidence supports that line of reasoning.
Sophistication	0–1 point available	• You will get 1 point if your essay demonstrates sophistication of thought and/or develops a complex literary argument. • You will get 0 points if your essay oversimplifies the prompt, uses ineffective language, only hints at interpretations of the selected work, or makes sweeping generalizations about the prompt.

Stay Up to Date!
For late-breaking information about test dates, exam formats, and any other changes pertaining to AP English Lit and Comp, make sure to check the College Board's website at apstudents.collegeboard. org/courses/ap-english-literature-and-composition

THE READER WANTS AN ESSAY THAT'S EASY TO SCORE

Readers are dedicated high school and university instructors who take a week out of their year to come to one site and grade essays. Of course, they are compensated for their time, but at times the grading can become monotonous. You need to make sure that your essay stands out from the hundreds of essays that each Reader scores.

Your job is to write an essay that's obviously better than average. You have to let the Reader feel confident about giving you at least a 5. Usually, the essays are generic and have no distinctive style to them. Often the essays are plot summaries that barely address the question. In many cases, the question is rewritten and the essay does not explore the topic adequately or with skill. Slogging through these medio-cre essays, the Reader gives a score and turns to the next essay hoping for that out-standing paper. Readers want to reward the writers for what they do well, but the topic must be addressed. If an essay starts out dull and poorly written but makes one completely original point right at the very end, the writer can be rewarded. Sometimes, however, there are too many grammar and spelling errors that distract the Reader and the one important statement that the writer makes is lost among the myriad errors on the paper. If you merely summarize the plot of the passage or do not adequately address the question, the Reader may have to give you a 2 or a 3, based on the grading rubric. You want to make it as easy as possible for the scorer to think your essay is good.

ANALYSIS OF THE SCORING RUBRIC

Look carefully over the Scoring Rubrics from earlier in this chapter. What do you see?

The College Board has shared an exact formula for how you can score a 6. You can rack up point by point following those scoring rubrics. The recurring theme is to go deeper, give more examples, flesh out those examples, and put things in context. But also, more than anything, be clear.

High-scoring essays aren't necessarily inspiring or life-changing but they are very clear. They establish a clear thesis and bolster that point throughout. Note that in their scoring rubric, the College Board says that your thesis may appear anywhere within your essay, but we find it's easiest to share it up front. Lay down your thesis and then build on that, tallying points along the way as you layer on the evidence and commentary (again, from their rubric). Finally, dazzle them with your sophistication.

> **Here's a Tip!**
> It doesn't hurt to think like a reader as you prac-tice the essays. In the free-response essays, you're going to see the following verbs. Be sure to under-stand what they mean to the people who will be scoring you.
>
> **Analyze:** Examine methodically and in detail the structure of the topic of the question in order to interpret and explain the passage.
>
> **Choose:** Select a literary work from among provided choices.
>
> **Read:** Look at or view printed directions and provided passages.

If you understand what you read and can write in grammatical English, a 3 is your absolute low-end score. You will almost certainly do better than that with our help.

The Adequate Essay Formula

Almost every adequate essay is written by a student who doesn't know how to craft a real essay idea based on the question and thinks that the "essay formula" can somehow save him. Here's the thought process that invariably leads to a middle score: "Let's see…they want me to write about the language…well, what *else* would I write about? The whole *thing* is language. This is crazy. And 'how the author dramatized the story'—well, with *language* of course—great, that's about one sentence worth of essay. What am I going to say? I don't know what they want! Yikes! I can't sit here forever; *I've got to write something.* I know! I'll restate the question as a statement and then come up with three examples: one for diction, one for imagery, and one for point of view. Then I'll summarize it all for a conclusion. *That's the essay formula, right?* Okay, here goes."

Panic + No Idea of What Is Wanted = The Adequate Essay

This student is perfectly intelligent. The "formula" isn't crazy; in fact, it's taught all over the place. Restate the question as a statement. Support the statement with three examples from the passage. Summarize it for a conclusion.

It sounds good, but when a student tries to use it, he'll realize he still doesn't have one interesting thing to say. From beginning to end he'll feel lost, and writing the essay will feel like one big, meaningless exercise. He'll struggle and pick out bits of the passage that catch his eye and try to discuss them. He won't be exactly sure why they catch his eye, but he'll make up something. The discussion will be vague, overly generalized, and mechanical. (That's the description of adequate essays in the AP scoring guide, remember.) The adequate essay has to be vague, because if it were precise, the student would reveal that he has no precise understanding of what he's supposed to be writing about. The formula results in a weak, boring essay.

The formula, however, is actually a heroic effort on the student's part, because no student is used to writing this way. When a student is writing from this place of panic and simply fulfilling a formulaic structure, a 3 is a success.

HOW TO MAKE IT EASY FOR THE READER TO GIVE YOU A HIGH SCORE

The most important part of your essay is the content. Your goal is to write meaty, content-filled essays that just blow the Reader away. But the Reader has to get to that content. There are a few vital things you must do to let your excellence come shining through with full impact. These basics have to do with the surface of your writing. That might seem cheap, but it's not. If the surface of your essay is clean and clear, the Reader can see through to the depths.

Neatness Counts

Studies have shown that neatly written essays earn higher scores. It's not fair, but it's a fact of life. Do everything in your power to make your essays readable. Write slowly. Write large. Write dark. Your writing doesn't have to be pretty, but it must be legible.

Take pains to be as neat as you possibly can. When a neatly written essay shows up, the wave of relief, of *love*, flooding the Reader is difficult to describe. A clearly written essay makes the Reader think, "Ah, now I can do my job!" A messy essay, however, will probably annoy Readers; they generally will try not to let poor handwriting affect the score, but if your essay is messy and difficult to read, they'll likely lose patience quickly.

If your penmanship isn't great and you've been writing essays on a computer for years, seriously consider printing or writing in italics, which is a sort of hybrid of cursive and printing. Trust us here. You may think this advice is ridiculous and that your handwriting shouldn't matter. The fact is, it does. As persecuted as you feel writing these essays, the Reader feels twice as persecuted reading them. Script is harder to read than print. If it weren't, this book would be written in a nice cursive typeface. If your normal handwriting looks like that on a wedding invitation or you're president of the Calligraphy Club at school, then you can use cursive. Otherwise, you should probably print (neatly!).

Indent

Keep It Clean
Don't underestimate the power of a tidy-looking essay. Write neatly, and write in paragraphs. No one wants to read a single paragraph that goes on for pages!

Your Reader's first impressions are crucial. Think about that character at the job interview with gum in his hair. If his battle isn't already lost, it's definitely an uphill fight the rest of the way. The overall look of your essay is a first impression. It's the smile on your face as you walk in the door. Your essay should look neat, organized, and clear. Make your paragraphs obvious. Indent twice as far as you normally would. When in doubt, make a paragraph. Ever look at a book, flip it open, and see nothing but one long paragraph? Your next thought is usually, "Oh please, don't make me have to read this!" That's exactly what Readers think when they see an essay without paragraphs. Neat presentation, clear handwriting, and indented paragraphs will show the Reader that you're super organized and you've got some great thoughts to share.

Write Perfectly…for the First Paragraph

Your "second first impression" (in case you were wondering, that's an **oxymoron**—see the glossary) is the first paragraph of the essay. Take extra care with your first paragraph. If you're unsure about the spelling of a word, don't use it. If you're unsure how to punctuate a sentence, rewrite it in a way that makes you feel confident. Don't make any mistakes in the first paragraph. Don't fret as much about the rest of the essay; the Readers expect mistakes. But the first paragraph needs to be strong because it sets the tone. If you try to write the whole essay perfectly, you'll write so slowly, or fill up your brain with so much worry, that you'll probably run out of time.

All you need is a few sentences to convince the Reader that you can write a good sentence when you want to. The glow of a good beginning carries over to the whole essay. Mistakes later on look like minor errors not even worth bothering with. After all, the Reader's already seen that you can write. Mistakes at the very beginning do just the opposite—they look like telling signs of inability and a weak grasp of fundamental English mechanics. Take extra care at the beginning of your essay; then relax and just write (*neatly*).

Show Off Your Literary Vocabulary

Readers do not give great grades to students who merely parrot the prompt. A good way to show that you understand what the question is asking is by paraphrasing the prompt in your response. If the prompt asks about diction, knowing that diction means "word choice" is great. Articulating how the author uses a particular form of diction is even better. Be sure that you know the meaning of key literary terms that frequently appear on the exam (see glossary of literary terms on page 335), and have some good synonyms at hand so you can display varied word choice.

Vital Vocab
Key words to use in your essays include *diction, imagery, metaphor, rhyme, form, point of view,* and *characterization.*

For poetry analysis, the big words are **diction**, **imagery**, **metaphor**, **rhyme**, and **form**. For prose fiction, substitute **point of view** and **characterization** for rhyme and form. Using the word "speaker" to refer to the poetry narrator and "narrator" when dealing with prose fiction is a convention worth employing because it will show that you are comfortable with the modes of writing that Readers will recognize from teaching students about literature. Remember, an entire point is dedicated to sophistication and that means both sophistication of thought and of language.

Use Snappy Verbs and Tasty Nouns

Spice up your writing. Try to write with some pizzazz. Don't let the test environment, the tension, or the anxiety caused by writing for a stranger take over your brain. Take risks. You may fall flat every so often, but the Reader will appreciate your effort and reward it. When you've gotten our essay techniques down, you'll understand that 90 percent of dull student writing on AP essays comes from confusion about what to write, which leads to inhibition. Don't be inhibited. Jazz it up a little. Show some stylistic flair.

Obviously, it's possible to go overboard here and if the Reader gets the impression you're just being silly, it won't help your score. It is important to write about the task at hand, not just your musings on life. But a dash of glitter is much better than none at all. By the way, big, important-sounding phrases are not your ticket to a high score. They're an obvious sign that you're full of it. So please don't try to write this kind of gibberish: "When Judy initially perceived Roger's rapid ambulatory movement along the pedestrian walkway bordering the automotive thoroughfare, she experienced tachycardia."

Impressing Your Readers

If you write like someone who enjoys writing, the Readers will be impressed. Going back to the example from the previous page, a student might write, "When Judy first sees Roger going down the street, she thinks he seems interesting." That's probably true, but what a bore! There are a thousand ways to liven up that sentence. It all depends on your personality and what is really happening in the story. How about, "When Judy first glimpses Roger dashing through the shadows of Sullivan Street, her heart flutters; she's already in love, she just doesn't know it yet." Or, "When Judy spots Roger flying down the sidewalk with the Sullivan Street gang nipping at his heels, she's dumbstruck by the wild vitality of his whirling limbs and blazing eyes." Cheesy? Over the top? Who cares? Nobody expects you to write like Marcel Proust. Actually, the Readers expect you to write like someone who's suffering through a tedious, nerve-wracking exercise, because that's exactly how most of the essays are written.

We aren't saying you have to write tangled, complex sentences either; in fact, you should try to avoid them. Great, long, looping sentences usually just wander off into error and confusion. All you need to do is pay attention to your word choice. When you find yourself using a generic verb like *look*, *see*, *says*, *walk*, *go*, *take*, or *give*, or a generic noun like *street*, *house*, *car*, or *man*, ask yourself whether there isn't a more precise, more colorful word you can use. Why write *house* when you're referring to a *mansion*, or *car* when you're really writing about a *jalopy*? Just a little bit of this goes a long way. It shows you're not scared and it might even look like you're having fun, which is very good.

The Questions

Each passage will be preceded by instructions to "Read the passage below carefully and then write a well-organized essay about...." These instructions may also contain some additional material orienting you to the passage, telling you things like who wrote it, the novel it was drawn from, and any other special information the test-writers feel you need to know in order to understand the passage. Be sure to give the instructions a complete look in case there's any useful information there.

Answer the Question

If you write a great essay that the Reader doesn't think addresses the question, you'll get a lousy score. All three essays, even the literary argument, will be directed, and the questions will tell you exactly what the test-writers want—that's the theory, anyway. In reality, the questions can be infuriatingly vague but at the same time, not answering the question is the ultimate sin. Understanding and answering the question are crucial to writing a high-scoring essay.

Timing

Just like the passages in the multiple-choice section, the essay prompts should be answered in the order that works best for you. The one that appears easiest should be your first feat. Get your writing juices flowing, and soak up some of your confidence as you write. You want to write all three essays; therefore, you have to keep a handle on your time. Completing the easiest essay topic (for you) first will help you to save time for the harder responses. You're handed an essay booklet and given 120 minutes (2 hours) to complete all three essays. Ideally, you'll use only 40 minutes for each essay; however, how you choose to delegate your time between essays may mean more time for one writing task and less for another. Again, keep a watch close. Set it to 12:00. It's easy to see how much time has progressed and how much is left if you keep up with your time in this manner.

The Two Most Important Things to Ask Yourself When Tackling an AP Essay

1. What is the meaning?
2. How do I know it?

When you sit down to write an essay, you really can't write word one until you've deciphered what the prompt is asking you to do. Find the actual command and underline it, highlight it, or put a star by it. Remind yourself as you write exactly what you're working to accomplish with your essay.

Certain members of the Big Six are your friends when you're answering questions like "what is the meaning?" and "how do I know it?" Do the character, settings, structure, and narration inform your answers? They certainly can; give them a whirl.

Summary

General Essay Information

o   There are three essays: one essay on a prose fiction passage, one essay on one or two poetry analysis passages, and one essay on a work that you select (the literary argument).

o   You have two hours to complete all three essays. Time yourself. Spend approximately 40 minutes on each essay.

o   The essays are a great place to improve your score.

Essay Scoring

o   Each essay is given a score from 0 to 6.

o   The essays are scored "analytically" according to a scoring rubric. Familiarize yourself with this rubric so you can learn how to tally up points, one by one, on exam day. The three categories of the rubric are thesis, evidence and commentary, and sophistication.

o   The Reader wants to read an essay that's easy to score.

o   High-scoring essays are interesting, clear essays. Middle-scoring essays are generic and boring. Low-scoring essays are plain old bad.

Presentation

o   Do everything in your power to make your essays readable.

o   Write carefully in large, dark handwriting. Your writing doesn't have to be pretty, but it must be clear.

o   Make your paragraph indentations easy to spot.

o   When in doubt, create a new paragraph.

o   Your first paragraph should be grammatically perfect. Your Reader will make a very quick judgment about your ability to write. Once the Reader has decided you can write a sentence, you'll get some slack later on (as long as you write neatly).

o   Have a solid literary vocabulary. You'll express yourself with greater clarity.

o   Try to use interesting, snappy verbs and nouns. It will impress the Reader and make her or him think you're comfortable, confident, and smart. Don't stress too much about overdoing the jazzy language, but don't go bananas.

o   Don't confuse interesting, snappy verbs and nouns with ten-dollar vocabulary words. Use the best, most precise word you can think of, not the one with the most syllables.

o   Understand the question. (Don't worry; there's much more on this subject in Part V.)

o   If you write a great essay that doesn't address the question, you won't get a great score.

o   Order the section. Do the essay you like best first, and save the worst one for last.

o   Manage your time—try to complete each essay in about 40 minutes.

Part V
Content Review and Practice for the AP English Literature and Composition Exam

Chapter 6
An Overview
of Literary
Movements

> "
> That is part of the beauty of all litera-
> ture. You discover that your longings are
> universal longings, that you're not lonely
> and isolated from anyone. You belong.
>
> —F. Scott Fitzgerald
> "

USING THIS OVERVIEW

If you have allotted yourself enough time before the test, this section gives you the opportunity to familiarize yourself with the potential content of the exam. If you are reading this book months before you are to take the test, you can use this section in a methodical, poem-by-poem manner. By reading the 200 representative poems listed in this chapter, you will gain a thorough sense of the kinds of poems that the College Board chooses from when writing its tests. If you are using this book during crunch time and the test is a few weeks away, our suggestion is to read a poem or two from each movement and to familiarize yourself more broadly with the ideas associated with each movement. If you are picking up this book for the first time when you have only a few days left to study for the exam, then skip this section and make sure you're familiar with the material in Part III and Part IV, which address cracking the test.

You may notice that this chapter is almost exclusively poetry-based. We have done it this way for two main reasons. First, students typically have more difficulty with poetry analysis than with prose friction. Reviewing this chapter will allow you to freshen up your knowledge on poets and poems, as well as the ideas associated with specific movements.

Second, if you are short on time, you can read more poems in a shorter amount of time than you can read full-length novels, plays, and short stories. Even reading a few poems from each movement will give you a sense of the notable characteristics of a specific period or genre.

Before getting into the overview, let's answer some questions you may have.

Does the AP English Exam Require Certain Readings?

A lot of students wonder if there's an AP English Lit and Comp reading list of specific books, poems, plays, and authors that they should be reading. While the College Board does not release an exact list of works or authors you should or must know, there are some books that crop up time and time again as classics, "the canon," and works expressing important themes that AP level students should be able to explore.

The test will choose texts from a variety of time periods and literary movements. While this chapter gives you a historical survey you should learn, the College Board will be including a greater number of 20th-century and contemporary works than those published before the 20th century.

For Further Exploration

It's not a list, but some specific works DO crop up in the College Board's AP English Literature and Composition Classroom Resources, which is posted on their website here: apcentral.collegeboard.org/courses/ap-english-literature-and-composition/classroom-resources?course=ap-english-literature-and-composition

Though the Advanced Placement English curriculum avoids requiring any specific list of authors or texts to be taught, there are certainly seminal works with which you should be familiar. Reading these works is important for the AP English Literature and Composition Exam, but also useful to become a well-read human who is aware of cultural references, certain popular metaphors and parables, characters, archetypes, and such. A list of these important authors to know is below, plus many additional works are tallied up later in this book.

W. H. Auden
Elizabeth Bishop
William Blake
Anne Bradstreet
Edward Kamau Brathwaite
Gwendolyn Brooks
Samuel Taylor Coleridge
H. D. (Hilda Doolittle)
Emily Dickinson
John Donne
John Dryden
T. S. Eliot
Robert Frost
Seamus Heaney
George Herbert
Langston Hughes

John Keats
Robert Lowell
Andrew Marvel
Marianne Moore
Sylvia Plath
Alexander Pope
Adrienne Rich
Anne Sexton
Percy Bysshe Shelley
Walt Whitman
William Carlos Williams
William Wordsworth
William Butler Yeats

For a more complete list, see pages 44–46.

How Can a List of Representative Authors Help Me Prepare for the Exam?

By itself, a list of authors or poets will not help you. To someone who doesn't know much about poetry, it will be more daunting than illustrative. However, when the list is reformatted to grouping writers by literary movement rather than listing them alphabetically, you may find that the once intimidating list has become much more understandable and helpful. You will still need to do a good deal of reading in order to apply the concepts of each literary movement to this exam, as no shortcut exists for becoming well-read. This chapter, however, will give you an efficient and organized method to follow, and a good overview of each movement.

What Is a Literary Movement?

A literary movement (or school of literature or poetry) is a grouping of writers who share similar aims, years of publication, and bases of operation. Some writers acknowledge or even encourage the idea of being seen as members of a single group, such as William Wordsworth and Samuel Taylor Coleridge, who consciously published some of their earlier poems in a volume that also included essays about their shared aesthetic ideals. Other writers actively reject the notion of being grouped. One such person was John Ashbery, who often maintained a bemused wariness when the term "New York School of poetry" is applied to his work.

How Can Knowing the Literary Movement of a Poem Help Me?

Regardless of whether or not the poets acknowledge their participation in a movement, you can put the following information to good use. For example, if you recognize that a poem is in the metaphysical tradition, you will have some immediate, ready-made ideas about form, structure, narration, content, figurative language, and overall meaning. You will know to look for witty, surprising pairings of concrete and abstract ideas. You will expect irony and paradox to percolate beneath even the most religious content. And you will pay special attention to the ornate quality of the conceits. On the other hand, the moment you recognize that a poem is from the romantic tradition, you will be able to call up the phrases "sublime transcendence," "redemptive nature," and "imaginative power." If you have practiced using these phrases, you can use them appropriately for part of a meaningful and attentive analysis of the concrete particulars of a poem. Studying poems within the framework of their literary movements may also help you on the multiple-choice section. If you are familiar with the period of a poem provided in the multiple-choice section, you may more easily recognize the correct answer (or at least be able to eliminate answers that are obviously incorrect).

LITERARY MOVEMENT OVERVIEW

In the following overview, you will find some of the most important poets and poems of each movement as well as a list of what to look for in these poems. The best way to use these lists to help you crack the exam is to read some of the suggested poems and note where specific features of each movement show up. Practice writing an analytical essay on one poem from each movement, using at least two of the features from the list somewhere in your essay, and you'll be off to a great start. Or draft outlines of possible essays using different poems to familiarize yourself with the poems and relevant themes. The more familiar you are with some key phrases, the more likely you'll be to smoothly incorporate them into your analytical prose. Be warned: if you only adopt them without actually considering what they mean or without practicing using them, they are likely to seem artificial and may even hurt your score.

The following list concentrates on the schools of literature that are most commonly included on AP English Literature and Composition Exam, and ignores other important movements that the College Board is less likely to emphasize. An excellent website for further study of the whole idea of literary movements is www.poets.org. It includes many links to brief poet biographies and sample poems from the movements listed in our overview. In fact, many of the representative poems in our overview were chosen because they are easily accessible through links from this website. Another great online resource is www.poetryfoundation.org.

Poetry Online

There are a bunch of great websites you can use to brush up on your knowledge of poems and poets. Check out www.poets.org and www.poetryfoundation.org

Metaphysical Poetry

Representative Metaphysical Poets and Poems

- John Donne (1572–1631)—"A Valediction: Forbidding Mourning"; "The Sun Rising"; "Death Be Not Proud—Holy Sonnet X"; "Woman's Constancy"; "Love's Alchemy"
- George Herbert (1593–1633)—"Easter Wings"; "The Collar"; "Jordan (I)"; "Love (III)"; "The Windows"
- Andrew Marvell (1621–1678)—"The Mower's Song"; "The Mower to the Glow-Worms"; "The Mower Against Gardens"; "The Garden"; "To His Coy Mistress"

A Quick Definition

Metaphysical poetry is a mostly 17th-century English poetic mode that breaks with earlier Renaissance ideas about romantic poetry. Instead of following in the footsteps of the troubadours, Petrarch and Shakespeare, who often wrote love poetry that placed the object of their poems on a pedestal, metaphysical poems often exhibit introspective meditations on love, death, God, and human frailty. The poems of John Donne, for example, are much more realistic about sexual relationships. Metaphysical poetry is famous for its obscurity (and therefore a favorite choice of the College Board).

What to Look for in Metaphysical Poetry

- Wit, irony, and paradox are paramount—wit is often seen in the pairing of dissimilar objects into the service of a clever, ironic analogy or paradoxical conceit. For example, see how Donne's speaker in "A Valediction: Forbidding Mourning" uses astronomy and math to illustrate his deep abiding love for his wife.
- Elaborate stylistic maneuvers (ornamental conceits, dazzling rhymes) are pulled off with aplomb. For example, look at how Herbert uses relative line length, stanza shape, rhyme, and repetition in "Easter Wings" to underscore the importance of human humility.
- Huge shifts in scale proliferate (for example, ants to planets). Consider how Marvell's speaker in "The Mower to the Glow-Worms" conflates glow-worms and comets, for example.
- These formal tendencies are used by metaphysical poets to talk about deep philosophical issues: the passage of time; the difficulty of ever being sure of any one thing; the uneasy relationship of human beings to one another and to God; the fearful, obsessive qualities that death often inspires in human consciousness. Sometimes, after all of the elaborate style is reduced and its content summarized, the truism that is left can seem clichéd. Most of the beauty of metaphysical poetry is in the dramatic unfolding of that truth through techniques like irony, conceits, and scale shifts.

Get It Donne

If metaphysical poetry comes up on the test (and it probably will), think John Donne. Review some of the poems listed here before test day if you need a refresher.

Augustans

Representative English Augustan Poets and Poems
- John Dryden (1631–1700)—"Mac Flecknoe"; "Marriage a-la-mode"; "Absalom and Achitophel"
- Alexander Pope (1688–1744)—"The Rape of the Lock"; "Windsor Forest"; "Epitaph on Sir Isaac Newton"

Related Prose Fiction and Plays
- *Gulliver's Travels* and "A Modest Proposal" by Jonathan Swift (1667–1745)
- *A Beggar's Opera* by John Gay (1685–1732)

A Quick Definition

Augustan poetry is best known for its rhymed, heroic-couplet satire. These pairs of lines in iambic pentameter often produce great forward propulsion, and most students report that reading them aloud helps with comprehension. Coming between the baroque metaphysical poets and the enthusiastically sincere romantic poets, the wickedly funny Augustan poets went back to antiquity for their inspiration. They translated Greek and Roman epics into English using heroic couplets and wrote their own original work based on classical forms.

What to Look for in Augustan Poetry

- Wit, irony, and paradox are still as important here as they were for the metaphysical poets, but one must also add brevity to the list when discussing the Augustans. Their poems can be quite long but because they employ the heroic couplet so pointedly, their observations are often quite pithy. As Pope put it in his poem "Essay on Criticism," "True wit is nature to advantage dress'd,/What oft was thought, but ne'er so well express'd."
- The ongoing subject of Augustan poetry is human frailty. Even when these poets used biblical subjects and allusions for their plots, as Dryden does in "Absalom and Achitophel," the tone taken often mocks human behavior: "What cannot praise effect in mighty minds, When flattery soothes, and when ambition blinds!"
- These poets were also likely to dress absurdly mundane plots (such as the secret cutting of a noble maiden's hair in "Rape of the Lock") in the outward appearance of heroic epic poetry for comic effect.
- Current events figure in these poems, either allegorically or directly. In his famous epitaph for Sir Isaac Newton, Pope wrote: "Nature and nature's laws lay hid in night; God said 'Let Newton be' and all was light," which addresses the ongoing controversies between the forces of religion and science in 18th century Europe. John Dryden's poem "Mac Flecknoe" satirizes another prominent poet of his day and takes sides in contemporary political debates, similar to how a present-day poet with Democratic leanings might make fun of Republican leaders.

Romantic Poetry

Representative English Romantic Poets and Poems

- William Wordsworth (1770–1850)—"I Wandered Lonely as a Cloud"; "Composed Upon Westminster Bridge Sept. 3, 1802"; "Lines Composed a Few Miles Above Tintern Abbey"; "My Heart Leaps Up When I Behold"; "Lucy"
- Percy Bysshe Shelley (1792–1822)—"Ozymandias"; "Ode to the West Wind"; "Adonais—An Elegy on the Death of John Keats"; "The Cloud"; "Hymn to Intellectual Beauty"
- John Keats (1795–1821)—"Ode on a Grecian Urn"; "When I Have Fears That I May Cease to Be"; "To Autumn"; "La Belle Dame Sans Merci"; "Ode to a Nightingale"
- William Blake (1757–1827)—"The Tiger"; "The Lamb"; "A Poison Tree"; "The Sick Rose"

Got a Question?
For answers to test-prep questions for all your tests and additional test taking tips, subscribe to our YouTube channel a www.youtube.com/ThePrincetonReview

Representative American Transcendental Poets and Poems

- Ralph Waldo Emerson (1803–1882)—"Ode to Beauty"; "The World-Soul"; "Song of Nature"
- Walt Whitman (1819–1892)—"When I Heard the Learn'd Astronomer"; "A Noiseless Patient Spider"; "Crossing Brooklyn Ferry"; "There Was a Child Went Forth"; "Song of the Open Road"

Related European Prose Fiction

- *Ivanhoe* by Sir Walter Scott (1771–1832)
- *Les Misérables* by Victor Hugo (1802–1885)

Related American Prose Fiction

- *The Scarlet Letter* by Nathaniel Hawthorne (1804–1864)
- "The Poet," an essay by Ralph Waldo Emerson that inspired Whitman to become a poet;
- "Walking," an essay by Henry David Thoreau (1817–1862)

A Quick Definition

Romantic poetry written in English is a (mostly) 19th-century English and American poetic mode that breaks with earlier neoclassical ideas about poetry by specifically emphasizing that these poems were written in, as Wordsworth calls it, "the real language of men" and were about "common life." This poetry is emotional and often enthusiastic in its embracing of the large, impressive forces of nature and the infinite resources of the human imagination. Famous for having given us the image of tormented poets idly strolling over moors, looking through their wind-whipped hair at a tulip, these poems are often used on AP Exams because of their strong thematic content.

What to Look for in Romantic Poetry

- Natural imagery redeems the imagination of the individual stuck in the crowded, industrial torment of the city. See Wordsworth's "I Wandered Lonely as a Cloud," in which the speaker, on a couch, imagines himself floating above a "host of golden daffodils."

In a Nutshell
Romanticism summed up: nature imagery, imagination, and transcendence.

- The human imagination empowers the individual to escape from society's strictures, established authority, and even from fear of death. Think about how Whitman's speaker in "When I Heard the Learn'd Astronomer" needs to leave the room where the lecture is happening in order to better understand the perfect silence of the stars.

- The sublime (impressively big, obscure, or scary) is the main descriptive mode rather than the "merely beautiful." Look at how the speaker in Shelley's "Ozymandias" relies on words such as "vast," "colossal," and "boundless" to create a sense of how intimidating the statue must have been, and actually is.

- Transcendence is the ultimate goal of all the romantic poets. Wordsworth turns a city into a beating heart in "Composed Upon Westminster Bridge Sept. 3, 1802"; in "Ode to the West Wind," Shelley turns the west wind into poetic inspiration; Keats turns an old urn into a meditation on life and death in his "Ode on a Grecian Urn"; Whitman in his "Noiseless Patient Spider" turns a spider into a human soul surrounded by a vacant, vast expanse, yearning to be connected. What do all these poems have in common? Each finds transcendence in the ordinary.

The Symbolists

Representative French Symbolist Poets and Poems

- Charles Baudelaire (1821–1867)—"Spleen"; "*Harmonie du soir* (Harmonies of Evening)"; "*Correspondances* (Correspondences)"
- Stéphane Mallarmé (1842–1898)—"*L'Apres-midi d'un faune* (The Afternoon of a Faun)"; "*Soupir* (Sigh)"; "*Salut* (Salutation)"
- Paul Verlaine (1844–1896)—"*Il pleure dans mon couer* (It Rains in My Heart)"; "*Chanson d'automne* (Autumn Song)"; "*Langueur* (Languor)"
- Arthur Rimbaud (1854–1891)—"*Le bateau ivre* (The Drunken Boat)"; "*Voyelles* (Vowels)"

Symbolist-Influenced Poets Who Wrote in English

- Oscar Wilde (1854–1900)—"Chanson"; "Impression du Matin"; "Harmony"
- W. B. Yeats (1865–1939)—"The Lake Isle of Innisfree"; "Towards Break of Day"; "Broken Dreams"; "Leda and the Swan"; "Sailing to Byzantium"

- Arthur Symons (1865–1945)—"White Heliotrope"; "Colour Studies"; "Perfume"
- T. S. Eliot (1888–1965)—"The Love Song of J. Alfred Prufrock"; "Ash Wednesday"

Related Symbolist Prose Fiction
- *A Rebours* (Against the Grain) by Joris-Karl Huysmans (1848–1907)
- *The Picture of Dorian Gray* by Oscar Wilde (1854–1900)

A Quick Definition

The symbolists are often considered the link between the schools of romanticism and modernism. Full of the yearning for transcendence, which they inherited from the romantic poets, the symbolists took this yearning in a more decadent and sensual direction, foreshadowing the kind of sexual frankness one often finds in modernist work. Many of their poems will seem obscure on the first few readings, and College Board test makers are probably not going to use any of the French symbolists on the exam, but if you take the time to analyze the deep symbols and intuitive associations found in their work, you will be in a better place when you are asked to interpret a poem by Yeats or Eliot, whose work often does show up on the exam.

What to Look for in Symbolist Poetry

- Many symbolist poems deal with the crepuscular (dusk and dawn), and with the time between waking and sleep. Consider Wilde's "*Impression du Matin.*" Dreams or dream states figure prominently in many symbolist works of art, as dream experiences afford human beings one of the best opportunities to explore the relationship between states.
- *Synaesthesia*, the using of one sense to describe another, proved to be a favorite mode of the symbolists. For example, Rimbaud attributes colors and sounds to the different vowels in his poem "*Voyelles.*"
- The French symbolists proved particularly adept at using words with three or four simultaneous meanings, creating a resonance among groups of these words. For example, Mallarmé in "*Salut*" toasts younger poets gathered around a white tablecloth that can simultaneously be seen as a white sail for a boat and a white, blank page upon which these poets will eventually write. By carefully choosing his words, the speaker of this poem keeps all three meanings viable throughout this beautifully dense piece.
- Often associated with the "art for art's sake" movement that placed aesthetics and form above political relevance or reducible message, symbolist poetry finds its artistic counterparts in these kinds of paintings: Whistler's *Nocturne Blue and Gold—Old Battersea Bridge*, Turner's *Moonlight,* and Monet's *Waterloo Bridge in Grey Weather.*

Symbolists and Music
As you can tell from the items in this list, symbolists were drawn to the properties of music and attempted to create some of the same effects in their poetry by concentrating on simultaneous effects (similar to harmony) and by choosing mellifluous words meant to inspire a kind of languor in the reader.

Modernism

Representative Modernist Poets and Poems

- Wallace Stevens (1879–1955)—"Thirteen Ways of Looking at a Blackbird"; "The Snow Man"; "Peter Quince at the Clavier"; "Anecdote of the Jar"
- William Carlos Williams (1883–1963)—"Red Wheelbarrow"; "This Is Just To Say"; "Danse Russe"; "Spring and All"; "The Great Figure"; "The Yachts"; "Desert Music"; "The Descent"
- H. D. (Hilda Doolittle) (1886–1961)—"Star Wheels in Purple"; "Helen"; "Heat"
- Marianne Moore (1887–1972)—"Poetry"; "Baseball and Writing"; "To a Snail"
- T. S. Eliot (1888–1965)—"Love Song of J. Alfred Prufrock"; "Ash Wednesday"
- e. e. cummings (1894–1962)—"anyone lived in a pretty how town"; "next to of course god america i"; "spring is like a perhaps hand"; "i sing of Olaf glad and big"
- Ezra Pound (1885–1972)—"In Durance"; "In a Station of the Metro"; "Hugh Selwyn Mauberley"; "The Cantos"

Related Modernist Prose Fiction

- *A Portrait of the Artist as a Young Man* by James Joyce (1882–1941)
- *Mrs. Dalloway* by Virginia Woolf (1882–1941)
- *As I Lay Dying* by William Faulkner (1897–1962)
- *Heart of Darkness* by Joseph Conrad (1857–1924)
- *The Awakening* by Kate Chopin (1851–1904)

A Quick Definition

Modernism is often characterized as a revolutionary force. In the field of science, Einstein was reassessing time, space, and our relationship to these concepts. In global politics, two calamitous world wars bracketed decades of intense technological advances in the mass killing of soldiers and civilians. In the field of visual arts, surrealism, futurism, abstraction, and cubism overthrew most accepted traditional ideas about pictorial representation. Not surprisingly, literature in the 20th century also saw a thorough questioning of what had come before and a willingness to experiment with new forms, a goal shared with the symbolists but one with which the modernists were much more daring. Modern poets valued the idea of "make it new." Ezra Pound coined the phrase and encouraged writers to take old topics and revamp them with a modern twist. Modernists believed that poetry should be valuable and understandable. Some, like Marianne Moore, even argued that a poet who writes convoluted and frustrating verse just for the purpose of complexity is no poet at all. Modern poets and writers were often expatriates disillusioned with American life.

What to Look for in Modernist Poetry

- Chock full of allusions, these poems reduce human experience to fragments. For example, e.e. cummings breaks language down into its component parts, using pieces of overheard conversation alongside more grandiose pronouncements. In Hilda Doolittle's 18-line poem entitled "Helen," she assumes the reader has a working knowledge of the incident that prompts the Trojan War (chronicled in *The Iliad* by Homer) to make sense of why "All Greece hates/the still eyes in the white face."

- Some of these poems are influenced by cubism, and they try to see the world from as many points of view as possible at the same time. Wallace Stevens's "Thirteen Ways of Looking at a Blackbird" comes in thirteen sections, each of which refers explicitly or implicitly to a blackbird, and can be seen as a kind of analogue to Picasso's cubist presentation of a still life in *Guitar, Bottle, Bowl of Fruit and Glass on Table*.

- Romantic notions of the importance of individuality were overtaken by systematic representations of human consciousness in the emerging fields of psychology and sociology, so poems from this time are often concerned with how an individual relates to his environment (see Eliot's "The Love Song of J. Alfred Prufrock") or how the environment and setting help to create the individual (see Stevens's "The Snow Man").

- Romantic yearning for freedom (the bloody excesses of the French Revolution are an extreme example) was usurped by proponents of political systems, such as socialism or fascism, that saw human beings not as individuals but as servants of the state (see the Russian Revolution and the rise of the Third Reich). Modernist poems sometimes efface individuality, choosing to focus on machines or other inanimate objects rather than nature or human beings. For example, William Carlos Williams's "The Yachts" contains brutal imagery: "Arms with hands grasping seek to clutch at the prows/Bodies thrown recklessly in the way are cut aside./It is a sea of faces about them in agony, in despair/until the horror of the race dawns staggering the mind." But this use of imagery does not ever really feel personal; it feels more like a representation of mass death.

Looking to Guarantee a 5 or Your Money Back?

We now offer one-on-one tutoring for a guaranteed 5 on the AP English Literature and Composition exam. For information on rates and availability, visit https://www.princetonreview.com/college/ap-test-prep

The Harlem Renaissance

Representative Poets and Poems of the Harlem Renaissance
- Paul Laurence Dunbar (1872–1906)—"Frederick Douglass"; "Sympathy"; "We Wear the Mask"
- Claude McKay (1889–1948)—"If We Must Die"; "The White House"; "The Tropics in New York"
- Langston Hughes (1902–1967)—"I, Too, Sing America"; "The Negro Speaks of Rivers"; "Theme for English B"; "Montage of a Dream Deferred"
- Countee Cullen (1903–1946)—"Incident"; "For A Lady I Know"; "Yet Do I Marvel"

Related Prose Fiction from the Harlem Renaissance
- *Their Eyes Were Watching God* by Zora Neale Hurston (1891–1960)
- *Passing* by Nella Larsen (1891–1964)
- *Black Boy* and *Native Son* by Richard Wright (1908–1960)
- *Invisible Man* by Ralph Ellison (1913–1994)

A Quick Definition
Art associated with the Harlem Renaissance was mostly created in the first half of the 20th century, after World War I, during the movement of African Americans to northern industrial cities (called the Great Migration). Harlem in New York City was one of the most famous African American neighborhoods during this time. Jazz, poetry, painting, novels, dance, electrified blues, and the study of folk lore thrived in these neighborhoods and took on many of the same concerns as the modernists.

What to Look for in Harlem Renaissance Poetry
- Content is often directly related to African American concerns and issues of the time. Consider Dunbar's "Frederick Douglass," which elegizes the famous abolitionist in such a way as to draw attention to his continuing positive influence on the culture: "Oh, Douglass, thou hast passed beyond the shore,/But still thy voice is ringing o'er the gale!"
- Many Harlem Renaissance poems rely on repetitive structure similar to blues lyrics (see Dunbar's "Sympathy") or on fragmented structure similar to jazz improvisation (see Hughes's "Montage of a Dream Deferred").
- Several of these poets, especially Langston Hughes, consciously sought a new American idiom alongside other African American artists such as blues singer Bessie Smith. Other poets combined European forms like the sonnet with content and tone more related to African American concerns, such as McKay's "If We Must Die."

Postmodernism

A Quick Definition

Academic controversy continues as to whether works labeled postmodern are merely a later version of the modernist tendencies developed in the 20th century or whether they are actually part of a new and separate movement. Usually the most that academics can agree on regarding postmodernism is that the term "postmodern" is insufficient. Most postmodern works were created in the second half of the 20th century, and though they share some of the concerns and motivations of modernists, they often take these principles to a much different end. If Einstein's theory of relativity represents the modern era, Heisenberg's uncertainty principle is the emblem of the postmodern. In reductive terms, the uncertainty principle holds that one cannot know both the speed and the location of an object simultaneously, which introduces a note of chance or chaos into scientific inquiry.

Even more so than other literary labels, "postmodern" is a label that is rejected by the majority of artists who are labeled as such. Instead, smaller contingents of writers exist, often in conflict with other postmodern groups. These smaller groups include the **Beats**, the **confessional** poets, the **New York School of poets**, the **Black Arts movement**, and the **Black Mountain school**. Each of these groups is addressed separately below because each had such a different aesthetic program. A few statements can be applied to postmodern art in general, however, and will be discussed before going into the specific sub-movements.

What to Look for in Postmodern Poetry

- Parody, irony, and narrative instability often inform the tone.
- Allusions are just as likely to be made to popular culture as they are to classical learning.
- Strictly binary concepts (hot and cold; black and white) often collapse. Here, the predominant ideas are ones that spread across a spectrum rather than fit strictly into one box or the other.
- There is no real center. The Internet is a perfect example of a postmodern invention.
- The surface is often more interesting to postmodern artists than any ideas of depth. The following quote is attributed to Andy Warhol, a kind of patron saint of postmodernism and a notorious wig wearer: "Wear a wig and people notice the wig. Wear a silver wig and people notice the silver."

The Beats

Representative Beat Poets and Poems
- Lawrence Ferlinghetti (b. 1919–2021)—"A Coney Island of the Mind"; "The Changing Light"; "Vast Confusion"; "Wild Dreams of a New Beginning"
- Allen Ginsberg (1926–1997)—"Howl"; "America"; "A Supermarket in California"; "Kaddish"
- Gregory Corso (1930–2001)—"Marriage"; "Bomb"; "The Mad Yak"
- Gary Snyder (b. 1930)—"Four Poems for Robin"; "For All"; "Hay for the Horses"

Need More Help on Essays?

We've got just the book for that! *How to Write Essays for Standardized Tests* contains advice and examples of best practices on an assortment of AP exams, plus ACT, and others!

Related Beat Prose Fiction
- *Naked Lunch* by William S. Burroughs (1914–1997)
- *On the Road* by Jack Kerouac (1922–1969)

A Quick Definition

A post–World War II phenomenon, the Beats used different settings over the years to practice their brand of hallucinogenic, visionary, and anti-establishment art: New York City (many of the original group were Columbia University students or dropouts), San Francisco, Tangiers, Prague, and Mexico City witnessed Beat events, as did many places in between.

Beat poets were quite good at mythologizing themselves, sharing a sense of personal frankness with the confessional poets and a sense of interdisciplinary energy (especially in its overlap with music) with the New York School. Buddhism was important to many members (especially Gary Snyder) as were many of the tenets of William Blake's version of romanticism, such as the importance of the individual, the imagination freed from society's constraints, and the yearning for transcendence. In Ferlinghetti's "The Changing Light," a reader can feel the deep connection Beats often felt to nature even as the speaker of this poem is describing a city scene. In Corso's "Marriage," the oppositional stance the Beats took toward the suburban bourgeoisie is in bold relief. Ginsberg's "America" shares much of the same satirical tone, but Ginsberg was also capable of writing angry, ranting, Whitmanesque masterpieces like "Howl" and a tender, meditative elegy for his mother in "Kaddish."

"First thought, best thought" describes the aesthetic ideal of the Beat poet. Moved by jazz improvisation and Buddhist ideas of impermanence, these poets considered themselves the chroniclers of their age. Politics directly informs many of their poems, either through specific references to members of the government or specific references to issues important to them, such as Gary Snyder's commitment to the environment.

Confessional Poets

Representative Confessional Poets and Poems

- John Berryman (1914–1972)—"Dream Song 1"; "Dream Song 4"; "Dream Song 29"
- Robert Lowell (1917–1977)—"Skunk Hour"; "For the Union Dead"; "Memories of West Street and Lepke"; "Home After Three Months Away"
- Anne Sexton (1928–1967)—"Wanting to Die"; "The Truth the Dead Know"; "For My Lover, Returning to his Wife"
- Sylvia Plath (1932–1963)—"Daddy"; "Lady Lazarus"; "Balloons"; "Ariel"

Related Confessional Prose Fiction

- *The Bell Jar* by Sylvia Plath

A Quick Definition

As the name suggests, confessional poets took the personal pronouns (I, me, my) seriously and explored intimate content in their poetry. Love affairs, suicidal thoughts, fears of failure, ambivalent or downright violent opinions about family members, and other autobiographically sensitive material moved front and center in these poets' works. As Berryman wrote, using his alter ego "Henry" as a mask for his own feelings of distress in "Dream Song 1," "I don't see how Henry, pried/ open for all the world to see, survived." These poets "pried open" their innermost thoughts and opened them for all the world to see, even if it meant sharing one's troubled feelings about one's father, as Plath did in a poem full of Holocaust imagery entitled "Daddy," writing "Daddy, I have had to kill you./You died before I had time…"

In a cultural milieu much more discreet than that of the current era, these poets ripped the façade off an outwardly comfortable suburban life to reveal the doubts and anxieties that kept the occupants awake at night behind white picket fences. For example, Robert Lowell wrote in "Home After Three Months Away" how he felt when faced with the details of his life such as the recent birth of his child: "I keep no rank nor station./Cured, I am frizzled, stale and small." And Anne Sexton wrote with existential dread, "Since you ask, most days I cannot remember./I walk in my clothing, unmarked by that voyage./Then the almost unnameable lust returns." The "unnameable lust" is the speaker's desire for death, and she writes eloquently about it at a time when mental illness was much less understood or validated by society than it is today.

More than just poets who shared personal stories with their readers, these poets also invested a good deal of time and effort in their craft, constructing verse that paid careful attention to rewritten prosody.

New York School of Poets

Representative New York School Poets

Poetry and Art
Many of the New York School poets wrote art criticism, while Frank O'Hara even rose to the rank of assistant curator for the Museum of Modern Art.

- Barbara Guest (1920–2006)—"The Blue Stairs"; "Wild Gardens Overlooked by Night Lights"; "Sound and Structure"; "Echoes"
- Kenneth Koch (1925–2002)—"One Train May Hide Another"; "Talking to Petrizia"; "To Various Persons Talked to All at Once;" "Variations on a Theme by William Carlos Williams"
- Frank O'Hara (1926–1966)—"In Memory of My Feelings"; "The Day Lady Died"; "A Step Away from Them"; "Lines to a Depressed Friend"
- John Ashbery (b. 1927–2017)—"The Painter"; "The Instruction Manual"; "Daffy Duck in Hollywood"; "The New Higher"

A Quick Definition

New York School poets saw themselves as fellow travelers of the abstract expressionist school of painters. Their aesthetic mode overlapped with Beat spontaneity and confessional-poet frankness, but was much more ironic and more interested in the surreal combination of high art and popular art allusions. Many of their poems, especially those called "Lunch Poems" by Frank O'Hara, seem to be catalogs of what one might see on a walk in midtown Manhattan. The urban environment, of course, allows for many spontaneous intersections. A taxi goes by a construction site. A billboard advertising tourism to a natural paradise hovers over a traffic jam, providing ironic contrast.

These poets often viewed themselves as artists who could help the reader see the world in new and different ways. For example, Guest writes "The Blue Stairs" in an ekphrastic mode (or a mode based on putting visual art into words), "Now I shall tell you/why it is beautiful/Design: extraordinary/color: cobalt blue" while O'Hara writes in "The Day Lady Died," an elegy for Billie Holiday, "and I am sweating a lot by now and thinking of/leaning on the john door in the 5 SPOT/ while she whispered a song along the keyboard/to Mal Waldron and everyone and I stopped breathing." Guest's speaker describes looking at a painting while O'Hara's speaker describes hearing a song at a jazz club, but both speakers are interested in inspiring us to look or listen again.

Surrealists wanted to jar their audience's senses by juxtaposing uncommon objects. John Ashbery mixes "Rumford's Baking Powder, a celluloid earring, Speedy Gonzales, the latest from Helen Topping Miller's fertile Escritoire" in his poem "Daffy Duck in Hollywood," and Kenneth Koch consciously mixes tones in his poem "To Various Persons Talked to All at Once," writing, "I suppose I wanted to impress you./It's snowing./The Revlon Man has come from across the sea./This racket is annoying./We didn't want the baby to come here because of the hawk./ What are you reading?/In what style would you like the humidity to explain?" These poets reveled in the combination of the serious and the silly, the profound and the absurd, the highly formal and the casual.

Black Arts Movement

Representative Black Arts Movement Poets and Poems

- Gwendolyn Brooks (1917–2000)—"The Bean Eaters"; "We Real Cool"; "The Lovers of the Poor"; "The Mother"
- Amiri Baraka (also known as LeRoi Jones) (1934–2014)—"Preface to a Twenty Volume Suicide Note"; "Black Art"; "Ka'Ba"; "In the Funk World"
- Sonia Sanchez (b. 1934)—"Ballad"; "Malcolm"; "I Have Walked a Long Time"; "For Sweet Honey in the Rock"
- Ntozake Shange (1948–2018)—"My Father Is a Retired Magician"; "For Colored Girls Who Have Considered Suicide When the Rainbow Is Enuf"

A Quick Definition

Poets of the Black Arts were often associated with members of the Black Power movement who grew frustrated with the pace of the changes enacted by the civil rights movement of the 1950s and 1960s. These poems are often politically charged, unrepentant challenges to the white establishment.

Black Mountain Poets

Representative Black Mountain Poets and Poems

- Charles Olson (1910–1970)—Excerpts from *The Maximus Poems*
- Denise Levertov (1923–1997)—"The Mutes"; "In California During the Gulf War"; "When We Look Up"
- Robert Creeley (1926–2005)—"Age"; "For Love"; "A Wicker Basket"; "America"

A Quick Definition

Besides teaching in the same place (Black Mountain College in Black Mountain, North Carolina) for some time and sharing an abiding interest in process over product, these poets seem quite different. Olson's poems spill across the page while Creeley's lines compress into tight corners. Levertov tackled political issues head-on, but Olson delved deeply into the archeology and history of Gloucester, Massachusetts.

Other Important Representative Poets and Poems

The poets and poems listed below are important but do not fit easily into the structure of literary movements.

Emily Dickinson (1830–1886). Writing in near absolute isolation during the transcendental period, this astonishingly prolific and powerful poet does not easily fit into the transcendental rubric, and shares many more attributes with the compressed wit and irony of the metaphysical poets. Poems: "Because I could not stop for death"; "I heard a fly buzz when I died"; "Tell all the truth but tell it slant"; "I measure every grief I meet."

Robert Frost (1874–1963). Frost was active during modernism's heyday, concerning himself with more traditionally minded verse forms and local color (the customs, manner of speech, dress, or any specificities of a place or period that contribute to its unique character) that cloaked a profound philosophical vein. Poems: "Out, Out"; "Birches"; "The Death of the Hired Man"; "Mending Wall"; "Design"; "Stopping by Woods on a Snowy Evening."

W. H. Auden (1907–1973). Auden, one of the giants of 20th-century literature, wrote the first half of his poems as an English citizen before World War II, and the second half as an American citizen after World War II. His work is more similar to the modernists than to any other school, but he really transcends labels. Poems: "As I Walked Out One Evening"; "In Memory of W. B. Yeats"; "The Unknown Citizen"; "Musée des Beaux Arts."

Elizabeth Bishop (1911–1979). Sometimes placed with the confessional poets because of her friendship with Robert Lowell, Bishop is more reticent than the confessional poets. Poems: "In the Waiting Room"; "Filling Station"; "At the Fishhouses"; "One Art"; "The Moose."

Adrienne Rich (1929–2012). An important feminist and political poet, Rich shared some background with the confessional poets, but took the role of the poet in society so seriously that she transcended the personal and became an icon. Poems: "Diving into the Wreck"; "North American Time"; "Aunt Jennifer's Tigers"; "Miracle Ice Cream."

Seamus Heaney (1939–2013). Heaney uses rural imagery to take on issues of identity, from the post-colonial confusion of what it means to be Irish to the late 20th-century confusion of what it means to be a poet. Poems: "Digging"; "The Harvest Bow."

REFLECT

Respond to the following questions:

- For which content topics discussed in this chapter do you feel you have achieved sufficient mastery to answer multiple-choice questions correctly?

- For which content topics discussed in this chapter do you feel you have achieved sufficient mastery to discuss them effectively in an essay?

- For which content topics discussed in this chapter do you feel you need more work before you can answer multiple-choice questions correctly?

- For which content topics discussed in this chapter do you feel you need more work before you can discuss them effectively in an essay?

- What parts of this chapter are you going to re-review?

- Will you seek further help, outside of this book (such as from a teacher, tutor, or AP Students), on any of the content in this chapter—and, if so, on what content?

Summary

○ There are many literary movements that you should be aware of. Be sure that you are familiar with:
- Metaphysical Poetry
- Augustan Poetry
- Romantic Poetry
- Symbolist Poetry
- Modernism
- Harlem Renaissance
- Postmodernism
- The Beats
- Confessional
- New York School
- Black Arts Movement
- Black Mountain

Chapter 7
Poetry Analysis
Questions

> "
> There is no Frigate like a Book To take us Lands away
>
> —Emily Dickinson
> "

READING POETRY LIKE A PRO

Answering multiple-choice questions about poetry analysis passages involves many of the same principles as does answering questions about prose fiction. There are some differences, however.

First, the poetry analysis passages tend to contain more questions that rely on knowledge than the prose fiction passages. You will certainly see a question or two on the literary devices (for example, personification or metaphor) in the poem. You might see a question about the way a line scans or what the rhyme scheme is called, but these are nothing to worry about. Recent tests have not included a single question on scansion or the names of classical poetic forms. The test-writers do, however, like to use poetry for questions about grammar, because poets use the kind of tangled syntax that makes for challenging grammar questions.

Second, the poetry you'll see on the AP Exam tends to make for harder reading than the prose fiction passages. Hard, but not impossible. There's a certain style of poetry that tends to appear on the AP English Literature and Composition Exam. In order to write questions properly, the test-writers are limited in the kind of material they can use. As a result, you won't see poems that stretch language and meaning to its limits, or poems that are open to such a variety of interpretations that asking meaningful multiple-choice questions about them is too difficult. Nor will you see beautiful and elegant but direct and simple poems. Also, you won't see any especially "out there" or experimental postmodern poetry on the exam. The AP Exam generally features poems of 100 to 300 words that use difficult language to make a precise point. The poem below and the questions that follow should give you a good idea of what to expect on the test. This is an excellent place to practice what you've learned in previous chapters. For even more practice, work through the two poetry analysis drills and the bonus questions at the end of this chapter.

Use all of the techniques we've taught you.

- Read the poem as prose.
- Focus on the main idea.
- When answering the questions, use POE and Consistency of Answers.
- Be sure to read before and after line references.

SAMPLE POETRY ANALYSIS PASSAGE AND QUESTIONS

Andrew Marvell's "On a Drop of Dew"

Read the following poem carefully and choose answers to the questions that follow.

	See how the orient[1] dew,
	Shed from the bosom of the morn
	Into the blowing[2] roses,
Line	Yet careless of its mansion new,
(5)	For the clear region where 'twas born
	Round in itself incloses:
	And in its little globe's extent,
	Frames as it can its native element.
	How it the purple flow'r does slight,
(10)	Scarce touching where it lies,
	But gazing back upon the skies,
	Shines with a mournful light,
	Like its own tear,
	Because so long divided from the sphere.
(15)	Restless it rolls and unsecure,
	Trembling lest it grow impure,
	Till the warm sun pity its pain,
	And to the skies exhale it back again.
	So the soul, that drop, that ray
(20)	Of the clear fountain of eternal day,
	Could it within the human flow'r be seen,
	Remembering still its former height,
	Shuns the sweet leaves and blossoms green,
	And recollecting its own light,
(25)	Does, in its pure and circling thoughts, express
	The greater heaven in an heaven less.
	In how coy[3] a figure wound,
(30)	Every way it turns away:
	So the world excluding round,
	Yet receiving in the day,
	Dark beneath, but bright above,
	Here disdaining, there in love.

(35)	How loose and easy hence to go,
	How girt and ready to ascend,
	Moving but on a point below,
	It all about does upwards bend.
	Such did the manna's sacred dew distill,
(40)	White and entire, though congealed and chill,
	Congealed on earth: but does, dissolving, run
	Into the glories of th' almighty sun.

1. The overall content of the poem can best be described by which statement?

(A) The characteristics of a drop of dew are related to those of the human soul.

(B) The life cycle of a drop of dew is contemplated.

(C) The human soul is shown to be a drop of dew.

(D) The physical characteristics of a drop of dew are analyzed.

(E) The poet offers a mystical vision of a drop of dew as a spiritual entity that has all the qualities of the human soul.

2. In context, "careless of its mansion new" (line 4) most nearly means

(A) the dew drop does not understand the value of its beautiful surroundings

(B) the dew drop does not assist the flower in any way

(C) the dew drop is unconcerned with its beautiful surroundings

(D) the human soul does not value the body

(E) the human soul does not take part in the care of the body

3. The speaker's metaphor for the human body is

(A) "the orient dew" (line 1)

(B) "the sphere" (line 14)

(C) "the clear fountain" (line 20)

(D) "the sweet leaves and blossoms green" (lines 23–24)

(E) "th' almighty sun" (line 42)

[1] pearly, sparkling

[2] blooming

[3] modest

4. Which of the following is the antecedent of "its" in "Does, in its pure and circling thoughts,/ express" (lines 26–27)?

   (A) "soul" (line 19)
   (B) "day" (line 20)
   (C) "flow'r" (line 21)
   (D) "height" (line 22)
   (E) "leaves" (line 23)

5. All of the following aspects of the dew drop are emphasized in the poem EXCEPT

   (A) its disregard for the physical world
   (B) its desire to regain the heavens
   (C) its purity
   (D) its will to live
   (E) its roundness

6. Lines 9–14 suggest the drop of dew is

   (A) frightened of death
   (B) full of unhappy longing
   (C) envious of the rose's vitality
   (D) part of a larger body of water in the sky
   (E) uncertain of the future

7. Lines 19–28 make explicit

   (A) the analogy between the drop of dew and the soul
   (B) the actual differences between the drop of dew and the soul
   (C) the true nature of the drop of dew
   (D) the soul's need for the body
   (E) the soul's thoughts

8. Each of the following pairs of phrases refers to the same action, object, or concept EXCEPT

   (A) "mansion new" (line 4)…"purple flow'r" (line 9)
   (B) "globe's extent" (line 7)…"the sphere" (line 14)
   (C) "that drop" (line 19)…"that ray" (line 19)
   (D) "exhale" (line 18)…"dissolving" (line 41)
   (E) "Every way it turns away" (line 30)…"It all about does upwards bend" (line 38)

9. Which of the following best paraphrases the meaning in context of "So the world excluding round,/ yet receiving in the day" (lines 31–32)?

   (A) Although the dew drop evaporates in the sun, it arrives anew each day.
   (B) The world evaporates the drop of dew when it receives the light of the sun.
   (C) The dew drop is impervious to everything but time.
   (D) Although the dew drop and the soul shut out the material world, they let in the light of heaven.
   (E) The only thing that matters to the dew drop is light.

10. In line 42, the sun is symbolic of

    (A) fire
    (B) rebirth
    (C) the soul
    (D) God
    (E) time

11. Which of the following sets of adjectives is best suited to describing the poem's tone?

    (A) Mysterious, moody, and spiritual
    (B) Pious, proper, and academic
    (C) Intricate, delicate, and worshipful
    (D) Witty, clever, and ironic
    (E) Straightforward, impassioned, and sincere

12. In the final four lines of the poem, the poet suggests that

    (A) the dew drop will ultimately be destroyed by the sun
    (B) the cycle of life and death is continual
    (C) the dew drop will return to earth in the form of "manna"
    (D) souls as pure as a drop of dew will ascend to heaven
    (E) death brings spiritual unity with God

13. Which of the following adjectives is LEAST important to the poem's theme?

    (A) "blowing" (line 3)
    (B) "clear" (line 20)
    (C) "pure" (line 26)
    (D) "bright" (line 33)
    (E) "loose" (line 35)

About Andrew Marvell's "On a Drop of Dew"

This poem is challenging but absolutely typical of what you will find on the AP Exam. Marvell (1621–1678) was one of the metaphysical poets (check your overview of literary movements), and the previous poem is an excellent example of this school of poetry's verse. The metaphysical poets were a loosely connected group of 17th-century poets who fashioned a type of elaborately clever, often witty verse with a decidedly intellectual twist. The metaphysical poets are noted for taking a comparison—for example, "a drop of dew is like the soul"—and developing it over dozens of lines. Lots of metaphysical poetry appears on the multiple-choice section, not because metaphysical poetry is necessarily great but because unlike most poetry, it lends itself well to multiple-choice questions. So, reading any of the metaphysicals' poetry is great practice for the AP Exam.

Let's Get Metaphysical
Others from the metaphysical school include John Donne, George Herbert, Thomas Carew, Abraham Cowley, and Richard Crashaw.

Answers and Explanations to the Questions

1. The overall content of the poem can best be described by which statement?

   (A) The characteristics of a drop of dew are related to those of the human soul.
   (B) The life cycle of a drop of dew is contemplated.
   (C) The human soul is shown to be a drop of dew.
   (D) The physical characteristics of a drop of dew are analyzed.
   (E) The poet offers a mystical vision of a drop of dew as a spiritual entity that has all the qualities of the human soul.

Here's How to Crack It

This is a main-idea question. Remember, you could have left it alone and come back to it if you hadn't found the main idea yet, but chances are you didn't have too much trouble. If you had any trouble eliminating choices, it was probably with (C). Does the poet really show that the human soul is a drop of dew? No. Marvell uses a drop of dew to speak about the human soul, but he isn't suggesting that a person's inner spirit is actually composed of condensed water. In fact, in the poem the drop of dew isn't so much a water droplet as it is a receptacle for light. This point becomes important in later questions. You should have eliminated (B) on the premise that it is much too literal to be correct; you're looking for the deeper main idea of the poem. If (D) threw you, then you weren't paying attention to the word *physical*. You should have asked yourself, "Wait a minute, this dew drop trembles with fear at the thought of becoming impure: Can I call that a physical analysis?" Marvell's drop of dew is a being with a personality and desires; all of these things are studied, not just its physical characteristics. Although (E) looks good at first glance, there's no way to prove that the author is offering a "mystical" vision. Choice (A) is similar in concept but without any added stuff to throw you off, so it's the best answer.

2. In context, "careless of its mansion new" (line 4) most nearly means

   (A) the dew drop does not understand the value of its beautiful surroundings
   (B) the dew drop does not assist the flower in any way
   (C) the dew drop is unconcerned with its beautiful surroundings
   (D) the human soul does not value the body
   (E) the human soul does not take part in the care of the body

Here's How to Crack It

Question 2 is a straightforward line-reference question. After reading around the line reference, you can easily eliminate (D) and (E). The line in question discusses only the dew drop upon a rose petal. It does not refer to the human soul. Of the remaining choices, (A) and (B) both imply that in context, "careless" means that the dew drop does not take care of the rose, which is simply a misreading. Chances are you didn't have much trouble on this question. The correct answer is (C).

3. The speaker's metaphor for the human body is

   (A) "the orient dew" (line 1)
   (B) "the sphere" (line 14)
   (C) "the clear fountain" (line 20)
   (D) "the sweet leaves and blossoms green" (lines 23–24)
   (E) "th' almighty sun" (line 42)

Here's How to Crack It

To answer this question you must either trace Marvell's involved metaphor, noting that in lines 19–21 he describes the soul as being housed within the "human flow'r," or use POE. All four incorrect answers refer to either a spiritual entity (the dew) or its source (the sphere, fountain, and sun) and so can be eliminated. The correct answer is (D).

4.   Which of the following is the antecedent of "its" in "Does, in its pure and circling thoughts,/ espress" (lines 26–27)?

   (A) "soul" (line 19)
   (B) "day" (line 20)
   (C) "flow'r" (line 21)
   (D) "height" (line 22)
   (E) "leaves" (line 23)

Here's How to Crack It

Question 4 is a typical grammar question and hinges on your knowing the term **antecedent**. That term, and other grammatical terms you need for the test, can be found in the glossary at the end of this book. By asking for the antecedent, the question is simply asking what the word *its* stands for in the given phrase. Analyzed grammatically, the only correct usage (and you'll only be asked about correct usage) is the soul. You might also have reasoned, "For which of the choices would it make sense to have 'pure and circling thoughts'?" Only (A) makes sense.

5.   All of the following aspects of the dew drop are emphasized in the poem EXCEPT

   (A) its disregard for the physical world
   (B) its desire to regain the heavens
   (C) its purity
   (D) its will to live
   (E) its roundness

Here's How to Crack It

Question 5 is an EXCEPT question. An excellent way to proceed is to disregard the EXCEPT; cross EXCEPT out.

Eliminate any choice that fits the remaining question, which now reads: All [Which] of the following aspects of the drop of dew are emphasized in the poem.

To do this you *must* refer back to the passage. Remember: Never work from memory! "Careless of its mansion new" lets you eliminate (A). "Like its own tear/ Because so long divided from the sphere" takes care of (B). "Trembling lest it grows impure" lets you eliminate (C). The dew drop's roundness is emphasized in several places; (E) was easy to eliminate. This leaves only (D), which is the correct answer.

6. Lines 9–14 suggest the drop of dew is

(A) frightened of death
(B) full of unhappy longing
(C) envious of the rose's vitality
(D) part of a larger body of water in the sky
(E) uncertain of the future

Here's How to Crack It

Question 6 is a line-reference question that tests your comprehension of a set of lines. If you had trouble with this question, you should practice reading poetry for comprehension. You can eliminate (C) and (E) easily as they have nothing to do with the poem. The other choices can almost be justified from the poem, but *almost* means *wrong*. Choice (A) could be eliminated because of the word *frightened*. The drop of dew is perhaps frightened of earthly life (remember, it "trembles" at the thought of becoming "impure") but as a metaphor for the soul, it is not afraid of death. Certainly no such statement can be found in the poem. Choice (D) is incorrect because Marvell treats the dew drop not only as water, but also as a container of light and as a metaphor for the soul. For Marvell the drop comes from the sky, not a body of water in the sky. The correct answer is (B).

7. Lines 19–28 make explicit

(A) the analogy between the drop of dew and the soul
(B) the actual differences between the drop of dew and the soul
(C) the true nature of the drop of dew
(D) the soul's need for the body
(E) the soul's thoughts

Here's How to Crack It

The key here is to understand the question. When something is made explicit, it is stated or spelled out. *Explicit* is the opposite of *implicit*. Your task is to see what lines 19–28 show clearly. Using POE, you should eliminate (D) immediately; it talks only about the drop of dew, whereas the lines in question refer primarily to the human soul. Choice (E) is a trap answer. The lines in question do refer to the soul's thoughts, but they do not spell them out; the thoughts are not made explicit. Choice (C) is similarly wrong. The drop of dew's "true nature" is not the subject of these lines; only the similarity of the drop of dew and the soul is. Choice (B) talks about differences between the soul and the drop of dew. This answer choice is the exact opposite of the lines' intent. They discuss the similarities of the drop and the soul. In fact, they make the analogy between the drop of dew and the soul explicit—therefore, (A) is the correct answer.

Go Online!
Check out us out on YouTube for test taking tips and techniques to help you ace your next exam at www.youtube.com/ThePrincetonReview

8. Each of the following pairs of phrases refers to the same
    action, object, or concept EXCEPT

    (A) "mansion new" (line 4)…"purple flow'r" (line 9)
    (B) "globe's extent" (line 7)…"the sphere" (line 14)
    (C) "that drop" (line 19)…"that ray" (line 19)
    (D) "exhale" (line 18)…"dissolving" (line 41)
    (E) "Every way it turns away" (line 30)…"It all about does
         upward bend" (line 38)

Here's How to Crack It

This is another EXCEPT question, a common type on the exam. Cross out
EXCEPT and eliminate answers that satisfy the remaining statement: Each of
the following pairs of phrases refers to the same action, object, or concept. Use
POE. In (A), "mansion new" and "purple flow'r" both refer to the rose the drop
of dew perches on. Eliminate it. In (C), "that drop" and "that ray" seem to refer
to different things but both in fact refer to the soul—so eliminate (C). In (D),
"exhale" and "dissolving" both refer to the process by which the drop of dew van-
ishes (evaporation, if you want to be scientific about it). In (B), "globe's extent" and
"sphere" seem to both refer to the dew drop, but in fact, the sphere refers to the
skies above—the "heavenly sphere." Thus, (B) is the correct answer.

Nitpicky? Maybe, but this question is an excellent example of the kind of careful
reading you'll be called upon to do on the actual test.

Practice, Practice, Practice
On the College Board's
website they share real
AP questions for you
to practice with. Check
out apstudents.college-
board.org/

9. Which of the following best paraphrases the meaning in
    context of "So the world excluding round,/ yet receiving
    in the day" (lines 31–32)?

    (A) Although the dew drop evaporates in the sun, it arrives
         anew each day.
    (B) The world evaporates the drop of dew when it receives
         the light of the sun.
    (C) The dew drop is impervious to everything but time.
    (D) Although the dew drop and the soul shut out the
         material world, they let in the light of heaven.
    (E) The only thing that matters to the dew drop is light.

Here's How to Crack It

This kind of comprehension question is probably the most common type of poetry
analysis question on the AP Exam. In essence, you'll be given a line and asked to
answer the question, "So, what does it mean?" As always, read around the line and
then use POE. Paraphrase "the world excluding round" as "the drop that turns

away from the world" and you can eliminate (A), (B), and (E). None of those choices include that idea. Choice (C) mentions that the drop of dew is impervious. That isn't a good paraphrase of "world excluding round," and you can eliminate it with confidence by reasoning that *time* is not mentioned in the lines in question at all. That leaves only the correct answer, (D).

10. In line 42, the sun is symbolic of

   (A) fire
   (B) rebirth
   (C) the soul
   (D) God
   (E) time

Different Levels of Difficulty

Get used to the range of difficulty on the AP Exam. Some of the questions are subtle and challenge even the most experienced readers, while others are a piece of cake. Don't freak out and think you must have missed something when a question seems easy: just collect the point. Don't miss the easy questions by over-thinking. And don't worry about missing difficult questions. If those are all you miss, you're on your way to earning a score of 5.

Here's How to Crack It

On this question, we hope you saw that the sun symbolized God. The word *almighty* should have been a big clue. Additionally, metaphysical poets are often concerned with spiritual issues. If you've used your overview of literary movements to prepare for this exam, the answer may be even more obvious. The correct answer is (D).

11. Which of the following sets of adjectives is best suited to describing the poem's tone?

   (A) Mysterious, moody, and spiritual
   (B) Pious, proper, and academic
   (C) Intricate, delicate, and worshipful
   (D) Witty, clever, and ironic
   (E) Straightforward, impassioned, and sincere

Here's How to Crack It

This is a tone question. On tone questions, always use POE, and remember that "half wrong equals all wrong." Every answer choice has something right in it but only the correct answer choice has *nothing* wrong in it. In (A), yes, the poem's tone is spiritual, but is it mysterious and moody? Not really. Eliminate it. Choice (B) has one promising word—*pious,* as the poem discusses God—but *proper* and *academic* do not fit. That isn't right. Eliminate it. In (D), well, it's true that the poem is witty and clever, but is it also ironic? Metaphysical poets typically are ironic— that is, hidden messages and contradictions often lurk below the surface of a metaphysical poem's text, but "On a Drop of Dew" is an exception. Marvell says what he means in a clever way, but not ironically. Choice (E) should just sound wrong. "On a Drop of Dew" is an intensely crafted work, but it is not impassioned or straightforward. That leaves (C), which sums things up fairly well: intricate, delicate, and worshipful.

12. In the final four lines of the poem, the poet suggests that

    (A) the dew drop will ultimately be destroyed by the sun
    (B) the cycle of life and death is continual
    (C) the drop of dew will return to earth in the form of "manna"
    (D) souls as pure as a drop of dew will ascend to heaven
    (E) death brings spiritual unity with God

Here's How to Crack It

If you answered question 10 correctly, this one shouldn't be much tougher. If you understand that the sun symbolizes God, then you should also understand that the dew's dissolving into the sun is a metaphor for the soul's ascent to heaven. The incorrect answer choices all add extraneous points or misconstrue the emphasis of this essentially simple idea. Choice (A) suggests that the dew would be destroyed. That misses the point. The dew's evaporation is not a destruction, but a reunion with the divine. Choice (B) is extraneous: the cycle of life is not a thematic point of the poem. Choice (C) tries to trap you by confusing the manna with the dew drop. The poem suggests that the dew drop is like manna in that both are distilled from the spiritual realm. The poem does not suggest that the dew will somehow become manna. Choice (D) should have been easy to eliminate. Nowhere does the poem talk about whether or not souls are as pure as a drop of dew. The correct answer is (E).

13. Which of the following adjectives is LEAST important to the poem's theme?

(A) "blowing" (line 3)
(B) "clear" (line 20)
(C) "pure" (line 26)
(D) "bright" (line 33)
(E) "loose" (line 35)

Here's How to Crack It

The test-writers are fond of asking questions about theme, despite the fact that pinning down the theme of many poems is problematic. When you're asked about the theme, don't try to come up with an exact definition. Just think about the main point, the important stuff. Again, POE is the way to work. Cross out LEAST and work with the remaining question, eliminating choices that are important to the theme. An important aspect of the poem is the metaphor of the dew drop and the soul. A good way to start would be to eliminate those choices that describe any aspect of that relationship. In this way you could eliminate (B), (C), and (D), because all are qualities of the dew drop that relate to qualities of the soul. A moment of study should tell you that (E) is also important. The dew drop is "loose," or ready to ascend; it grips this world only lightly. That is a thematic point. And (A)? Well, *blowing* means blooming. Is it important that the rose is in bloom? Does Marvell return to the fact of the rose being in bloom later in the poem? Does blooming somehow relate to the soul? No. Choice (A) is least thematically important, and thus (A) is the correct answer.

Bonus Grammar Questions

Try these for strenuous, but excellent, practice. They're harder than real AP questions, but not by much. The following is an excerpt from Percy Bysshe Shelley's "Alastor; or, The Spirit of Solitude."

> Nature's most secret steps
> He like her shadow has pursued, wher'er
> The red volcano overcanopies
> Its fields of snow and pinnacles of ice
>
> *Line*
> (5) With burning smoke, or where bitumen lakes
> On black bare pointed islets ever beat
> With sluggish surge, or where the secret caves
> Rugged and dark, winding among the springs
>
> Of fire and poison, inaccessible
> (10) To avarice or pride, their starry domes
> Of diamond and of gold expand above
> Numberless and immeasurable halls,
>
> Frequent with crystal column, and clear shrines
> Of pearl, and thrones radiant with chrysolite.

1. The word "inaccessible" (line 9) modifies which of the following words?

   (A) "lakes" (line 5)
   (B) "caves" (line 7)
   (C) "springs" (line 8)
   (D) "poison" (line 9)
   (E) "avarice" (line 10)

You should recognize that *inaccessible* is an adjective (the ending *-ible* gives it away). That observation means that you need to decide which noun or pronoun it modifies. Unfortunately, all of the choices are nouns. If you look carefully, you will see that *or* (in line 7) introduces an independent clause. Because of the use of commas, the participial phrase *winding among the springs* modifies *caves*. *Of fire and poison* is a prepositional phrase modifying *springs*. *To avarice or pride* is another prepositional phrase that limits *inaccessible*. The correct answer, then, is (B), *caves*. Tough, isn't it?

Try this poem by Emily Dickinson.

> There's a certain Slant of light,
> Winter Afternoons—
> That oppresses, like the Heft
> Of Cathedral Tunes—
>
> *Line*
> (5) Heavenly Hurt, it gives us—
> We can find no scar,
> But internal difference,
> Where the meanings, are—
>
> None may teach it—Any—
> (10) 'Tis the Seal Despair—
> An imperial affliction
> Sent us of the Air—
>
> When it comes, the Landscape listens—
> Shadows—hold their breath—
> (15) When it goes, 'tis like the Distance
> On the look of Death—

2. In line 5, "it" refers to

   (A) "Cathedral Tunes" (line 4)
   (B) "Heavenly Hurt" (line 5)
   (C) "Slant of light" (line 1)
   (D) "look of Death" (line 16)
   (E) "imperial affliction" (line 11)

Asking what a pronoun refers to is a favorite of the AP Exam writers. Do you see that this isn't so much a question of grammatical analysis as it is of comprehension? The correct answer is (C). The *slant of light* is the antecedent.

Poetry Analysis Passage Drill 1

Suggested time: 12 minutes

Questions 1–11. Choose your answers to questions 1–11 based on a careful reading of the following poem by Phillis Wheatley.

"On the Death of J.C. an Infant"

NO more the flow'ry scenes of pleasure rise,
Nor charming prospects greet the mental eyes,
No more with joy we view that lovely face
Smiling, disportive, flush'd with ev'ry grace.

Line
(5) The tear of sorrow flows from ev'ry eye,
Groans answer groans, and signs to sighs reply;
When sudden pangs shot thro' each aching heart,
When, Death, thy messenger dispatch'd his dart?
Thy dread attendants, all-destroying Pow'r,
(10) Hurried the infant to his mortal hour.
Could'st thou unpitying close those radiant eyes?
Or fail'd his artless beauties to surprize?
Could not his innocence thy stroke controul,
Thy purpose shake, and soften all thy soul?

(15) The blooming babe, with shades of Death o'er-spread,
No more shall smile, no more shall raise its head,
But, like a branch that from the tree is torn,
Falls prostrate, wither'd, languid, and forlorn.
"Where flies my James?" 'tis thus I seem to hear
(20) The parent ask, "Some angel tell me where
"He wings his passage thro' the yielding air?"
Methinks a cherub bending from the skies
Observes the question, and serene replies,
In heav'ns high palaces your babe appears:
(25) Prepare to meet him, and dismiss your tears."
Shall not th' intelligence your grief restrain,
And turn the mournful to the chearful strain?
Cease your complaints, suspend each rising sigh,
Cease to accuse the Ruler of the sky.
(30) Parents, no more indulge the falling tear:
Let Faith to heav'n's refulgent domes repair,
There see your infant, like a seraph glow:
What charms celestial in his numbers flow
Melodious, while the foul-enchanting strain
(35) Dwells on his tongue, and fills th' ethereal plain?

Enough—for ever cease your murm'ring breath;
Not as a foe, but friend converse with Death,
Since to the port of happiness unknown
He brought that treasure which you call your own.
(40) The gift of heav'n intrusted to your hand
Cheerful resign at the divine command:
Not at your bar must sov'reign Wisdom stand.

1. Taken as a whole, the poem is best understood to be

   (A) an epitaph
   (B) an elegy
   (C) a parable
   (D) a dirge
   (E) a sestina

2. The poet's use of syncope throughout the poem serves

   (A) to save copying time, since this poet wrote
       in longhand
   (B) to form alliteration with the surrounding words
   (C) to make the line fit the poem's meter
   (D) to make it evident that a new subject is
       being addressed
   (E) to represent the dialect of the speaker

3. Line 29 contains an example of

   (A) an apostrophe
   (B) an allusion
   (C) free verse
   (D) a metaphor
   (E) a euphemism

4. The poet makes use of all of the following literary
   devices in lines 1–4 EXCEPT

   (A) metaphor
   (B) consonance
   (C) iambic pentameter
   (D) enjambment
   (E) parallelism

5. Grammatically, the word "wings" (line 21) is a

   (A) noun
   (B) direct object
   (C) adjective
   (D) adverb
   (E) verb

6. The tone in lines 1–21 is best characterized as

   (A) disdainful
   (B) nostalgic
   (C) reverential
   (D) woeful
   (E) earnest

7. Lines 30–31 can best be paraphrased as

   (A) "Dismiss your tears and return your faith
       to heaven"
   (B) "Your tears are important: know that heaven will
       heal you"
   (C) "The angels of heaven will mend the tears in
       your heart"
   (D) "Your faith, not your tears, will replace the repugnant
       structures of heaven"
   (E) "Parents, repair your faith so you too may see your
       infant in the vaults of heaven"

8. Each clause in lines 28–29 is best described as a

   (A) question
   (B) command
   (C) concession
   (D) invitation
   (E) declaration

9. The primary purpose of lines 22–25 is to

   (A) engage the listeners by offering a peaceful
       anecdote
   (B) remind the parents they will see their infant in
       heaven
   (C) recount the infant's words to those left on earth
   (D) console the grieving parents
   (E) speculate where the infant has gone

10. In lines 13–14, "thy" refers to

   (A) each aching heart
   (B) the poet
   (C) Death
   (D) the attendants
   (E) the infant

11. Which course of action would the speaker most wish the
    audience to take?

   (A) Be resigned to the harsh realities of life
   (B) Stop indulging in misery
   (C) Understand the gift that has been sacrificed
   (D) Accept that the loss of a child is inevitable
   (E) Entrust the infant to a higher power

POETRY ANALYSIS PASSAGE DRILL 1: ANSWERS AND EXPLANATIONS

Sold into slavery at age seven, Phillis Wheatley was educated by her Boston slave owner and in 1773 became the first published African American poet. Her preferred poetic form was the couplet, and elegies comprised more than one-third of her published works.

1. **B** This is a definition question. An elegy is a poem that mourns the death of someone, which makes the correct answer (B). None of the remaining answers would work. An epitaph is the inscription on a tombstone, so eliminate (A). A parable is a story that instructs, so (C) is also incorrect. A dirge is a song lamenting the dead, so (D) can be eliminated. A sestina has a different rhyme scheme and is only 39 lines long, so eliminate (E).

2. **C** This question is tricky if you don't know the definition of syncope. *Syncope* involves the shortening of a word by removing internal letters and inserting an apostrophe. Poets often employ this technique, and Wheatley uses it frequently in this poem. By modifying the sound of certain words, the poet ensures that the line's metrical rhythm is kept intact. The correct answer is (C).

3. **B** This is another definition question. The use of the word *Ruler* makes this line an example of an allusion, specifically a biblical allusion as "Ruler" refers to God. Wheatley often wrote about her Christian faith in her poems, so it would not be surprising to find such allusions in her poems. The correct answer is (B).

4. **A** One example of consonance, (B), in lines 1–4, is the repetition of the s sound (scenes, rise, prospects, smiling, grace). The poem is written in iambic pentameter, (C). The end of line 3 contains an example of enjambment, (D). Lines 1 and 3 contain parallel structure, (E). The device not appearing in these four lines is metaphor. The correct answer is (A).

5. **E** Make sure to read the entire sentence, not just line 21. Start with line 20 at the beginning of the quotation: "Some angel tell me where He wings his passage thro' the yielding air?" The word *wings* is not being used as a noun, as it is normally used. Eliminate (A) and (B). The parent is asking where the infant wings (or flies) through the air (i.e., where did he go?). Thus, the word *wings* is being used as a verb. The correct answer is (E).

6. **D** Remember that this poem is an elegy. Elegies are written about someone who has died, so the tone is likely sorrowful. Lines 1–12, for example, confirm this. The poet expresses great sadness through the use of phrases like *no more joy, tear of sorrow, Death*, and *Hurried the infant to his mortal hour*. The tone is indeed sorrowful, which makes the best answer (D).

7. **A** The meaning of the word *repair* in this context is to return to or to go to a place, not to fix something. Knowing that, eliminate (B), (C), and (E). If you know what *repugnant* means (repulsive), then eliminate (D), since there is nothing in these lines that suggests the "heav'n's refulgent domes" are repulsive or offensive. (By the way, *refulgent* means "shining brightly.") This leaves the correct answer, which is (A).

8. **B**   The three clauses begin with cease, suspend, and cease, which are all verbs in the imperative mood. The imperative mood is used when a speaker makes a command. In this poem, the speaker is requesting that the parents stop complaining about, sighing/crying for, and implicating God in the loss of their infant. There are no questions asked in these lines, so eliminate (A). The speaker doesn't ask them to give up something—the parents have already lost something—in order to reach an agreement, so (C) is also incorrect. The speaker is not inviting the parents to stop, so eliminate (D). A declaration would fall under the indicative mood, and declaratives usually express statements and contain a subject, which is not the case in these lines; (E) is incorrect. The speaker is clearly telling the parents to do something, so the best answer is (B).

9. **D**   With purpose questions, ask yourself why are these lines here, not what did the writer say. If you do the latter, you will likely pick (B) or (E), neither of which is the purpose of these lines. The speaker is offering the mourning parents solace and, to do so, offers them a peaceful thought: a cherub telling the parents their child is safe in heaven. Therefore, the speaker's purpose is to comfort them. The correct answer is (D). These lines are not an example of anecdote, (A), and the words are that of the cherub, not the infant, (C).

10. **C**   The word *thy* is a possessive pronoun. When dealing with pronouns, you want to locate the antecedent. Whose stroke controlled? Whose purpose should be shaken? Whose soul should be softened? You will need to go back to line 8 to find the antecedent, which is Death. It is Death who hurried the infant to his mortal hour and with whom the speaker is pleading. The correct answer is (C).

11. **E**   The speaker, in an effort to comfort the grieving parents, is reminding them that the child is in heaven and urging them to put their faith in God. Choices (A), (B), and (D) are all too negative and do not align with the message of the speaker. While the speaker does acknowledge the sacrifice, the takeaway message is more than their sacrifice—it is to hold fast to their faith in God.

Poetry Analysis Passage Drill 2

Suggested time: 12 minutes

<u>Questions 1–9.</u> Choose your answers to questions 1–9 based on a careful reading of the following poem by Carl Sandburg.

"Skyscraper"

By day the skyscraper looms in the smoke and sun and has
    a soul.
Prairie and valley, streets of the city, pour people into
Line   it and they mingle among its twenty floors and are
(5)   poured out again back to the streets, prairies and
    valleys.
It is the men and women, boys and girls so poured in and
    out all day that give the building a soul of dreams and
    thoughts and memories.
(10)   (Dumped in the sea or fixed in a desert, who would care
    for the building or speak its name or ask a policeman
    the way to it?)

Elevators slide on their cables and tubes catch letters
    and parcels and iron pipes carry gas and water in and
(15)   sewage out.
Wires climb with secrets, carry light and carry words,
    and tell terrors and profits and loves—curses of men
    grappling plans of business and questions of women in
    plots of love.

(20)   Hour by hour the caissons reach down to the rock of the
    earth and hold the building to a turning planet.
Hour by hour the girders play as ribs and reach out and
    hold together the stone walls and floors.
Hour by hour the hand of the mason and the stuff of the
(25)   mortar clinch the pieces and parts to the shape an
    architect voted.
Hour by hour the sun and the rain, the air and the rust, and
    the press of time running into centuries, play on the
    building inside and out and use it.

(30)   Men who sunk the pilings and mixed the mortar are laid
    in graves where the wind whistles a wild song without
    words
And so are men who strung the wires and fixed the pipes
    and tubes and those who saw it rise floor by floor.
(35)   Souls of them all are here, even the hod carrier begging at
    back doors hundreds of miles away and the bricklayer
    who went to state's prison for shooting another man
    while drunk.
(One man fell from a girder and broke his neck at the end
(40)   of a straight plunge—he is here—his soul has gone
    into the stones of the building.)

On the office doors from tier to tier—hundreds of names
    and each name standing for a face written across with a
    dead child, a passionate lover, a driving ambition for a
(45)   million dollar business or a lobster's ease of life.

Behind the signs on the doors they work and the walls tell
    nothing from room to room.
Ten-dollar-a-week stenographers take letters from corpora-
    tion officers, lawyers, efficiency engineers, and tons of
(50)   letters go bundled from the building to all ends of the
    earth.
Smiles and tears of each office girl go into the soul of the
    building just the same as the master-men who rule the
    building.

(55)   Hands of clocks turn to noon hours and each floor empties
    its men and women who go away and eat and come
    back to work.
Toward the end of the afternoon all work slackens and all
    jobs go slower as the people feel day closing on them.
(60)   One by one the floors are emptied… The uniformed
    elevator men are gone. Pails clang… Scrubbers work,
    talking in foreign tongues. Broom and water and mop
    clean from the floors human dust and spit, and machine
    grime of the day.
(65)   Spelled in electric fire on the roof are words telling miles
    of houses and people where to buy a thing for money.
    The sign speaks till midnight.
Darkness on the hallways. Voices echo. Silence holds…
    Watchmen walk slow from floor to floor and try the
(70)   doors. Revolvers bulge from their hip pockets… Steel
    safes stand in corners. Money is stacked in them.
A young watchman leans at a window and sees the lights
    of barges butting their way across a harbor, nets of
    red and white lanterns in a railroad yard, and a span
(75)   of glooms splashed with lines of white and blurs of
    crosses and clusters over the sleeping city.
By night the skyscraper looms in the smoke and the stars
    and has a soul.

1. What is implied by lines 10–12 ("Dumped . . . to it")?

   (A) The building depends on people.
   (B) It would be just as easy to tear down the skyscraper and dump its bricks and mortar and steel girders as it is to let it stand.
   (C) The skyscraper is important only because of the city in which it is located.
   (D) There would be no point in having the building unless people used it.
   (E) The speaker doesn't think the building has any value.

2. It can be inferred that the poet

   (A) admires the workers who built the skyscraper
   (B) would prefer it if the skyscraper were gone
   (C) works in the skyscraper or in a building much like it
   (D) venerates the skyscraper
   (E) is critical of the contemporary social order

3. The image in line 28, "the press of time running into centuries," suggests

   (A) the speaker's attitude of awe for the building
   (B) one of the poem's themes
   (C) the central metaphor of the poem
   (D) an allusion to the city itself
   (E) the negative quality of the building

4. According to the poem, which of the following is NOT true of the skyscraper?

   (A) It has outlasted its original creators.
   (B) It carries advertising messages to surrounding residents.
   (C) It is permanent but not eternal.
   (D) It is empty at night.
   (E) It has systems that mirror those of a living being.

5. How do the first and last lines contribute to the structure of the poem?

   (A) They reinforce the fact that the skyscraper has a soul.
   (B) They give the poem a formal, "bookended" quality, stating and then restating an image.
   (C) They reinforce the theme of time passing while the skyscraper endures.
   (D) They present the skyscraper's connection to major objects in the universe.
   (E) They paint a vivid picture of the building's enduring nature.

6. What can you infer from the poet's diction?

   (A) His intended audience was ordinary people, like the blue-collar construction workers, the watchmen and the "Ten-dollar-a-week stenographers" (line 48) in the poem.
   (B) He was writing primarily for men.
   (C) He was accustomed to writing novels and short stories, not poetry.
   (D) He wanted his writing to appeal to "the master-men who rule the building" (lines 53-54) and the "corporation officers, lawyers, efficiency engineers" (lines 48–49).
   (E) He didn't have much formal education.

7. In line 22, the statement that "the girders play as ribs" is an example of which literary device?

   (A) An allusion
   (B) A double entendre
   (C) A simile
   (D) Pathos
   (E) Hyperbole

8. The watchmen, the office girls, the night cleaners, and the construction workers have all of the following characteristics in common EXCEPT

   (A) They are enablers.
   (B) They won't outlast the skyscraper.
   (C) They won't end up in an office with their name on the door.
   (D) They give the building its soul.
   (E) They are proud of their association with the building.

9. Which of the following best summarizes the significance to the poem of lines 16–19 ("Wires...love")?

   (A) Just as the skyscraper gives people a place to work, so the telephone lines give them a way to make plans to achieve what they want.
   (B) It reinforces the poet's assertion that it is the people using the skyscraper who give it life and soul.
   (C) The telephone wires in the skyscraper may be inanimate, but they carry dramatic conversations and plans for action.
   (D) Although the stenographers are faceless and the executives are behind identical doors on identical floors, these people are not bland and ordinary. Their lives are filled with secrets and intrigue and ambition.
   (E) It explains what is hinted at in lines 46–47: "Behind the signs on the doors they work and the walls tell nothing from room to room."

POETRY ANALYSIS PASSAGE DRILL 2: ANSWERS AND EXPLANATIONS

About "Skyscraper"

Skyscrapers—a solution to the shrinking amount of land in big city downtown areas—were still a relatively new phenomenon when American poet Carl Sandburg wrote this in 1916. The Wainwright Building in St. Louis, Missouri, built only 25 years earlier, is often considered the first such building. They were called "skyscrapers" because, in comparison to the surrounding buildings, they appeared tall enough to scrape the sky.

1. **A** Remember, when a question stem sends you to a specific line in a poem, always read at least a line before and a line after in order to understand the context. If you looked only at lines 10–12, you might think the correct answer is (C). In this case, you only need to read one line before—"It is the men and women, boys and girls so poured in and out all day that give the building a soul of dreams and thoughts and memories"—to see that the correct answer is (A). The skyscraper has value, permanence, and a sense of life by virtue of the people who work in it, maintain it, and consider it important, not because of the city in which it stands. Choice (D) is too narrow—people do more than use the building. Choices (B) and (E) aren't implied: the speaker doesn't suggest that dumping the skyscraper in the sea would be easy, and doesn't give his own opinion of the building's value.

2. **E** This question calls for two things: an understanding of the poem as a whole, and an ability to distinguish the poet from the narrator. The first requirement eliminates (C)—there is much more to the descriptions in the poem than an obvious familiarity with the day-to-day routine of working in a downtown office building. Choice (A) is gone for the same reason—the original construction crew is only one of the groups of people the poet describes. In addition, there is no suggestion that he particularly admires them. The poet's tone is too neutral to suggest either hostility, (B), or veneration, (D), for the building, so eliminate those two choices. That leaves (E). He juxtaposes the "Ten-dollar-a-week stenographers" (line 48) and "the master-men who rule the building" (lines 53–54). He states that, at night, "Scrubbers work, talking in foreign tongues" (lines 61–62) and refers to the blue-collar workers who erected the building so white-collar "corporation officers, lawyers, efficiency engineers" (lines 48–49) could work there. The poet is suggesting a criticism of the class system and gender inequality of his time. Although the narrator's tone is relatively neutral when he refers to these groups, it is the author who chose to include them in the poem.

3. **B** POE works well on this question. The quoted phrase is neither a metaphor nor an allusion, so (C) and (D) can be eliminated. When you read the line before and after, there is no mention of the speaker's opinion, which eliminates (A). The only negative word in line 27 is "rust"; otherwise the description is neutral, so (E) can also be eliminated. That leaves (B) and indeed, when you consider the poem as a whole, one of the themes running through it is time. For example, the builders ended their short lives long ago, but the skyscraper they constructed still stands. "Hands of clocks turn" (line 55); day turns into night turns into day. The skyscraper "has a soul" (lines 1–2), which is eternal.

4. **D**   In this EXCEPT/LEAST/NOT format question, first eliminate the "NOT," leaving the standard format question, "which of the following is true of the skyscraper?" Then eliminate the four choices that would be correct answers to that question. Choices (A) (lines 30–32), (B) (lines 65–65), and (E) (lines 22–23) are all true of the building. So is (C)—the skyscraper may be anchored to the planet (lines 20–21), but time and weather are wearing it down (lines 27–29). It is "permanent" compared to the long-gone men who built it, but not "eternal" as the sun and stars are. That leaves (D) as the correct answer. Scrubbers (line 61) and watchmen (line 69) work in the building at night, so it is not empty. This is the only statement that is NOT true of the building.

5. **B**   The key words in the question stem are "contribute to the *structure*." This is an example of how reading the question stem carefully, word for word, pays off. All of the answer choices are true of the first and last lines, but only one concerns the poem's structure. That's (B). The first line presents the skyscraper and its soul, looming "in the smoke and sun." The poem then goes on to develop the building's relationship to people, past and present, and its own life-like qualities. Then the last line returns to recap the first line; the building and its soul now loom "in the smoke and the stars."

6. **A**   This question asks you to assess the poet's vocabulary and choice of words throughout the entire poem and then make an inference from your assessment. What do you see in the language he chooses? Is it dominated by sophisticated words that only well-educated people would understand? No, so you can eliminate (D). Is it filled with lyrical references to dewdrops and cherubs? Is it overflowing with symbols and imagery and obscure references to ancient Greek gods? No, Sandburg uses concrete, down-to-earth, everyday language. Even words that seem unusual now ("caissons," or foundations, and "hod carrier," or a low-level laborer who brought supplies to tradesmen) were common in 1916. That accessible vocabulary points to ordinary, everyday people as his intended audience (A). The poet doesn't describe many women (only the office girls in line 52 and possibly the stenographers in line 48 and the scrubbers in line 61). However, that's not surprising; in 1916 men held most of the jobs. Nothing in the choice of language seems particularly aimed at either men or women, eliminating (B). The unrhymed free verse in this poem might make (C) seem like an attractive choice. However, the question asks about diction, not about poetic form, so (C) is incorrect. Using plain, everyday language doesn't necessarily point to a lack of formal education, (E). In fact, Sandburg did attend college and West Point, although the progression of his education was erratic. Therefore, you can eliminate (E).

7. **C**   A simile compares two unlike things (here, inanimate steel girders and living ribs of bone), using "as" or "like." This particular simile reinforces the concept of the skyscraper having life. None of the other choices would apply to the quote in the question stem. An allusion, (A), is a brief reference to a significant person, place, or thing (such as a character in a Shakespearean play, or a place in a Greek myth). It depends on readers being familiar with the reference. A double entendre, (B), refers to a word or statement which can be interpreted in different ways. It is often used for humor or irony. Pathos, (D), is designed to trigger feelings of pity or sympathy in the reader. Hyperbole, (E), is an exaggeration intended to create emphasis.

8. **E** This is a tricky question that requires careful reading of the question stem. It says these four groups "have" characteristics in common—not "likely have" or "probably have." This stem isn't asking for inference or interpretation; it allows for only what the poem directly and specifically says. Since this is an EXCEPT/LEAST/NOT format question, cross out the EXCEPT and find the four answer choices that would be correct for the resulting standard format question. Choice (A) is correct: the construction workers enabled the skyscraper to exist, the office girls enable executives to send out their letters, the night cleaners enable workers to return the next day to an environment free of "human dust and spit, and machine grime" (lines 63–64), and the watchmen with their revolvers enable protection from intruders and from thieves who want the money in the steel safes. The construction workers didn't outlast the skyscraper they built; none of the other human groups will outlast it, either, so (B) is correct. Only the members of the privileged class—the "corporation officers, lawyers, efficiency engineers" (lines 48–49)—get an office with their name on the door. In the poet's 1916 class society, no one from the other four groups would have that chance, so (C) is correct. Choice (D) is correct; the building has a soul in virtue of the "[men and women, boys and girls]… poured in and out all day" (lines 7–8) and the workers who built it (lines 30–32), while the scrubbers and watchmen who take over at night, after the "floors are emptied" (line 60), give the skyscraper its soul in the stars (lines 77–78). That leaves (E) as the correct EXCEPT answer. The narrator is neutral about the relationships between each of the four groups and the building. They may be proud of their association with it; they may not. From what the poem says, we don't know, and the question stem doesn't allow inferences.

9. **B** Again, careful reading of the question stem is essential. You're asked about the *significance* of lines 16–19 to the poem, not about what the words mean (C) or what the poet might be implying (D). Those two choices are both incorrect. Choice (E) has some merit in presenting lines 46–47 as an expansion. However, it's too narrow. The question asks for the best summary of the significance to the poem as a whole, not just to part of it. Choice (A) is also too narrow; it misses the connection between the life of people and the soul of the skyscraper that runs throughout the poem. Only (B) makes that connection.

REFLECT

Respond to the following questions:

- Which types of multiple-choice questions discussed in this chapter do you feel you have achieved sufficient mastery to answer correctly?

- On which types of multiple-choice questions discussed in this chapter do you feel you need more work before you can answer correctly?

- What strategies discussed in this chapter do you feel you will be able to apply effectively when taking the exam?

- What parts of this chapter are you going to re-review?

- Will you seek further help, outside of this book (such as from a teacher, tutor, or AP Students), on any of the content in this chapter—and, if so, on what content?

Summary

o Don't worry about scansion (you know: iambic pentameter, dactyls, spondees, and the like). You probably won't see even one question on it.

o Remember:
   • Read the poem as prose.
   • Focus on the main idea.
   • When answering the questions, use POE and Consistency of Answers.

o Be sure to read around line references.

o Metaphysical poetry is excellent practice for the kind of poetry you'll see on the AP Exam. John Donne, Andrew Marvell, George Herbert, Thomas Carew, Abraham Cowley, and Richard Crashaw are all poets whose work provides excellent AP practice. Also, the poetry of Emily Dickinson and Robert Frost is rich in intricate grammatical structures.

o On EXCEPT, NOT, and LEAST questions, cross out the negative word and eliminate any choice that fits the remaining question.

Chapter 8
Prose Fiction
Analysis Questions

“

Books are a form of political action.
Books are knowledge. Books are
reflection. Books change your mind.

—Toni Morrison

”

USING THE SAMPLE PASSAGES AND QUESTIONS

There's no limit to the different kinds of questions that ETS can (and does) write for the AP English Literature and Composition Exam. As a result, we can't show you every type of question that may show up on the test. We can come pretty close, though, as questions are often reused from year to year. The best way to study these questions is by practicing on examples, but to understand and use the example questions, you need a passage.

There's no need to complete the questions immediately because we're going to take you through them one step at time, discussing the best approaches and specific techniques to use in answering them. Of course, if you want to see how you do on them before referring to our instructions, go right ahead.

After you've looked over the passages, read each question, try to answer it, and then follow our explanations. The correct answer to each question is given in the explanation, but don't just skim through the explanation looking for the answer to see whether you chose correctly. Read all of each explanation, regardless of whether you got the question right. Our explanations will point out details you overlooked and discuss how you might have approached the question differently.

At the end of this chapter, you'll have the opportunity to try a full passage and set of questions so that you can practice using the techniques and approaches discussed in this chapter.

TAKING CONTROL OF PROSE FICTION ANALYSIS PASSAGES

Expect anything from mystery to humor to fantasy (and a host of other literary genres, or categories) in the exam's prose fiction analysis passages, representing periods ranging from the 16th century to modern times. Moreover, each prose fiction analysis passage is just a piece of a larger work, sometimes with bits truncated (cut out) in order to fit the exam's roughly 500–700 word average length. So, you may feel that you've been dropped into the middle of something when you first start reading, and that you've been left hanging when you reach the end. As disorienting as that may seem, each passage is a self-contained selection that holds the answers you need.

You'll find two or three prose fiction analysis passages (interspersed with poetry analysis) in the multiple-choice section, with about 10 to 12 minutes to answer 8 to 13 questions about each one. That's around a minute or a bit more than a minute per question, and you need time to read the passage, too. How can you accomplish that?

First, *work* (don't *read*) the passage, using the active reading techniques described in Chapter 1. Your only objective is to answer the questions correctly, so use your active reading skills to take control and make the passage give you the information you need. Practice active reading until it becomes second nature.

Second, use the time management and pacing techniques explained in Chapter 2. Work at a steady pace, and don't waste time on questions you can't answer. Guess (using your Letter of the Day) and move on, quickly noting the question number in case you have a chance to go back to it.

Third, learn to recognize the question types, question formats, and the best way to approach each one. Review the information in Chapter 4, and practice with the passages in this book. That way, when you see a particular type of question on the exam, you'll be well prepared with a plan of attack.

A Passage in 12–15 Minutes

1. Work—don't just read—the passage. Read actively.
2. Manage your time; pace yourself.
3. Learn the question types.

GETTING TO KNOW THE QUESTIONS

Typical prose fiction analysis passage questions are designed to test your critical reading skills. They give you an opportunity to show that you can grasp both the overall theme (the main point), and how various elements of the passage function to develop that theme. These questions assess your ability to analyze, interpret, and make inferences—to "read between the lines" and dissect *how* the author conveys his or her meaning. It also checks that you can do all of that quickly and accurately.

Prose fiction analysis passage questions tend to focus on elements that are likely familiar to you from previous literature studies, such as

- characters (their significance and function in the passage, as well as the relationships among them)
- setting and its significance
- situation and its significance
- narration
- plot
- theme(s)
- structure (how the passage progresses)
- perspectives (the narrator's and the author's) and the relationships of part to whole and parts to each other

Sound Familiar?
The items listed right here (well, left here, heh), are the Big Six, plus some guest stars.

- style (vocabulary and syntax, devices the author uses to convey his or her meaning)
- tone (the author's or narrator's attitude) and the elements that reveal it
- literary devices (figurative language such as allusions, metaphors, and symbols) and their functions in the passage

Need More Help on Essays?

We've got just the book for that! *How to Write Essays for Standardized Tests* contains advice and examples of best practices on an assortment of AP exams, plus ACT, and others!

In the rest of this chapter, you can practice taking control of two prose fiction analysis passages and making them give you the correct answers. First is a sample passage. Try using active reading techniques and answering the questions. Then read the answer explanations that follow; they describe not only how to reach the correct answer, but also how to approach this type of question when you encounter it in other passages. At the end of this chapter is a prose fiction analysis passage drill with questions and answer explanations to give you more practice.

SAMPLE PROSE FICTION ANALYSIS PASSAGE AND QUESTIONS

Edgar Allan Poe's "The Duc De L'Omelette"

Keats fell by a criticism. But who ever died of inept poetry? Ignoble souls!—De L'Omelette perished of an ortolan[1]. The story then, in brief:

Line
(5) That night the Duke was to sup alone. In the privacy of his bureau he reclined languidly on that ottoman for which he sacrificed his loyalty in outbidding his king—the notorious ottoman of Cadet.

He buries his face in the pillow. The clock strikes! Unable to restrain his feelings, his Grace swallows an olive.
(10) At this moment the door gently opens to the sound of soft music, and lo! the most delicate of birds is before the most enamored of men! But what inexpressible dismay now overshadows the countenance of the Duke? *"Horreur! Dog! Protestant! —the bird! Ah Good God! This modest*
(15) *bird you've quite unclothed and served without paper!"* It is superfluous to say more:—the Duke expired in a paroxysm of disgust....

"Ha! ha! ha!" said his Grace on the third day after his decease.
(20) "He! he! he!" replied the Devil faintly, drawing himself up with an air of hauteur.

"Why surely you are not serious," retorted De L'Omelette. "I have sinned—that's true—but, my good sir, consider!—you have no actual intention of putting such—
(25) such—barbarous threats into execution."

"No what?" said his Majesty—"come, sir, strip!"

"Strip, indeed! very pretty i' faith! no, sir, I shall not strip. Who are you, pray, that I, Duke De L'Omelette, Prince de Foie-Gras, just come of age, author of the
(30) 'Mazurkiad,' and member of the Academy, should divest myself at your bidding of the sweetest pantaloons ever made by Bourdon, the daintiest dressing gown ever put together by Rombert—take say nothing of undressing my hair—not to mention the trouble I should have in drawing
(35) off my gloves?"

"Who am I?—ah, true! I am Baal-Zebub, Prince of the Fly. I took thee, just now, from a rosewood coffin inlaid with ivory. Thou wast curiously scented, and labeled as per invoice. Belial sent thee—my Inspector of Ceme-
(40) teries. The pantaloons, which thou sayest were made by Bourdon, are an excellent pair of linen drawers, and thy dressing gown is a shroud of no scanty dimensions."

"Sir!" replied the Duke, "I am not to be insulted with impunity!—Sir! you shall hear from me! In the meantime
(45) au revoir!"—and the Duke was bowing himself out of the Satanic presence, when he was interrupted and brought back by a gentleman in waiting. Hereupon his Grace rubbed his eyes, yawned, shrugged his shoulders, reflected. Having become satisfied of his identity, he took a bird's-
(50) eye view of his whereabouts.

The apartment was superb. Even De L'Omelette pronounced it "quite well done." It was not its length nor its breadth—but its height—ah, that was appalling!—there was no ceiling—certainly none—but a dense whirling
(55) mass of fiery-colored clouds. His Grace's brain reeled as he glanced upward. From above, hung a chain of an unknown blood-red metal—its upper end lost. From its nether extremity swung a large cresset. The Duke knew it to be a ruby; but from it there poured a light so intense, so
(60) still, so terrible. Persia never worshipped such, no great Sultan ever dreamed of such when, drugged with opium, he has tottered to a bed of poppies, his back to the flowers, and his face to the God Apollo. The Duke muttered a slight oath, decidedly approbatory.

(65) The corners of the room were rounded into niches, and these were filled statues of gigantic proportions. But the paintings! The paintings! O luxury! O love!—who gazing on those forbidden beauties shall have eyes for others.

The Duke's heart is fainting within him. He is not, how-
(70) ever, as you suppose, dizzy with magnificence, nor drunk with the ecstatic breath of the innumerable censers. (It's true that he thinks of these things to no small degree—but!) The Duke De L'Omelette is terror-stricken; for, through the lurid vista which a single uncurtained window
(75) is affording, lo! gleams the most ghastly of all fires!

The poor Duke! He could not help imagining that the glorious, the voluptuous, the never-dying melodies which pervaded that hall, as they passed filtered and transmuted through the alchemy of the enchanted window-panes,
(80) were the wailings and the howlings of the hopeless and the damned! And there, too!—there!—upon the ottoman!— who could he be?—he, the Deity—who sat as if carved in marble, and who smiled, with his pale countenance, bitterly?

(85) A Frenchman never faints outright. Besides, his Grace hated a scene—De L'Omelette is himself again. Hadn't he read somewhere? wasn't it said "that the devil can't refuse a card game?"

But the chances—the chances! True—desperate; but
(90) scarcely more desperate than the Duke. Besides wasn't he the slyest player in the craftiest card-club in Paris?—the legendary "21 club."

"Should I lose," said his Grace "I will lose twice—that is I shall be doubly damned—should I win, I return to my
(95) ortolan—let the cards be prepared."

His Grace was all care, all attention, his Majesty all confidence. His Grace thought of the game. His majesty did not think; he shuffled. The Duke cut.

The cards are dealt. The trump is turned—it is—it is—

---

[1]An ortolan is a small dove-like bird considered a supreme delicacy by nineteenth-century gourmets.

(100) the king! No—it was the queen. His Majesty cursed her masculine habiliments. De L'Omelette placed his hand upon his heart.

They play. The Duke counts. The hand is out. His majesty counts heavily, smiles and is taking wine. The Duke *(105)* palms a card.

"It's your deal," said his Majesty, cutting. His Grace bowed, dealt, and arose from the table—turning the King. His Majesty looked chagrined.

Had Alexander not been Alexander, he would have been *(110)* Diogenes; and the Duke assured his antagonist in taking his leave, "Were one not already the Duke De L'Omelette one could have no objection to being the Devil."

1. The primary purpose of the passage is to portray

   (A) the characteristics of an exaggerated type through the figure of De L'Omelette
   (B) a reassuringly humorous vision of hell through a narrative in which the Devil himself is bested
   (C) the evil consequences of excessive pride
   (D) the developing relationship between De L'Omelette and the Devil
   (E) the pivotal change that occurs in De L'Omelette through his encounter with the Devil

2. Which of the following best describes the Duke De L'Omelette?

   (A) He is a typical eighteenth-century nobleman.
   (B) He is a caricature of a snob.
   (C) He is a man more wicked than the Devil.
   (D) He is a man with perfect aesthetic judgment.
   (E) He is a man transformed by his encounter with a power greater than his own.

3. In context, lines 27–35 serve to reinforce the reader's impression of the Duke's

   (A) quick temper
   (B) exquisite taste
   (C) sense of self-importance
   (D) accomplishments and social position
   (E) misunderstanding of his situation

4. The author's portrayal of the Duke De L'Omelette is best described as

   (A) a sympathetic portrait of a man with overly delicate sensibilities
   (B) a comically ironic treatment of an effete snob
   (C) a harshly condemnatory portrait of a bon vivant
   (D) an admiring portrait of a great artist
   (E) a farcical treatment of the very rich

5. Which of the following descriptions is an example of the narrator's irony?

   (A) "Unable to restrain his feelings, his Grace swallows an olive." (lines 8–9)
   (B) "I took thee, just now, from a rosewood coffin inlaid with ivory." (lines 37–38)
   (C) "The Duke knew it to be a ruby; but from it there poured a light so intense, so still, so terrible." (lines 58–60)
   (D) "And there, too!—there!—upon the ottoman!—who could he be?—he, the Deity—who sat as if carved in marble, and who smiled, with his pale countenance, bitterly?" (lines 81–84)
   (E) "His Grace was all care, all attention, his Majesty all confidence." (lines 96–97)

6. In line 53, the word "appalling" suggests the Duke

   (A) has found the room's decor unacceptable
   (B) has approbation for clouds
   (C) suffers from insomnia
   (D) finds the apartment extraordinary
   (E) suffers from a paroxysm

7. Which of the following best implies the contextual meaning of the phrase "sacrificed his loyalty" (line 6) within the context of the story?

   (A) The Duke has fallen into disfavor with the King by outbidding him.
   (B) The Duke has betrayed his country.
   (C) The Duke has allowed his desire for the ottoman to override his deference to the King.
   (D) The Duke recognizes no one as more powerful than himself.
   (E) The Duke values the ottoman more greatly than his prestige.

8. In which of the following lines is the narrator most clearly articulating the Duke's thoughts?

   (A) "Ignoble souls!" (line 2)
   (B) "It is superfluous to say more:—"(lines 15–16)
   (C) "Having become satisfied of his identity, he took a bird's-eye view of his whereabouts." (lines 49–50)
   (D) "But the chances—the chances! True—desperate;" (line 89)
   (E) "They play." (line 103)

9. Which of the following lines implies a speaker other than the narrator?

(A) "But who ever died of inept poetry?" (lines 1–2)
(B) "That night the Duke was to sup alone." (line 4)
(C) "The apartment was superb." (line 51)
(D) "His majesty did not think, he shuffled." (lines 97–98)
(E) "Had Alexander not been Alexander, he would have been Diogenes." (lines 109–110)

10. Which of the following best describes the situation in lines 22–25 and the events that came immediately *before* it?

(A) The Duke has just noticed the Devil and laughs at him. The Devil returns the laugh, but quietly because he feels insulted.
(B) The Duke has just heard the Devil explain the tortures that lie in store for him. He believes the Devil is joking and laughs. The Devil mocks his laughter, implying that it is no joke.
(C) The Duke and the Devil have been talking, but the exact topic has purposefully been left vague.
(D) The Duke has just heard the Devil's plans for him and laughs defiantly at the Devil. The Devil puns on the Duke's use of the word "Ha!" by saying "He!" By doing so, the devil indicates "He," that is the Duke, will be punished for his sins.
(E) The Duke, believing he speaks with a lowly servant, laughs at the threats the Devil has made. The Devil plays along, laughing with the Duke in order to draw out the Duke's eventual humiliation.

11. Which of the following reinforces the effect of the passage most strongly?

(A) Lighthearted situations narrated with deep seriousness
(B) Humorous irony in the introduction, contrasted with serious reflection in the conclusion
(C) Calculated objectivity offset by occasional interjections of subjective emotion
(D) Underlying contempt partially concealed by objectivity
(E) First-person outbursts of effusive emotion in an otherwise third-person narration

12. The narrator's attitude toward the Duke can be best described as

(A) complete objectivity
(B) ambiguous pity
(C) slight distaste
(D) bemused confusion
(E) satiric glee

13. The phrase "as if carved in marble" (lines 82–83), is an example of

(A) an apostrophe
(B) irony
(C) lyricism
(D) a metaphor
(E) a simile

About Poe's "The Duc De L'Omelette"

This passage was adapted from a short story called "The Duc De L'Omelette." You'll sometimes see adapted passages on the AP English Literature and Composition Exam. All it means is the passage was edited to make it appropriate for all high school students and to meet the test's length requirements. The actual Poe story uses a great deal of French, but keeping the French parts would give an unfair advantage to those who studied French.

The passage demonstrates the kind of language and stylistic devices you'll see on prose fiction analysis passages on the AP English Literature and Composition Exam, but they aren't all this weird. If it seemed long, don't panic—it is about one-third longer than the usual AP passage. (We wanted to use a long passage in this example to give you plenty to work with and to provide abundant fodder for our sample questions. Keep in mind that with a total of 55 questions, some of the passages will have fewer than 13 questions.) If you see a passage of this length on the test, there will then be a shorter passage somewhere to compensate.

Answers and Explanations to the Questions

We give detailed explanations to the 13 questions that followed the passage. The passages and questions on our practice test are designed to imitate the actual exam. Here, we've chosen the questions with an eye toward teaching you our techniques, but even so, the mix of the types of questions is fairly representative of the questions you'll see on an AP passage.

We've broken the questions down into small groups in order to illustrate specific types of questions you're likely to see. We don't want you to memorize the names of these types or spend a lot of time practicing identifying these types. There are no points for doing that. If you do remember them, great, but all we want is for you to become familiar with the most common types of questions on the test and to see how the same techniques, applied in slightly different ways, work on question after question.

GENERAL COMPREHENSION QUESTIONS

The first question is a general question and as you know, general questions ask about the whole passage, not just some detail of the passage.

The question sets will often (but not always) start out with general questions. We've placed the questions on this passage in the order that lets us best explain them to you. Remember that when you actually take the test, you should attempt the questions in the order given (if you feel comfortable with your comprehension of the passage). If you feel pretty lost, then you should put any general questions off until last, in the hope that working with the specific questions will give you more confidence about your comprehension of the passage and its main idea.

Primary Purpose

The classic general question is the primary purpose question:

————————○————————

1. The primary purpose of the passage is to portray
   (A) the characteristics of an exaggerated type through the figure of De L'Omelette
   (B) a reassuringly humorous vision of hell through a narrative in which the Devil himself is bested
   (C) the evil consequences of excessive pride
   (D) the developing relationship between De L'Omelette and the Devil
   (E) the pivotal change that occurs in De L'Omelette through his encounter with the Devil

Here's How to Crack It

Understand the question by understanding the answer choices. What does "primary purpose" mean?

When you see a primary purpose question, it means you must look for an answer that covers the broad outline of the story. This advice goes for all general questions; it is what makes them general. Remember that you are looking for a choice that accurately describes some facet of the entire passage.

Now use the answer choices themselves to focus on exactly what primary purpose the test-writers are looking for.

The question itself indicates that the primary purpose of the passage is to portray something. What is it portraying? Use POE.

Take (A). Does the whole passage deal with an exaggerated type? Well, the Duke is an exaggeration of something. This is a guy who takes time to approve of the decor in hell. Choice (A) seems to be a reasonable summation of the whole passage. Leave it. Now take each of the remaining choices in turn.

Now to (B). The whole passage is not all about a "reassuringly humorous vision of hell." Each paragraph does not point out how harmless hell is. The humorous part is the Duke's taking it all more or less in stride. Eliminate (B).

Choice (C) talks about "the evil consequences of excessive pride." The passage is all about the Duke's excessive pride, but what are the consequences? There are none. The end of the story finds the Duke returning to his ill-prepared ortolan, which is right where he started, so you have to wonder whether it's going to kill him all over again. Remember, *half wrong equals all wrong*. Eliminate (C).

POE In Action
Here's how you might approach a question using the POE strategy. Look for the *wrong* answers first.

And while you're at it, eliminate (D) unless you think that the whole passage is about the relationship between De L'Omelette and the Devil. It isn't. The Devil doesn't have much personality in the story at all. He serves as a foil for the Duke, little else.

Eliminate (E) because the Duke doesn't change at all. When the point of a passage is to show a dramatic change, you'll know it. The whole passage will build to that change.

You're left with (A), the correct answer.

What phrase have we kept repeating? "The whole passage." General questions call for you to consider the whole passage, not one small piece of it.

Another thing we did was focus on key phrases in the answer choices. "What consequences?" we asked when we looked at (C). We didn't get taken in by the phrase "excessive pride." Learning how to focus on an answer choice is a skill that comes with practice. As you follow our explanations, your skill will improve. In fact, after that discussion, the next question should be a breeze.

―――――――――○―――――――――

Overall Character

AP passages tend to be focused on one thing. Here the focus is on the Duke. A passage might focus on the description of an event or a place, but the most common focus is on a character. Yes, here's where the first of the Big Six comes in handy.

―――――――――○―――――――――

2.   Which of the following best describes the Duke De L'Omelette?

   (A)   He is a typical eighteenth-century nobleman.
   (B)   He is a caricature of a snob.
   (C)   He is a man more wicked than the Devil.
   (D)   He is a man with perfect aesthetic judgment.
   (E)   He is a man transformed by his encounter with a power greater than his own.

Here's How to Crack It

The correct answer is (B) and finding it probably didn't cause you much trouble. The only problem might have been the term *caricature*, which means "exaggerated portrait." It is a term you should know (it's in our glossary). Do you notice any similarities between the correct answer to question 1 and the correct answer here? You should. One speaks of an exaggerated portrayal of a type, and one speaks of a caricature of a snob. These are almost the same answer. The only difference is that the second question spells out what "type" is being caricatured: the snob. This is an example of Consistency of Answers. Both answers are consistent with the main idea, and when answers are consistent with the main idea, they are consistent with each other. In this case the answers are extremely similar. If you thought the Duke was an exaggerated portrayal in question 1, why would he suddenly become a "typical eighteenth-century nobleman" in question 2? That would be inconsistent, so eliminate (A). The Duke is either exaggerated or he's typical, but he can't be both. Choice (C) is for students who read into things too much. The Duke wins the card game at the end. Does that mean he's more wicked than the Devil? No. Choice (D) is too strong. "Perfect?" De L'Omelette thinks his tastes are perfect, but does the story suggest that his tastes are perfect? No, only that they are extremely, almost comically, particular. Choice (E) isn't supported by the passage. You'd think the Duke would be transformed by his encounter with the Devil, but he isn't. At the end of the story you should have gotten the feeling that De L'Omelette is going to go right back to his old ways.

Consistency of Answers doesn't just apply to general questions. It is just as helpful with detail questions.

Try This Tip
When in doubt, make your answers agree with each other.

DETAIL QUESTIONS

Detail questions (aka specific questions) make up the majority of questions on the multiple-choice section of the test. These are questions (or answer choices) that direct you to a specific place in the passage and ask about your comprehension of the details.

Line-Reference Questions

Most of the time (but not always), the detail questions give you a line number or a range of lines with which to work. We call these line-reference questions. For line-reference questions there are just two things you need to keep in mind:

- Go back to the passage and reread the lines in question. Don't rely on your memory, particularly under the time pressure of the exam. Your memory will likely lead you astray. Also, read at least one full sentence before the line reference and one full sentence after the line reference. Keep in mind that a word or phrase you are being asked to define may not have the meaning you would infer from the wording of the question. It is important that you refer to the word in the context of the line.
- Keep the main idea in mind, and use Consistency of Answers whenever possible.

Try This One

_____○_____

3. In context, lines 27–35 serve to reinforce the reader's impression of the Duke's

    (A) quick temper
    (B) exquisite taste
    (C) sense of self-importance
    (D) accomplishments and social position
    (E) misunderstanding of his situation

Here's How to Crack It

This question calls for you to go back and read a fairly large range of lines—a whole paragraph. Go back and read it. Because the several lines referred to in this question make up a more or less self-contained paragraph, reading a full sentence before and after the reference doesn't make a big difference in getting the question right, but it doesn't hurt, either, and takes just an extra two or three seconds. Make it a habit to read a little above and below the lines referred to; it'll be worth a couple of points in the long run.

Essentially, the lines in question discuss the Duke's outrage at the Devil's command to disrobe.

If you misunderstand the question, you have a good chance of getting the answer wrong. The passage shows aspects of all the answer choices. The Duke shows a quick temper, mentions his tastes (which are not so much exquisite as they are ostentatious), mentions his accomplishments, and misunderstands his situation. But the correct answer is (C).

All the answer choices seem right, so what gives? The solution lies in understanding the question and how the question relates to the main idea. The question asks: What does the passage serve to reinforce? Nearly everything in this very compact story serves to reinforce the central impression of the story—the Duke's outrageous sense of self-importance. He isn't merely a snob; he's completely besotted with his own fabulous self. The Duke thinks he's the apex of human intellectual and social development. In fact, (A), (B), (D), and (E) are all facets of the Duke's vanity. His anger is angered vanity. His tastes are flawless; they must be, thinks the Duke, because they're his. When the Duke mentions his work, the "Mazurkiad," you can almost see him puff up with the greatness of it all. Even his misunderstanding is an aspect of his vanity. The Duke doesn't quite comprehend his surroundings because he can't imagine being in a position to take orders from anyone. All these things revolve like planets around the Duke's sense that he's the center of the universe.

If you had a solid grasp on the central theme of the story, the Duke's self-love, you might have found this question easy. Choices (A), (B), (D), and (E) are details. Choice (C) is the main thing. If you had trouble, all you had to do to get this question correct was muse, "Hmm, they all look possible, but which one is most consistent with the main idea?" Well, a snob thinks he's better than everyone and is very important. Choice (C), sense of self-importance, is most in agreement with that.

Question 3 is an example of using Consistency of Answers. Here's another:

4. The author's portrayal of the Duke De L'Omelette is best described as

    (A) a sympathetic portrait of a man with overly delicate sensibilities
    (B) a comically ironic treatment of an effete snob
    (C) a harshly condemnatory portrait of a bon vivant
    (D) an admiring portrait of a great artist
    (E) a farcical treatment of the very rich

Here's How to Crack It

Take each answer a word at a time and remember, half wrong equals all wrong. If any part of the answer is wrong, don't hesitate to eliminate it. Yes, it's true that the portrait is of a man with delicate sensibilities (A), but is it sympathetic? Hardly. Get rid of it. You might not understand "effete" in (B), so hold on to it. However, "harshly condemnatory" in (C) should sound wrong to you. The Duke is harshly condemnatory of the servant who brings in his meal, but the passage itself does not disapprove of either of them. Half bad equals all bad, so eliminate it. Now look at (D): John Keats was a great artist, but the Duke? From this passage you sure can't say that, so cross this one off too. On to (E). "Farcical?" Perhaps. But is this passage about the "very rich"? No, it's about the Duke De L'Omelette. Half bad equals all bad, so you're left with (B) even if you're not quite sure what it means. But here's a pop quiz: What technique tells you the answer must be (B)? Consistency of Answers.

Now we aren't saying every single question uses Consistency of Answers. It should be one of the first things you think about when you approach a question, but there are definitely questions that focus on a detail in such a way that Consistency of Answers doesn't come into play.

Here's an example:

_____ ○ _____

5.　Which of the following descriptions is an example of the narrator's irony?

(A)　"Unable to restrain his feelings, his Grace swallows an olive." (lines 8–9)

(B)　"I took thee, just now, from a rosewood coffin inlaid with ivory." (lines 37–38)

(C)　"The Duke knew it to be a ruby; but from it there poured a light so intense, so still, so terrible." (lines 58–60)

(D)　"And there, too!—there!—upon the ottoman!—who could he be?—he, the Deity—who sat as if carved in marble, and who smiled, with his pale countenance, bitterly?" (lines 81–84)

(E)　"His Grace was all care, all attention, his Majesty all confidence." (lines 96–97)

Here's How to Crack It

Notice that in this question the line references come in the answer choices. That's not uncommon. Properly speaking, this isn't a specific question or a general question or a literary-term question. The answer choices send you back to the passage to find a specific example of something that occurs throughout the whole passage: irony, which is a literary term. But, you don't get points for putting questions in categories anyway; the important thing is to get the question right, efficiently.

The way to get this question right is to know what irony is. Learn to recognize its many forms. We discuss irony in our glossary of literary terms for the AP English Literature and Composition Exam. (Yep, we're going to say that every time we mention irony.)

The correct answer is (A). You should have noticed the entire tone of the piece is somewhat ironic. Most of the passage is written with a deliberate undercurrent of meaning that changes the effect of the literal meaning of the lines. This, above all, is the hallmark of irony; there's more than meets the eye. But let's get back to (A). Why is it ironic? Let's take the statement "Unable to restrain his feelings, his Grace swallows an olive." At face value, the Duke's feelings became so strong that he had to swallow an olive. Now, in no way can swallowing an olive be the outcome of unrestrained feelings unless one has pretty unusual feelings, which is precisely the point. The Duke's anticipation of dinner having reached a fevered pitch, he buries his face in a pillow. The clock bangs out the long-awaited hour and unable to restrain himself, the Duke swallows an olive. One thing this shows is how fanatically the Duke takes his meals. At the same time, the juxtaposition (to _juxtapose_ means to place things side by side) of the Duke's unrestrained feelings and his act of swallowing an olive show something else: the Duke's biggest feelings are actually puny; the Duke's crescendo of passion is capped by swallowing an olive. That's the ironic part. The author in effect says, "In the Duke's opinion this is something big, but we can all see that it's rather small." When the literal meaning of a word or phrase implies its opposite, you're dealing with irony.

Count on This
You can count on only a very few specific things showing up on the exam. One of them is irony.

Hey, didn't we say that the whole piece was ironic? If that's true, what makes the other choices wrong? Well, okay, the whole piece *is* ironic. In effect, the passage tells us that the Duke thinks he's absolutely first-rate but we can see that he's really quite laughable. However, for this question you must consider the answer choices in isolation. None of them alone carry the double meaning that is so crucial to irony. Choice (B) is a description of a coffin. Choice (C) describes the ruby that illuminates the Devil's chamber in hell. Choice (D) describes the moment the Duke realizes, at last, that the creature he's dealing with is truly the Devil himself. Choice (E) simply describes the Duke's and the Devil's attitude as they begin the card game.

Okay, enough about irony, on to the next kind of question.

Single Phrase or Word Questions

AP questions will often ask you to look at a single word or phrase:

---

6. In line 53, the word "appalling" suggests the Duke

    (A) has found the room's decor unacceptable
    (B) has approbation for clouds
    (C) suffers from insomnia
    (D) finds the apartment extraordinary
    (E) suffers from a paroxysm

Here's How to Crack It

It's true that for the AP English Literature and Composition Exam, a strong vocabulary helps a lot. If you did not know the meaning of *decor* in (A), *approbation* in (B), *insomnia* in (C), or *paroxysm* in (E), you may have been at a loss. You could eliminate (A) because you know that the Duke found the apartment "superb," and you could have guessed that the referenced line has nothing to do with the Duke's inability to sleep (that he suffers from insomnia). Then you would be left with (B), (D), and (E).

Keep in mind that you are only to answer the question being asked—to examine the contextual meaning of one word. You can safely eliminate (E) from the list because in the sentence that contains the word "appalling," a reference to the Duke's suffering or discomfort is not implied. Even if you don't know what *paroxysm* means (a convulsion), you can use POE to get rid of this answer choice. Now look carefully at (B). In line 53, "appalling" refers to the room, not the clouds. So you can eliminate this choice too, even if you don't know that *approbation* is approval. You're left with the correct answer, (D), in which the two words, which may seem very different, have a commonality in how they both describe something shocking.

Questions 5 and 6 are two questions in a row that don't use Consistency of Answers. The streak's over. Here's a question that asks about a single phrase, yet you can still use Consistency of Answers to assist your POE.

7. Which of the following best implies the contextual meaning of the phrase "sacrificed his loyalty" (line 6) within the context of the story?

(A) The Duke has fallen into disfavor with the King by outbidding him.

(B) The Duke has betrayed his country.

(C) The Duke has allowed his desire for the ottoman to override his deference to the King.

(D) The Duke recognizes no one as more powerful than himself.

(E) The Duke values the ottoman more greatly than his prestige.

Here's How to Crack It

When approaching this question, you should first go back and read around the citation. Because the citation is a fragment of a sentence, you should read at least a full sentence before and after the reference. (If you want to read more, by all means, do. The full sentence before and after is just a guideline. If it takes you a little more reading to get your bearings in the passage, that's fine.)

Now, use POE to get rid of what is obviously wrong. If you stay focused on what the phrase in question means it should be easy to eliminate a few answers. Does "sacrificed his loyalty" mean the Duke has betrayed his country? That should sound a little too intense: We're talking about buying a couch here (an ottoman is a kind of couch). Eliminate (B). Does the Duke recognize no one as more powerful than himself? That may or may not be true, but how could you get that meaning from "sacrificed his loyalty"? Of course, if you try really hard, you can talk yourself into anything. Don't talk yourself into answers. This is POE. Eliminate (D).

Can you eliminate two more answer choices? The best way is to ask yourself which answer choice is most in keeping with the Duke's character. Do you think the Duke cares about his prestige more than his couch? Of course he does. He would never sacrifice his prestige. L'Omelette thinks of appearances above all else. Eliminate (E). What about (A)? It is certainly reasonable that the Duke fell into disfavor with the King for outbidding him. But is this what "sacrificed his loyalty" means? No. And if you have any doubts, ask yourself what that interpretation has to do with the rest of the passage. Is the rest of the passage about the Duke's loss of favor with the King? No. That leaves (C), the correct answer. It is perfectly in keeping with the other answers and the rest of the passage: the Duke shows little deference to the Devil; why would he defer to the King?

The next two questions ask for your comprehension of a detail, but the questions center less on the meaning of the words than on what they indicate about the narrator.

Question-Comprehension Questions

Some questions are straightforward, some are vague, and a few are downright tricky. You need to pay close attention to the wording of questions and when you see an unusual phrase, it's a good idea to ask yourself why the phrase is worded that way. For many questions, just understanding what the question is asking is half the battle.

———○———

8. In which of the following lines is the narrator most clearly articulating the Duke's thoughts?

   (A) "Ignoble souls!" (line 2)
   (B) "It is superfluous to say more:—" (lines 15–16)
   (C) "Having become satisfied of his identity, he took a bird's-eye view of his whereabouts." (lines 49–50)
   (D) "But the chances—the chances! True—desperate." (line 89)
   (E) "They play." (line 103)

Here's How to Crack It

This question has little to do with the main idea. Your first task is to understand the question. What is meant by "articulating the Duke's thoughts"? Well, try to put it in your own words. The question could be rewritten as "When is the narrator speaking for the Duke?" There's nothing wrong with putting a question in your own words so as to understand it better. In fact it's a good idea as long as you're careful and don't just drop off the parts of a question that confuse you. Reading the questions accurately is just as important as reading the passages. The passage isn't worth any points; the questions are.

Use POE. Eliminate what you can right away. When is the narrator clearly speaking as himself? Choices (B), (C), and (E) all seem like examples of straightforward narration, so eliminate them. That leaves just (A) and (D). In (A), the narrator responds to a question. He exclaims in a very Duke-like way, but the Duke hasn't even been introduced yet. How could the reader know it was the Duke speaking? The reader couldn't. All that's left is (D), the correct answer. In (D), the narrator steps into the Duke's mind for a moment to record his thoughts, and then just as quickly steps out with the words "but no more desperate than the Duke."

———○———

Question 9 picks up where question 8 left off; a variation on the same theme:

---○---

9. Which of the following lines implies a speaker other than the narrator?

(A) "But who ever died of inept poetry?" (lines 1–2)
(B) "That night the Duke was to sup alone." (line 4)
(C) "The apartment was superb." (line 51)
(D) "His majesty did not think, he shuffled." (lines 97–98)
(E) "Had Alexander not been Alexander, he would have been Diogenes." (lines 109–110)

Here's How to Crack It

Read the questions carefully. The difference between question 8 and question 9 is that question 8 asks which answer choice shows the Duke's speech (or thoughts), whereas question 9 wants to know which implies a speaker other than the narrator. Question 9 is tougher. If your approach to question 9 got stuck somewhere back on question 8 and you were still looking for the narrator to speak the Duke's thoughts (or perhaps the Devil's), you might have easily gotten this question wrong.

As always, use POE. Clearly, (B), (C), (D), and (E) are spoken by the narrator. What about (A)? Well, (A) is spoken by the narrator as well but *implies* another speaker, someone who asks the question, "Who ever died of poor poetry?" The narrator, speaking as himself, responds to that question: "Ignoble souls!" If the structure of this interchange wasn't clear to you, here's an explanation: "Who ever died of poor poetry?" is a rhetorical question (a question to which the answer is obvious—of course, most people would say, no one has ever been killed by a bad poem). That's where the narrator jumps in and says, "Oh ho, you think the answer to that question is so very obvious but that's because your souls have no finer qualities; it may seem unbelievable to you but some very delicate spirits have died of immaterial things like bad poetry. De L'Omelette, for example, died of a badly prepared meal." All that (and a little more) is contained in the first paragraph of the passage. This paragraph is a good example of how gifted writers make every word count.

---○---

Ready for one more detail question? It's a good example of how weird things can get on the AP Exam, as it asks about the meaning of a piece of the passage that isn't there.

Weirdness

10. Which of the following best describes the situation in lines 22–25 and the events that came immediately *before* it?

    (A) The Duke has just noticed the Devil and laughs at him. The Devil returns the laugh, but quietly because he feels insulted.

    (B) The Duke has just heard the Devil explain the tortures that lie in store for him. He believes the Devil is joking and laughs. The Devil mocks his laughter, implying that it is no joke.

    (C) The Duke and the Devil have been talking, but the exact topic has purposefully been left vague.

    (D) The Duke has heard the Devil's plans for him and laughs defiantly at the Devil. The Devil puns on the Duke's use of the word "Ha!" by saying "He!" By doing so, the devil indicates "He," that is the Duke, will be punished for his sins.

    (E) The Duke, believing he speaks with a lowly servant, laughs at the threats the Devil has made. The Devil laughs in order to play along with the Duke and draw out the Duke's eventual humiliation.

Here's How to Crack It

You may sometimes run across a weird or unexpected question on the test. In this case, you're being asked to make sense of an abrupt shift in the story, from the Duke's death to his meeting the Devil, and essentially to fill in the blanks.

Use POE and remember to read at least one sentence before and one sentence after, so as to piece things together. Choice (A) can be eliminated outright, as there is no indication in the text that the Devil feels insulted. (The "hauteur" in line 21 hints that the opposite may be true.) Choice (C) is vague, but what the Duke and Devil have been discussing is not—the Duke refers to a specific topic, "barbarous threats," and elaborates in the next paragraph. Choice (D) suggests that "He!" is being used as a bizarre pun, but there's nothing to support that in the text. Finally, Choice (E) can also be eliminated, for although the Duke may not know that he speaks to the Devil, he also does not suggest that he speaks to a "lowly servant." Choice (B) is correct, and is the best (and simplest) explanation of the Devil's mocking reply.

Staying simple doesn't just apply to poetry analysis. Many students get into trouble when reading the answer choices and think about the wrong answers so much that they get led into outer space. This comes from looking at every answer choice as though it could be correct. Four out of the five answer choices are wrong. At least one answer choice is usually wildly wrong. If something looks nuts, don't spend five minutes trying to figure it out. If it looks nuts, it is.

11. Which of the following describes the effect of the passage most strongly?

(A) Lighthearted situations narrated with deep seriousness
(B) Humorous irony in the introduction, contrasted with serious reflection in the conclusion
(C) Calculated objectivity offset by occasional interjections of subjective emotion
(D) Underlying contempt partially concealed by objectivity
(E) First-person outbursts of effusive emotion in an otherwise third-person narration

Here's How to Crack It

Again, from the question alone you can't know exactly what the question asks. That's fine. Look over the answer choices. You can see that they refer to the tone, style, and structure of the passage. The test-writers like to throw these mixtures at you. The way to work on this kind of question is to break the answer choices into bite-size parts, and then check the passage to see whether you can find an example of that part. For example, are there lighthearted situations, (A)? Well, going to hell isn't exactly lighthearted. (So the choice is already wrong, but let's keep going.) Are the situations narrated with deep seriousness? No, not exactly. Narrated with a straight face perhaps, but not deeply serious. The idea is to break the choices into pieces you can use. Remember, half wrong equals all wrong.

The correct answer is (E). As always, use POE and look at the whole passage. Make your initial eliminations. Choice (A) is wrong because the situations are not so much lighthearted as absurd and the narrator is not deeply serious, but nearly as bizarre and out of control as the Duke. Choice (B) isn't worth a second look unless you really think cheating the Devil at cards is deadly serious. Choice (D) should be unappealing as well. What "contempt"? What "objectivity"? Eliminate it. Although the Duke shows contempt for his situation, this isn't the overall effect of the passage that the question asks for.

This leaves (E) and (C). Take each answer choice and go back to the passage. Do you see any "calculated objectivity"? Not really; almost every sentence is loaded with one of the Duke's preposterous emotions. Almost everything comes to us through a filter of the Duke's impressions, especially in the longer sentences. It isn't accurate to call the subjective (first-person element) "occasional." That is enough to eliminate (C), leaving you with just one remaining choice, (E). For safety's sake you should now examine it. "Outbursts of effusive emotion"? Well, there are all those exclamation points all over the place. As a matter of fact, half of the time the author seems to be shouting. The story is told in the third person, yet much of the time the Duke's persona, his voice, or the attitude behind his voice seems to be speaking. Choice (E) is correct.

The Complexity of the Test
It's unlikely that you'll see an AP question this complex and multi-layered, but it's better to expect the unexpected and over-prepare than to be caught off guard. Think of it this way: if you can parse a question like this, you're ready for the AP Exam.

Use the Glossary
If any of the terms we've used in this explanation—*first person, third person, subjectivity*—gave you trouble, you should refer to their definitions in the glossary, which is located at the end of this book.

Attitude questions are just like tone questions; they ask about the underlying emotional content of the passage:

———————————◯———————————

12. The narrator's attitude toward the Duke can be best described as

(A) complete objectivity
(B) ambiguous pity
(C) slight distaste
(D) bemused confusion
(E) satiric glee

Here's How to Crack It

The correct answer is (E). POE, as usual, helps a great deal. On tone questions, there are usually a couple of answer choices that you can dismiss without a second glance. There's no way you could call the passage an example of (A), complete objectivity; it's much too weird. Doesn't the whole passage feel high-strung, as though old Edgar A. Poe had a few too many cups of coffee on top of whatever else he was drinking that day? That feeling never goes with objectivity. Choice (B), pity, is just off the wall. Choice (C) might have been appealing because it didn't sound too extreme. In general, mild is better than extreme on tone questions but unfortunately, "slight distaste" is wrong; there's no evidence that the narrator feels a slight distaste for the Duke. Remember, you wanted to pick what the *narrator* feels. You might have felt slight distaste, but the question didn't ask how you felt. Speaking of how you felt, (D) is a type of answer choice that occasionally appears on the exam. When students are struggling, they're drawn to answers that suggest their own mental state, such as *confused*, *depressed*, *anxious*, and *fearful,* even when such words are plain wrong. The answer feels right, not because it's correct but because it's how the student feels taking a test. There's no evidence in the story that the narrator is confused or doesn't understand the Duke; in fact, he seems to understand the Duke a little too perfectly.

This brings up (E), the correct answer. "Glee" may seem a bit strong, but it fits. The narrator tells the story with energy, enthusiasm, and a completely unabashed use of exclamation points—that's a tip-off right there. Good writers don't overuse exclamation points. (The great Irish novelist James Joyce called them, derisively, "shriek marks.") Poe doesn't overuse them here, but it could easily seem like it. Poe uses exclamation points because, if for the Duke a badly prepared bird is upsetting enough to kill him, the Duke's life must be filled with exclamation points. This is one of the elements (and there are many) which make the passage satiric. *Satire* (see the glossary) is an important concept for the AP Exam. When a passage pokes fun at an exaggeratedly foolish type (in this case, the type of arrogant man who considers himself supreme in all things), you can be sure it's satire. The gleefulness stems from the evident enjoyment Poe takes in describing the Duke's peculiar foolishness. Of course, Poe has the Duke win in the end, which makes sense because Poe himself had a lot of the Duke in him.

———————————◯———————————

Literary Term Questions

13. The phrase "as if carved in marble" (lines 82–83) is an example of

    (A) an apostrophe
    (B) irony
    (C) lyricism
    (D) a metaphor
    (E) a simile

Here's How to Crack It

This is an absolutely straightforward literary term question. You are sure to see a few questions like it on the test. Of course you should use POE, but the best solution for literary term questions is to know the terms. That's why we've included our glossary. As we mentioned earlier, there are just a few things you can be sure will make an appearance somewhere on the test. Among those things are the terms *simile* and *metaphor*.

The correct answer here is (E). The phrase is a simile. A comparison that uses *like* or *as* is a simile. Even if these terms don't show up on your test as the best answers to a question (and chances are that's exactly how they will show up), at the very least they'll show up as answers you'll be able to eliminate. If you aren't aware that the phrase in question is a simile, eliminate what you can and take your best guess. Believe it or not, all the terms in the question are defined in our glossary.

A FEW FINAL WORDS

If you worked through the passage as we instructed, you just learned a great deal about how to take the multiple-choice questions on the AP English Literature and Composition Exam. It probably took close to five times longer here than working on a real passage would, but that's to be expected—you're learning. This does bring up an important point though: time. We've taken you through the passage and familiarized you with some typical questions so that when you're on your own, you can work efficiently and accurately, answering all the questions in about 12–15 minutes.

But what if it doesn't work that way? Let's say you had reasoned that this passage was the most difficult on the test and decided to do it last. By the time you got to it, you had only seven minutes left. Seven minutes to do that passage! You would use up most of that time just reading it. Should you give up?—No! This is where all the study you've put into the questions can really pay off. Check out the Art of the Seven-Minute Passage—and enjoy!

The Art of the Seven-Minute Passage

When you hit the last passage on the test, check your time. If you have seven minutes or fewer left, you have to change your strategy. You don't have enough time to do the passage the normal way. It's time for emergency measures. What is the worst thing to do in an emergency? Panic. Don't. The best defense against panic is preparation. Know exactly what you're going to do. Here it is:

7 Minutes to Go!
If you find yourself in a situation in which you have only 7 minutes left but several questions still unanswered, don't panic. Instead, follow this simple six-step system.

- Don't read the passage. Just *don't* do it.

- Go straight to the questions.

- Answer the questions in the following order:

  1. **Answer any literary term or grammar questions.** You barely need the passage at all for these questions. If you know the point at issue, you'll just snap up a point. Otherwise apply as much POE as you can and guess.

  2. **Go to any question that asks for the meaning of a single word or phrase.** These questions always include a line reference. Go to the passage and read a sentence before and after the reference. Answer the question.

  3. **Go to any other question that gives you a line reference in the question.** (Not line-reference answer choices, but questions.) Read the reference and answer the question.

  4. **Go to any question on tone or attitude.** By this time, you've read quite a bit of the passage just by answering questions. You've read enough to be able to make a good guess about where the author's coming from.

  5. **Go to any questions that have line references in the answer choices.** Answer them all.

  6. **Do whatever is left over**—character questions, primary purpose questions, weird questions, and so on. If you need to, read some of the passage to get them. Go ahead and read. Keep working until the proctor tells you to put down your pencil.

That's the Art of the Seven-Minute Passage. It works in six, five, four, three, two, or one-minute too; with less time, you don't get as far down the list, that's all.

What If I Have Seven Minutes and Fifteen Seconds Left?

Seven minutes or fewer is a good rough guideline for when to use the Don't Read the Passage technique. Your pace on multiple-choice passages should be about 12 minutes a passage. If you have an awkward amount of time left for the last passage—that is, somewhere between 7 and 15 minutes—you'll have to decide which approach to use. You have two choices. The first is to just read and work faster, to step on the gas big-time. The other choice is to go straight to the questions, that is, to use the Art of the Seven-Minute Passage technique. It's your call. At the seven-minute mark (or 7 minutes and 3 seconds, whatever), you should go straight to the questions. With 10 minutes left you should probably try to read the passage fast but then attempt the questions in the seven-minute order. At, say, 14 minutes, you should just work normally, but keep in mind that you don't have any time to waste worrying about those silly things students worry about, like whether you've guessed too many (C)'s, or ponder the occult meaning of the pattern of dots you've made.

Prose Fiction Analysis Passage Drill

Suggested time: 12 minutes

Questions 1–14. Choose your answers to questions 1–14 based on a careful reading of the following passage. (The passage, an excerpt from *Anna Karenina* by Leo Tolstoy, describes one of the central characters and his dog.)

Getting on his boots and stockings, taking his gun, and carefully opening the creaking door of the barn, Levin went out into the road. It was still gray out-of-doors.

Line
(5) "Why are you up so early, my dear?" the old woman, their hostess, said, coming out of the hut and addressing him affectionately as an old friend.

"Going shooting, granny."

Laska ran eagerly forward along the little path. Levin
(10) followed her with a light, rapid step, continually looking at the sky. He hoped the sun would not be up before he reached the marsh. But the sun did not delay. In the transparent stillness of morning the smallest sounds were audible. A bee flew by Levin's ear with the whizzing sound
(15) of a bullet. He looked carefully, and saw a second and a third. The marsh could be recognized by the mist which rose from it, thicker in one place and thinner in another, so that the reeds and willow bushes swayed like islands in this mist. Laska walked beside her master, pressing a little
(20) forward and looking round. … Levin examined his pistols and let his dog off. Levin patted Laska, and whistled as a sign that she might begin.

Laska ran joyfully and anxiously through the slush that swayed under her.

Running into the marsh among the familiar scents, Las-
(25) ka detected at once a smell that pervaded the whole marsh, the scent of that strong-smelling bird that always excited her more than any other. Sniffing in the air with dilated nostrils, she felt at once that not their tracks only but they themselves were here before her, and not one, but many.
(30) They were here, but where precisely she could not yet determine. To find the very spot, she began to make a circle, when suddenly her master's voice drew her off. "Laska! here?" he asked, pointing her to a different direction. She stopped, asking him if she had better not go on doing as
(35) she had begun. But he repeated his command in an angry voice, pointing to a spot covered with water, where there could not be anything. She obeyed him, pretending she was looking, so as to please him, went round it, and went back to her former position, and was at once aware of
(40) the scent again. Now when he was not hindering her, she knew what to do, and without looking at what was under her feet, and to her vexation stumbling over a high stump into the water, but righting herself with her strong, supple legs, she began making the circle which was to make all
(45) clear to her. The scent of them reached her, stronger and stronger, and more and more defined, and all at once it became perfectly clear to her that one of them was here, behind this tuft of reeds, five paces in front of her; she

(50) stopped, and her whole body was still and rigid. Her tail was stretched straight and tense, and only wagging at the extreme end. Her mouth was slightly open, her ears raised. One ear had been turned wrong side out as she ran up, and she breathed heavily but warily, and still more warily
(55) looked round, but more with her eyes than her head, to her master. He was coming along with the face she knew so well, though the eyes were always terrible to her. He stumbled over the stump as he came, and moved, as she thought, extraordinarily slowly. She thought he came
(60) slowly, but he was running.

Noticing Laska's special attitude as she crouched on the ground, as it were, scratching big prints with her hind paws, and with her mouth slightly open, Levin knew she was pointing at grouse, and with an inward prayer for luck,
(65) especially with the first bird, he ran up to her. Coming quite close up to her, he could from his height look beyond her, and he saw with his eyes what she was seeing with her nose. In a space between two little thickets, to a couple of yards' distance, he could see a grouse. Turning
(70) its head, it was listening. Then lightly preening and folding its wings, it disappeared round a corner with a clumsy wag of its tail.

"Fetch it, fetch it!" shouted Levin, giving Laska a shove from behind.

(75) She darted forward as fast as her legs would carry her between the thick bushes.

Ten paces from her former place a grouse rose with a guttural cry and the peculiar round sound of its wings. And immediately after the shot it splashed heavily with its
(80) white breast on the wet mire. Another bird did not linger, but rose behind Levin without the dog. When Levin turned towards it, it was already some way off. But his shot caught it. Flying twenty paces further, the second grouse rose upwards, and whirling round like a ball, dropped
(85) heavily on a dry place.

When Levin, after loading his gun, moved on, the sun had fully risen, though unseen behind the storm-clouds. The moon had lost all of its luster, and was like a white cloud in the sky. Not a single star could be seen. Crows
(90) were flying about the field, and a bare-legged boy was driving the horses to an old man. The smoke from the gun was white as milk over the green of the grass.

One of the boys ran up to Levin.

"Uncle, there were ducks here yesterday!" he shouted to him, and he walked a little way off behind him.

(95) And Levin was doubly pleased, in sight of the boy, who expressed his approval, at killing three snipe, one after another, straight off.

1. One effect of lines 85–88 is to emphasize

   (A) the author's ability to create a sense of foreboding
   (B) the passage of time explicitly
   (C) the use of specific details to frame the passage
   (D) the impact of the weather on the events
   (E) Levin's desire to seek shelter

2. How is the word "vexation" used in line 42?

   (A) To demonstrate Levin's confusion about Laska's clumsiness
   (B) To underscore the danger of Laska's mission
   (C) To reveal Laska's bewilderment as to why she stumbled
   (D) To emphasize Laska's single-mindedness
   (E) To highlight her irritation toward Levin's command

3. The passage suggests that Levin

   (A) is visiting with family
   (B) is anxious about his ability to provide for his family
   (C) has a strained relationship with Laska
   (D) prefers to spend time alone
   (E) is on familiar terms with those whom he encounters

4. What is the function of lines 64–67 in relation to lines 30–31?

   (A) Levin's hunting skills are superior to Laska's.
   (B) Laska requires Levin's supervision when hunting.
   (C) Laska finds Levin's proximity to her helpful.
   (D) The author highlights the synergistic relationship between Laska and Levin.
   (E) The author underscores Levin's dependence on Laska.

5. Which lines demonstrate Laska's relationship to Levin?

   (A) Lines 20–21
   (B) Lines 37–40
   (C) Lines 55–56
   (D) Lines 70–71
   (E) Lines 72–73

6. The author views Levin

   (A) with impartial objectivity
   (B) with wry optimism
   (C) as a domineering master
   (D) as a boastful hunter
   (E) through a critical lens

7. The passage as a whole is most indebted to which literary tradition?

   (A) Romanticism
   (B) Realism
   (C) Modernism
   (D) Transcendentalism
   (E) Naturalism

8. In context of the passage as a whole, lines 8–23 serve to

   (A) provide a description of the setting
   (B) foreshadow later events
   (C) build anticipation
   (D) establish perspective
   (E) establish the characters' contentment in nature

9. In lines 95–97, the author characterizes Levin as

   (A) proud and content
   (B) pleased and exhausted
   (C) powerful and victorious
   (D) astonished and boastful
   (E) approving and dignified

10. The narrator suggests that the individuals Levin encounters are characterized by

    (A) envious curiosity about Levin's excursion
    (B) exuberant pleasure for Levin's skill
    (C) pious respect for Levin's hunting prowess
    (D) warm regard for Levin
    (E) affectionate approval for his day's accomplishments

11. What dominant technique is the author using in lines 31–40?

    (A) Personification
    (B) Irony
    (C) Anthropomorphism
    (D) Dialogue
    (E) Metaphor

12. The sentence in lines 40–45 contains all of the following EXCEPT

    (A) a character flaw
    (B) alliteration
    (C) suspense
    (D) juxtaposition
    (E) complex syntax

13. Lines 32–37 suggest

    (A) Levin's temperamental nature
    (B) Laska's submissive nature toward Levin
    (C) Laska's ability to speak to Levin
    (D) Laska's inexperience with hunting
    (E) Levin's deftness in hunting

PROSE FICTION ANALYSIS PASSAGE DRILL: ANSWERS AND EXPLANATIONS

Considered one of the greatest writers of all time, Leo Tolstoy was a Russian author, and *Anna Karenina* was his second novel. This novel, along with *War and Peace*, are hallmark examples of realism in literature.

1. **C** Coming at the end of the passage, this description of the sun bookends the passage nicely (lines 85–88). Therefore, the correct answer is (C). The passage ends on a pleasant note, so the author is not creating a sense of foreboding, so eliminate (A). The effect of these lines is not to highlight the passage of time explicitly or implicitly, so (B) is incorrect. Rather, these lines offer further description of the setting and are written in such a way that they parallel the description provided at the beginning of the passage. The weather is not impacting Levin's hunting—he's done quite well so far—and he does not appear to be seeking shelter at the conclusion of the passage, so (D) and (E) are also incorrect.

2. **D** *Vexation* means annoyance or irritation, not confusion, so eliminate (A) and (C). This word highlights Laska's desire to find the source of the smell, and she's irritated that the stump got in her way. However, she does not let it or her stumble impede her forward progress for very long. She is focused on the task at hand and does not let this event distract her, making (D) the correct answer. She is not irritated that Levin has asked her to find the bird, (E), nor is there evidence in the passage that she's in danger, (B).

3. **E** Although Levin refers to the old lady as "granny" (note the lower case g), and the boy calls Levin "Uncle," Levin is not related to either of them. The old woman is the hostess of the place at which he is staying, and he comes across the boy while he is hunting, so eliminate (A) and (B). There is no evidence in the text to support (C) or (D). Since he does speak with the old woman in a friendly way, and the boy addresses him in a casual way, we can infer that Levin treats those whom he encounters in an informal and warm way. Therefore, (E) is the answer.

4. **D** The first line reference illustrates the advantage Levin's height gives him. From his vantage point, Levin can see what Laska's nose has tracked. The second line reference demonstrates Laska's ability to put the pair in close proximity to the bird—a tracking skill she has but Levin does not. Therefore, these lines emphasize how the combined efforts of the pair allow them to pinpoint the bird's exact location. The correct answer is (D). In (A), the cooperative interaction is minimized. The fact that Levin, not Laska, can actually see the bird makes (E) wrong. Finally, (B) and (C) do not reflect the purpose of these lines, nor are they supported by the text.

5. **B** Laska is obedient to her master. She follows his commands and seeks to please him. The correct answer is (B). Choice (D) is referring to the grouse, not Laska, and is incorrect. Choice (A) does not answer the question—it asks for Laska's relationship to Levin. This choice is from Levin's perspective. In the context of the whole passage, there is no evidence to support (C) and (E). She does obey Levin, she moves "eagerly" and "joyfully," and she does want to please him. She is not afraid of him or threatened by him.

6. **A** The author shows Levin's friendly exchanges with the people he encounters, his manner toward Laska, and his thoughts as he hunts. The reader is given a wide range of information from which to draw his or her own conclusions about Levin. Therefore, the author provides a neutral view, and (A) is the best answer. Choices (C) and (D) could be inferred at certain parts, but there are moments that undermine both. We see a softer side of Levin, for example, when he pats Laska on the head and allows her to run off leash, both of which would discount (C). There's a moment when he prays for luck on his bird, which undermines (D). The author is not sarcastic, (B), nor is he critical toward Levin, (E), overall.

7. **B** Tolstoy is classified as a writer of realism, so the correct answer is (B). Note that the naturalism movement did not occur until well after Tolstoy wrote *Anna Karenina*. Literature from the realism movement is notable for its use of detail, transparent language, truthfulness, and omniscient narrator. Writers of realism sought to reflect the true, daily reality of life—this passage is a prime example of realism.

8. **A** The last question helps with this question: this passage is representative of the realism movement, so thorough descriptions of the setting and characters will be present in the work. The purpose of this section of the text is to give the reader a vivid description of what the characters are experiencing and doing, so the correct answer is (A). There is no foreshadowing, (B), or rising anticipation, (C). The perspective changes in this passage, thereby eliminating (D), and while the characters may seem content in nature, it is not the purpose of this part of the text, so (E) can be eliminated as well.

9. **A** Levin is quite pleased with himself and satisfied with his haul, at what appears to be just the start of his day of hunting. Therefore, the correct answer is (A). There is no evidence in the text that he feels exhausted, (B), powerful, (C), astonished, or boastful, (D). Furthermore, it is the boy who approves of Levin, so eliminate (E) as well.

10. **D** Use the answer to question 3 to help you on this question. His interactions with the old woman and boy are both friendly and cordial. Everyone is getting along nicely and both seem to enjoy Levin's presence, so the correct answer is (D). There is no evidence of envy, (A). The old woman makes no comment regarding Levin's skill, so eliminate (B) and (C). Levin encounters the old woman before he shoots any birds, so there is no way to know whether she approves of his accomplishments, (E).

11. **C** This is a pure definition question, and you need to know the difference between personification and anthropomorphism. When an animal is given human characteristics, behavior, or motivation, anthropomorphism is at work. Personification requires that the nonhuman quality or thing take on a human shape. In this case, Laska seems to have human thoughts (asking him if she had better not go on doing as she had begun) and motivations (pretending she was looking, so as to please him) but never takes on human form. The correct answer is (C). Note that in order for there to be dialogue, both characters would have to be speaking. Since only Levin is actually speaking, (D) cannot be correct.

12. **A** There is evidence of alliteration, (B), since the initial s sound is repeated in stumbling, stump, strong, supple, she, and circle. She has an intense desire to find the bird, and each event presented in this sentence adds a layer of light suspense, (C). The idea of Levin hindering her (sending her off in the wrong direction) and the stump acting as an impediment, presented with her desire to reach the source of the scent, is an example of juxtaposition, (D). Note the use of compound, complex sentence structure—complex syntax is present, (E). Laska stumbling is not a character flaw, nor is Levin hindering her a flaw in his character, so the correct answer is (A).

13. **B** Use the earlier questions to help you here, especially question 5. Laska obeys her master despite not feeling his command is correct, which makes her obedient and submissive, so keep (B). She cannot actually speak to Levin—remember, this is realism—so eliminate (C). There is no evidence that Laska is inexperienced, (D). If anything, there is evidence to the contrary, since she knows she needs to go on doing as she had begun, which could reveal a slight flaw in Levin's skill as a hunter and would thus disprove (E). Choice (A) might be tempting, but this answer has been wrong before—the rest of the passage does not indicate that Levin has an erratic or volatile disposition. The answer that is best supported by the text is (B).

REFLECT

Respond to the following questions:

- Of which types of multiple-choice questions discussed in this chapter do you feel you have achieved sufficient mastery to answer correctly?

- On which types of multiple-choice questions discussed in this chapter do you feel you need more work before you can answer correctly?

- What strategies discussed in this chapter do you feel you will be able to apply effectively when taking the exam?

- What parts of this chapter are you going to re-review?

- Will you seek further help, outside of this book (such as from a teacher, tutor, or AP Students), on any of the content in this chapter—and, if so, on what content?

Summary

- When a question seems unclear, the answer choices can help you make sense of it.

- On general questions, you are looking for a choice that accurately describes some facet of the entire passage.

- Learn to focus on key phrases in the answer choices in order to eliminate using the "half wrong equals all wrong" technique.

- Use Consistency of Answers.

- For line reference questions, keep the main idea in mind and use Consistency of Answers whenever possible. Also, go back to the passage and reread the lines in question, as well as one full sentence before and after the line reference.

- Pay close attention to the wording of questions. Put questions in your own words if that makes things easier for you. Be careful not to just ignore confusing parts, though.

- Expect a weird question or two. The test-writers like to get creative on the AP English Literature and Composition Exam. We can't prepare you for everything, just almost everything.

- Our glossary of terms has many valuable definitions and will get you some points; flip to the back of this book to brush up on important key terms!

- Use the Seven-Minute Passage technique for the last passage if you have seven minutes or fewer left: don't read the passage, and answer the questions starting with those that require no knowledge of the passage or those that can be answered by referring to specific lines.

Chapter 9
The Idea Machine: Starting Your Essays with a High Score

> " Reading is my inhale, and writing is my exhale.
>
> —Glennon Doyle "

FROM IDEA TO EXECUTION

We're going to take you through our AP English writing process, one we've designed specifically for AP essays. The most stressful part of writing essays under time pressure is coming up with something to say quickly. In this chapter, we'll show you how to get the ideas that give you something to write about in the first place. We aren't going to teach you how to write; you've already spent years learning to write. However, AP essays are unlike anything you've had to write before, and you probably haven't spent years learning how to write them.

Approximately 90 percent of this chapter is about how to get an overall idea of your essay and create a great first paragraph. If you can get off to a good start, you're more than halfway to a great score.

THE APPROACH

Just as with the multiple-choice section, you want to have a common-sense, step-by-step approach to the essay section (and know how to use it). Here it is:

- Take a watch and note the time. Remember: 40 minutes per essay.
- Pick the essay (prose fiction analysis, poetry analysis, literary argument) you want to write first.
- Identify the key words in the essay prompt.
- Skim the passage.
- Work the passage, make notes, and identify quotations you will want to use.
- Use the Idea Machine (explained in this chapter) to plan your first paragraph.
- In your body paragraphs, support and develop the points you made in your first paragraph.
- Get a solid conclusion on the page. Your conclusion can be as important as your introduction, and it usually is.
- Repeat the process with the other essays.

Don't Write a Formal Outline

You don't have time to write an outline. Outlines are for organizing longer, more complex pieces of writing, like research papers, when you have the time to revise and plan. We know you've probably had outlining drummed into you by your teachers. But short essays, like the ones you'll write for the AP Exam, don't call for an outline. You don't even have time to rewrite. Our method shows you how to come up with a solid beginning from which you can build so that you can just write the rest of the essay without an outline.

The Idea Machine

We've developed a method of approaching AP essays that we call the "Idea Machine." Hey, don't get us wrong, the *real* idea machine is in your skull. The point here is to focus your brain, imagination, and analytical skills in a way that's productive for the AP Exam. This approach won't let you down. Use it, and your essays will shine.

The Idea Machine is a series of questions that direct your reading to the material needed to write an essay. Take these questions, apply their answers to the essay question, and in the end you'll find you've written the kind of essay the Readers want to see.

The Idea Machine

1. What is the meaning of the work?
   a. What is the literal, face-value meaning of the work?
   b. What feeling (or feelings) does the work evoke?
2. How does the author get that meaning across?
   a. What are the important images in the work and what do those images suggest?
   b. What specific words or short phrases produce the strongest feelings?
   c. What do the characters, setting, structure, or narrators tell you about the passage?

That may not look like much, but when we put all the pieces together in this chapter and the next, you'll see just how powerful of a tool we're giving you.

The Classic Essay Question

Whether you are working on a prose fiction analysis or poetry analysis passage, there is a classic essay question that you will be asked to address. Here it is in its most basic form:

> Read the following work carefully. Then, in a well-written essay, analyze the manner in which the author conveys ideas and meaning. Discuss the techniques the author uses to make this passage effective.

In your response you should do the following:

- Respond to the prompt with a thesis that presents an interpretation and may establish a line of reasoning.
- Select and use evidence to develop and support your line of reasoning.
- Explain the relationship between the evidence and your thesis.
- Use appropriate grammar and punctuation in communicating your argument.

The classic essay question actually breaks down into three questions. The first two should look familiar because they're part of the Idea Machine.

1. What does the poem or passage mean?
2. How did the author get you to see that? Were elements like character, setting, structure, narration, and figurative language deployed? Which ones?
3. How do the answers to questions 1 and 2 direct your knowledge to adequately answer the question?

The first question is hidden, but totally important. It's the foundation on which you build the rest of your essay. Your (high-scoring) essay should answer those three questions in that order. Question 2 is the one you'll be asked on the exam; the test-writers feel that question 1 is implied.

If the first question is "What does the passage or poem mean?" Well...what does that mean? What is *meaning*?

The Meaning of *Meaning*

For the AP essays, the meaning of a work of prose fiction or poetry is the most basic, flat, literal sense of what is said plus the emotions and passions behind that sense.

The passages and poems they ask you to write about on the AP English Literature and Composition Exam will present some event or situation in the same way a newspaper article presents an event or a situation. But AP essay passages will, of course, do more than that. They will make the event or situation "come alive" by bringing in human emotions and passions in such a way that those emotions and passions are as important as the facts.

Let's consider an example:

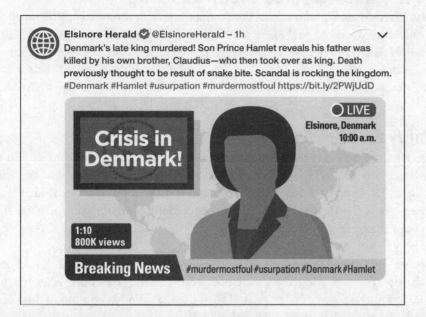

Think of how much will be lost by the Twitter version. Can the tweets really let us know Hamlet's suffering, his frantic (and occasionally crazed) attempts to figure out what is going on with his father and his uncle? Of course not, but those emotions are part of what the story means. They are the most important part of your essay.

Avoid Summary

You must absolutely avoid writing only a newspaper or social media version. Doing that amounts to a summary, something the AP Readers do not want. Discuss the way emotions are involved in the story and focus on the feelings the language produces, and you'll be discussing meaning in the right way. Always identify point of view, tone, and figurative language usage. Discussing these literary elements will ensure that you are moving beyond a summary.

Just Say No...
...to summaries! AP Readers want to see you analyze a literary work, not rehash what you read.

The Modified Classic Essay Question

Your AP Exam may well have the classic question on it almost word for word, but probably not. What you will likely see is a modified classic essay question. There are an endless number of modifications for the test-writers to throw at you. For example, the question might ask you to analyze "the narrator's attitude toward the nature of war," "the speaker's attitude toward society," or "the author's use of repetition."

Identify the Key Words in the Prompt

Of course, the specifics mentioned in the essay prompt are what you should pay close attention to when you read. Just as in the multiple-choice section, where looking at the questions can help you read the passages more actively, identifying precisely what the Readers want you to write about can help you focus on those aspects of the poem or prose fiction.

However, even if you're responding to a modified essay prompt, you should begin just as if you're answering the classic one. You want to talk about what meaning you found in the poem or passage, and then use that as a foundation to discuss the topic about which the question specifically asks.

Let's look at an example. (You don't need the actual passage to understand our discussion of the question here.)

> Read the following passage carefully. Write a well-organized essay that discusses the interrelationship of humor, pity, and horror in the passage.

This seems like a simple enough question—until you try to answer it. How do you go about discussing the interrelationship of humor, pity, and horror? Most students start out something like this:

> The story X by writer Z mixes humor pity and horror in an interesting way. It begins with a father meeting his son. The father seems like a funny guy because of things he does, but then we see that he is actually a person who arouses our pity because he goes too far, so far in fact, that the father becomes almost horrible.

The student who writes this response knows he's basically flailing. He's just trying to answer the question without looking foolish. If the student uses reasonable examples, writes with some organization and only a few grammatical errors, then the student will get a 3, a "limbo" score—not passing, but not failing.

On the other hand, the student who understands that this question is a modified form of the classic question and knows how to use the Idea Machine will break it down.

What does the passage mean? What was I supposed to get from it? What did I get from it? Okay, I got that the passage was about a father and son and that the son feels his father is basically embarrassing. Yeah, that sounds about right. Now, let's see, how does the author get that across using humor, pity, and horror?

Notice how this student has taken the question, turned it into the classic question, and simply used the modification to focus on the point to be developed. The student began by describing the meaning of the story. ("The son feels his father is basically embarrassing" is the meaning. Remember that the meaning doesn't have to be complicated.) Then this student wondered, *How does the author get that across using humor, pity, and horror?* This student's opening is going to look something like this:

> In story X, writer Z shows us a son confronted by the embarrassing spectacle of his father. By shifting the son's perspective of his father from humor and pity, to horror, we see and feel the son's fluctuating, uncertain responses to his father's vulgarity and ignorance.

This student is writing about something and it shows. She's on the way to a score of at least 4, and if the essay stays this clear and focused, it's going to earn a score of 6. Do you see how slight an alteration has been made between this response and the one that came before it? Yet there's a world of difference. The first student rephrased the question without really saying anything, and then began to work his way through the points, ticking them off...first humor, then pity, then horror. The second student began by answering the implied question in every essay: *What does this story mean?* Then she began to show how the author brought that meaning across.

The best part is that the second essay is easier to write than the first one. It's easier to write an essay about something than nothing. Writing a bogus essay is like trying to wind up a ball of string with nothing to wrap it around. The second essay is going to wrap itself neatly around the core of the story's meaning—the son's uncertain embarrassment at his father's behavior.

No Fear!

Sometimes the questions can be fairly intimidating, but don't let them throw you. Remember to use the Idea Machine. What does the passage mean? How does that meaning come across?

Once you've got that under your belt, you can think about how to focus on the points in a question about a poem. Let's look at an example:

> Read the poem below carefully. Notice that the poem is divided into two stanzas and that the second stanza reapplies much of the first stanza's imagery. Write a well-organized essay in which you discuss how the author's use of language, including his use of repetition, reflects the content and tone of the poem.

You should look at the question and remember that it's just a modified version of the classic essay question. Ask yourself "What is the meaning?" and "How do I know it?" Then you can think about how the author uses imagery and figurative language to convey that meaning. In fact, this question almost organizes itself once you break it down. Your first paragraph should talk about what you get from the whole poem, and your subsequent paragraphs should discuss the language and meaning of each stanza. Your conclusion should look at the poem as an entire piece and reiterate your emphasis about why and how repetition is important in understanding the overall tone and theme of the poem.

A Great Start

The key to a great essay is a great start and the key to a great start is having an overall idea of what you're doing. We've shown you how to address the meaning (literal and emotional) of the poem right from the beginning, and that you must then address the "how" of the author's method. Taken together, these things will form your opening and the central idea around which you will write—the idea you will explain and support. If you're already a sharp, sensitive reader, following these instructions will lead you to high-scoring essays.

Sounds easy in principle. But are you ready? Let's go back to that tough, intimidating question we just looked at in the No Fear section, this time along with the poem that goes with it. We'll use our approach to come up with a good first paragraph for a high-scoring essay. Then we'll show you two powerful tools you can use to open up a passage and get the kinds of ideas that blow AP Readers away.

Dylan Thomas's "In My Craft or Sullen Art"

Read the following poem carefully. Notice that the poem is divided into two stanzas and that the second stanza reapplies much of the first stanza's imagery. Write a well-organized essay in which you discuss how the author's use of language, including his use of repetition, reflects the content and tone of the poem.

In My Craft or Sullen Art by Dylan Thomas

In my craft or sullen art
Exercised in the still night
When only the moon rages
Line And lovers lie abed
(5) With all their griefs in their arms,
I labor by singing light
Not for ambition or bread
Or the strut and trade of charms
On the ivory stages
(10) But for the common wages
Of their most secret heart.

Not for the proud man apart
From the raging moon I write
On these spindrift pages
(15) Nor for the towering dead
With their nightingales and psalms
But for the lovers, their arms
Round the griefs of the ages,
Who pay no praise or wages
(20) Nor heed my craft or art.

So, where do you begin? Well, before you begin to consider the repetition mentioned in the essay instructions, get the answers to the questions that let you write a classic essay. Use the Idea Machine.

- **What does the poem say, literally?** That shouldn't be too tough to answer, even if you don't know exactly what Dylan Thomas is trying to say. Put it in your own words. What does the poet say about his "craft or sullen art"? Take a moment to think about it and then read on.

You should have come up with something like this: "Dylan Thomas explains that he isn't writing for money or fame but for lovers who don't even care about his writing."

- **Okay, now what is the feel of the poem?** What emotions are conveyed? Is there an overall emotion? Again, think about it a moment before you read on.

It's a tougher question, isn't it? You probably went back to the poem to look at it again, thinking, "Just what emotion was I supposed to get? There's something there, but what?"

You might have picked up on a few aspects of the tone: pride, grief, loneliness, perhaps futility, and also perhaps the opposite of futility—a sense of total purpose. The poem has a truly complex emotional range. Don't let that scare you off; it only gives you more to write about.

- **What is the meaning of the poem for your AP essay?** Take your literal sense and your emotional sense, and combine them:

  > Dylan Thomas's "In My Craft or Sullen Art" explores the pride, grief, loneliness, futility, and yet sense of total purpose that come from the author's struggle to write not for fame or for wealth but for "the lovers, their arms round the griefs of ages."

So far so good. But don't think we're finished. This sentence is just the answer to question 1 of the Idea Machine—what does the poem mean? If you're particularly astute, you may even notice that we haven't completely answered that question. We've only said what Thomas "explores." We haven't come out and taken a stand on exactly where Thomas's exploration has led him. Don't worry. You don't have to try to pin everything down all at once. If this essay were an assignment due at the end of the week, you'd want to write a rough draft that you could revise carefully later. Here on the AP Exam, you don't have the opportunity for careful revision. You don't have to write a perfect essay. The Readers don't expect you to, not even for a score of 6. Just stay with our method: what does the work mean, how does the author achieve his effects, and what does the question ask you to address?

The "Perfect" Essay
No one, not even the AP Readers, expects you to write the perfect essay. But what they DO want you to write is an essay that discusses the meaning of a literary work, how the author conveys that meaning, and how all of that ties into the question you are being asked.

Now you have the second part of our three-part approach to consider:

- **How does the author achieve his effects?** Perhaps in answering that question we can take more of a stand. How does Thomas bring his emotions into his sense of what writing means to him and (because the essay instructions demand we consider it) what does the repetition have to do with it?

How indeed? Thomas gets his message across in so compact a fashion that you may feel a little lost and overwhelmed. Remember, you're just trying to write a 40-minute essay on a poem you've never seen before. The Readers don't expect perfection or profound originality. They want to see you focus on saying *something*, and then say it as clearly as you can. In brief, they want to see you confidently develop your ideas as best you can.

Here's how we'd complete our opening statement and answer the question of how Thomas explores his sense of what, to him, it means to write:

> Dylan Thomas's "In My Craft or Sullen Art" explores the pride, grief, loneliness, futility, and yet sense of total purpose that come from the author's struggle to write not for fame or for wealth but for "the lovers, their arms round the griefs of ages." Thomas gives us an image of himself, laboring alone "by singing light" and contrasts this with an image of self-contained completeness, of lovers wrapped in each other's arms, oblivious to all the world and even to his poetry. By repeating these images, and key words like "moon," "rage," and "grief," he emphasizes the power of his emotions and the intensity of his need to define himself and the purpose of his art.

This opening gets our essay off to a great start. Of course, you might have had different ideas, and you undoubtedly would have phrased your ideas another way, even if you saw exactly what we saw in the poem. You might even have written two or three better sentences—although you wouldn't have had to in order to score well. This brings up our next point.

Have Confidence in Your Answer

Many other insights about Dylan Thomas's poem are waiting between the lines. It all depends on what you got from it. If you ask yourself, "How can I describe the subject of this poem in one word?" You will find that your answer, in this case, reflects the title of the poem. It is his writing. Then, ask yourself this question: "What is Dylan Thomas saying about the craft of writing?" The answer is the theme of the poem. If you look at the last few lines of the poem, you will discover the answer in those lines. Usually if you look at the title of the poem, the last few lines of the poem, and combine that with the one word that accurately describes the subject of the poem, you are on your way to accurately describing the theme of the poem. You want to make sure that you are on track with your interpretation because the Readers want to see that you have understood the point of the poem and can explain how this understanding helps you answer the essay question.

Use that literary vocabulary you've been building by studying the glossary. The Readers are paying attention to your craft of writing as you address the question. They want to see how the literary work you've been asked to write about acted on your imagination and how well you've managed to convey the impressions you've received.

Imagery and Words

Speaking of *imagination*, notice what we've done in the "how" part of our opening paragraph about the Dylan Thomas poem. We've discussed imagery and part of figurative language. We chose to mention the contrasting images of the author working alone and of the lovers in their self-enclosed togetherness. You might have chosen something else but the point to remember is this: *It's always a safe bet to talk about imagery.*

In writing (as opposed to cinema or theater or painting), an image is made of words. Is that obvious? Yes, it is. But just because it's obvious doesn't mean all students pay attention to that important fact. On the AP essays, your job is to discuss writing. Remember then that whenever you're discussing the imagery in a passage, you're discussing words. If a word sticks out as unusual or particularly vivid, think about it. Ask yourself, why did the author use *that* word? What effect does that word have? If you can think of something to say about the words an author has used to create an image and the specific effect those words have, by all means put it in your essay. You'll have the AP Readers eating out of your hand. One easy method of discussing imagery is to try to create a short film clip with your words based on what the poet has written.

Notice that in our sample opening, we zeroed in on the two most striking word choices in the poem: *rage* and *grief*. It's odd (and poetic) to say lovers have their arms around their griefs. And when was the last time you saw the moon raging? A lot of students run from unusual language like that. They think that the poet is just being a typical crazy artist who can't really be understood or that they'll misinterpret the phrase anyway and look dumb. But when you see unusual usages like that, consider them. Why that word? What does that word do to the feel of the piece? Thinking this way will jog ideas loose and result in material that makes for great AP essays. Notice also that both *rage* and *grief* have strong emotional content. Writing about the emotional content is the best way to let the Reader know you're really reading and not simply enacting some dry, mechanical exercise.

When in Doubt
The most important, most open-ended, most easily discussable aspect of a poem is almost always the imagery.

Opposition

If you've been following our discussion so far, you should see that you need to be able to pull ideas from the text you're working with so that you have ideas for your essay. Considering imagery and word choice is a good start, but there's one more concept we want you to think about as you read, something that should really help you find the ideas that you need to write a great essay.

How can you get to the heart of what you read on the AP English Literature and Composition Exam? How can you find something interesting and important to say about a passage quickly? What do you look for to see what makes a passage or a poem "tick"?

The answer is *opposition*.

Opposition vs. Conflict

Some people call opposition *conflict*, but we think that's too narrow a term. *Conflict* sounds like two people having a fight. Don't be crude. Be subtle. Opposition is everywhere in good writing, and the passages on the AP Exam will always be good sources. Seek it out as you read because opposition leads you to the important parts of a passage or poem.

Attune your reading to seeing opposition and you'll open up AP passages like cans of sardines. You'll have something around which to center your discussion of the way an author uses language, imagery, and tone to make their point. If you carefully read the question, you will notice that there is usually a comparison or contrast that it directs you to address. Sometimes it is subtle, but sometimes you are directed to focus your answer on a comparison or contrast noted within the passage or two passages.

So, What's Opposition?

Opposition occurs when any pair of elements contrast sharply. Another way to think about opposition is tension—think of the two opposing elements as if they were magnetized poles, attracting and repelling each other. Opposition provides a structure underneath the surface of the poem, which you will unlock by discovering the oppositional elements. Opposition might be as blatant as night and day. Or it might be less obvious: a character who's naïve and a character who's sophisticated. Opposition might be found in a story that begins with a scene in a parlor but ends with a scene around a campfire, which would be the opposition of indoors and outdoors. It would be easy to miss if you weren't looking for it, but it can often be found between the author's style and his subject. For example, a cerebral, intellectual style that's heavy on analysis in a story about a hog farmer would be opposition. Your essay should address why the author wrote that way and what effect it has on the story. Keep an eye out for any elements that are in contrast to each other as they'll often lead you to the heart of the story.

Let's look at that Dylan Thomas poem again. Notice what we went after in our opening paragraph: the image of the author working alone and the image of lovers in each other's arms. That's an opposition. Do you see how it's not exactly a conflict? It's a pairing of images whereby each becomes more striking and informative when placed against the other. Doesn't that pair of images seem central to the poem? Doesn't it seem there's something to talk about there? What it means exactly is open to interpretation, and that's exactly what you should do when you see elements opposed to each other: *interpret*. Don't worry about getting it right; there is no single right answer. The AP Reader will see that your searching intelligence has found the complexity of the material and is making sense of it. That's exactly what the Reader wants you to do. (And it's what very few students attempt to do.)

Opposition creates tension and mystery. What's the most mysterious line in "In My Craft or Sullen Art"? We think it's "And lovers lie abed/With all their griefs in their arms." That line alone has an opposition: if they're lovers, why do they have their griefs in their arms?

So your job is to figure out what Thomas means by that. The answer? Nothing simple, but something you can write about. Realize that you don't have to resolve opposition. You don't have to interpret that line (or the poem) in a concrete way that makes absolute perfect sense. It's a poem, not a riddle.

Our opening paragraph mentioned a third opposition: Thomas's sense of futility and his sense of total purpose. The sense of futility in the poem comes from the statements that the lovers "pay no praise or wages," nor do they heed Thomas's "craft or art." Describing how Thomas gets across his deep sense of purpose is more difficult even though it is the stronger of the two impressions. In many ways the entire poem is about conveying the sense of purpose Thomas feels when writing poetry.

We found these things because we looked for the oppositions. Some oppositions are obvious. Like a tiger in a bus station, they catch your attention immediately and make you wonder what's going on. Good writers boldly toss together mismatched concepts, objects, and tones all the time. But good writers also work with quiet oppositions that aren't nearly so easy to spot. If you aren't paying attention, you'll feel what's going on without realizing where it's coming from. Many literary oppositions come from within one character. The character who wants two totally opposite things at the same time is a classic case of opposition, as is the character who badly wants something that he just isn't cut out for.

Another important opposition is *tone*. Some writers will write about the silliest thing possible in a deadly serious way. (This is generally done to make a situation funnier.) Still another opposition, one that is often handled with supreme delicacy and with seemingly infinite repercussions, is *time*. Writers will often let the past stand in opposition to the present. The story of a once proud family that has fallen on hard times is an example of a plot that uses the changes time brings to develop oppositions.

We could come up with hundreds of specific examples of oppositions in literature, but those examples won't do you any good if you haven't read the works. Our point here is to give you a tool with which to generate ideas for your AP essays.

You're probably still a little unclear as to how to apply this concept of oppositions to a short AP essay, but don't worry. The samples and examples in Chapter 10 will take you through several AP passages and point out how you might use oppositions to find ideas (while also boosting your essay scores into the 5's and 6's).

Opposition in Your Essay
An AP essay won't get to all of these oppositions; it shouldn't try to. But you can be sure we'll mention that repetition plays a part.

After the First Paragraph—Do an Essay Check

Looking back at our overall approach to the Essay section, you'll see that the second to last point is the recommendation to do an essay check. That sounds fancy, but all it means is that you should think briefly about the points you need to make in your essay.

The time to do this thinking is after you've written that first paragraph. The first paragraph comes from using the Idea Machine: discussing the meaning of the passage or poem (remember, the newspaper version plus emotion) and beginning to talk about how the author gets her point across. This method gives you a first paragraph that establishes the foundation on which the rest of your essay will be built. If it's hyperfocused, it will already set out the overall points you intend to cover, but even if it just gives you a general platform on which to build, you've got plenty, enough to put you miles ahead of the majority of other (flailing) students. The essay check is just a spot check, a place to pause, make sure you're on the right track, and haven't forgotten anything important. When you finish your first paragraph, stop and ask yourself the following questions:

> - What points does my first paragraph indicate I'm going to cover?
> - Do those points address the specifics the essay question calls for?
> - In what order am I going to put my points?

One More Reminder About Our Essay Book
If you need more help on essays in a test setting, our book *How to Write Essays for Standardized Tests* contains advice and examples for best practices on an assortment of AP exams, plus ACT, and others!.

When you've decided the order of your points, get back to writing. Your check shouldn't take more than a minute. The least important part of the check is deciding the order of your points. It's the closest thing to an outline you need to do, but don't overdo it. As long as you've paused to think about addressing the question, it makes sense to form a rough plan of how you'll proceed. But the idea is to make it easier for you to write, not to suffocate your writing. Be flexible. If it's convenient to change the order of your points as you write, change them. If you think of new things to say, say them!

Developing Your Essay

As you write, you'll notice things that you hadn't seen at first, things that will depart from your original ideas and take you in unexpected directions. Should you include these things? YES!

Many, many students are intimidated by the test. They think their writing has to be truly organized and tight and end up writing short, dry, little essays—essays that receive a score of 3. Go with the flow. As long as your ideas have some connection to the question that was asked, include them. Write a great first paragraph that sets you out in the right direction and then loosen up—you'll score high.

Once you've finished your first paragraph and your essay check, it's time to develop your essay. When it comes to development, each essay is unique. The best way to study development is through examples. The next chapter is devoted to sample essays; we'll show you how to put our method (and your ideas) into practice.

Remember...
It is impossible to write a tight, well-organized essay in 40 minutes—impossible. Style and flair aren't as important here as substance and the clarity of your ideas.

REFLECT

Respond to the following questions:

- On which AP essay-writing strategies discussed in this chapter do you feel you have achieved sufficient mastery to write high-scoring essays?

- On which AP essay-writing strategies discussed in this chapter do you feel you need more work before you can write high-scoring essays?

- What parts of this chapter are you going to re-review?

- Will you seek further help, outside of this book (such as from a teacher, tutor, or AP Students), on any of the content in this chapter —and, if so, on what content?

Summary

○ If you can get off to a good start, you're more than halfway to a great score.

○ Use our approach:
  - Note the time. Remember, 40 minutes per essay.
  - Pick the essay (prose fiction, poetry analysis, literary argument) you want to write first.
  - Identify the key words in the essay prompt.
  - Skim the passage.
  - Work the passage, making notes and identifying quotations you will want to use.
  - Use the Idea Machine to plan your first paragraph.
  - In your body paragraphs, support and develop the points you made in your first paragraph.
  - Get a solid conclusion on the page.
  - Repeat the process with the other essays.

○ Don't write an outline.

○ Identify key words in the prompt.

○ Understand the question and how to turn the question into an *essay idea*.

- Use the Idea Machine:
  - What is the meaning of the work? *Meaning* is literal meaning plus the emotions the work evokes.
  - How does the author get that meaning across?
    - important images
    - specific words or short phrases
    - opposition

- The Idea Machine is the tool that will help you apply your skills specifically to a 40-minute essay.

- Any student who can write an adequate essay can write an AP essay that scores a 4 or higher.

- Don't worry about being wrong. Have confidence in your interpretation.

- Unusual language and imagery are great places to find essay ideas.

- *Opposition* is created when any pair of elements in a story or poem contrasts sharply or subtly.

- Look for elements that are in opposition. They'll lead you to the heart of the passage and give you material for the kinds of ideas that make AP Readers give out sixes.

- Go with the flow. It is impossible to write a tight, well-organized essay in 40 minutes. Write a great first paragraph that sets you out in the right direction, and then loosen up. Don't digress, however, and start talking about irrelevant topics. Always stay focused on the text.

Chapter 10
Sample Poetry Analysis and Prose Fiction Analysis Essays

> " I see things with my own eyes, just as if they were the first eyes that ever saw, and then I set about to tell, as best I can, just what I've seen.
>
> —Edna St. Vincent Millay "

Here's a poem that relies a great deal on irony, similar to Robert Browning's "My Last Duchess," which you worked on back in Chapter 3. This time, the poem we are studying comes with an essay question. Read the question and the poem and think about how you might write a response.

SAMPLE POETRY ANALYSIS ESSAY

William Blake's "The Chimney Sweeper" (Two poems)

Essay (Suggested Time—40 Minutes)

In the following poems by William Blake, the speaker, most likely a small child known as a chimney sweep, has been forced to work inside chimneys cleaning the interiors. Read the poems carefully. Then, in a well-written essay, compare and contrast the two poems and the ways that Blake uses poetic elements and techniques to express the plight of the chimney sweep.

The Chimney Sweeper

When my mother died I was very young,
And my father sold me while yet my tongue
Could scarcely cry " 'weep! 'weep! 'weep! 'weep!"*
So your chimneys I sweep and in soot I sleep.

Line
(5)   There's little Tom Dacre, who cried when his head
That curled like a lamb's back, was shaved, so I said,
"Hush, Tom! never mind it, for when your head's bare,
You know that the soot cannot spoil your white hair."

And so he was quiet, and that very night,
(10) As Tom was a-sleeping he had such a sight!
That thousands of sweepers, Dick, Joe, Ned, and Jack,
Were all of them locked up in coffins of black;

And by came an Angel who had a bright key,
And he opened the coffins and set them all free;
(15) Then down a green plain, leaping, laughing they run,
And wash in a river and shine in the Sun.

Then naked and white, all their bags left behind,
They rise upon clouds, and sport in the wind.
And the Angel told Tom, if he'd be a good boy,
(20) He'd have God for his father and never want joy.

And so Tom awoke; and we rose in the dark
And got with our bags and our brushes to work.
Though the morning was cold, Tom was happy and warm;
So if all do their duty, they need not fear harm.

*The child's lisping attempt at the chimney sweep's
street cry, "Sweep! Sweep!"*

(1789)

The Chimney Sweeper

A little black thing among the snow,
Crying "'weep! 'weep!" in notes of woe!
"Where are thy father and mother? say?"
"They are both gone up to the church to pray.

Line
(5) Because I was happy upon the heath,
And smil'd among the winter's snow,
They clothed me in the clothes of death,
And taught me to sing the notes of woe.

And because I am happy and dance and sing,
(10) They think they have done me no injury,
And are gone to praise God and his Priest and King,
Who make up a heaven of our misery."
(1794)

Poetry Analysis Answers in General

Before we delve into this specific poem, we want to discuss some differences between prose fiction and poetry analysis. Poems are special cases because they deal in compressed language. Lyric poems (most of the poems on the AP English Literature and Composition Exam are lyric poems) often use a convention, simple on the surface but infinite in its varieties and depth. In this convention, the speaker of the poem (the "I") is addressing the reader directly, as prompted by a certain occasion or dramatic situation. If you pay attention to this lyric convention and its component parts, you may be able to understand a seemingly difficult poem more quickly. Not all poems on the AP Exam will exactly fit into this convention, but most will. The two poems we've chosen to discuss here definitely do.

In the previous chapter, we introduced the Idea Machine—three questions to consider when looking at a work of literature. Do you remember them?

1. What does the poem or passage mean?
2. How did the author get you to see that?
3. How do the answers to questions 1 and 2 direct your knowledge to adequately answer the question?

The same three questions also apply to the poetry analysis essay. Question 2, however, should be considered more like a drop-down kind of menu when you are writing about poetry.

Go Online!
Check out us out on YouTube for test taking tips and techniques to help you ace your next exam at www.youtube.com/ThePrincetonReview

Here are the three Idea Machine questions modified for the poetry analysis essay:

> 1. What's the literal meaning of the poem?
> 2. How did the author get you to see that?
>   - What is suggested by the title?
>   - Who is the speaker and who is the audience?
>   - What is the dramatic situation that prompted the speaker to speak?
>   - What problem is being explored in the poem, and does the poem find a solution?
>   - What feelings do you get from the poem?
>   - What is the overall effect of the poem?
> 3. How do the answers to the first two questions direct your knowledge to adequately answer the exam question?

You don't have to ask or answer all of the secondary questions under question 2, but the more answers you can find to these questions, the better your essay. Let's see how this method works by looking at a specific poem.

Idea Machine in Action
On the following pages, we break down how to implement the Idea Machine strategy on the day of the exam.

Discussion of "The Chimney Sweeper" by William Blake

Like many poems, these two could be the focus of a long discussion. A full class period could be spent analyzing these coupled poems as a group of interested students slowly circled them, discovered small details, and found ways to express their discoveries to each other. You don't have that time.

We won't be delving deeply into the many possible interpretations of these poems. The point here is to figure out what you could say about these poems in order to write an essay that answers the question. Let's use the poetry analysis essay Idea Machine—the simple, orderly process that you should apply to every AP English Literature essay.

First, tackle the question.

> What's the literal meaning of the poem?

It is the classic AP essay question. That makes our lives a little easier. The Idea Machine will work perfectly here.

Here is some background that may prove helpful to your understanding. The speaker in both poems is a chimney sweep. In the late 18th and early 19th centuries, boys as young as six were indentured to masters as chimney sweeps by their families, who were too impoverished to keep the children at home. Young children were considered useful as chimney sweeps because they were small enough to get up into the chimneys to clean them. But the dark, soot-encrusted chimneys were likely terrifying, and the sweeps were subject to a number of hazards, including cancer, broken bones, respiratory diseases, and even suffocation. It was common to see them on the streets of London, as coal-burning fireplaces were perhaps the most common way of heating homes and businesses. The plight of chimney sweeps was the subject of a report to British Parliament in 1817, more than 25 years after Blake's first poem was published. Ultimately, employment of young children in the chimney-sweep trade became illegal.

Both poems are from a larger project by William Blake, *The Songs of Innocence and of Experience*. The first poem is one of innocence; the second, one of experience.

If the AP exam writers were to use these poems or others that could benefit from historical background or allusions, the chances are that they wouldn't provide the historical or publication background as we just did. You will be provided with the years of publication (1789 and 1794, respectively), and a note that the poems were written in response to the poor conditions that caused young chimney sweeps to suffer. Most versions of the poem will carry a footnote to the first poem indicating that " 'weep! 'weep! 'weep!" is a child's version of the common chimney-sweep cry, "Sweep! Sweep!" But unless you've read about the plight of the chimney sweeps, the years, brief explanation, and footnote will provide very minimal explication of the historical background.

Fortunately, you don't need to know the background to understand these poems well enough to write a high-scoring essay on the AP exam. Recognizing the importance of the historical background helps, which is why many versions of the published poem include a brief note about it. But the AP exam writers will never choose a poem that relies on knowledge about historical context or allusions to historical events for its very sense.

Here's a quick summary of what you should have in mind after reading the first poem.

In the first three stanzas, a chimney sweeper speaks about how he came to be a sweep. He introduces a fellow chimney sweeper, Tom Dacre, and tells us a dream Tom had. The dream seems to comfort Tom about being a sweep. The poem ends with an injunction that chimney sweeps should do their duty, which will keep them from harm.

Let's look at the first poem in more detail. In its first stanza, the speaker tells us important information: his mother is dead and his father sold him while he, the speaker, was very young (lines 1–2), and that he is a chimney sweeper (line 4). As we saw in the footnote, the chimney sweeper's " 'weep! 'weep! 'weep! 'weep! "(line 3) resemble his cries of "sweep!"

In the next four stanzas, we receive important information about the chimney sweeper's environment, through the treatment and dream of Tom Dacre. Tom's hair is shaved (line 6), which he finds distressing; Tom cries, which reminds readers of the weeping in the first stanza. Told that a shaved head will at least protect his hair, Tom calms down, falls asleep, and has a dream which is both sinister and comforting. In it, "thousands of sweepers" (line 11) are "locked up in coffins of black" (line 12). In Tom Dacre's dream, the sweeps are released by an "Angel" with a "bright key" (line 13) who "set them all free" (line 14). They run, bathe in a river, and play in the sun (lines 15 and 16).

In the next stanza, they are not just free and playing, but leaving the earth. They leave their bags behind (line 17) and rise on the clouds (line 18). Tom is told, in line 20, that "He'd have God for his father and never want joy."

In the last stanza, we return to earth and to the narrator addressing us directly. Tom wakes up, along with the other chimney sweeps (line 21) and prepares to go to work along with the other boys (line 22). In the last two lines, the narrator's voice shifts to a more omniscient tone, telling us that Tom, in contrast to his fear and tears in the second stanza, was "happy and warm" (line 23). Further, the narrator tells us "if all do their duty, they need not fear harm" (line 24). The line seems comforting. Yet the comfort is conditional; the sweeps must do their duty—work as a sweep without tears or complaint—to be without fear of being hurt.

Now let's look at the second poem. Here's a quick summary of what you should have in mind after reading the second poem. In the first stanza, an unnamed person overhears a chimney sweep crying " 'weep!' " Asked where his parents are, he says they have gone to church. The next two stanzas are the sweep talking: he seems angry that his parents have put him to work and becomes overtly condemnatory in the last stanza.

Now, let's look at the second poem in more detail. The narrator at first seems to be omniscient, talking about "A little black thing among the snow" (line 1) "crying 'weep! weep' " (line 2). Because we are reading this poem in juxtaposition with the 1789 "The Chimney Sweeper" and because the title of this poem is also "The Chimney Sweeper," we might immediately think of the former poem's cry of the chimney sweeps. But, unlike the narrator of the first poem, this chimney sweep seems to have both parents, because when asked where his parents are by an unnamed interlocutor (line 3), he replies that they've gone to church (line 4).

In the next stanza, the sweep speaks, addressing the audience directly. He says that his parents "clothed me in the clothes of death, / And taught me to sing the notes of woe" (lines 7–8). Although readers are not told what the clothes of death and notes of woe are, they can infer from the similarity of titles that they are the chimney sweep's black clothes and the street cry.

Yet in this poem, we are not given direct biographical detail, as we are in the first poem. The "father and mother" in line 3 are not only not dead, we are never told that they have "sold" their children, as line 2 of the first poem tells us. Then the speaker reiterates that his parents are currently in church, "to praise God and his Priest and King" (line 11).

Then there's an abrupt shift in tone in the last line. With "Who make up a heaven of our misery" (line 12), the speaker accuses the authority figures of church and state cited in the penultimate line of creating misery for the chimney sweeps.

In fact, the reader is to understand that perhaps those figures' ultimate realm of influence and authority, heaven, is created out of that pain.

The paragraphs preceding this one are a summary of the two poems. They are not an essay. In fact, you can use the paragraphs as a good example of what not to write on your AP essay. A literal reading is only a first step. Nothing is more mechanical or commonplace than a simple retelling of the passage. This kind of essay is going to score in the range of a 2 or a 3. If we apply the rest of the Idea Machine to this literal reading, we can move the score much higher. Let's continue with the Idea Machine. We're at question 2 of the Idea Machine: How did the author get you to see that?

- What is suggested by the title?

- Who is the speaker and who is the audience?

- What is the dramatic situation that prompted the speaker to speak?

- What problem is being explored in the poem, and does the poem have a solution?

- What feelings do you get from the poem?

- What is the overall effect of the poem?

What is suggested by the title? The title is simple on the surface. It's just three words, almost like the title of a painting in a museum. It indicates that the poem will be about a chimney sweeper. In the first poem, it lets the audience know that the "I" of the first stanza is a chimney sweeper. In the second poem, it provides a clue as to who the "little black thing among the snow" is and offers a clue about the "I" in the second stanza. Finally, the fact that the title is the same in both poems unifies them, and suggests that they are to be read in conjunction if readers don't already know.

Who is the speaker and who is the audience? The answer to this question is crucial for many poems. The primary speaker in both poems is a chimney sweep. He is telling the audience about his life as a chimney sweep, and what came before it. He is also discussing the plight of the chimney sweep with reference to spiritual and authority figures, such as the Angel and God (in the first poem) and God, Priest, and King (in the second poem). The chimney sweep in neither case appeals directly to the audience for sympathy, but makes clear that the life can be a miserable one. The audience is the reader. The audience is also presumed to be sympathetic with the plight of the chimney sweeps, or at least to be susceptible to sympathy.

What is the dramatic situation that prompted the speaker to speak? If you can put the dramatic situation of this poem into your own words, you are off to a good start. While we know from our reading of literature that first-person narrators are not always trustworthy, in this case, they initially seem to be. There is nothing in a surface read of the poem to indicate otherwise. In the first poem, the speaker is talking about his own situation as a chimney sweep and his back story. Then, he discusses a boy presumably new to the trade, Tom Dacre, who is having his head shaved for the first time. The speaker comforts Tom about his hair. Tom's dream, narrated by the speaker, seems partly to be a comforting vision of heaven. The speaker then comes back to offer an adage: if the sweeps do their duty, they needn't fear any harm. In the second poem, the speaker seems also to be discussing his own life as a sweep, but his tone is dark and angry. His parents and other authority figures have seemingly all worked together to take him from the happiness of lines 5 and 9, believing they have not done him injury. But the last line, which directly indicates the sweeps suffer from their "misery," indirectly condemns parents and authority figures for using the sweeps' unhappiness to create "a heaven" from it.

What problem is being explored in these poems, and do the poems find a solution? It's clear that a social problem is being discussed in the poems. First, the chimney sweeps are deprived of parental comfort by being sold into a job in which they sweep chimneys (lines 2 and 4) and carry bags (lines 17, 22), in the first poem. Second, it's a painful existence, in which they sleep in soot (line 4) and cry. In the second poem, they are deprived of happiness as well, and feel misery even more overtly.

The first poem seems initially to find a solution to the problem of their misery: they are presumably to find comfort in dreams of God as a father and doing their duty. Tom, after all, is "happy and warm" after the dream, despite the fact that it's cold outside. But can the reader fully trust this solution? There's disquieting coffin imagery in the third stanza of the first poem. If you follow the thread of metaphor, the later "clouds" they rise on may be heaven. They may be dead, then. So yes, their comfort might still be God, but they find comfort and release in death. Plus, of course, the coffins are black (line 12), a color associated with the sweeps' profession and its discomfort—and also frequently associated with death and mourning.

This might lead the reader to question whether the solution in the first poem—trust God as a father and do one's duty—is actually meant as a solution. Could it be ironic? After all, the last line says the sweeps "need not fear harm," but in the first stanza, the narrator has already suffered harm, in being sold and sleeping in soot.

If the conclusion of the first poem contains some irony, the reader might start to wonder if another problem is being addressed: religion and its role vis-à-vis the social problem. Is it really a comfort?

In the second poem, it clearly is not a comfort, at least to the narrator. The trappings of religion, such as the church, represent parental figures to the sweeps. But the actions of the parents, rather than exhibiting parental concern, endanger their children. His parents "clothed me in clothes of death/ And taught me to sing the notes of woe," the narrator tells us. Not only that, but they are oblivious, believing they have "done him no injury."

As the second poem comes to its final two lines, in fact, the narrator seems to move beyond the parents to higher authorities, the "God and his Priest and King" the parents praise. They, too, exhibit none of the care usually associated with these positions. In fact, the narrator says that these three nouns—collectively referred to by the pronoun "who" in the final line—"make up a heaven of our misery." So God in the second poem definitely isn't the comforting father of the first poem. In fact, if the reader sees the pronoun "our" here as referring to the chimney sweeps, God and his Priest and King may have made up heaven as a comforting fiction for the chimney sweeps or may even be the *cause* of the sweeps' plight. So religion itself is part of the problem being explored.

In neither poem is there a specific solution to the problems explored.

What feelings do you get from the poem? You probably already noticed that the tool of "finding oppositions," which we discussed at great length in the preceding chapter, is coming into play in our discussion of this poem. There are several possible ways to interpret the first poem, for example. One could read it as a religious poem in which God and heaven are offered as a genuine comfort and refuge for Tom Dacre and the other chimney sweeps. Or one could see the ending as ironic—something Tom himself is expected to believe, but that the reader is not expected to find persuasive. Or one could go further, especially when juxtaposed with the second poem, and believe that religion is created as a false comfort by church and other authorities.

Don't let the discovery of two (or more!) possible interpretations to any poem unnerve or confuse you. The AP Exam will feature complex poems full of these kinds of tensions. If they didn't, you'd have nothing to write about.

Readers of these poems sometimes feel that the first does offer a solution. Most think that the second poem is much darker. Some feel that the second poem is very cynical. Readers feel moved by the plight of the chimney sweepers, but some feel that the failure to offer a solution makes the poems unsatisfying.

What is the overall effect of the poem? Many readers have found great depth in these poems because they evoke such sympathy and because they can be so productively analyzed. The speaker in the first poem shows us his life and the life of Tom Dacre and offers a resolution of sorts. The speaker in the second poem shows us his life and offers a bleaker vision. Neither case offers a full resolution.

We came to all these points by thinking about the answers to the questions and by looking for oppositions. But we also had the time we needed, and we've had some practice at this kind of thing before. So....

Relax

Are you supposed to pick this all up in one or two readings? In between checking your watch to make sure you have time for the next two essays? Not likely. We just wanted to show you how much there is to unearth in a typical AP Exam passage or poem and how much our techniques can dig up for you. All you'd need to see about this poem on the actual test is that the speakers are in some kind of opposition—and that the narrator of the first one might be in opposition with Blake himself. If you saw that and looked for the ways Blake got that across, you'd find enough to write a great essay.

A Strong Beginning

You should be ready to finalize your opening. Here's an example.

> "The Chimney Sweeper" is a pair of poems written in the late eighteenth-century about the plight of young children forced to work as chimney sweeps. Although the narrators in each seem to have profoundly different perspectives, the stylistic unity and similarities in figurative language indicate that William Blake blames social and religious authorities for the fate of the chimney sweeps in both.

Is this great writing? No. It won't win any prizes. But for the AP Exam, such writing is well on its way to a high score. Anything beyond this will impress your Reader. Let's take it apart for a moment, and then we'll finish the essay.

The beginning paragraph is a first pass at writing about meaning. We wanted to start with something more meaningful than "In 'The Chimney Sweeper' by William Blake…." If you start that way, it's okay, and if the rest of your essay is any good, you'll score high. But the readers like to see something more than that. We opened with the idea that it's a pair of poems on a similar topic, but that the narrator's perspectives are very divergent. Then, we link that to an opposition: the author's use of style and imagery, *not* what the narrators say, suggests a unity between the two poems, not a divergence. The Reader will be impressed that you forecast the main point so quickly.

Unfortunately, we ran out of steam before we could satisfy the overall goal of our beginning: to get at the meanings of the poems (literal and emotional) and explain how Blake gets the meanings across (we've barely started this process).

Keep Going

In the next section of our essay, we describe (not summarize!) what Blake's poem is, what it does, and how. This is a poem in which the overt statements of the narrator may not reflect what readers are expected to believe, nor what William Blake truly believes, or what he thinks the reader might think he believes (did you get that?). There's a double meaning. On the AP English Literature and Composition Exam, any time you can show that a writer has created a double meaning, you have risen in the estimation of the Reader, who has likely been dealing with single meanings for most of the last hour of reading assignments. But we can't stop there; we have to explain both meanings. We chose to talk about the fact that the narrators express very different viewpoints about their lives. So initially these poems seem very different, right? But then we are going to segue to the idea that Blake wants the reader to see that the plights of the sweeps are the same in both.

How do we do this? Let's look at the first two paragraphs. You want to set up the first part of the argument, which is that the narrators differ. We also need to support these assertions with concrete examples from the text. That's our evidence.

While Readers don't have specific checklists to use, one aspect of your writing that every Reader will look for is fluid use of specific evidence to prove your point. Without evidence, your essay is an empty series of assertions. With evidence, you're building your case. Like this:

> Both narrators are chimney sweeps, but the tone of each contrasts sharply with the other. The first speaker has been cruelly treated, as he was "sold" into work when he was very young. He nonetheless attempts to offer comfort to a fellow chimney sweep, Tom Dacre, who is upset when his hair is shaved. The speaker tells of a dream Tom has, in which an "Angel" tells him "he'd have God for his father, and never want joy." The narrator implies at the end that, not only can Tom be comforted by a vision of heaven, with God and the Angel, but all the hard-working sweeps can be as well, because "if all do their duty, they need not fear harm."
>
> The second speaker's tone is far more overtly unhappy. He doesn't see God as a beneficent parent, but condemns "God and his Priest and King" for causing the sweeps' plight—they "make up a heaven of our misery." His parents, who have "gone up to the church to pray," are responsible as well.

Ok. We've given evidence that there is contrast. But what about our friend double meaning? Time to introduce that idea. This is not a simple Case of the Two Contrasting Poems, as Nancy Drew might have called it. Let's introduce the opposition. And let's do it by pointing out the forms and shape of the poems, which tell us that the narrators' views aren't all there is.

> On the surface, then, the narrator in each poem expresses quite different beliefs. One is optimistic and one is quite bitter. Yet the poems are not completely different; they are unified by multiple stylistic elements. The first, of course, is the identical title. The unity continues into the first stanza, with both using the "'weep! 'weep!" cry the sweeps employed to announce their services. In each, "'weep!'" reminds the readers of the cry of a child, and thus appeals to their sympathy about the injustice done to the sweeps.
>
> Through this unity, Blake shows readers that, despite the stark contrast in each narrator's point of view, the poems are in fact a unit, not two widely divergent works of art.

And Going

Okay. We've started to talk about the literary methods that Blake uses to indicate to readers that something is going on beyond the surface of the poem. Let's talk more about those literary methods and tricks! Let's talk imagery and metaphor! Again, let's use abundant examples from the text as evidence for the Reader that we know what we're talking about.

> The imagery of the two poems echoes each other as well, with use of contrasting white and black. The sweeps are linked with "soot" and "black coffins" in Poem 1, in vivid contrast to being "naked and white" later on, in Tom's dream. The initial figure in Poem 2, line 1, mirrors this contrasting black and white, as the sweep is "a little black thing among the snow."

Then, we're going to pivot. Why does this imagery matter? Because it's the first indication we have that we are not to believe the narrator of the first poem. Let's hone in on that.

> An analysis of these unified images leads readers to question the first narrator's optimism. The chimney sweeps in Poem 1 are, after all, "locked up in coffins of black" in Tom's dream. Coffins and chimneys are similar: dark rectangles into which the boys' bodies are placed. The coffin is thus a metaphor for the chimneys. While the freedom given by the "Angel who had a bright key" to the coffins is associated with heaven (the boys "rise upon clouds" and go to a place where God is the father), it's also linked to death because of the coffins. The association with dying is repeated and made explicit in Poem 2, where the narrator is "clothed…in the clothes of death" by his parents.

Is the product of our Idea Machine complete? Not quite. We haven't yet fully stated how Blake gets the idea across that the poems are unified, although we're well on the road. We're going to talk further about the shaping of the poem's meaning through irony, which we realize only from our analysis of the imagery above.

Here's the rest.

> Once readers notice this imagery, they realize that Blake intends the first poem's conclusion to be ironic. Regardless of the speaker's attempt to reassure a fellow chimney sweep (and possibly himself) that things will be alright, it's ultimately death the boys in Poem 1 are sold into. The boys in each poem meet a miserable fate.

> But Blake does not intend the ending of Poem 2 to be ironic. The speaker indicts religion, the state ("King"), and parents in the system that condemns him to a bleak life. The end is abrupt—"our misery"—as Blake intends readers to sympathize with that view. Religion and duty are a false comfort in the first poem; in the second, religion and parents help nail the (figurative) coffin shut.

That's the end of our essay. It's not that long and much more could have been written. But that's it. That's all the time we had. So we wrote that and moved on. We checked our watch, and it said that we had used up 40 minutes. Is it the best piece of writing we've ever done? No. But will it earn a high score? Yes, high enough. Why?

First, as we said, the AP Readers are forgiving of some mistakes. The opening of the essay lets the Readers know that we understand some of the main aspects of the poem and are able to put this understanding into fairly clear sentences. Second, our essay continues to make good points. It talks about metaphor, irony, and the narrators' trustworthiness. We spread out well-chosen examples from most stanzas throughout each poem. We didn't digress for long, and we weren't overly repetitive. The Readers want to see your ideas. By making these insights clear and obvious to the Reader, you make it easy for the Reader to give you a better score.

Is this a well-organized essay? Not by the standards of the writing process. If you were writing for a take-home essay, this would be more like a free-writing, brainstorming session on the journey to a finished project. But by AP standards, this essay is pretty good. It begins with a clear direction, moves on to a consideration of oppositions, and finishes with specifically developed examples of style, imagery, and irony. For a first draft done in just 40 minutes top to bottom, the essay is admirable and will probably receive a 5.

SAMPLE ESSAY ON PROSE FICTION

Let's look at another sample. If you've got paper and pencil handy, try the question that follows and time yourself. At the very least, before you go to our sample essays (we've written two sample responses to this passage, one great and one fair), think about your first paragraph and try writing it in your head. But you really should practice writing a whole essay under time constraints.

Essay (Suggested Time—40 Minutes)

The following excerpt is from *Ultramarine* by Malcolm Lowry (published in 1933). Read the passage carefully. Then, in a well-written essay, analyze how Lowry uses literary elements and techniques such as imagery and interior monologue to paint a picture of Dana Hilliot, a young lad from a well-off family, as he ventures to sea as a sailor.

In your response you should do the following:

- Respond to the prompt with a thesis that presents an interpretation and may establish a line of reasoning.
- Select and use evidence to develop and support your line of reasoning.
- Explain the relationship between the evidence and your thesis.
- Use appropriate grammar and punctuation in communicating your argument.

From *Ultramarine* by Malcolm Lowry.

This 1933 novel follows Dana Hilliot, a young lad from a well-off family, as he ventures to sea as a sailor.

Puella mea[1]…No, not you, not even my supervisor would recognise me as I sit here upon the number six hatch drinking ship's coffee. Driven out and compelled
Line
(5) to be chaste. The whole deep blue day is before me. The breakfast dishes must be washed up: the forecastle and the latrines must be cleaned and scrubbed—the alleyway too—the brasswork must be polished. For this is what sea life is like now—a domestic servant on a treadmill in hell! Labourers, navvies, scalers rather than sailors. The
(10) firemen[2] are the real boys, and I've heard it said there's not much they can't do that the seamen can. The sea! God, what it may suggest to you! Perhaps you think of a deep gray sailing ship lying over in the seas, with the hail hurling over her: or a bluenose skipper who chewed glass
(15) so that he could spit blood, who could sew a man up alive in a sack and throw him overboard, still groaning! Well, those were the ancient violences, the old heroic days of holystones; and they have gone you say. But the sea is none the less the sea. Man scatters even farther and farther
(20) the footsteps of exile. It is ever the path to some strange land, some magic land of faery, which has its extraordinary and unearthly reward for us after the storms of ocean. But it is not only the nature of our work which has changed, Janet. Instead of being called out on deck at all
(25) hours to shorten sail, we have to rig derricks, or to paint the smokestack: the only thing we have in common with Dauber, besides dungarees, is that we still "mix red lead in many a bouilli[3] tin." We batter the rusty scales off the deck with a carpenter's maul until the skin peels off our hands

(30) like the rust off the deck….Ah well, but this life has compensations, the days of joy even when the work is most brutalising. At sea, at this time, when the forecastle doesn't need scrubbing, there is a drowsy calm there during the time we may spend between being roused from our bunks
(35) and turning out on deck. Someone throws himself on the floor, another munches a rasher; hear how Horsey's limbs crack in a last sleepy stretch! But when bells have gone on the bridge and we stand by the paintlocker, the blood streams red and cheerful in the fresh morning breeze,
(40) and I feel almost joyful with my chipping hammer and scraper. They will follow me like friends, throughout the endless day. Cleats are knocked out, booms, hatches, and tarpaulins pulled away by brisk hands, and we go down the ladder deep into the hold's night, clamber up along
(45) the boat's side, where plank ends bristle, then we sit down and turn to wildly! Hammers clap nimbly against the iron, the hold quivers, howls, crashes, the speed increases: our scrapers flash and become lightning in our hands. The rust spurts out from the side in a hail of sharp flakes, always
(50) right in front of our eyes, and we rave, but on on! Then all at once the pace slackens, and the avalanche of hewing becomes a firm, measured beat, of an even deliberate force, the arm swings like a rocking machine, and our fist loosens its grip on the slim haft—And so I sit, chipping,
(55) dreaming of you Janet, until the iron facing shows, or until eight bells go, or until the bosun comes and knocks us off. Oh, Janet, I do love you so. But let us have no nonsense about it.

---

[1] My girl (Latin)

[2] The men that tend the steam engines and boilers of the ship

[3] bullion

Discussion

Did you practice writing the essay on this passage? Did you time yourself? If so, great; if not, we hope you at least read the passage carefully and thought about how you would go about writing your first paragraph.

Oddly enough, writing about prose fiction can actually be more difficult than writing about poetry. Poetry often presents many difficulties to the reader caused by the density and complexity of poetic language. However, once interpreted, those same difficulties give you material to write about. Prose fiction presents the opposite problem. In general, assimilating the passage is pretty easy; the challenge is finding something worth saying about it. It is useful to remember that the literary devices you look for in poetry can also be pointed out in your essays on prose fiction.

As always, start out with the classic question and let the Idea Machine guide your thinking process. Of course, make sure that you allow the question to focus the development of your essay, and also note the time so that you don't go overboard and come up short on the last essay.

Below you'll find two responses to the passage. One is excellent, the other is mediocre. We'll discuss both responses after the samples are given. By the way, in these two essays we've taken out the annoying errors of diction and spelling that creep into every student's essay. We want you to read the essays for what they say and how they say it without distracting errors. The sentence construction reflects student writing, but in reality, both essays would have more language mistakes.

Sample Response to *Ultramarine*—Essay 1

In the passage, Malcolm Lowry effectively uses the resources of language to create an interior monologue (a mental speech) to dramatize the adventures a young English boy has aboard a ship, and shows the character of the boy, Dana Hilliot, as well. He uses vivid imagery and many details from the boy's life to show who Hilliot is and what he thinks, and captures the different rhythms of life aboard a ship.

First Hilliot thinks that no one, "not even my supervisor would recognise me…" This shows that Hilliot thinks that he has changed and that life at sea has changed him. But he's happy, he likes the change, as he says, "The whole deep blue day is before me." But there are many conflicting feelings in Hilliot as he sits and drinks his coffee. For he quickly screams out, "this is what sea life is like now—a domestic servant on a treadmill in hell!" This shows the conflict that Hilliot undergoes. He doesn't know whether he thinks life at sea is great or a stinking hell. Lowry shows this by switching all the time between images that are pleasant, and images that are full of misery and despair and heartbreak. He really misses Janet and it shows. A sailor's life is lonely, and Lowry shows that. Lonely and boring sometimes, as hard as that may be to believe. But the boredom is broken up by danger and hardship. "We batter the rusty scales off the deck with a carpenter's maul until the skin peels off our hands like the rust off the deck…" is an example of the hardship. But immediately, the conflict shows up again. The very next sentence is, "Ah well, but this life has compensations, the days of joy even when the work is most brutalising."

Through it all though, Hilliot thinks of Janet. He begins thinking of her "Puella mea…," which is Latin for "my girl" and ends saying "Oh, Janet, I do love you so." This tells us a great deal about Hilliot. He misses his girlfriend and is probably homesick for England too. These are normal reactions for the character of a young Englishman far from home, and by framing the story between these statements Lowry shows that the character of Dana Hilliot hasn't changed as much as he thinks it has. Hilliot is still a lonely young man with a great deal to learn.

Sample Response to *Ultramarine*—Essay 2

Who hasn't dreamed of throwing everything away and running off to sea? And yet very few people actually do run off to sea, probably because, at least in part, they realized (around the time they're packing all those wool sweaters into a duffle bag) that life at sea isn't just dropping anchor at exotic ports and gazing at the moon setting over the Indian Ocean. It's a hard, dangerous life. Better unpack the sweaters.

The passage shows the inner thoughts of one young man who actually did run off, and as he sits and thinks of the life he's leading and the life he's left behind, we get a picture of what a young sailor's life is really like. We get something else as well, a detailed portrait of a young, confused man, Dana Hilliot, and all the swirling emotions that he carries in his young heart. Hilliot is lonely, defiant, excited, bored, romantic, and cynical all at once.

The passage begins, "Puella mea…" Although that's Latin for "my girl," the translation isn't so important as the fact that it's Latin. Right from the beginning, Lowry shows us a fish out of water. Dana's educated, but how many of Dana's shipmates speak Latin? Probably none. Dana talks about how unrecognizable he's become. Maybe he really is unrecognizable to his old friends, but it's more likely that he can't recognize himself. He's gotten more than he bargained for, "this is what sea life is like now—a domestic servant on a treadmill in hell!" This is one of the recurring themes of the passage. Hard, dull, work. Polishing brass. Chipping paint. Scrubbing and cleaning. It isn't a very romantic scenario. This theme tells us not just about sea-life, but about Dana. He must have been pretty naïve to not know that a sailor works from daybreak into the night, and it's all manual labor.

Lowry gives us a picture of the wild, terrifying, intense life that Dana thought he was going to lead. He describes it to his girlfriend, to correct her and tell her the truth, but you can be sure that these were Dana's ideas of life at sea before he came to the ship. "Perhaps you think of a deep gray sailing ship lying over in the seas, with the hail hurling over her: or a bluenose skipper who chewed glass so that he could spit blood…" Well, Dana has learned that it isn't anything like that at all. His romantic dreams have been squashed, all except the sea. He still finds poetry in the sea. It is "ever the path to some strange land, some magic land of faery…" This is the beauty that Dana really got on board for.

The passage then takes us even deeper into Dana's character. In the beginning, he talked about how horrible it was to be just a lackey, scrubbing decks. As he thinks deeper though, we see a real change in him. He loves the moments of calm, and is such a sensitive experiencer of the life around him that he even notes the way one of his fellows' joints crack, but the amazing thing is that he's learned to love the work. He describes it with relish, "I feel almost joyful with my chipping hammer and scraper. They will follow me like friends…The rust spurts out from the side in a hail of sharp flakes, always right in front of our eyes, and we rave, but on on!" The work, the hard relentless work, is the real adventure, and in those words "on on!" you can hear almost hear Dana's amazement at the fact that he can do it, he can keep going on.

In the end Dana's loneliness, cut off from his familiar life, returns him to being a moody "Romeo," dreaming of his girlfriend, imagining sweet-talking her. It wells up in him with the line, "Oh, Janet, I do love you so." But then comes the very last line of the passage, another abrupt change, "But let us have no nonsense about it." He's still a young person, pouring out his love to his girlfriend but then a second later he's pretending to be a tough guy, a sailor, who wants "no nonsense." By putting these lines, one after the other, Lowry shows Dana in the midst of growing up, and pretending to be more hardened than he is.

Discussion of Sample Responses 1 and 2

It shouldn't be too difficult to tell which is the better of the two responses. Essay 1 is clearly an average response from an intelligent student struggling to write a response about a passage he didn't get much from. Notice the mechanical repetition of the question and the mechanical, plodding way he works through the passage, not so much interpreting as it is summarizing. He did manage to address the question somewhat and did pull together a few simple insights into the passage. He would receive a score of 4. Not a terrible score by any means, but you can do better.

The biggest mistake the author of the first essay made was to choose to emphasize the life-at-sea aspect of the question. Unless an author is just setting the stage for what is to come, or planting some enormous symbol, almost every sentence in a novel or a story *is intended to reveal character*. This is especially true of the kind of masterful writers you'll be dealing with on the AP Exam. When you read prose fiction on the AP Exam, always ask yourself what the sentences tell you about the people in the passage. In the Lowry passage, everything Dana thinks tells us something about Dana. The first student missed most of the psychological details of the passage and ended up floundering.

The author of the second essay worked with the Idea Machine. She asked herself about both the literal and emotional content of the passage. She kept an eye out for strong imagery and evidence of opposites. In doing so, she saw that the passage was filled with conflicting images. Dana loves Janet, but then wants "no nonsense." Dana thinks the work is beneath him ("domestic servant"—Dana's the kind of kid who's used to having servants, not being one) and makes his shipboard life hell, but at the same time he realizes that when he's lost in the physical frenzy of the labor, he finds the work exhilarating. The author of the second essay tried to put these oppositions together in a meaningful way. Most important, she knew to focus on character. By tying everything back to Dana's character she assured herself of a high score. In fact, the second essay would be scored a 6—the top score.

Also notice that the second essay does not begin with the typical restatement of the question. That doesn't mean that a Reader would look at the beginning of the second sample essay and think, "Oh my, what an original opening—this essay gets a high score." A nice opening isn't enough. You still have to write the essay. But, the Reader would think, "Hmm, this kid isn't writing like a robot…now if she can show me she understood the passage and communicate her understanding with anything like the flair of this opening, I'll give her a high score." In other words, yes, your opening can be a little stiff and dull (yes, you can paraphrase the question if you want to) if you write an otherwise good, insightful essay, but an original, interesting opening is better if you can write one without wasting a lot of time.

Essay Do's and Don'ts to Remember

After reviewing some sample essays, you probably have a good sense of what you need to accomplish to achieve a solid score. Some of this may seem basic and verge on the formulaic. Remember that your good ideas do need to be clear and well-organized. The following are tips for reviewing your own practice essays.

Your first paragraph should

- grab the reader (don't worry if you can't do this, but it helps)
- answer the question in the prompt
- preview the evidence you'll use to support your ideas

Your first paragraph should not

- go off on a tangent
- ignore the prompt
- merely restate the wording of the prompt

Your body paragraphs should

- have clear transitions and topic sentences
- provide evidence, in the form of quotations from the text, that supports your opinion
- explain how that evidence supports your point of view

Your body paragraphs should not

- rely on plot summary
- let quotation outweigh analysis
- ramble

Your conclusion should

- exist
- sum up the evidence for the jury
- contain any profound insights about the work that may have occurred to you while writing

Your conclusion should not

- suggest you didn't budget your time
- merely restate the introduction or prompt

REFLECT

Respond to the following questions:

- Which aspects of poetry analysis essays do you feel you have achieved sufficient mastery of to write a high-scoring essay based on a poem?

- Which aspects of poetry essays do you feel you need more work on before you can write a high-scoring essay based on a poem?

- Which aspects of prose fiction essays do you feel you have achieved sufficient mastery of to write a high-scoring essay based on a work of prose fiction?

- Which aspects of prose fiction essays do you feel you need more work on before you can write a high-scoring essay based on a work of prose fiction?

- What parts of this chapter are you going to re-review?

- Will you seek further help, outside of this book (such as from a teacher, tutor, or AP Students), on any of the content in this chapter—and, if so, on what content?

Summary

o   Avoid summary.

o   Get a feel for the passage.

o   Notice imagery.

o   Notice oppositions.

o   Your essay doesn't have to be great, but you do have to show command of the English language. An AP essay that scores a 6 might not even be an "A" paper in English class. Of course not. It's a 40-minute essay on a story or poem you've never seen before.

o   Whenever possible, show your verbal flair.

o   It's okay to establish the foundation of your essay in two or three short opening paragraphs, if necessary.

o   Your first paragraph should be free of error, but nobody writes an error-free paper. That doesn't mean be careless and sloppy. It means write as well as you can and don't worry about mistakes.

o   If the question gives you the opportunity, write about character. The writing in AP passages almost always says something about character. This is especially true in the dialogue of a character, or in a first-person narration.

o   A nice opening is icing on the cake.

o   Make sure you leave yourself enough time to write a complete conclusion.

Chapter 11
Literary Argument

"
Art is a lie that makes us realize truth.

—Pablo Picasso
"

HOW DO YOU PREPARE FOR AN ESSAY ON *ANYTHING*?

The literary argument usually appears as the last of the three essays on the AP Exam. Unlike the prose fiction analysis or poetry analysis essays, the literary argument does not give you a text to work with; you must write an essay on a given theme using support drawn from your own reading.

Most people assume that the literary argument is the most difficult of the three essays but this assumption is false. Even though the average score on the literary argument tends to be a little lower than on the other two essays, a close look at the data suggests that students who attempt the literary argument earn higher scores. Many students skip this essay altogether, so there are more scores of 0 here than on the prose fiction analysis and poetry analysis essays. On the other hand, more students earn scores of 5 and 6 on this essay than on the other two. The scores still tend to bunch up around the middle (the mean), but they spread out more across all the score ranges (a greater standard deviation). All the same, the literary argument is the most dreaded and anticipated portion of the AP Exam. It isn't worth any more than the other questions, but unlike the rest of the test, the literary argument question feels like the one you *have to* study for. At the same time, it's the question that most students feel like they *haven't* studied for, at least not enough.

We've shown you that you can and should study for the rest of the test. We *hope* we've shown you that knowing what you're doing on the Essay section is the way to shoot your scores through the roof. Now, what about the literary argument—how do you prepare for it?

The answer is simple. Use all the techniques we've already described for writing the prose fiction analysis and poetry analysis essays. Use the Idea Machine to direct your thoughts and answer the classic question as you go about answering the specifics of the question. The literary argument is no different from the other essays. There's just one more bit of preparation you need for the literary argument: three well-chosen works of literature that you know backward and forward.

WHAT THE TEST-WRITERS REALLY WANT FROM YOUR LITERARY ARGUMENT

You can, should, and *must* study a literary work for the literary argument. But what if the literary argument question asks for a theme that the work you've prepared doesn't address? Don't worry. The test-writers aren't trying to persecute you (although it does feel that way sometimes). Follow our instructions and you'll be prepared.

What the test-writers would really like to do is say, "Write an essay about any major literary work that you enjoyed. We just want to see how well you can write on a longer work that you've read and studied." Unfortunately, they can't ask you that directly because there would be no way to stop students from writing essays ahead of time (or having their dear Aunt Donna, the Pulitzer Prize–winning novelist, write an essay ahead of time) and memorizing them. The literary argument question is just a way of making sure that the student hasn't prepared the whole essay in advance.

However, the test writers don't want to ask literary argument questions that are too restrictive, either. They won't ask a question that points to just a handful of literary works, for example. They won't ask for an essay about "a character who may or may not be insane and who sees ghosts that may or may not be there." A few hundred students would get sixes by writing about Henry James's *The Turn of the Screw*. A few thousand would struggle to make this question make sense for *Hamlet* or *Macbeth*. The rest would just leave it blank.

The test writers go out of their way to make sure the literary argument question is truly open and provides an opportunity for a student who has read challenging literary works to write a good essay.

Let's look at the types of themes the literary argument question asks about. Remember, you can see real, previously asked essay questions at https://apcentral.collegeboard. org/courses/ap-english-literature-and-composition/exam.

Sample Themes for the Literary Argument

According to The College Board, the literary argument question assesses students' ability to do the following:

- Respond to the prompt with a thesis that presents an interpretation and may establish a line of reasoning.

- Select and use evidence to develop and support the line of reasoning.

- Explain the relationship between the evidence and the thesis.

- Use appropriate grammar and punctuation in communicating the argument.

As you can see, these tasks are things that you have been doing in class throughout the year, and can all be applied to thousands of literary works. At the same time, these tasks must be performed on command and you cannot go ahead and write an essay ahead of time. The key to a great literary argument is having the right work for the theme, and knowing it cold.

So what works should you study?

Preparing for the Literary Argument

To be really ready for the literary argument, you should know at least three works very well. Two of them should be longer works that you've studied in class. We'll call these the *primary* works. The third work is a safeguard in case, for some reason, you can't apply your knowledge of the first works to the question at all, or in case you need to back up your points with another example. You have no idea what specific titles will be listed in that tally of potential works just beneath the Literary Argument question, so it's good to be well-versed in at least three important literary works. That way, you may see one of those three listed and it can be your primary work; then you can also discuss another important piece of literature. Trust us, the question stem may say that you need to choose only one work to discuss, but a Reader will be hugely impressed if you can adeptly discuss two or three pieces of literature. We'll provide you with a list of short *secondary* works that are useful for the AP Exam.

THE PRIMARY WORKS

Have two primary works that you know well. Your primary works should be fairly hefty. One of Shakespeare's plays or a thick, complex novel will do. The full-length works of the following authors are all good choices: Jane Austen, James Joyce, Joseph Conrad, Emily and Charlotte Brontë, Charles Dickens, Nathaniel Hawthorne, Herman Melville, Toni Morrison, Thomas Hardy, George Eliot, Fyodor Dostoyevsky, and Thomas Mann. The object in choosing your primary works is to come up with two novels or plays that are so rich in incident and form that no matter what the literary argument question asks, you have something to say.

Choose Works You Already Know (and Love)

Just Say No... to Nonfiction
Remember: You must choose a work of fiction to write about in your literary argument.

You've already studied some literary works in school. Pick two and go over your notes. Read the books again or at least spend a few hours looking them over thoroughly. Pick your favorite work. If you fell in love with Shakespeare's *Hamlet*, great; use *Hamlet*. If you felt sleepy every time the word Shakespeare was mentioned but thought Dostoyevsky's *Crime and Punishment* might change your life, then that's the work to use.

There are just a couple of exceptions to the favorite-work rule. Do not pick a short story, a work of nonfiction, or a poem. The literary argument questions, as a rule, say, "Choose a play or a novel: Do not choose a poem or short story." There have been very few exceptions to this rule, and the exception is that they'll allow complete epic poems. Now, if your favorite work of literature is really-honestly-no-I-loved-it Milton's *Paradise Lost* or Spenser's *The Faerie Queene*…well, okay, you could prepare those novel-length poems for the literary argument, but you'd still be better off with a novel. Short stories are wonderful reading material, but they are practically useless for the AP Exam; you're just not allowed to use them. They don't want students preparing to write literary arguments on short stories; they think it's too easy.

If you don't have a usable favorite work or are for some reason undecided about what to choose for your primary work, we highly recommend Shakespeare's plays, particularly *Hamlet, A Midsummer Night's Dream, King Lear, Othello,* and *The Tempest.* All of these plays are intricately plotted, contain elements of comedy and tragedy, and are incredibly rich in the kind of material about which literary arguments are written. The object in choosing your primary work is to find a work that can support any number of questions, and Shakespeare's works fit that bill better than any others of comparable length. As tough as Shakespeare's plays can be to read, they are considerably shorter than say, *Crime and Punishment* or *David Copperfield.* If you decide to go with Shakespeare, you could easily prepare to write about two plays in the time it takes to prepare to write about a longer novel. Just remember, we said we recommend Shakespeare. If you already know the work of another writer better, by all means prepare something else. But remember that we strongly recommend using a book you've already studied in class.

You'll be happy to know that in the past few years many contemporary books have appeared on the list of accepted sources for the literary argument. *The Kite Runner* by Khaled Hosseini, *Life of Pi* by Yann Martel, and *The Bonesetter's Daughter* by Amy Tan are a few contemporary works that fall outside of the traditional primary works list but might be strong choices as one of your primary works.

Suggestions for Primary Works

Here are some other books we think make for good primary works. This list is not even close to complete, but it's a start. If you happen to know and love another long work inside and out, that's fine.

Emma by Jane Austen

Jane Eyre by Charlotte Brontë

Wuthering Heights by Emily Brontë

Don Quixote by Miguel Cervantes

White Noise by Don DeLillo

Bleak House by Charles Dickens

David Copperfield by Charles Dickens

Great Expectations by Charles Dickens

A Tale of Two Cities by Charles Dickens

Crime and Punishment by Fyodor Dostoyevsky

Invisible Man by Ralph Ellison

The Sound and the Fury by William Faulkner

Tess of the D'Urbervilles by Thomas Hardy

The Scarlet Letter by Nathaniel Hawthorne

The Kite Runner by Khaled Hosseini

Their Eyes Were Watching God by Zora Neale Hurston

A Portrait of the Artist as a Young Man by James Joyce

Sons and Lovers by D. H. Lawrence

The Magic Mountain by Thomas Mann

One Hundred Years of Solitude by Gabriel García Márquez

Moby Dick by Herman Melville

Frankenstein by Mary Shelley

The Catcher in the Rye by J. D. Salinger

The Grapes of Wrath by John Steinbeck

Of Mice and Men by John Steinbeck

The Bonesetter's Daughter by Amy Tan

Anna Karenina by Leo Tolstoy

The Adventures of Huckleberry Finn by Mark Twain

Black Boy by Richard Wright

THE SECONDARY WORK

The secondary work is your just-in-case work and perhaps a bit more. The question just may not fit any aspect of your primary works. This is highly unlikely, but if this happens, you need to have something prepared. You don't want to be stuck trying to remember some book you haven't looked at since ninth grade. The other reason to prepare a secondary work is simply to have more options. If the question fits your secondary work perfectly, you'll want to use it. Prepare your secondary work well and in effect, you have three primary works. With well-chosen and well-prepared primary and secondary works, you would have to be extremely unlucky to find yourself faced with a literary argument question that did not fit any of the works.

Choose Something Different from Your Primary Works

Ideally, you want your secondary work to be as different as possible from your primary works. If you pick *Hamlet* as one of your primary works, you don't want to pick another Shakespearean tragedy starring a messed-up, confused, violent hero. In other words, don't pick *Macbeth*. You'd be much better off picking a comedy such as *A Midsummer Night's Dream*. Even better would be to pick a 20th-century comic novel like *Catch-22* by Joseph Heller or *A Confederacy of Dunces* by John Kennedy Toole. If you pick an extremely male-oriented work for one of your primary works, say *Invisible Man*, then Kate Chopin's *The Awakening* makes an excellent choice for a secondary work, as would Henry James's *The Turn of the Screw*, both of which feature female main characters.

Suggestions for Secondary Works

We've put together a list of secondary work books. These are all short novels, novellas, and plays that are acceptable to the AP Readers. Some works are not acceptable. Writing about *Family Guy*, episode 56, will result in a low score, as will writing about a Danielle Steele or Stephen King novel. Don't push it. You may think William Gibson's *Neuromancer* is a great book, but the AP committee probably won't be impressed and they'll lower your score.

The books on the following list were chosen according to the following guidelines: they're all recognized classics of which the AP Readers will highly approve. They're all short. Most important, they're all works that have been perfect fits with many literary argument questions.

We strongly recommend studying at least one of the works listed here. If you've read one of these works in class (and there's a good chance you have), by all means look it over again and prepare it for the AP Exam. An asterisk (*) means that the work is most highly recommended reading for the exam. Pick one of these and you won't go wrong.

Finally, if you really don't feel comfortable with any of the longer works that you've studied in class, are thinking of taking the AP Exam without having taken an AP course, or, well, slacked off in class—don't try to prepare a longer work for the AP Exam. Go straight to the list below and knock off two or three or four titles (remember, these are short works). You'll be prepared.

Novellas and Short Novels:

The Stranger by Albert Camus

The Awakening by Kate Chopin*

Heart of Darkness by Joseph Conrad*

Notes from the Underground by Fyodor Dostoyevsky

The Old Man and the Sea by Ernest Hemingway

The Turn of the Screw by Henry James*

Death in Venice by Thomas Mann

Ballad of the Sad Café by Carson McCullers

Billy Budd by Herman Melville

A Sentimental Journey by Lawrence Sterne

The Death of Ivan Ilyich by Leo Tolstoy

Candide by Voltaire

Plays:

Who's Afraid of Virginia Woolf? by Edward Albee

Waiting for Godot by Samuel Beckett

A Man for All Seasons by Robert Bolt

The Cherry Orchard by Anton Chekhov

The Seagull by Anton Chekhov

Uncle Vanya by Anton Chekhov

Medea by Euripides*

A Doll's House by Henrik Ibsen*

Hedda Gabler by Henrik Ibsen*

The Crucible by Arthur Miller

Death of a Salesman by Arthur Miller

Emperor Jones by Eugene O'Neill

Hughie by Eugene O'Neill

Long Day's Journey Into Night by Eugene O'Neill

Antigone by Sophocles*

Oedipus Rex by Sophocles*

A Streetcar Named Desire by Tennessee Williams

The Glass Menagerie by Tennessee Williams

What Does "Prepare the Work" Mean?

We keep telling you to *prepare* your primary and secondary works. What does this mean? Two things:

1. Study the work as thoroughly as you can.
2. Write a first paragraph based on the classic question for each work you prepare.

Studying Your Primary and Secondary Works

Study the works you've chosen. Take notes. Record impressions. Map out different themes and examples of these themes within the work. Imagine important scenes as movies in your head. If you're reading this book early in the school year or in the summer before your AP English Lit course begins, you should consider prepping every work you read for class. This strategy will not only give you a broad array of works to select from on test day, but will also improve your study habits. If you have a few months or a few weeks to prepare, then selecting two or three works you have studied will put you in a good place. If it's the week before the test, looking over the books to remind yourself of the plot lines and the names of the main characters might forestall those moments you lose when you're racking your brain, thinking, "Gatsby's girlfriend's name...Rose...Iris...Violet?"

How should you prepare the works?

- **Reread** your primary and secondary works within four weeks of the test. You want to have each one fresh in your mind.
- **Work from critical editions.** The books you should prepare for the AP Exam are the kinds of works that have been studied and restudied over the years. Although you can easily find your chosen texts in small, inexpensive reading editions, you should look for them in larger, critical editions that contain full introductions, notes, annotations, and sometimes appendices containing background material, biographical information, and samplings of past critical commentary. Whenever possible, use these fuller editions. Read as much of the supplementary material as you can stand. If you can put the work in a cultural context and discuss the political or sociological happenings of the time, the Reader's socks will undoubtedly be knocked off. No AP Reader is going to downgrade your essay because the points you make about the novel seem influenced by the opinions of other authors and critics. On the contrary, they'll think you're a genius. One student in a hundred actually bothers to read literary criticism about the book he or she has prepared, but that's about the percentage of students who score a 6 on the literary argument. Coincidence?
- **Write your own study guide.** As much as some teachers might disparage store-bought or online study guides, they can be an invaluable supplement to your own study. (Note that we said "supplement." You still need to read the books.) Even better than a store-bought study guide, however, is one you've written yourself. You'll accomplish a lot of your review just by writing it. Moreover, once you're done, you'll have a study guide that highlights the aspects of a work you find most interesting—and those are the things you're most likely to write about on the exam.

Your custom study guide should be no longer than one page and should contain the following:

12 Is Key
The College Board suggests that AP English Lit teachers have their students read at least 12 works closely in class.

- **Plot**—You want to avoid plot summary in your literary argument, but it's still important to remember what happens—and *why*. Chapter by chapter or scene by scene, note what happens but focus on the major conflicts of the book. The details help you remember the specific chronology of the narrative; thinking about the larger conflicts puts the story into perspective.

- **Character**—Who's who? This list could be as simple as remembering how they spell their names or it can be as detailed as you want.

- **Themes**—What's the message or moral of the story? Avoid oversimplification.

- **Symbols**—Scarlet letters, green lights, white whales: what do they stand for and how do they help the author achieve his or her purpose?

- **Quotations**—"If you have tears, prepare to shed them now." (That's from *Julius Caesar*, in case you were wondering.) In the literary argument, it's important to provide support for your assertions, and even more important to avoid plot summary. Quoting your chosen work and explaining how the quote relates to the prompt demonstrates to the reader that you know and understand the work. Memorizing the quotes—and understanding what each means—allows you to write with more confidence.

A sample page of your self-made study guide might look like this:

The Seagull by Anton Chekhov

Act I—Lots of complaining (Masha's in mourning for her life, Treplev's mother Arkadina doesn't love him) as preparations are made for Treplev's play, starring Nina. The chain of unrequited lovers is introduced. Treplev loves Nina, Nina has a crush on Trigorin, Arkadina's acknowledged lover. Masha's mother Polina has the hots for Dorn, the local doctor. The play is experimental and a flop. Arkadina laughs at it, and Treplev's feelings are hurt. Trigorin takes an interest in Nina. Masha confesses to Dorn that she loves Treplev.

Act II—Midsummer squabbles on the estate—can Arkadina take the horses out or not. Nina thinks the great actress's demands are the most important thing. Treplev shoots a seagull and lays it at Nina's feet, threatening that one day he will do the same to himself. Nina dismisses his concerns, and Trigorin promptly begins seducing her. The dead seagull inspires Trigorin—a young girl lives by the lake like a seagull, but one day a man comes along and, for lack of anything better to do, destroys her.

Act III—Three big scenes: Masha tells Trigorin she's going to destroy her love for Treplev by marrying Medvedenko, the schoolmaster who pines for her. Arkadina changes Treplev's bandages (he's attempted suicide offstage between the acts). Arkadina fights with Trigorin, who wants to stay behind and complete his seduction of Nina, but Arkadina wants him out of there. As they're leaving together, Trigorin goes back for his walking stick. Nina goes to him; she's run away from home and heading to Moscow to become an actress. Trigorin gives her his address and asks her to come to him.

Act IV—Two years later. Masha has married Medvedenko, but she's still in love with Treplev and miserable. She's hoping Medvedenko's transfer will tear the love from her heart. Treplev brings Dorn up to date on Nina. She had a child by Trigorin, who managed to stay with Arkadina the whole time, and has returned to her. Meanwhile, Nina's acting career has been a disaster. Trigorin and Arkadina arrive. Trigorin is kind to Treplev's face, but behind his back, disparages his writing. After a quick game of lotto, the party relinquishes the study to Treplev. He struggles with his writing, then is surprised by Nina. He's been trying to see her. They reminisce about old times, and Nina compares herself to a seagull. She leaves as abruptly as she arrived. Treplev tears up his manuscripts and exits, just as Shamreyev shows Trigorin the stuffed seagull. A shot is heard offstage. Treplev has shot himself.

Characters

ARKADINA, an actress. 42 years old. Petty, vain, involved with writer Trigorin.
KONSTANTIN TREPLEV, Arkadina's son, an aspiring writer.
SORIN, Arkadina's brother and the owner of the estate where the play is set.
NINA, a young local girl and aspiring actress. Romantically involved with Treplev at the outset, later falls in love with Trigorin.
SHAMRAYEV, Sorin's estate manager.
POLINA, Shamrayev's wife. In love with Dorn.
MASHA, Shamrayev's daughter. In love with Treplev, but will marry Medvedenko.
TRIGORIN, a writer. Spineless.
DORN, a doctor.
MEDVEDENKO, a schoolteacher. Obsessed with money.

Themes

Unrequited love and lots of it. Idealistic youth spoiled by the corruption of the real world. Struggle to create new art forms (Chekhov creating a new kind of drama in this play).

Symbols

The seagull: symbolic of youth. Trigorin sees it as emblematic of Nina and her innocence, which he will proceed to spoil. Treplev, who has shot a seagull, thinks it represents himself, and he shoots himself at the end of Act IV, just as he threatened when he laid the seagull at Nina's feet in Act II. Nina is a little confused about whether she's the seagull or not, as we see in her Act IV monologue.

Quotations

"I'm in mourning for my life; I'm depressed."—Masha, Act I. Opening lines of play, sets tone for what is to follow.

"I am a seagull; no, that's not it; I am an actress."—Nina, Act IV.

This study guide isn't perfect—it isn't very thorough—but it forces you to think about how the work is structured and how the author achieves his effects. While prepping this, you might note that each act begins with Masha, a minor character. In looking at criticism about the play, you might note that it was a failure when originally produced, possibly because Chekhov's effects are so subtle. Finally, after prepping the work in this way, you'll be certain about the names of the characters and what happens when, which will allow you to write with more clarity.

Prepare for the Literary Argument Ahead of Time

In addition to prepping the works, you should also write the first paragraph of a literary argument a couple of nights before the test. (Remember to use the Idea Machine: What does the work mean? What are the emotional contents of the work?) Writing the first paragraph shouldn't take you longer than 30 minutes, and when you consider how much time and stress it will save you on test day, surely you can see why it's a winning strategy.

While it's true that you have no idea what aspect of the work the prompt will ask you to address, we've supplied you with plenty of sample prompts with which to practice. Once you've seen a few, you'll be familiar with the kind of questions that appear on the exam and should see how altering one or two sentences in your sample introduction will probably save the day. And, even if you do end up writing an entirely new introduction on test day, you'll write with more confidence and skill if you've had some recent practice.

RECENT CHANGES

The literary argument prompt is a little intimidating, but since you've been studying all year for this test, you should have a pretty solid knowledge base regarding various themes in literature. Over the last few decades, this prompt has taken on various forms and it was recently changed by The College Board from the "open prompt" to the "literary argument" prompt. Despite the name change, this prompt remains quite open, so you'll want to be sure that you have read an assortment of books, you have explored the themes, symbolism, and meanings of said books, and you can express your thoughts well. Because we can't see the test in advance, it's impossible to know just how simple or complex the prompt will be; therefore, it might help to consider some previous prompts so that you can prepare yourself with an arsenal of knowledge that will help you to answer appropriately and quickly.

The College Board released a new Course Description for AP English Literature and Composition and they mapped out lots of specifics, thankfully. Here is a sample question that they share:

> Many works of literature feature characters who have been given a literal or figurative gift. The gift may be an object, or it may be a quality such as uncommon beauty, significant social position, great mental or imaginative faculties, or extraordinary physical powers. Yet this gift is often also a burden or a handicap.
>
> Either from your own reading or from the list below, choose a work of fiction in which a character has been given a gift that is both an advantage and a problem. Then, in a well-written essay, analyze how the gift and its complex nature contribute to an interpretation of the work as a whole. Do not merely summarize the plot.

In addition, the College Board has shared the wording that you will see in the Literary Argument question. The text in italics will vary by question, while the remainder of the prompt will be consistently used in all Literary Argument essay questions.

> *[Lead that introduces some concept or idea that students will be asked to apply to a text of their choosing.]*
>
> Either from your own reading or from the list below, choose a work of fiction in which *[some aspect of the lead is addressed]*. Then, in a well-written essay, analyze how *[that same aspect of the lead]* contributes to an interpretation of the work as a whole. Do not merely summarize the plot.

REFLECT

Respond to the following questions:

- Which AP essay-writing strategies discussed in this chapter do you feel you have achieved sufficient mastery of to write a high-scoring literary argument?

- Which AP essay-writing strategies discussed in this chapter do you feel you need more work on before you can write a high-scoring literary argument?

- What parts of this chapter are you going to re-review?

- Will you seek further help, outside of this book (such as from a teacher, tutor, or AP Students), on any of the content in this chapter—and, if so, on what content?

Summary

- When writing the literary argument, use all the techniques we've described for writing the prose fiction analysis and poetry analysis essays.

- Don't worry about having to face an open question that doesn't apply to the works you've prepared. The test writers try to make the literary argument question broad enough so that you won't be lost—as long as you have *something* prepared.

- Prepare two primary works and a secondary work.

- If you've studied Shakespeare's work in class (and enjoyed it), we strongly recommend using a Shakespeare play as one of your primary works. His plays are chock-full of the material that literary arguments call for.

- Choose a work that you've already studied in class.

- Our list of secondary works suggests novellas and plays that have proven useful on many AP literary arguments in the past.

- Your secondary work should be as different as possible from your primary works. For example, if one of your primary works is a Shakespearean tragedy, pick a modern comic novella for your secondary work.

- If possible, reread your primary and secondary works within four weeks of the test. Otherwise, at least skim the book and look over any class notes you have. Use critical editions if you can find them.

- Write a sample first paragraph of the literary argument ahead of time. It's great practice for the real thing.

Part VI
Additional Practice Tests

Practice Test 2

The Exam

AP® English Literature and Composition Exam

SECTION I: Multiple-Choice Questions

DO NOT OPEN THIS BOOKLET UNTIL YOU ARE TOLD TO DO SO.

At a Glance

Total Time
1 hour
Number of Questions
55
Percent of Total Grade
45%
Writing Instrument
Pencil required

Instructions

Section I of this examination contains 55 multiple-choice questions. Fill in only the ovals for numbers 1 through 55 on your answer sheet.

Indicate all of your answers to the multiple-choice questions on the answer sheet. No credit will be given for anything written in this exam booklet, but you may use the booklet for notes or scratch work. After you have decided which of the suggested answers is best, completely fill in the corresponding oval on the answer sheet. Give only one answer to each question. If you change an answer, be sure that the previous mark is erased completely. Here is a sample question and answer.

Sample Question   Sample Answer

Chicago is a
(A) state
(B) city
(C) country
(D) continent
(E) village

Use your time effectively, working as quickly as you can without losing accuracy. Do not spend too much time on any one question. Go on to other questions and come back to the ones you have not answered if you have time. It is not expected that everyone will know the answers to all the multiple-choice questions.

About Guessing

Many candidates wonder whether or not to guess the answers to questions about which they are not certain. Multiple-choice scores are based on the number of questions answered correctly. Points are not deducted for incorrect answers, and no points are awarded for unanswered questions. Because points are not deducted for incorrect answers, you are encouraged to answer all multiple-choice questions. On any questions you do not know the answer to, you should eliminate as many choices as you can, and then select the best answer among the remaining choices.

GO ON TO THE NEXT PAGE.

ENGLISH LITERATURE AND COMPOSITION

SECTION I

Time—1 hour

<u>Directions:</u> This section consists of selections from literary works and questions on their content, form, and style. After reading each passage or poem, choose the best answer to each question and then completely fill in the corresponding oval on the answer sheet.

Questions 1–11. Choose your answers to questions 1–11 based on a careful reading of the following passage. The passage, an excerpt from a novel by Charlotte Brontë, discusses curates, members of the clergy in charge of a parish, in the nineteenth century.

Of late years an abundant shower of curates has fallen upon the north of England: they lie very thick on the hills; every parish has one or more of them; they are young enough
Line to be very active, and ought to be doing a great deal of good.
(5) But not of late years are we about to speak; we are going back to the beginning of this century: late years— present years are dusty, sunburnt, hot, arid; we will evade the noon, forget it in siesta, pass the midday in slumber, and dream of dawn.
(10) If you think, from this prelude, that anything like a romance is preparing for you, reader, you never were more mistaken. Do you anticipate sentiment, and poetry, and reverie? Do you expect passion, and stimulus, and melodrama? Calm your expectations; reduce them to a lowly
(15) standard. Something real, cool, and solid lies before you; something unromantic as Monday morning, when all who have work wake with the consciousness that they must rise and betake themselves thereto. It is not positively affirmed that you shall not have a taste of the exciting, perhaps
(20) towards the middle and close of the meal, but it is resolved that the first dish set upon the table shall be one that a Catholic— ay, even an Anglo-Catholic— might eat on Good Friday in Passion Week: it shall be cold lentils and vinegar without oil; it shall be unleavened bread with bitter herbs,
(25) and no roast lamb.
Of late years, I say, an abundant shower of curates has fallen upon the north of England; but in eighteen-hundred-eleven-twelve that affluent rain had not descended.
….
(30) The present successors of the apostles, disciples of Dr. Pusey and tools of the Propaganda, were at that time being hatched under cradle-blankets, or undergoing regeneration by nursery-baptism in wash-hand basins. You could not have guessed by looking at any one of them that the Italian-
(35) ironed double frills of its net-cap surrounded the brows of a preordained, specially-sanctified successor of St. Paul, St. Peter, or St. John; nor could you have foreseen in the folds of its long night-gown the white surplice in which it was hereafter cruelly to exercise the souls of its parishioners, and
(40) strangely to nonplus its old-fashioned vicar by flourishing aloft in a pulpit the shirt-like raiment which had never before waved higher than the reading-desk.

Yet even in those days of scarcity there were curates: the precious plant was rare, but it might be found. A certain
(45) favoured district in the West Riding of Yorkshire could boast three rods of Aaron blossoming within a circuit of twenty miles. You shall see them, reader. Step into this neat garden-house on the skirts of Whinbury, walk forward into the little parlour. There they are at dinner. Allow me to introduce them
(50) to you: Mr. Donne, curate of Whinbury; Mr. Malone, curate of Briarfield; Mr. Sweeting, curate of Nunnely. These are Mr. Donne's lodgings, being the habitation of one John Gale, a small clothier.

Mr. Donne has kindly invited his brethren to regale with
(55) him. You and I will join the party, see what is to be seen, and hear what is to be heard. At present, however, they are only eating; and while they eat we will talk aside.

These gentlemen are in the bloom of youth; they possess all the activity of that interesting age— an activity which
(60) their moping old vicars would fain turn into the channel of their pastoral duties, often expressing a wish to see it expended in a diligent superintendence of the schools, and in frequent visits to the sick of their respective parishes. But the youthful Levites feel this to be dull work; they prefer
(65) lavishing their energies on a course of proceeding which, though to other eyes it appear more heavy with *ennui*, more cursed with monotony, than the toil of the weaver at his loom, seems to yield them an unfailing supply of enjoyment and occupation.
(70) I allude to a rushing backwards and forwards, amongst themselves, to and from their respective lodgings— not a round, but a triangle of visits.

—Published 1849.

GO ON TO THE NEXT PAGE.

1. "An abundant shower of curates" (line 1) is an example of

   (A) satire
   (B) metaphor
   (C) oxymoron
   (D) irony
   (E) paradox

2. The lines 6–9, "present years are dusty, sunburnt, hot, arid; we will evade the noon, forget it in siesta, pass the midday in slumber, and dream of dawn," most likely serve all of the following purposes EXCEPT

   (A) disengaging the reader from the present that opens the passage
   (B) exerting a hypnotic spell on the reader via parallelism
   (C) equating novel reading with sleep and dreaming
   (D) exercising authorial control
   (E) characterizing the past as arid and dusty

3. The tone of the description of the curates in paragraphs 1 and 2 is

   (A) realistic
   (B) admiring
   (C) surprised
   (D) arch
   (E) fearful

4. Which best describes the difference in the way the reader is addressed in paragraph 1 versus paragraph 4?

   (A) The reader is told the type of tale versus confidingly brought into a specific scene
   (B) The reader is promised an exotic romance versus given a prosaic scene
   (C) The reader is subtly placed on the side of the curates versus invited to laugh at them
   (D) The narrator is straightforward at first and ironic later
   (E) The narrator is trying to win the reader to her point of view versus distancing the reader from it

5. What does "lowly" in line 14 most nearly mean in context?

   (A) Mean
   (B) Poor
   (C) Prosaic
   (D) Meek
   (E) Humble

6. Which of the following best conveys the effect of the references to curates in lines 30–37, "successors of the apostles," "disciples of Dr. Pusey and tools of the Propaganda," "specially sanctified successor of St. Paul, St. Peter, or St. John" in the context of paragraph 4?

   (A) They reinforce the earlier reference to Passion Week and Easter.
   (B) The tone is admiring of the effort to keep religious beliefs alive in the current day.
   (C) The phrases use parallelism and alliteration to convey the progression of religious life through history.
   (D) The exalted comparisons mock curates in the current day.
   (E) The curates are ennobled by comparison with religious figures.

7. Which of the following statements best conveys the effect of lines 37–42 ("nor could you have foreseen…the reading-desk")?

   (A) The imagery links "gowns" worn by christened babies and the "surplices" of curates
   (B) The imagery expresses the cruelty of young curates
   (C) The exaggerated diction makes religious life seem silly
   (D) The ironic diction makes religious life seem cruel
   (E) The allusions indicate that aristocrats no longer attend church

GO ON TO THE NEXT PAGE.

8. The narrator's perspective in this passage is

   (A) disinterested journalist
   (B) diffident investigator
   (C) ironic chronicler
   (D) sentimental storyteller
   (E) nonplussed resident

9. The settings toward the end of the passage are described as a "neat garden-house" (47–48) a "little parlour" (48–49), and the "habitation of … a small clothier" (52–53). What do these settings primarily convey?

   (A) The middle-class, bourgeois existence of the curates
   (B) A diminishment from the religious predecessors of the curates
   (C) The stifling and confining propriety the curates must abide by
   (D) The historical conditions of nineteenth-century England
   (E) A realistic portrayal of the north of England

10. The word "affluent" in line 28 most nearly means

    (A) abundant
    (B) wealthy
    (C) liquid
    (D) streaming
    (E) opulent

11. What do the last two paragraphs indicate about the characters of the curates Mr. Donne, Mr. Malone, and Mr. Sweeting?

    (A) They are virtually indistinguishable from each other.
    (B) They are exuberant and boisterous.
    (C) They are devoted to their duties.
    (D) They are dull and monotonous.
    (E) They are sociable with each other.

GO ON TO THE NEXT PAGE.

Questions 12–23. Read the poem below, "Planetarium" by Adrienne Rich, then choose answers to the questions that follow.

Planetarium

Thinking of Caroline Herschel (1750–1848)
astronomer, sister of William; and others.

A woman in the shape of a monster
a monster in the shape of a woman
the skies are full of them

Line a woman   'in the snow
 (5)   among the Clocks and instruments
       or measuring the ground with poles'

       in her 98 years to discover
       8 comets

       she whom the moon ruled
(10)   like us
       levitating into the night sky
       riding the polished lenses

       Galaxies of women, there
       doing penance for impetuousness
(15)   ribs chilled
       in those spaces   of the mind

       An eye,

              'virile, precise and absolutely certain'
              from the mad webs of Uranusborg

(20)   encountering the
       NOVA

       every impulse of light exploding

       from the core
       as life flies out of us

(25)   Tycho whispering at last
           'Let me not seem to have lived in vain'

       What we see, we see
       and seeing is changing

       the light that shrivels a mountain
(30)   and leaves a man alive

       Heartbeat of the pulsar
       heart sweating through my body

The radio impulse
pouring in from Taurus

(35)   I am bombarded yet   I stand

I have been standing all my life in the
direct path of a battery of signals
the most accurately transmitted most
untranslatable language in the universe
(40) I am a galactic cloud so deep   so invo-
luted that a light wave could take 15
years to travel through me   And has
taken   I am an instrument in the shape
of a woman trying to translate pulsations
(45) into images   for the relief of the body
and the reconstruction of the mind.

12. What does the reverse parallelism of lines 1–2, "a woman in the shape of a monster/ a monster in the shape of a woman" most nearly convey?

(A) That monsters and accomplished women like Caroline Herschel are viewed as similar
(B) That explosions in astronomy can be monstrous
(C) That women who go outside traditional occupations are monsters
(D) That women in science were at one time viewed as monstrous
(E) That only monsters can make scientific discoveries

13. What does "the skies are full of them" in line 3 convey in the context of the poem?

(A) There are many more women in science waiting to be discovered.
(B) There are many monstrous women.
(C) The skies are full of witches.
(D) The skies are full of stars.
(E) We need telescopes to see history clearly.

14. In line 13, "Galaxies of women, there", the word "there" most nearly seems to be everywhere EXCEPT

(A) the night sky
(B) a planetarium
(C) the cosmos
(D) Taurus
(E) the moon

GO ON TO THE NEXT PAGE.

15. The speaker likely says women are "doing penance" to highlight

    (A) the risks of scientific knowledge
    (B) the penalties for violating social constraints
    (C) women's traditional association with the home
    (D) the analogies between religious vocation and astronomy
    (E) the moral purpose of scientific knowledge

16. What metaphor is conveyed in the poem in lines 9–12, "she whom the moon ruled/ like us/ levitating into the night sky/ riding the polished lenses"?

    (A) That women are witches
    (B) That scientists are witches
    (C) That witches violate male power
    (D) That scientists court death and destruction
    (E) That geniuses appear and reappear like comets

17. What poetic device is used in lines 45-46 ("for the relief…and mind")?

    (A) Cacophony
    (B) Enjambment
    (C) Hyperbole
    (D) Alliteration
    (E) Paradox

18. The narrative "I" in the poem can best be described as

    (A) sorrowful that women astronomers were not appreciated at one time
    (B) angry that a women astronomer was not appreciated in her lifetime
    (C) eager to finish the analysis of the universe that Caroline Herschel started
    (D) pensive about the nature of the universe and the sweep of history
    (E) receptive to knowledge about the universe and hoping to contribute

19. The overall tone of the poem is

    (A) anguished and militant
    (B) peaceful and restrained
    (C) satiric and demonic
    (D) searching and analytical
    (E) ironic and distanced

20. The first 10 stanzas are best understood as

    (A) a tribute to Caroline Herschel and women like her
    (B) a plea to appreciate early women in science
    (C) a comparison of Caroline Herschel with Tycho Brahe
    (D) a paean to the vision required to discover comets
    (E) a discussion of women's contributions to science

21. What does the unusual space in line 16, "in those spaces of the mind," convey in the context of the poem?

    (A) Poems open new spaces in the mind.
    (B) The poem is like a galaxy, with open spaces.
    (C) The poem is like the universe, with shifting spaces.
    (D) It represents a pause for reading the poem aloud.
    (E) The women in the night sky are expanding their minds.

22. Lines 43–45, "I am an instrument in the shape/ of a woman trying to translate pulsations/ into images" most clearly mirror the sense of which earlier line in the poem?

    (A) 6, "poles"
    (B) 5, "instruments"
    (C) 12, "lenses"
    (D) 19, "Uranusborg"
    (E) 17, "eye"

23. One of the effects of the last stanza's shift in focus is to

    (A) extoll the speaker's making of images
    (B) lament that scientific data is more valued than images
    (C) imply that people can be instruments for understanding the universe
    (D) express fear about pulsations' effect on people
    (E) imply that pulsations can cause a psychological breakdown

GO ON TO THE NEXT PAGE.

Questions 24–34. Choose answers to questions 24–34 based on a careful reading of the passage below. The selection is an excerpt from the novel *Quicksand* by Nella Larsen.

Helga Crane sat alone in her room, which at that hour, eight in the evening, was in soft gloom. Only a single reading lamp, dimmed by a great black and red shade, made a pool
Line of light on the blue Chinese carpet, on the bright covers of
(5) the books which she had taken down from their long shelves, on the white pages of the opened one selected, on the shining brass bowl crowded with many-colored nasturtiums beside her on the low table, and on the oriental silk which covered the stool at her slim feet. It was a comfortable room,
(10) furnished with rare and intensely personal taste, flooded with Southern sun in the day, but shadowy just then with the drawn curtains and single shaded light. Large, too. So large that the spot where Helga sat was a small oasis in a desert of darkness. And eerily quiet. But that was what she liked after
(15) her taxing day's work, after the hard classes, in which she gave willingly and unsparingly of herself with no apparent return. She loved this tranquility, this quiet, following the fret and strain of the long hours spent among fellow members of a carelessly unkind and gossiping faculty, following
(20) the strenuous rigidity of conduct required in this huge educational community of which she was an insignificant part. This was her rest, this intentional isolation for a short while in the evening, this little time in her own attractive room with her own books. To the rapping of other teachers,
(25) bearing fresh scandals, or seeking information, or other more concrete favors, or merely talk, at that hour Helga Crane never opened her door.

An observer would have thought her well fitted to that framing of light and shade. A slight girl of twenty-two
(30) years, with narrow, sloping shoulders and delicate but well-turned arms and legs, she had, none the less, an air of radiant, careless health. In vivid green and gold negligee and glistening brocaded mules, deep sunk in the big high-backed chair, against whose dark tapestry her sharply cut face, with
(35) skin like yellow satin, was distinctly outlined, she was—to use a hackneyed word—attractive. Black, very broad brows over soft yet penetrating dark eyes, and a pretty mouth, whose sensitive and sensuous lips had a slight questioning petulance and a tiny dissatisfied droop, were the features on
(40) which the observer's attention would fasten; though her nose was good, her ears delicately chiseled, and her curly blue-black hair plentiful and always straying in a little wayward, delightful way. Just then it was tumbled, falling unrestrained about her face and on to her shoulders.

(45) Helga Crane tried not to think of her work and the school as she sat there. Ever since her arrival in Naxos she had striven to keep these ends of the days from the intrusion of irritating thoughts and worries. Usually she was successful. But not this evening.
(50) ....

She was a failure here. She had, she conceded now, been silly, obstinate, to persist for so long. A failure. Therefore, no need, no use, to stay longer. Suddenly she longed for immediate departure. How good, she thought, to go now,
(55) tonight!—and frowned to remember how impossible that would be. "The dignitaries," she said, "are not in their offices, and there will be yards and yards of red tape to unwind, gigantic, impressive spools of it."

And there was James Vayle to be told, and much-needed
(60) money to be got. James, she decided, had better be told at once. She looked at the clock racing indifferently on. No, too late. It would have to be tomorrow.
....

To relinquish James Vayle would most certainly be social
(65) suicide, for the Vayles were people of consequence. The fact that they were a "first family" had been one of James's attractions for the obscure Helga. She had wanted social background, but—she had not imagined that it could be so stuffy.

(70) She made a quick movement of impatience and stood up. As she did so, the room whirled about her in an impish, hateful way. Familiar objects seemed suddenly unhappily distant. Faintness closed about her like a vise. She swayed, her small, slender hands gripping the chair arms for support.
(75) In a moment the faintness receded, leaving in its wake a sharp resentment at the trick which her strained nerves had played upon her. And after a moment's rest she got hurriedly into bed, leaving her room disorderly for the first time.

Books and papers scattered about the floor, fragile
(80) stockings and underthings and the startling green and gold negligee dripping about on chairs and stool, met the encounter of the amazed eyes of the girl who came in the morning to awaken Helga Crane.

GO ON TO THE NEXT PAGE.

24. The tone of the beginning of the passage implies that Helga Crane is

    (A) reflective
    (B) sad
    (C) lonely
    (D) constricted
    (E) romantic

25. In lines 13–14, the words "the spot where Helga sat was a small oasis in a desert of darkness" is an example of what type of figurative language?

    (A) Synecdoche
    (B) Apostrophe
    (C) Metaphor
    (D) Simile
    (E) Personification

26. The narrator views Helga Crane as

    (A) confused and unhappy
    (B) isolated and temperamental
    (C) snobbish and arrogant
    (D) attractive and intelligent
    (E) depressed and dissatisfied

27. In line 16, the word "unsparingly" most nearly means

    (A) ruthlessly
    (B) generously
    (C) unmercifully
    (D) indecisively
    (E) uncharitably

28. In relation to the first paragraph (lines 1–27), the fourth paragraph (lines 51–58) represents a shift from

    (A) realism to parody
    (B) historical fiction to personal narrative
    (C) an omniscient narrator's perspective to a character's thoughts
    (D) an omniscient narrator to stream of consciousness
    (E) a specific setting to a more general setting

29. In lines 71–72, the phase "the room whirled about her in an impish, hateful way" uses which of the following to convey a sense of the room?

    (A) Metaphor
    (B) Metonym
    (C) Onomatopoeia
    (D) Hyperbole
    (E) Personification

30. The primary purpose of the passage is to

    (A) establish the personality of Helga Crane
    (B) examine the relationship of Helga Crane and James Vayle
    (C) describe the social life of an educational institution
    (D) describe the setting Helga Crane is leaving
    (E) present a pivotal moment for Helga Crane

31. What does "yards and yards of red tape to unwind, gigantic, impressive spools of it" (lines 57–58) refer to?

    (A) The bureaucratic offices of Naxos
    (B) Evidence that the institution is impressive
    (C) Breaking off her relationship to James Vayle
    (D) The process of resigning from her work
    (E) Leaving the teaching profession

32. What is conveyed by the narrator saying that the clock was "racing indifferently on" (line 61)?

    (A) Helga Crane feels that time has gotten away from her.
    (B) The outside world is indifferent to Helga Crane's decision.
    (C) It doesn't matter when Helga Crane gives notice of her departure.
    (D) Helga Crane feels out of sync with time at Naxos.
    (E) Helga Crane feels the world disapproves of her decision.

33. The style of the passage as a whole can best be described as

    (A) subjective and judgmental
    (B) analytic and precise
    (C) descriptive and figurative
    (D) ironic and distanced
    (E) satiric and harsh

34. In line 81, the negligee "dripping about on chairs and stool" conveys all of the following EXCEPT

    (A) it's falling from the chairs and stools
    (B) Helga Crane has washed it
    (C) it's made from a fluid material
    (D) it's been thrown at the furniture
    (E) it's between several different places, like Helga Crane

GO ON TO THE NEXT PAGE.

Questions 35–45. Choose your answers to questions 35–45 based on a careful reading of the following passage. The selection is an excerpt from the poem *Paterson* by William Carlos Williams.

Paterson lies in the valley under
the Passaic Falls
its spent waters forming the out-
Line line of his back. He
(5) lies on his right side, head near the
thunder
of the waters filling his dreams!
Eternally asleep,
his dreams walk about the city
(10) where he persists
incognito. Butterflies settle on his
stone ear.
Immortal he neither moves nor
rouses and is seldom
(15) seen, though he breathes and the
subtleties of his
machinations
drawing their substance from the
noise of the pouring
(20) river
animate a thousand automatons.
Who because they
neither know their sources nor
the sills of their
(25) disappointments walk outside
their bodies aimlessly
for the most part,
locked and forgot in their desires
—unroused.

(30) —Say it, no ideas but in things—
nothing but the blank faces of
the houses
and cylindrical trees
bent, forked by preconception
(35) and accident—
split, furrowed, creased, mot-
tled, stained—
secret—into the body of the
light!

(40) From above, higher than the
spires, higher
even than the office towers, from
oozy fields
abandoned to grey beds of dead
(45) grass,
black sumac, withered weed-
stalks,
mud and thickets cluttered with
dead leaves—
(50) the river comes pouring in above
the city
and crashes from the edge of the
gorge
in a recoil of spray and rainbow
(55) mists—

(What common language to un-
ravel?
… combed into straight lines
from that rafter of a rock's
(60) lip.)

By William Carlos Williams, from PATERSON, copyright ©1946, 1948,1949,1951,1958 by William Carlos Williams. Reprinted by permission of New Directions Publishing Corp.

35. What literary comparison is being used in lines 1–4, "Paterson lies in the valley under / the Passaic Falls / its spent waters forming the out-/ line of his back"?

(A) Zeugma
(B) Personification
(C) Pastoral
(D) Conceit
(E) Epitaph

36. What effect does the author likely intend with the repetition of sounds in line 21, "animate a thousand automatons"?

(A) Underscore the multiplicity of the automatons that is the explicit subject of the lines
(B) Impart a musical and sing-song quality to the lines
(C) Portray the number of automatons as disquieting
(D) Emphasize the irony of inhuman creatures being animated
(E) Cast aspersions on the inhuman nature of modern life

GO ON TO THE NEXT PAGE.

37. What is being conveyed by "no ideas but in things," line 30?

    (A) The individual elements of nature are more important than any idea.
    (B) The automatons are more concerned with ideas than emotions.
    (C) The only way to understand ideas is through things.
    (D) Sleeping Paterson can't be woken up with ideas, but responds to things.
    (E) Concrete things like houses and trees are more important than any idea.

38. In context, describing the "cylindrical trees" as "bent, forked by preconception / and accident" (lines 34-35) conveys which of the following?

    (A) The heaviness of nature that would bend a tree mirrors the strength of the pouring river.
    (B) All nature is cut in two ("forked"); one side is biology and one side is random events.
    (C) Trees are formed by a combination of biology and random events.
    (D) Trees are analogous to machines that have cylinders.
    (E) Trees can make us think of how humans influence nature.

39. In lines 40–50 ("From above…the river comes pouring in above"), what does the use of "even" most nearly convey in context?

    (A) The river is more important than either religion (the "spires") or work ("office towers").
    (B) Work ("office towers") is more important than religion ("spires").
    (C) All natural elements contribute to the river.
    (D) The river contributes to Paterson's abundance.
    (E) The river is the most important element in Paterson.

40. The poem as a whole is best understood as

    (A) a eulogy for a fading town
    (B) an analysis of modern society
    (C) a pledge of faith to a waterfall and a town
    (D) a celebration of a waterfall and a town
    (E) a rhapsody about the natural world around a town

41. One effect of the shift in the speaker's focus in the third stanza is to

    (A) imply that the river is mightier than Paterson
    (B) introduce the river as distinct from Paterson
    (C) argue that the river creates automatons
    (D) emphasize the river's central position in the poem
    (E) extoll the beauty of nature around the river

42. What best characterizes the relationship of the automatons and Paterson in lines 1–29 ("Paterson lies…. unroused"?)

    (A) Both their dreams walk around the city unseen
    (B) Both are roused by the pouring, thundering river
    (C) The automatons are being drained by industrialization and Paterson is being invigorated
    (D) Paterson is the antithesis of the automatons
    (E) Paterson resides in his body, while the automatons walk around outside theirs

43. The tone of lines 22–29 indicates that the speaker feels what about the automatons?

    (A) Fear, as they are neither human nor natural
    (B) Disinterest, as they are little more than statues
    (C) Approval, as they are linked with the river's power
    (D) Sadness, as they cannot express human emotions
    (E) Disdain, as they cannot connect with their disappointments

44. Grammatically, the word "recoil" (line 54) is

    (A) a verb
    (B) an adjective
    (C) an adverb
    (D) a noun
    (E) a direct object

45. The unusual use of punctuation in lines 36–37 ("split, furrowed, creased, mot-/ tled,") and lines 56–57 ("What common language to un-/ ravel?") could be interpreted to suggest

    (A) the speaker feels the world is fragmenting around the river and town, as the punctuation fragments language
    (B) the speaker is emphasizing splitting and unraveling by making the words themselves split and unravel
    (C) the words are moving to and fro as objects in a pouring river would move to and fro
    (D) the speaker is conveying potential unexpected fragmentation in the city and the town
    (E) the speaker's difficulty in finding a common language

GO ON TO THE NEXT PAGE.

Questions 46–55. Choose your answers to questions 46–55 based on a careful reading of the following excerpt from Jonathan Swift's essay *A Modest Proposal For preventing the Children of Poor People From being a Burthen to Their Parents or Country, and For making them Beneficial to the Publick.*

It is a melancholy object to those, who walk through this great town, or travel in the country, when they see the streets, the roads, and cabbin-doors crowded with beggars of the female sex, followed by three, four, or six children,
Line all in rags, and importuning every passenger for an alms.
(5) These mothers, instead of being able to work for their honest livelihood, are forced to employ all their time in stroling to beg sustenance for their helpless infants who, as they grow up, either turn thieves for want of work, or leave their dear native country, to fight for the Pretender in Spain, or sell
(10) themselves to the Barbadoes.

I think it is agreed by all parties, that this prodigious number of children…is in the present deplorable state of the kingdom, a very great additional grievance; and therefore whoever could find out a fair, cheap and easy method of
(15) making these children sound and useful members of the commonwealth, would deserve so well of the publick, as to have his statue set up for a preserver of the nation.

But my intention is very far from being confined to provide only for the children of professed beggars: it is of a
(20) much greater extent, and shall take in the whole number of infants at a certain age, who are born of parents in effect as little able to support them, as those who demand our charity in the streets.

….

(25) The question therefore is, How this number shall be reared and provided for? which, as I have already said, under the present situation of affairs, is utterly impossible by all the methods hitherto proposed. For we can neither employ them in handicraft or agriculture; they neither build houses, (I
(30) mean in the country) nor cultivate land: they can very seldom pick up a livelihood by stealing till they arrive at six years old….

I shall now therefore humbly propose my own thoughts, which I hope will not be liable to the least objection.
(35) I have been assured by a very knowing American of my acquaintance in London, that a young healthy child well nursed, is, at a year old, a most delicious nourishing and wholesome food, whether stewed, roasted, baked, or boiled; and I make no doubt that it will equally serve in a fricasee, or
(40) a ragoust.

I do therefore humbly offer it to publick consideration, that of the hundred and twenty thousand children, already computed, twenty thousand may be reserved for breed, whereof only one fourth part to be males; which is more
(45) than we allow to sheep, black cattle, or swine, and my reason is, that these children are seldom the fruits of marriage, a circumstance not much regarded by our savages, therefore, one male will be sufficient to serve four females. That the remaining hundred thousand may, at a year old, be offered

(50) in sale to the persons of quality and fortune, through the kingdom, always advising the mother to let them suck plentifully in the last month, so as to render them plump, and fat for a good table. A child will make two dishes at an entertainment for friends, and when the family dines alone,
(55) the fore or hind quarter will make a reasonable dish, and seasoned with a little pepper or salt, will be very good boiled on the fourth day, especially in winter.

….

I grant this food will be somewhat dear, and therefore
(60) very proper for landlords, who, as they have already devoured most of the parents, seem to have the best title to the children.

46. What does the "melancholy object" in line 1 most likely refer to?

(A) Mothers and children begging
(B) The great numbers of poor people
(C) The roads, streets, and doors
(D) The problems poor people cause for wealthier people
(E) The unclean conditions on the roads

47. In relation to the first three paragraphs (lines 1–24), the remainder of the passage serves primarily to

(A) provide reasons for overpopulation and poverty
(B) document data toward implementing the solution
(C) reassure readers of a solution to overpopulation and poverty
(D) propose a solution for overpopulation and poverty
(E) invite wealthy aristocrats to invest in Ireland once overpopulation and poverty are solved

48. The narrator evidently believes someone should hit upon a "fair, cheap and easy method of making these children sound and useful members of the commonwealth" (lines 15–17). What does the narrator believe that method might be?

(A) Selling children to Barbadoes
(B) Training children as mercenary soldiers
(C) Teaching children about agriculture
(D) Permitting children to become thieves
(E) Eating children as food

GO ON TO THE NEXT PAGE.

49. What is the narrator's tone throughout the passage?

    (A) Patriotic and reverent
    (B) Satiric and ironic
    (C) Data-driven and scientific
    (D) Reasonable and prudent
    (E) Ridiculous and outlandish

50. What is the narrator conveying in lines 61–63, in saying that the food is "very proper for landlords, who, as they have already devoured most of the parents, seem to have the best title to the children"?

    (A) A foreshadowing that the parents might be next to be consumed
    (B) A realistic look at how poorly the parents are treated by the landlords
    (C) A satiric view of the avarice of landlords
    (D) A comprehensive indictment of the landlords' greed
    (E) A call for landlords to provide justice

51. Lines 31–33, "they can very seldom pick up a livelihood by stealing till they arrive at six years old," represents a shift from

    (A) a dismissal of potential careers for the poor to a recommendation of the age at which working should begin
    (B) a shared concern for the poor between the narrator and his readers to a satiric jab at the readers, who think of poor children with fear rather than sympathy
    (C) a series of potential remedies for the commonwealth to an aside to readers contemptuous of the poor
    (D) condescension toward poor children to contempt for poor children
    (E) a discussion about why poor children can't be employed to a satiric acceptance that they may turn to stealing once they're six years old

52. In line 60, "I grant this food will be somewhat dear," what does "dear" most nearly mean?

    (A) Precious
    (B) Expensive
    (C) Heartfelt
    (D) Affectionate
    (E) Immense

53. Which of the following statements best conveys the effect of the sentences in lines 42–49 ("I do therefore humbly… four females")?

    (A) The narrator is drawing an analogy between the children and livestock such as sheep and cattle in an attempt to make the proposal seem normal.
    (B) The diction employs mathematics to make the proposal seem as if it would make money.
    (C) The narrator points out that the children may be born outside marriage to make it seem as if the church would approve the proposal.
    (D) The diction uses historical analogies to argue that the proposal is workable.
    (E) The argument portrays the poor as immoral.

54. The passage as a whole is best understood as a

    (A) patriotic solution to a contemporary challenge
    (B) veiled plea for the poor to receive aid
    (C) satiric attack on proposals attempting to do good
    (D) political attack on the aristocracy
    (E) call for the poor to be trained to work

55. What is the overall effect of lines 54–58, "A child will make two dishes…especially in winter"?

    (A) Clarifying just how horrifying the proposal is, by giving recipes for cooking the children
    (B) Underscoring how mundane solutions to poverty can seem, even if the effects are cruel
    (C) Equating the proposal to murder, by emphasizing what the children will undergo
    (D) Reassuring the aristocrats that the proposal will not be harmful
    (E) Exhorting readers to understand how much the proposal will help the commonwealth

STOP
END OF SECTION I

IF YOU FINISH BEFORE TIME IS CALLED, YOU MAY CHECK YOUR WORK ON THIS SECTION.
DO NOT GO ON TO SECTION II UNTIL YOU ARE TOLD TO DO SO.

ENGLISH LITERATURE AND COMPOSITION

SECTION II

Total Time—2 hours

Question 1

(Suggested time—40 minutes. This question counts as one-third of the total essay score.)

Read the following poem (published in 2002) by Toni Morrison carefully. Then write a well-organized essay in which you discuss the author's use of poetic or literary elements, techniques, and language to convey her themes.

In your response you should do the following:

- Respond to the prompt with a thesis that presents an interpretation and may establish a line of reasoning.
- Select and use evidence to develop and support your line of reasoning.
- Explain the relationship between the evidence and your thesis.
- Use appropriate grammar and punctuation in communicating your argument.

Eve* Remembering

1

I tore from a limb fruit that had lost its green.
My hands were warmed by the heat of an apple
Fire red and humming.
Line I bit sweet power to the core.
(5) How can I say what it was like?
The taste! The taste undid my eyes
And led me far from the gardens planted for a child
To wildernesses deeper than any master's call.

2

Now these cool hands guide what they once caressed;
(10) Lips forget what they have kissed.
My eyes now pool their light
Better the summit to see.

3

I would do it all over again:
Be the harbor and set the sail,
(15) Loose the breeze and harness the gale,
Cherish the harvest of what I have been.
Better the summit to scale.
Better the summit to be.
　　　　　　　—Toni Morrison

From *Five Poems* by Toni Morrison, 2002.

* In the Bible, Eve is the first woman; Adam is the first man. Eve eats an apple from the tree of knowledge, which God had forbidden them to eat. As a consequence, they fall out of favor with God and are banished from the Garden of Eden.

GO ON TO THE NEXT PAGE.

Question 2

(Suggested time—40 minutes. This question counts as one-third of the total essay score.)

The following excerpt is from a short story entitled "An Anarchist" by Joseph Conrad, published in *A Set of Six* (1908). In this passage, the narrator is discussing a large company, its advertising, and its products. Read the passage carefully. Then, in a well-written essay, analyze how Conrad uses literary elements and techniques to portray the narrator's attitude toward the company and its activities.

In your response you should do the following:

- Respond to the prompt with a thesis that presents an interpretation and may establish a line of reasoning.
- Select and use evidence to develop and support your line of reasoning.
- Explain the relationship between the evidence and your thesis.
- Use appropriate grammar and punctuation in communicating your argument.

That year I spent the best two months of the dry season on one of the estates—in fact, on the principal cattle estate—of a famous meat-extract manufacturing company.

Line
(5) B.O.S. Bos. You have seen the three magic letters on the advertisement pages of magazines and newspapers, in the windows of provision merchants, and on calendars for next year you receive by post in the month of November. They scatter pamphlets also, written in a sickly enthusiastic style and in several languages, giving statistics of slaughter
(10) and bloodshed enough to make a Turk turn faint. The "art" illustrating that "literature" represents in vivid and shining colours a large and enraged black bull stamping upon a yellow snake writhing in emerald-green grass, with a cobalt-blue sky for a background. It is atrocious and it is an
(15) allegory. The snake symbolizes disease, weakness—perhaps mere hunger, which last is the chronic disease of the majority of mankind. Of course everybody knows the B. O. S. Ltd., with its unrivalled products: Vinobos, Jellybos, and the latest unequalled perfection, Tribos, whose nourishment is
(20) offered to you not only highly concentrated, but already half digested. Such apparently is the love that Limited Company bears to its fellowmen—even as the love of the father and mother penguin for their hungry fledglings.

Of course the capital of a country must be productively
(25) employed. I have nothing to say against the company. But being myself animated by feelings of affection towards my fellow-men, I am saddened by the modern system of advertising. Whatever evidence it offers of enterprise, ingenuity, impudence, and resource in certain individuals,
(30) it proves to my mind the wide prevalence of that form of mental degradation which is called gullibility.

In various parts of the civilized and uncivilized world I have had to swallow B. O. S. with more or less benefit to myself, though without great pleasure. Prepared with
(35) hot water and abundantly peppered to bring out the taste, this extract is not really unpalatable. But I have never swallowed its advertisements. Perhaps they have not gone far enough. As far as I can remember they make no promise of everlasting youth to the users of B. O. S., nor yet have they

(40) claimed the power of raising the dead for their estimable products. Why this austere reserve, I wonder? But I don't think they would have had me even on these terms. Whatever form of mental degradation I may (being but human) be suffering from, it is not the popular form. I am not gullible.
(45)   ....

The Maranon cattle estate of the B. O. S. Co., Ltd.... is also an island—an island as big as a small province, lying in the estuary of a great South American river. It is wild and not beautiful, but the grass growing on its low plains seems to
(50) possess exceptionally nourishing and flavouring qualities. It resounds with the lowing of innumerable herds—a deep and distressing sound under the open sky, rising like a monstrous protest of prisoners condemned to death....

But the most interesting characteristic of this island
(55) (which seems like a sort of penal settlement for condemned cattle) consists in its being the only known habitat of an extremely rare and gorgeous butterfly. The species is even more rare than it is beautiful, which is not saying little. I have already alluded to my travels. I travelled at that time,
(60) but strictly for myself and with a moderation unknown in our days of round-the-world tickets. I even travelled with a purpose. As a matter of fact, I am—"Ha, ha, ha!—a desperate butterfly-slayer. Ha, ha, ha!"

This was the tone in which Mr. Harry Gee, the manager
(65) of the cattle station, alluded to my pursuits. He seemed to consider me the greatest absurdity in the world. On the other hand, the B. O. S. Co., Ltd., represented to him the acme of the nineteenth century's achievement.

...I don't see why, when we met at meals, he should
(70) have thumped me on the back, with loud, derisive inquiries: "How's the deadly sport to-day? Butterflies going strong? Ha, ha, ha!"
                    —Joseph Conrad, "An Anarchist." *A Set of Six*. 1908.

GO ON TO THE NEXT PAGE.

Question 3

(Suggested time—40 minutes. This question counts as one-third of the total essay score.)

Many works of literature are concerned with loyalty. These concerns can take many forms. Characters may be struggling to decide who or what deserves their loyalty, and why. The objects of loyalty can be a person, place, or a concept. A character's feelings of loyalty may change over time. The work may depict a test of loyalty, or changes in the object of a character's loyalty. Either from your own reading or from the list below, choose a work of fiction in which characters struggle with loyalty. Then, in a well-written essay, analyze how the treatment of loyalty contributes to an interpretation of the work as a whole. Do not merely summarize the plot.

In your response you should do the following:

- Respond to the prompt with a thesis that presents a defensible interpretation.
- Provide evidence to support your line of reasoning.
- Explain how the evidence supports your line of reasoning.
- Use appropriate grammar and punctuation in communicating your argument.

A Doll's House	The Kite Runner
Age of Innocence	LaRose
Anna Karenina	Lonely Londoners
A Streetcar Named Desire	Lord Jim
The Adventures of Huckleberry Finn	Macbeth
Angels in America	Mambo Kings Play Songs of Love
The Awakening	Mansfield Park
Breath, Eyes, Memory	Medea
The Bonesetter's Daughter	Middlemarch
Cold Mountain	The Mill on the Floss
The Crucible	Of Mice and Men
David Copperfield	The Oresteia
Don Quixote	Paradise Lost
Father Comes Home from the Wars	Persuasion
The Goldfinch	The Piano Lesson
A Handmaid's Tale	The Scarlet Letter
Henry IV, Part 2	Sense and Sensibility
Homegoing	Sula
The Iliad	The Sympathizer
King Lear	Wuthering Heights

STOP
END OF EXAM
IF YOU FINISH BEFORE TIME IS CALLED, YOU MAY CHECK YOUR WORK ON THIS SECTION.

Practice Test 2:
Answers and
Explanations

PRACTICE TEST 2 ANSWER KEY

1.	B	21.	E	41.	A
2.	E	22.	C	42.	E
3.	D	23.	C	43.	E
4.	A	24.	A	44.	D
5.	C	25.	C	45.	B
6.	D	26.	D	46.	A
7.	A	27.	B	47.	D
8.	C	28.	C	48.	E
9.	B	29.	E	49.	D
10.	A	30.	E	50.	C
11.	E	31.	D	51.	E
12.	A	32.	A	52.	B
13.	B	33.	C	53.	A
14.	D	34.	B	54.	C
15.	B	35.	B	55.	B
16.	A	36.	A		
17.	D	37.	C		
18.	E	38.	C		
19.	D	39.	B		
20.	A	40.	D		

PRACTICE TEST 2 EXPLANATIONS

Questions 1–11

Charlotte Brontë (1816–1855) was a novelist. She initially published under the pseudonym Currer Bell; the initials were her own and the pseudonym was an attempt to disguise her identity, partly because women writers weren't generally accepted by the literary establishment at the time. This excerpt is from her novel *Shirley*, a regional novel about Yorkshire, labor unrest, and love in the early nineteenth century. Brontë was from a family of writers; her sisters Emily and Anne were both accomplished novelists as well.

1. **B** In context, "abundant shower of curates" means that curates are as abundant as raindrops in a rain shower. The correct answer is therefore (B), metaphor. Both (A) and (D), satire and irony, may tempt you slightly, as they are in the passage. But they aren't in the phrase, so cross them off. It's not (C), an oxymoron, because the phrase doesn't represent opposites. (It represents unalike things, but that's par for the course for metaphor, and they aren't opposites!) The phrase doesn't contradict itself, so is not a paradox (E).

2. **E** Remember that this is an EXCEPT/LEAST/NOT QUESTION. It's the *present* that is characterized as arid and dusty, so (E) is the correct answer choice.

3. **D** This is a classic question for Process of Elimination (POE). Is the description in paragraphs 1 and 2 realistic? The narrator tells you that the representations will be "real," but do you know they are? So much of the language is fanciful. Hmmm. Hold that thought, and don't choose this one right off the bat. Is it (B), admiring? Line 4, they "ought to be doing a great deal of good" holds the idea of their doing good in suspension rather than firmly stating that they do it—so it's not exactly admiring. Strike (B) out. Is the tone surprised? No, definitely not. Cross out (C). Is it (D), arch? Arch means mischievous or saucy. That comment on doing good is somewhat arch. Keep this one. Are the paragraphs fearful, (E)? The tone definitely doesn't convey fear. (D) it is.

4. **A** The narrator addresses the reader as an entity several times in this passage. Look carefully at the specific lines. Choice (A) looks very good as an answer, because the narrator tells the reader what to expect and then tells them they are about to see the characters. But always in this test, make sure you check the other answers briefly to make sure you aren't going astray. In (B), the reader is definitely *not* promised an exotic romance—quite the opposite. (B) bites the dust immediately on those grounds. If a part of the answer is wrong, it *can't* be the correct response. In (C), you aren't really placed on the side of the curates, so out it goes. For (D), the narrator is arguably ironic in the beginning, so that's not a correct choice. And (E) isn't it because the narrator is arguably trying to win readers to her point of view throughout by addressing them!

5. **C** Nicely enough, all the choices are potential meanings of *lowly* or closely aligned with it. So context is all; be sure to reread the lines surrounding the word. They imply that the narrator's tale will be *without* passion, stimulus, or melodrama; it will be, by contrast, *real, cool,* and *solid.* With that in mind, exercise your POE chops. Is it (A), mean? A definition that would work here is *miserly* or *stingy.* Is that what our narrator is trying to convey in context? It doesn't seem that close (and it definitely isn't "mean" as in *cruel*). Is it poor, (B)? That seems even further away from the context. How about (C), prosaic? Some synonyms of prosaic are *commonplace, every day,* even *dull.* This seems to most match

the context here so far. Is (D), meek, a contender? It's not as close as (C), certainly, and neither is (E), humble. Ah, the glories of utilizing POE, which lead you to (C) as the correct choice!

6. **D**   This can be a difficult passage to parse, especially given the fact that it isn't perfectly clear to contemporary readers what "Dr. Pusey and tools of the Propaganda" refer to! (Fun fact: he was a 19th-century theologian at England's Oxford University, engaged in religious controversies.) But it's good to know you don't have to know a thing about that to think through the phrases, right? Why? Just think about their effect on you as a reader vis-à-vis the paragraph, because that's what the question is asking. Is it (A)? It could be. Hold that thought. Is it (B)? Well…people often admire religion. But is that the effect of these passages in context? Hold that thought, too. Is it (C)? Answer (C) seems very broad—beware of the overly general answer. Is it (D)? Ah, this seems like firmer ground than the others, because "disciples" and "successors" do refer directly to the curates, in context. And the passage is somewhat mocking. Is it (E)? This paragraph does not ennoble curates; it pokes fun at them. (D) is closer than (A); in fact, it's the closest answer here, and so the correct answer choice.

7. **A**   What is going on here? The "gown" is a baby's christening gown and it is linked via imagery with the surplices of curates (although the author ironically disavows this). Choice (A) is the correct answer. Were you tempted by (B)? Although the word "cruelly" is used, it's ironic (and it's not imagery, either), so that answer goes by the wayside. Neither (C) nor (D) is as close as (A). (E) is irrelevant to the passage.

8. **C**   How does the narrator come across to readers? This is a good one to utilize POE on as well. It doesn't appear likely that the narrator is (A), a disinterested journalist, if only because she tells us in lines 8–9 we will "dream of dawn." Journalists deal in facts, not dreams. (Yes, she tells us the story will be "real," but the dreams are in there, too.) Choice (B), a diffident investigator, is not the tone, either, because nothing in particular is being investigated. Choice (C) appears to be closer than either of the first two, as she's chronicling two time periods, a present day and "eighteen-hundred-eleven-twelve," and the narrator's view of the curates is ironic. Is the narrator (D), a sentimental storyteller? There's no sentiment; in fact, she tells you it won't be romantic in lines 10–12. Is (E), nonplussed resident, a candidate? We have no evidence that the narrator is a resident of the north of England or not, so that can't be it. Choice (C) it is.

9. **B**   Look carefully at context. These descriptions of the setting do convey a middle-class existence with "neat" and "parlour," so (A) looms as a possibility. Let's move on to (B), a diminishment from the religious predecessors. Hmm, given that they are successors to St. Peter et al. (lines 36–37), diminishment is a distinct possibility. Mentally put (B) in the starting block. In (C), while "small" can be confining, "stifling" is too extreme, and we have no evidence that they are chafing under society's propriety. Yes, (D), the historical conditions, is a possibility, as parlors, clothiers, and garden houses likely existed. But it's not as close as (B). Neither is (E). Choice (B) wins the prize!

10. **A**   While *affluent* in the present day is often used to describe wealthy people, a look at the line cited will clue you in: that's not the case here, so (B) is not a correct answer choice. And while "affluent" does have a *meaning of river tributary*, context will tell you it's also not (C) or (D). Choice (E),

opulent, is a synonym for *lush* and *wealthy*, so you can cross that off just like you did (B). Choice (A), abundant, is the correct answer.

11. **E** While there is parallelism in the language that introduces Mr. Donne, Mr. Malone, and Mr. Sweeting, we don't have enough evidence to say whether (A) is true or not. To the wayside it falls. They are exuberant, but we don't know if that leads to boisterousness, so (B) falls, too. They are definitely *not* devoted by their duties; they'd rather be doing other things. Nor are they dull and monotonous; if this fooled you, re-read, because these adjectives are applied to certain duties, but not the people. (C) and (D) are both out. The answer is (E), sociable with each other—they prefer "rushing backwards and forwards, amongst themselves, to and from their respective lodgings–not a round, but a triangle of visits" (lines 70–72).

Questions 12–23

An iconic feminist poet, Adrienne Rich was one of the best-known U.S. poets from the mid-20th century to her death in 2012. Rich was particularly known for her emphasis on representing women's voices and re-envisioning women's lives and choices. In many instances, she observed their power and agency vis-à-vis the patriarchal culture, dominant before the feminist movement began in the 1970s. This poem is about Caroline Herschel, an early astronomer who worked with her better-known brother William.

12. **A** Be sure to always look at lines in context, reading the lines directly above and below. The closest answer here is (A), that the reverse parallelism in the lines suggests a similarity between monsters and accomplished women such as Caroline Herschel. Choice (C) might be tempting, but "traditional occupations" is too broad to be the answer—you know that the poem is talking about Caroline Herschel because of the epigraph, and while "others" are referred to, it's still not as close as (A). Choice (D) is also too broad. Choices (B) and (E) aren't relevant in context of the lines.

13. **B** The line directly follows the two lines "A woman in the shape of a monster/ a monster in the shape of a woman," so the sense is closest to (B). If you see monstrous women as scientists, (A) is a possible interpretation of the lines, but it's not as close as (B). Although witches and monsters are often linked, (C) is more relevant later in the poem, and is not the answer here. Choices (D) and (E) aren't close in context.

14. **D** This is an EXCEPT/LEAST/NOT question. "There" as a pronoun could refer to all of these except (D), Taurus. While Taurus is mentioned in the poem, it is not a reference for "there" in this context.

15. **B** You can definitely use Process of Elimination (POE) on this. Is it the risks of scientific knowledge, (A)? But risks such as explosions come later in the poem. Penalties for violating social constraints, (B)? That's closer, as social constraints were against women achieving significant scientific knowledge in Caroline Herschel's lifetime. Choices (C), (D), and (E) don't make sense in context. Choice (B) it is.

16. **A** Let's see. The lines use "she" and "us" to say that these pronouns are ruled by the moon, rise (levitate) into the sky, and ride an object…just like, hey, witches ride broomsticks. "She" and very likely "us" are meant as women, so the metaphor operating is (A), women are witches. Could it be (B), scientists are witches? But not all scientists are ruled by the moon—and linkage of women and the moon is a

common literary association, so the metaphor breaks down there. There's nothing specifically about witches violating male power in these lines, so it can't be (C) in context. Neither (D) nor (E) has contextual support in these lines either.

17. **D** The repetition of sounds close together, as "relief of the body/ and the reconstruction of the Mind" is (D), alliteration. It's none of the others. Review the Glossary if this wasn't clear.

18. **E** The narrative "I" in this poem is receptive to knowledge about the universe and hoping to contribute, especially in the last stanza. Choice (E) is the correct choice. Choice (A), sorrowful, does not fit the overall tone of the poem when the narrative "I" speaks, and neither does (B), angry. She is more receptive than eager, (C). The "I" does seem to be at times analyzing a piece of the universe, but those points aren't as widespread as (E). Is the speaker pensive, that is, musingly thoughtful? Yes, but not so much about the nature of the universe. Choice (E) it is.

19. **D** Use POE to cut your way through this. Is it anguished? Not really, so (A) is out. Peaceful doesn't describe the tone either, so (B) bites the dust. It certainly isn't (C) or (E). Choice (D) is the closest, conveying both the praise of Herschel and the contradictions of her.

20. **A** The poet is honoring Caroline Herschel and her achievements in the first 10 stanzas, so (A) is the closest answer. Choice (B) is too broad. In (C), although the text refers to "Tycho" in line 25, an AP test will never require you to have specific knowledge outside the poem. (Tycho Brahe was an early Danish astronomer, but you are free to slot that in as an irrelevant fun fact.) All you need to do is read the poem to figure out that (C) couldn't be the answer here, because it doesn't fit all of the first 10 stanzas. Neither (D) nor (E) fits the entire 10 stanzas' theme or tone.

21. **E** Be sure to read the lines immediately above and below and utilize POE throughout—it will be a big help here. In context, (A), (B), and (C) are too broad. Choice (D) is irrelevant—poets don't put in spaces to guide oral readers. Choice (E) is the correct answer choice.

22. **C** Careful with this one. Look at what the lines are doing in the poem, not just at the words themselves. In other words, the answer isn't (B), instruments, just because the same words are used. In the phrase "I am an instrument," (line 43), an instrument is being actively used to understand and translate emanations from the sky. Does (A) do that? No, because it's a ground measurement. Choice (B) is something Herschel walked among, not actively used in the line. Choice (C) refers to instruments Herschel "rode." Ah, now we're getting somewhere; they were actively used to see the sky by something trying to decipher the universe. The speaker in "I am an instrument" is also trying to do that. (D), Uranusborg, is not relevant here, and neither is (E). Choice (C) is the clearest answer choice.

23. **C** The narrative "I" moves to the foreground in this stanza. The speaker is trying to translate pulsations into images, but (A), extoll, is not the tone here. Strike out (A). In (B), there is no sense that lament is the correct tone. Is it (C), implying that people can be instruments for understanding? That's the closest, as the speaker says "I am an instrument in the shape of a woman." In (D), fear doesn't fit the tone. Although the speaker seems to be under some psychological pressure, "cause a psychological breakdown" doesn't fit, either, so (E) falls by the wayside.

Questions 24–34

This passage is from *Quicksand* by Nella Larsen (1891–1964), published in 1928. It is a novel of the Harlem Renaissance and delves into themes of African American racial categorization, discrimination, and attendant social constraint.

24. **A**   Many questions about tone on the exam require you to read and note vocabulary closely. The beginning of the passage carefully sets up several references to reflective light within a darkened environment; the reading lamp forms a "pool of light" (lines 3–4) and the brass bowl is "shining" (line 7), although the room is in "soft gloom" (line 2) and "dimmed" (line 3). This gives a sense that the character Helga Crane is herself reflective within a dim environment, making the answer (A). There is no textual evidence that she is sad, (B). Don't be fooled by the description of her as "alone"; that is not the same as lonely, (C). While the passage later gives a sense that she is constricted in her environment, (D), the question clearly asks for the beginning of the passage, so that's not the correct answer here either. The first part of the passage also gives you no evidence that Helga Crane is romantic, (E).

25. **C**   Metaphor, (C), is a comparison between two relatively unlike ideas in which one thing is likened to something else to convey a point. The room here is described as an oasis in a desert, but it's not actually a watering place, nor is Naxos the shifting sands of the Sahara. It's not (A), a synecdoche, which requires a part/whole relationship. Apostrophe, (B), occurs when a speaker addresses someone or something in a rhetorical manner, not expecting an answer. Is it a simile, (D)? It comes close, but a simile always uses *like* or *as* in making comparisons between the two things. Had the sentence read "was *like* a small oasis," this would have been the answer. Personification, (E), requires the figurative language to use human qualities in a description, which this does not. If you encountered difficulty with these, review the glossary.

26. **D**   Questions about the narrator's point of view rely on careful attention to vocabulary and tone. You are told in line 23 that she is "attractive" and her intelligence is conveyed by the books and environment, making (D) the answer. For the others, look at textual cues. Is she (A), confused and unhappy? She's not confused, because she clearly believes she made a mistake and needs to leave. If part of the potential answer is wrong, it's all wrong. She's not isolated, either, because of James Vayle and the colleagues that could have been knocking on her door, so (B) isn't the correct answer. While the narrator tells us that Helga does care about the Vayles being a "first family" and that could be an indicator of snobbishness, you have no textual evidence of arrogance, so it's not (C). Her resolution to leave does not indicate depression, so the answer isn't (E).

27. **B**   The word *unsparing* has two definitions: 1) not merciful (hard, ruthless) or 2) not frugal (liberal, generous). Look carefully at context to find answers like this. It's (B), generously, as it's allied with giving willingly. While (A), ruthlessly, and (C), unmercifully *could* be correct answers if you look solely at the vocabulary, context clearly rules those answers out in this instance. Indecisive, (D), and uncharitable, (E), don't make sense in the context.

28. **C** Look carefully at each section. It's definitely not (A), realism to parody, as there's no parody in the excerpt. Nor are either historical fiction or personal narrative (B) categories applicable to this excerpt. What you do have is (C), an omniscient narrator giving way to the character's thoughts and comments. Ding, ding! That's the correct answer. While (D) may seem tempting, the representations of Helga Crane's thoughts and comments don't add up to stream of consciousness, which is a flow of thoughts as the character thinks them. Choice (E), a change in settings, doesn't happen in this passage.

29. **E** When an object is described in a way that has human attributes, the author is using which element of figurative language? Personification, (E), that's what! It isn't (A) because metaphor is a comparison between two unlike things, such as the room being an oasis. It isn't (B) because metonym is a word used to stand for something that it is associated with, such as "you owe allegiance to the crown" as a stand-in for owing allegiance to the king or queen. Choice (C) refers to words that imitate sounds, such as "buzz." Choice (D) refers to exaggeration.

30. **E** The primary purpose in the passage is (E), to present a pivotal moment in which the character Helga Crane decides to leave where she is. Did (A) seem like a tempting choice? The passage does establish her personality, but it's much more a linkage between the setting and her personality— and the primary action we see is her suddenly deciding she's a failure and she must leave. The passage spends a few lines each on (B), (C), and (D), but none of them are the primary purpose.

31. **D** The answer is (D), the process of resigning. How do you know? Immediately before these lines, she wants to depart, but can't because the red tape needs to be unwound. Remember always to read a line above and below anything quoted in a question. You can infer that she wants to resign from the institution she's teaching at, Naxos. Choice (A) is related to the red tape, but is the location where the process takes place rather than the process itself, so it's not a correct answer choice. In (B), her use of the word "impressive" to describe the bureaucracy of quitting is somewhat ironic. The phrase is not about James Vayle, so (C) is not the correct choice. You have no evidence that she's leaving teaching, only one institution in which teaching takes place, so it's not (E) either.

32. **A** Look closely at the text to choose this answer. Choice (A) is the correct choice, as Helga wants to talk to the "dignitaries" about leaving, but then notices it's become too late. Both (D) and (E) possible answer choices, but (D) is a bit too broad and in (E), "indifferently," isn't consistent with disapproval. Choice (C) is not relevant to the passage, because it does matter, to her. And it's definitely not (B), because we know that at least James Vayle needs to be told—the entire world isn't indifferent to her.

33. **C** Choice (C) is the correct choice, because the passage both describes and uses a great deal of figurative language. If you're not sure, run through the answer choices. It doesn't seem to be judgmental, so (A) is out. While it does analyze to some degree, "precise" isn't nearly as good a characterization of the style as (C), so it's not (B). It's neither ironic nor satiric, so (D) and (E) can both be eliminated as answer choices.

34. **B** While "dripping" could mean it's wet, from context you really don't know that Helga Crane has washed it—there is no evidence. The line does convey that it's all (A), (C), and (D), and there is an implied linkage with (E). Choice (B) is the correct answer choice to this EXCEPT question.

Questions 35–45

This excerpt is from the poem *Paterson*, by William Carlos Williams (1883–1963). Williams was a modernist poet. He won the Pulitzer Prize in 1962. *Paterson* was written about a city in the region of his birth, northern New Jersey, where he also lived most of his life. It is a five-part epic published throughout the 1940s and 1950s. Williams was also a practicing physician and wrote essays and novels in addition to poetry.

35. **B** The lines use (B), personification, to identify the city Paterson with a man. Though parts of the poem are somewhat pastoral, (C), these lines are not, and pastoral is not a literary comparison, but a genre. No other answer choice comes close.

36. **A** (B) is a partial answer, but it's not as close as (A). While the automatons may be disquieting, (C), the textual support for that is not in these lines—and (A) is also closer. It's neither (D) nor (E).

37. **C** The "things" seem to refer at least in part to nature, as exemplified by trees. But it also refers to houses, so (A) is shaky as a potential answer. Also, does the passage indicate that nature is more important than any idea? Not really. Eliminate (A). The automatons are not associated with this line, so strike out (B). Ah, things like houses and trees illuminate ideas, such as the immortality implied by the "body of the light" (lines 38–39), so (C) seems to do the trick. Choice (D) doesn't comport with the idea of the passage. Were you tempted by (E)? Look carefully at the line again. It isn't elevating things above ideas so much as saying that ideas don't exist without things. The best answer is (C).

38. **C** POE away on these. Choice (A) seems a bit of a stretch. Is it (B)? Well, that is a potential reading. How about (C)? That seems much closer. Hold it. Choice (D) seems too much of a stretch as well, and (E) is just too broad. So if it's between (B) and (C), how do you choose? Can you be sure the speaker is talking about nature as a whole here? No, you can't, because the poem is full of nature that isn't forked. Choice (C) is the better choice.

39. **B** Be sure to read the question and specific lines carefully. The answer is (B), because the river is higher *even* than the office towers—which allows us to infer that the office towers are the second-highest edifice in the town, so the church spires are lower. Metaphorically, work has trumped religion in the life of the city, as measured by the height of their respective buildings. It's very possible that other answers drew your eye. Choice (A) might be a good general answer, but it is not related to the use of "even," so it doesn't match the question. The same is true of (C), (D), and (E).

40. **D** Although "dead" parts of nature are referred to several times, it's not a eulogy, so strike out (A). Analysis of society, (B), is too broad. Choice (C) doesn't represent the tone of the poem. The closest answer here is (D), a celebration of the waterfall and town. Choice (E) is too strong to describe the poem accurately.

41. **A** The closest answer is (A). The river and falls have already been introduced as distinct from Paterson, so (B) isn't it. Choice (C) doesn't come close. Is it (D)? The shift actually indicates that the poem will move between Paterson and the river, not that the river will be central. It's not (E), because while parts of nature are beautiful, other parts aren't.

42. **E** Close reading and Process of Elimination (POE) can help you with this one. Paterson's dreams "walk around the city" (line 9), but you have no textual evidence that the automatons dream. Strike out (A). Paterson "neither moves nor/ rouses" (lines 13–14) and the automatons are also "unroused" (line 29), so it can't be (B). For (C), the role of industrialization isn't fully clear in these lines, but Paterson is asleep, so he can't be invigorated. That eliminates (C). Paterson and the automatons aren't antithetical to each other; they have commonalities, such as the unroused state. That knocks out (D) as a correct answer choice. Ah, (E), has strong textual support! Paterson has a back, a right side, and an ear (lines 4–12), so he's in a body (even if a fanciful one), while you are explicitly told that the automatons "walk outside/ their bodies" (lines 25–26). (E) it is!

43. **E** The closest answer is (E), as we are told "they don't know…their disappointments." Always look for textual support! While it might be natural to feel fear about automatons walking around, the tone is not fearful, so (A) is out. Were you prone to believe the automatons are little more than statues, as automatons are a type of robot? But the speaker devotes too many lines to them for (B), disinterest, to be a correct choice. The speaker also isn't approving, so (C) is out. The tone of the lines isn't sad either, so (D) can't be a correct choice.

44. **D** Recoil is often a verb. But the line uses it as a noun, so (D) is correct. If you fell for the trap (A), be sure to remember to always look at the lines—and you might want to review the grammar section.

45. **B** Why are words hyphenated from line to line here? The sense of both lines is about splitting and unraveling, so (B) is the best choice. You have no evidence of (A), the hyphens representing fragmentation of city and town, nor of (C) or (D). It may be tempting to choose (E), but after all, the speaker is successfully unraveling a common language—so *difficulty* is the wrong word.

Questions 46–55

Jonathan Swift (1667–1745) was an Anglo-Irish writer of novels, tales, and essays. This excerpt is from *A Modest Proposal For preventing the Children of Poor People From being a Burthen to Their Parents or Country, and For making them Beneficial to the Publick*, an essay published in 1729. It was written in response to conditions of overpopulation and poverty in Ireland, and published anonymously.

46. **A** If you look carefully at the passage, you'll see that the "melancholy object" are "beggars" "importuning every passenger for an alms." The correct response is therefore (A). Were you tempted by (B) or (C)? Both are close, but the high numbers in (B) only serve to heighten the effect of the "melancholy object," and the roadways in (C) are where it takes place. They are part of the scene but not the center of it. Wealthier people, (D), are not discussed in these lines, and (E) is clearly not a correct answer choice here.

47. **D** What is the narrator doing in paragraphs 4 onward? Some reasons are provided, so (A) might be it. The narrator also documents data, so, hmmm, (B) could be the answer. (C) is also potentially it, since our narrator definitely wants a solution. Ah, (D), proposing a solution for overpopulation and poverty is definitely it. Once you see this, you see that (A), (B), and (C) are less on the mark than (D). Choice (E) doesn't occur in the passage.

48. **E** Although (A) and (B) are mentioned in the passage, these choices describe things that might be done with the children, not ways of making them useful members of society (and in any case, they'd no longer be members of the society they grew up in). Strike both of them out. Choice (C) is mentioned in the passage as something that *cannot* be done. Poor children becoming thieves is mentioned several times, but it is not the author's solution, so (D) bites the dust as well. The author suggests, in lines 38–39, that children make "a most delicious nourishing and wholesome food." Choice (E), outlandish as it may seem, is the correct answer.

49. **D** Be careful with this question. Remember, tone is composed of many different features of writing. Go through your choices. Is it (A), patriotic and reverent? The author is thinking about the commonwealth, so set that aside for now. Is it (B), satiric and ironic? There are flashes of satire, but can we say that the overall tone is? Set this one aside for now as well. In (C), the narrator is certainly giving us data at one point, but it's not the overall tone. Eliminate (C). Is the narrator reasonable and prudent, (D)? Well, the *tone* is reasonable and prudent. This is the closest so far. (The solution may not be, but that's not what you're being asked.) He is discussing a common problem and earnestly attempting to solve it. Is the tone ridiculous and outlandish, (E)? Not really. Again, the solution may be, but not the tone. Choice (D) is the correct answer.

50. **C** Is the answer (A)? Look at the tense; the parents have already been "devoured" (and it's a metaphor also, not literal eating!). Cross out (A). Is the narrator giving a realistic look, (B)? The narrator is also telling us with a straight face that eating children is "proper for landlords." Not realistic. Out it goes. Is it (C), a satiric view of the avarice of landlords? That's the closest, as the landlords are shown to have a propensity to devour the poor, despite the straightforward diction. It may be an indictment of landlord greed, (D), but it's not a comprehensive one, so (D) falls by the wayside. Nor is it a clear call to justice, so the choice isn't (E). Choice (C) is the correct answer.

51. **E** Right before these lines, the narrator has been discussing how poor children can't be employed in agriculture or building. So (A) begins promisingly, as a dismissal of potential careers has happened. But the shift is *not* to a recommendation, so once you get to the end of (A), you should realize it won't do. Choice (B) is out almost immediately, because the tone is not one of "shared concern." Choice (C) should also be eliminated, because what's going on is not a series of potential remedies. Choice (D) should go immediately, because the shift isn't from condescension to contempt. Choice (E) begins promisingly as well…and also ends promisingly, as the lines indicate a satiric acceptance that the poor may turn to stealing, even though they can't do so until they turn six. Choice (E) it is! Remember, satire makes us aware of ridiculous expectations, such as talking about thievery as potential employment in the same way we would talk about agriculture or building.

52. **B** Several of these are in fact dictionary definitions of *dear*, so context, as ever in AP English, is all. The answer is (B), expensive. Were you tempted by (A), precious or (D), affectionate? Could there be some double meanings there, as the children may have been precious or affectionate before being eaten? Ah, but not to the landlords, who follow directly in context, so the answer is clearly (B). Choices (C) and (E) don't make sense in context.

53. **A** What's going on in the passage? Review it and wield your POE! Yes, there are definition analogies made between livestock and the children. Hold on to (A). Choice (B) initially seems correct, as the narrator is using mathematical figures left and right. But slam on the brakes when you get to "make money." That's not in the passage at all. Out goes (B). Choice (C) looks good at first, too, as the passage mentions children born outside wedlock. But the church doesn't enter it, so eliminate (C). Choice (D) can be eliminated immediately because it's not relevant. Are the poor seen as immoral, (E)? Well, no marriage and the term "savages" are in there. But look at the question. Is that what is most conveyed? No, (A) is much closer to the effect of the lines overall.

54. **C** Use POE to eliminate a lot of these. The ironic and satiric flashes should alert you to the fact that (A) can't really be correct, although it purports (on the surface) to be. It's not really sympathetic to the poor, either, so (B) is out, and so is (E). That leaves us with (C) and (D). There are some satiric jabs at the aristocracy, who are to blandly purchase children to eat, but it's not central enough to be the correct choice for a question like this. Choice (C) is it. Remember that satire is used to ridicule human folly. Yep, that's what's going on here.

55. **B** Let's POE away. Choice (A) does give recipes for cooking, but is "horrifying" correct in context? It may seem tempting, but there's no blood or fear, as there is in horror. Let's hold that thought and move on to (B), emphasizing the mundanity of the solution. Yes, that seems possible—the recipes are very mundane. Let's keep (B) and move on to make sure the others aren't closer. Is it (C)? Nope, it's not that one. (Note that there's no reference to murder throughout.) Is it (D) or (E)? In both cases, definitely not. The choice is (B).

Practice Test 3

The Exam

AP® English Literature and Composition Exam

DO NOT OPEN THIS BOOKLET UNTIL YOU ARE TOLD TO DO SO.

At a Glance

Total Time
1 hour
Number of Questions
55
Percent of Total Grade
45%
Writing Instrument
Pencil required

Instructions

Section I of this examination contains 55 multiple-choice questions. Fill in only the ovals for numbers 1 through 55 on your answer sheet.

Indicate all of your answers to the multiple-choice questions on the answer sheet. No credit will be given for anything written in this exam booklet, but you may use the booklet for notes or scratch work. After you have decided which of the suggested answers is best, completely fill in the corresponding oval on the answer sheet. Give only one answer to each question. If you change an answer, be sure that the previous mark is erased completely. Here is a sample question and answer.

Sample Question   Sample Answer

Chicago is a
(A) state
(B) city
(C) country
(D) continent
(E) village

Use your time effectively, working as quickly as you can without losing accuracy. Do not spend too much time on any one question. Go on to other questions and come back to the ones you have not answered if you have time. It is not expected that everyone will know the answers to all the multiple-choice questions.

About Guessing

Many candidates wonder whether or not to guess the answers to questions about which they are not certain. Multiple choice scores are based on the number of questions answered correctly. Points are not deducted for incorrect answers, and no points are awarded for unanswered questions. Because points are not deducted for incorrect answers, you are encouraged to answer all multiple-choice questions. On any questions you do not know the answer to, you should eliminate as many choices as you can, and then select the best answer among the remaining choices.

GO ON TO THE NEXT PAGE.

ENGLISH LITERATURE AND COMPOSITION

SECTION I

Time—1 hour

<u>Directions:</u> This section consists of selections from literary works and questions on their content, form, and style. After reading each passage or poem, choose the best answer to each question and then completely fill in the corresponding oval on the answer sheet.

<u>Questions 1–12.</u> Choose your answers to questions 1–12 based on a careful reading of the following passage.

A green and yellow parrot, which hung in a cage outside the door, kept repeating over and over:

"*Allez vous-en! Allez vous-en! Sapristi!* That's all right!"

Line He could speak a little Spanish, and also a language
(5) which nobody understood, unless it was the mockingbird that hung on the other side of the door, whistling his fluty notes out upon the breeze with maddening persistence.

Mr. Pontellier, unable to read his newspaper with any degree of comfort, arose with an expression and an
(10) exclamation of disgust.

He walked down the gallery and across the narrow "bridges" which connected the Lebrun cottages one with the other. He had been seated before the door of the main house. The parrot and the mockingbird were the property of
(15) Madame Lebrun, and they had the right to make all the noise they wished. Mr. Pontellier had the privilege of quitting their society when they ceased to be entertaining.

He stopped before the door of his own cottage, which was the fourth one from the main building and next to the
(20) last. Seating himself in a wicker rocker which was there, he once more applied himself to the task of reading the newspaper. The day was Sunday; the paper was a day old. The Sunday papers had not yet reached Grand Isle. He was already acquainted with the market reports, and he glanced
(25) restlessly over the editorials and bits of news which he had not had time to read before quitting New Orleans the day before.

Mr. Pontellier wore eye-glasses. He was a man of forty, of medium height and rather slender build; he stooped a
(30) little. His hair was brown and straight, parted on one side. His beard was neatly and closely trimmed.

Once in a while he withdrew his glance from the newspaper and looked about him. There was more noise than ever over at the house. The main building was called
(35) "the house," to distinguish it from the cottages. The chattering and whistling birds were still at it. Two young girls, the Farival twins, were playing a duet from "Zampa" upon the piano. Madame Lebrun was bustling in and out, giving orders in a high key to a yard-boy whenever she got
(40) inside the house, and directions in an equally high voice to a dining-room servant whenever she got outside. She was a fresh, pretty woman, clad always in white with elbow

sleeves. Her starched skirts crinkled as she came and went. Farther down, before one of the cottages, a lady in black was
(45) walking demurely up and down, telling her beads. A good many persons of the *pension* had gone over to the *Chênière Caminada* in Beaudelet's lugger to hear mass. Some young people were out under the wateroaks playing croquet. Mr. Pontellier's two children were there—sturdy little fellows of
(50) four and five. A quadroon nurse followed them about with a faraway, meditative air.

Mr. Pontellier finally lit a cigar and began to smoke, letting the paper drag idly from his hand. He fixed his gaze upon a white sunshade that was advancing at snail's pace
(55) from the beach. He could see it plainly between the gaunt trunks of the wateroaks and across the stretch of yellow camomile. The gulf looked far away, melting hazily into the blue of the horizon. The sunshade continued to approach slowly. Beneath its pink-lined shelter were his wife, Mrs.
(60) Pontellier, and young Robert Lebrun. When they reached the cottage, the two seated themselves with some appearance of fatigue upon the upper step of the porch, facing each other, each leaning against a supporting post.

"What folly! to bathe at such an hour in such heat!"
(65) exclaimed Mr. Pontellier. He himself had taken a plunge at daylight. That was why the morning seemed long to him.

"You are burnt beyond recognition," he added, looking at his wife as one looks at a valuable piece of personal property which has suffered some damage. She held up her
(70) hands, strong, shapely hands, and surveyed them critically, drawing up her fawn sleeves above the wrists. Looking at them reminded her of her rings, which she had given to her husband before leaving for the beach. She silently reached out to him, and he, understanding, took the rings from his
(75) vest pocket and dropped them into her open palm. She slipped them upon her fingers; then clasping her knees, she looked across at Robert and began to laugh. The rings sparkled upon her fingers. He sent back an answering smile.

"What is it?" asked Pontellier, looking lazily and amused
(80) from one to the other. It was some utter nonsense; some adventure out there in the water, and they both tried to relate it at once. It did not seem half so amusing when told. They realized this, and so did Mr. Pontellier. He yawned and stretched himself. Then he got up, saying he had half a mind

GO ON TO THE NEXT PAGE.

(85) to go over to Klein's hotel and play a game of billiards.

"Come go along, Lebrun," he proposed to Robert. But Robert admitted quite frankly that he preferred to stay where he was and talk to Mrs. Pontellier.

"Well, send him about his business when he bores you, (90) Edna," instructed her husband as he prepared to leave.

"Here, take the umbrella," she exclaimed, holding it out to him. He accepted the sunshade, and lifting it over his head descended the steps and walked away.

"Coming back to dinner?" his wife called after him.

(95) He halted a moment and shrugged his shoulders. He felt in his vest pocket; there was a ten-dollar bill there. He did not know; perhaps he would return for the early dinner and perhaps he would not. It all depended upon the company which he found over at Klein's and the size of "the game."

(100) He did not say this, but she understood it, and laughed, nodding good-by to him.

Both children wanted to follow their father when they saw him starting out. He kissed them and promised to bring them back bonbons and peanuts.

Excerpt from *The Awakening* by Kate Chopin (pp. 1–6).
Copyright © 1899 by Herbert S. Stone & Co.

1. The tone of the beginning of the passage is

   (A) cacophonous
   (B) whimsical
   (C) brooding
   (D) satirical
   (E) pastoral

2. Lines 8–10 establish Mr. Pontellier as

   (A) fastidious and officious
   (B) intolerant and judgmental
   (C) restless and volatile
   (D) surreptitious and untrustworthy
   (E) ambitious and corrupt

3. The parrot's chatter made at the beginning of the passage helps to establish

   (A) the unpleasantness of the setting
   (B) Mr. Pontellier's restlessness and discomfort
   (C) the tension between Mr. Pontellier and Robert
   (D) the tension between Robert and Mrs. Pontellier
   (E) a sense of unease between man and nature

4. In line 26, the word "quitting" means

   (A) finishing
   (B) leaving
   (C) giving up
   (D) dismissing
   (E) setting free

5. Mr. Pontellier's attitude toward his companions on Grand Isle could be characterized as

   (A) aloof
   (B) curious
   (C) mistrustful
   (D) warm
   (E) antagonistic

6. In line 49, the word "sturdy" helps to establish

   (A) Mr. Pontellier's self-satisfaction with his children
   (B) the children's ability to withstand Mr. Pontellier's neglect
   (C) parallels between the children and their mother
   (D) suspicion that Mr. Pontellier is not the children's biological father
   (E) a contrast between the Pontellier children and the rest of the island's inhabitants

7. In lines 52–66, which word complements our understanding of Mr. Pontellier's personality?

   (A) Smoke
   (B) Idly
   (C) Gaunt
   (D) Folly
   (E) Plunge

8. Lines 58–66 reveal

   (A) Mr. Pontellier's thinly veiled dislike of Robert
   (B) Mr. Pontellier's powerfully athletic nature
   (C) Mr. Pontellier's envy of late risers
   (D) Mr. Pontellier's concern for his wife's health
   (E) Mr. Pontellier's self-righteous contempt toward his wife

GO ON TO THE NEXT PAGE.

9. In line 67, Mr. Pontellier uses which literary device to provoke a reaction from his wife?

   (A) Hyperbole
   (B) Onomatopoeia
   (C) Assonance
   (D) Understatement
   (E) Apostrophe

10. Lines 67–78 serve to introduce

   (A) Mrs. Pontellier's unattractive appearance
   (B) an indication that the relationship between Mr. and Mrs. Pontellier is strained
   (C) a suggestion that Robert is uncomfortable around Mr. Pontellier
   (D) Mrs. Pontellier's dominant position in the marriage
   (E) Mr. Pontellier's protectiveness toward his wife

11. The description of the interactions between Mrs. Pontellier and Robert convey a tone of

   (A) unapologetic intimacy
   (B) passionate longing
   (C) polite tolerance
   (D) underlying antagonism
   (E) conspiratorial secrecy

12. Lines 86–90 serve to further clarify

   (A) Mr. Pontellier's indifference toward his marriage
   (B) Mr. Pontellier's disdain for his children
   (C) Mr. Pontellier's fear of Robert's influence over his wife
   (D) Mr. Pontellier's loathing of idle chit-chat
   (E) Mr. Pontellier's desire to send Robert away

GO ON TO THE NEXT PAGE.

Questions 13–23. Choose your answers to each of the following questions based on careful reading of the following poem by Christina Rossetti.

Passing away, saith the World, passing away:
Chances, beauty and youth sapped day by day:
Thy life never continueth in one stay.
Line Is the eye waxen dim, is the dark hair changing to gray
(5) That hath won neither laurel nor bay?
I shall clothe myself in Spring and bud in May:
Thou, root stricken, shalt not rebuild thy decay
On my bosom for aye.
Then I answered: Yea.

(10) Passing away, saith my Soul, passing away:
With its burden of fear and hope, or labor and play;
Hearken what the past doth witness and say:
Rust in thy gold, a moth is in thine array,
A canker is in thy bud, thy leaf must decay.
(15) At midnight, at cockcrow, at morning, one certain day
Lo the bridegroom shall come and shall not delay:
Watch thou and pray.
Then I answered: Yea.

Passing away, saith my God, passing away:
(20) Winter passeth after the long delay:
New grapes on the vine, new figs on the tender spray,
Turtle calleth turtle in Heaven's May.
Tho' I tarry, wait for Me, trust Me, watch and pray.
Arise, come away, night is past and lo it is day,
(25) My love, My sister, My spouse, thou shalt hear Me say.
Then I answered: Yea.

13. How many speakers does the poem directly present?

(A) One
(B) Two
(C) Three
(D) Four
(E) Five

14. "Laurel" and "bay" (line 5) are allusions to

(A) flowers highly prized for their rarity which bloom briefly and beautifully and then die
(B) spices which add flavor to food and, metaphorically, to life
(C) leaves traditionally woven into wreaths to honor poets
(D) traditional symbols for Homer and Ovid, respectively
(E) traditional symbols for true faith and pious conduct, respectively

15. Which of the following lines contains an image NOT echoed closely elsewhere in the poem?

(A) Line 6
(B) Line 7
(C) Line 13
(D) Line 14
(E) Line 21

16. Which of the following choices best characterizes the speaker's attitude in each of the poem's three stanzas, respectively?

(A) Realization of death's inevitability; fear of physical decay; passive acceptance of what cannot be escaped
(B) Nostalgia for the earthly world that must be left behind; fear of physical decay; welcome acceptance of the afterlife
(C) Realization that death will come before one's ambitions have been achieved; dismay over the visible signs of physical decay; supplication for the healing powers of divine intervention
(D) Sorrow and mild surprise at the arrival of early death; deepening awareness of death's certainty; hopefulness for a place in the afterlife
(E) Acknowledgment of death's inevitability; understanding of the need to prepare oneself; happiness at the prospect of union with the divine

17. In the context of the poem, "a moth is in thine array" (line 13) is intended to imply that the

(A) narrator's attire is being eaten by moths
(B) narrator's body is being consumed by cancer, or a cancer-like disease
(C) narrator's soul contains a destructive element which, unless the narrator takes some action, will render it unworthy of the afterlife
(D) narrator's soul is corrupted with sin that only death can purge
(E) narrator's soul is getting ready for decay

GO ON TO THE NEXT PAGE.

18. Lines 15 and 16 ("At midnight...shall not delay:") suggest that

   (A) the principal narrator's final hour will come, despite the small uncertainty of knowing exactly what hour that will be
   (B) the bridegroom mentioned in line 16 will arrive at three distinct times
   (C) the hour when a deadly illness first infects the principal narrator cannot be avoided
   (D) a mysterious and evil stranger will arrive at some time between midnight and morning
   (E) the principal narrator's soul prophesies that she will eventually meet the man who will become her beloved husband

19. In the third stanza, "winter" can be taken to represent

   (A) long disease
   (B) earthly life
   (C) the coldness of the grave
   (D) mental despair
   (E) aging and loss of vigor

20. Which of the following statements most accurately characterizes the relationship of the imagery in the third stanza to that of the first and second stanzas?

   (A) The third stanza weaves together the wedding-day imagery of the second stanza and the springtime imagery of the first stanza, thereby reconciling those earlier stanzas' differing views.
   (B) Through its imagery, the third stanza further develops the themes which were advanced by the first stanza and then questioned by the second stanza.
   (C) The third stanza echoes much of the first two stanzas' imagery, but recasts that imagery so that what earlier had been likened to decay is instead characterized as renewal.
   (D) By echoing the imagery of the earlier stanzas, the third stanza reaffirms and repeats the views advanced by those stanzas.
   (E) By introducing the terms "love" and "sister," the third stanza continues the progression by which each stanza proposes its own unique central metaphor around which to further the poem's exploration of the themes of death and renewal.

21. Line 16 ("Lo the bridegroom shall come and shall not delay:") provides an example of

   (A) apostrophe
   (B) enjambment
   (C) personification
   (D) mixed metaphor
   (E) simile

22. In context, the word "spray" (line 21) most nearly means

   (A) tree
   (B) blanket
   (C) a small branch
   (D) a liquid mist
   (E) a holy spirit

23. The grammatical subject of the sentence that begins at line 24 ("Arise, come away") is

   (A) "Arise"
   (B) "night is past and lo it is day"
   (C) "My love, My sister, My spouse"
   (D) "thou"
   (E) "Me"

GO ON TO THE NEXT PAGE.

Questions 24–36. Read the following passage carefully before you choose your answers. The selection is an excerpt from the novel *Barchester Towers* by Anthony Trollope.

It is not my intention to breathe a word against Mrs Proudie, but still I cannot think that with all her virtues she adds much to her husband's happiness. The truth is that in
Line matters domestic she rules supreme over her titular lord, and
(5) rules with a rod of iron. Nor is this all. Things domestic Dr Proudie might have abandoned to her, if not voluntarily, yet willingly. But Mrs Proudie is not satisfied with such home dominion, and stretches her power over all his movements, and will not even abstain from things spiritual. In fact, the
(10) bishop is henpecked.

The archdeacon's wife, in her happy home at Plumstead, knows how to assume the full privileges of her rank, and express her own mind in becoming tone and place. But Mrs Grantly's sway, if sway she has, is easy and beneficent. She
(15) never shames her husband; before the world she is a pattern of obedience; her voice is never loud, nor her looks sharp; doubtless she values power, and has not unsuccessfully striven to acquire it; but she knows what should be the limits of a woman's rule.

(20) Not so Mrs Proudie. This lady is habitually authoritative to all, but to her poor husband she is despotic. Successful as has been his career in the eyes of the world, it would seem that in the eyes of his wife he is never right. All hope of defending himself has long passed from him; indeed,
(25) he rarely even attempts self-justification; and is aware that submission produces the nearest approach to peace which his own house can ever attain.

One other marked peculiarity in the character of the bishop's wife must be mentioned. Though not averse to the
(30) society and manners of the world, she is in her own way a religious woman; and the form in which this tendency shows itself is by a strict observance of Sabbatarian rule. Dissipation and low dresses during the week are, under her control, atoned for by three services, an evening sermon
(35) read by herself, and a perfect abstinence from any cheering employment on the Sunday. Unfortunately for those under her roof to whom the dissipation and low dresses are not extended, her servants namely and her husband, the compensating strictness of the Sabbath includes all. Woe
(40) betide the recreant housemaid who is found to have been listening to the honey of a sweetheart in the Regent's park, instead of the soul-stirring discourse of Mr Slope. Not only is she sent adrift, but she is so sent with a character, which leaves her little hope of a decent place. Woe betide the six-
(45) foot hero who escorts Mrs Proudie to her pew in red plush breeches, if he slips away to the neighbouring beer-shop, instead of falling in the back seat appropriated to his use. Mrs Proudie has the eyes of Argus for such offenders. Occasional drunkenness in the week may be overlooked, for six feet on
(50) low wages are hardly to be procured if the morals are always kept at a high pitch, but not even for grandeur or economy will Mrs Proudie forgive a desecration of the Sabbath.

24. Which of the following descriptions is an example of the narrator's use of irony?

(A) "It is not my intention to breathe a word against Mrs Proudie" (lines 1–2)
(B) "the bishop is henpecked" (lines 9–10)
(C) "doubtless she values power, and has not unsuccessfully striven to acquire it" (lines 17–18)
(D) "it would seem in the eyes of his wife he is never right" (lines 22–23)
(E) "a perfect abstinence from any cheering employment on the Sunday" (lines 35–36)

25. Mrs Proudie's authoritarian character is shown most pointedly in the phrase

(A) "not satisfied with such home dominion" (lines 7–8)
(B) "knows how to assume the full privileges of her rank" (line 12)
(C) "submission produces the nearest approach to peace" (line 26)
(D) "the soul-stirring discourse of Mr Slope" (line 42)
(E) "has the eyes of Argus for such offenders" (line 48)

26. The use of the word "titular" in line 4 is an example of

(A) hyperbole
(B) metonym
(C) onomatopoeia
(D) zeugma
(E) irony

27. In the context of the passage, the phrase "if not voluntarily, yet willingly" (lines 6–7) is used to show Dr Proudie's attitude toward

(A) the duties that the clergy are expected to assume
(B) entering the institution of marriage
(C) strict Sabbatarianism
(D) granting his wife some power
(E) the hiring of domestic help

GO ON TO THE NEXT PAGE.

28. The description of Mrs Grantly serves to

    (A) provide another example of the power of
         the aristocracy
    (B) prove that Mrs Grantly henpecks her husband
    (C) imply specific faults of Mrs Proudie
    (D) suggest a rivalry between her and Mrs Proudie
    (E) assert why women should be seen and not heard

29. The narrator's attitude toward Mrs Proudie can best be
    described as one of

    (A) pity
    (B) objectivity
    (C) emotional judgment
    (D) sardonic condemnation
    (E) jaded disgust

30. Which of the following best describes Dr Proudie's
    relationship to his wife?

    (A) Morally devoted
    (B) Completely servile
    (C) Awkwardly tender
    (D) Thoroughly uxorious
    (E) Bitterly tyrannical

31. The author attributes Dr Proudie's attitude and behavior
    most clearly to

    (A) ambition
    (B) pride
    (C) pacifism
    (D) spirituality
    (E) feudalism

32. In context, the word "character" (line 43) is best
    interpreted as meaning

    (A) dubious personage
    (B) reference
    (C) antagonist
    (D) conscience
    (E) footman

33. What is the effect of the repetition of the phrase "Woe
    betide…" in the final paragraph?

    (A) It retards the tempo of the prose.
    (B) It satirizes the fate of the servants.
    (C) It highlights the drama of the situation.
    (D) It changes the point of view of the narrator.
    (E) It emphasizes the moral consequences of the action.

34. In context, the adjective "recreant" (line 40) is best
    interpreted as meaning

    (A) unfaithful and disloyal
    (B) engaging in a pastime
    (C) refreshing
    (D) craven and cowardly
    (E) depraved

35. Which of the following best describes the effect of the
    last paragraph?

    (A) It suggests a cause of Mrs Proudie's
         moral transformation.
    (B) It introduces Mr Slope as an observer
         of Mrs Proudie's actions.
    (C) It counters speculations about Mrs
         Proudie's character.
    (D) It illustrates how Mrs Proudie's religious
         beliefs reflect her character.
    (E) It shows how hard it is to hire household servants.

36. The style of the passage as a whole can best be
    described as

    (A) humorless and pedantic
    (B) effusive and subjective
    (C) descriptive and metaphorical
    (D) terse and epigrammatic
    (E) witty and analytical

GO ON TO THE NEXT PAGE.

Questions 37–46. Read the following poem by Amy Lowell carefully, and then choose answers to the questions that follow.

You—you—
Your shadow is sunlight on a plate of silver;
Your footsteps, the seeding-place of lilies;
Your hands moving, a chime of bells across a windless air.

Line
(5) The movement of your hands is the long, golden running of
       light from a rising sun;
   It is the hopping of birds upon a garden-path.

   As the perfume of jonquils, you come forth in the morning.
   Young horses are not more sudden than your thoughts,
(10) Your words are bees about a pear-tree,
   Your fancies are the gold-and-black striped wasps buzzing
       among red apples.
   I drink your lips,
   I eat the whiteness of your hands and feet.
(15) My mouth is open,
   As a new jar I am empty and open.
   Like white water are you who fill the cup of my mouth,
   Like a brook of water thronged with lilies.

   You are frozen as the clouds,
(20) You are far and sweet as the high clouds.
   I dare to reach to you,
   I dare to touch the rim of your brightness.
   I leap beyond the winds,
   I cry and shout,
(25) For my throat is keen as is a sword
   Sharpened on a hone of ivory.
   My throat sings the joy of my eyes,
   The rushing gladness of my love.

   How has the rainbow fallen upon my heart?
(30) How have I snared the seas to lie in my fingers
   And caught the sky to be a cover for my head? How have you
       come to dwell with me,
   Compassing me with the four circles of your mystic
       lightness,
(35) So that I say "Glory! Glory!" and bow before you
   As to a shrine?

   Do I tease myself that morning is morning and a day after?
   Do I think the air is a condescension,
   The earth a politeness,
(40) Heaven a boon deserving thanks?
   So you—air—earth—heaven—
   I do not thank you,
   I take you,
   I live.
(45) And those things which I say in consequence
   Are rubies mortised in a gate of stone.

37. The phrase "I drink your lips,/I eat the whiteness of your hands and feet" (lines 13–14) serves to

(A) describe the antagonistic interactions of the speaker and her subject
(B) point out the beauty of the poem's subject
(C) make clear that the speaker's relationship to her subject is more physically based than it is emotionally significant
(D) underscore the speaker's delight in the physical characteristics of her lover
(E) provide a figurative contrast between the speaker and her subject

38. Which of the following best conveys the meaning in context of "How have I snared the seas to lie in my fingers/ And caught the sky to be a cover for my head?" (lines 30–31)?

(A) The speaker is impressed with the physical feats she can perform now that her relationship has blossomed.
(B) The speaker is impressed with how attuned her lover is to the natural world.
(C) The speaker cannot believe her good fortune at being in such a wonderful relationship.
(D) The sea and sky, representing the relationship, are protecting the speaker from harm.
(E) The speaker feels amazement at how beautiful the world around her looks because of the new perspective granted by her relationship with her lover.

39. The use of repetition and punctuation in the first line of the poem could be interpreted to suggest

(A) the speaker's amazement at the existence of her subject
(B) the difficulty that the speaker has communicating with the poem's subject, even though they are in love
(C) the speaker's inability to make her sentiments clear
(D) the speaker's thoughts are being interrupted by everyday life or other concerns
(E) the speaker wants to be very clear in terms of who her subject is and who she is speaking to within the context of the poem

GO ON TO THE NEXT PAGE.

40. The speaker compares her beloved to all of the following EXCEPT

   (A) the clouds
   (B) bees buzzing among fruit
   (C) heaven, the earth, and the air
   (D) the perfume of flowers
   (E) the clear water of a brook

41. The third stanza of the poem principally suggests that

   (A) the speaker of the poem is fragile, like a jar made out of pottery or glass
   (B) the speaker is ready and waiting to receive the experiences and emotions that her relationship and/or her lover provides for her
   (C) the speaker loves the flowers of which her lover reminds her
   (D) the poem's speaker is similar to many of nature's treasures, such as the lilies in the brook
   (E) the speaker is unable to resist her lover's advances even when she would like to do so

42. Which word is a metaphor for the poem itself?

   (A) Sun
   (B) Perfume
   (C) Morning
   (D) Rubies
   (E) Sword

43. Which stanza most suggests the religious level of devotion felt by the poem's speaker?

   (A) 2
   (B) 3
   (C) 4
   (D) 5
   (E) 6

44. "As the perfume of jonquils, you come forth in the morning" (line 8) is an example of

   (A) personification
   (B) metaphor
   (C) simile
   (D) hyperbole
   (E) metaphysical conceit

45. The poem's final stanza suggests which of the following?

   (A) The speaker is thankful for the gift of heaven.
   (B) The speaker sees the elements of the earth in her lover.
   (C) The speaker's lover is similar to the morning.
   (D) The speaker values her lover more than rubies.
   (E) The speaker fears she will outlive her lover.

46. The poem states or implies which of the following?

   (A) The speaker's lover is far away from her.
   (B) The speaker shows reverence for the natural world.
   (C) The speaker fears losing her lover to someone else.
   (D) The speaker believes that heaven is necessary to her well-being.
   (E) The speaker regrets pushing her lover away.

GO ON TO THE NEXT PAGE.

Questions 47–55. Read the following poem by Margaret Atwood carefully, and then choose answers to the questions that follow.

February
By Margaret Atwood

Winter. Time to eat fat
and watch hockey. In the pewter mornings, the cat,
a black fur sausage with yellow
Line Houdini eyes, jumps up on the bed and tries
(5) to get onto my head. It's his
way of telling whether or not I'm dead.
If I'm not, he wants to be scratched; if I am
He'll think of something. He settles
on my chest, breathing his breath
(10) of burped-up meat and musty sofas,
purring like a washboard. Some other tomcat,
not yet a capon, has been spraying our front door,
declaring war. It's all about sex and territory,
which are what will finish us off
(15) in the long run. Some cat owners around here
should snip a few testicles. If we wise
hominids were sensible, we'd do that too,
or eat our young, like sharks.
But it's love that does us in. Over and over
(20) again, He shoots, he scores! and famine
crouches in the bedsheets, ambushing the pulsing
eiderdown, and the windchill factor hits
thirty below, and pollution pours
out of our chimneys to keep us warm.
(25) February, month of despair,
with a skewered heart in the centre.
I think dire thoughts, and lust for French fries
with a splash of vinegar.
Cat, enough of your greedy whining
(30) and your small pink bumhole.
Off my face! You're the life principle,
more or less, so get going
on a little optimism around here.
Get rid of death. Celebrate increase. Make it be spring.

"February" from *Morning In The Burned House* by Margaret Atwood. Copyright © 1995 by Margaret Atwood. Reprinted by permission of Houghton Mifflin Harcourt Publishing Company. All rights reserved.

47. In the last line of the poem, the word "increase" is referring to

   (A) escalation
   (B) strength
   (C) intensification
   (D) growth
   (E) enhancement

48. The reference to "sharks" (line 18) is an example of

   (A) metonymy
   (B) apostrophe
   (C) synecdoche
   (D) personification
   (E) a simile

49. In line 4, the word "Houdini" serves the purpose of

   (A) revealing the magic found in having pets
   (B) elaborating on the cat's animosity towards the interloper
   (C) emphasizing the striking appearance of the cat's eyes
   (D) accentuating the cat's mystical qualities
   (E) creating an allusion to a bygone era

50. Lines 25–26 most directly suggest that

   (A) the narrator dreads February because of Valentine's Day
   (B) the narrator finds the dead of winter to be a trying time
   (C) paradoxically, life can sometimes emerge from death
   (D) there is a natural cyclical pattern of renewal that the narrator has forgotten
   (E) the narrator is gravely ill and certain to die before the spring

51. Overall, the speaker's attitude toward the subject of the poem is one of

   (A) pessimism and impatience
   (B) devotion and fear
   (C) love and anger
   (D) reverence and awe
   (E) piety and amazement

GO ON TO THE NEXT PAGE.

52. In lines 2–11, the relationship between the speaker and her cat is most directly implied to be

    (A) a miserable coexistence
    (B) one-sided on the narrator's part
    (C) neither happy nor unhappy
    (D) a necessary evil
    (E) marked by begrudging affection

53. In lines 27–28, the speaker

    (A) reveals her struggles through thoughts of food
    (B) loses herself in the experience of her meal
    (C) is driven solely by her lust for food
    (D) is unsure if she should indulge her craving
    (E) is metaphorically transported by her meal

54. Grammatically, the word "off" (line 31) functions as a

    (A) noun
    (B) adjective
    (C) direct object
    (D) verb
    (E) preposition

55. Which of the following best describes the use of rhetorical devices in the poem?

    (A) The author uses them to imply that the speaker is questioning the morality of pet ownership.
    (B) The author uses them as a juxtaposition with the poem's many similes and metaphors.
    (C) The author uses them to emphasize how overwhelmed the speaker is.
    (D) The author uses them to introduce new aspects of her characterization of her cat.
    (E) The author uses them to convey the speaker's awe of the natural world.

STOP
END OF SECTION I
IF YOU FINISH BEFORE TIME IS CALLED, YOU MAY CHECK YOUR WORK ON THIS SECTION.
DO NOT GO ON TO SECTION II UNTIL YOU ARE TOLD TO DO SO.

ENGLISH LITERATURE AND COMPOSITION

SECTION II

Total Time—2 hours

Question 1

(Suggested time—40 minutes. This question counts as one-third of the total essay score.)

In the following poems by Samuel Taylor Coleridge and William Blake, the speakers explore infancy. Read the poems carefully. Then, in a well-written essay, analyze how the authors use poetic elements and techniques such as imagery to reveal their attitudes toward infancy.

In your response you should do the following:

- Respond to the prompt with a thesis that presents an interpretation and may establish a line of reasoning.
- Select and use evidence to develop and support your line of reasoning.
- Explain the relationship between the evidence and your thesis.
- Use appropriate grammar and punctuation in communicating your argument.

To an Infant

Ah cease thy tears and sobs, my little life!
I did but snatch away the unclasped knife:
Some safer toy will soon arrest thine eye,
Line And to quick laughter change this peevish cry!
(5) Poor stumbler on the rocky coast of woe,
Tutored by pain each source of pain to know!
Alike the foodful fruit and scorching fire
Awake thy eager grasp and young desire;
Alike the good, the ill offend thy sight,
(10) And rouse the stormy sense of shrill affright!
Untaught, yet wise! mid all thy brief alarms
Thou closely clingest to thy mother's arms,
Nestling thy little face in that fond breast
Whose anxious heavings lull thee to thy rest!
(15) Man's breathing miniature! thou mak'st me sigh—
A babe thou art—and such a thing am I!

To anger rapid and as soon appeased,
For trifles mourning and by trifles pleased;
Break friendship's mirror with a tetchy blow,
(20) Yet snatch what coals of fire on pleasure's altar glow!

Oh thou that rearest with celestial aim
The future seraph in my mortal frame,
Thrice holy Faith! whatever thorns I meet
As on I totter with unpractised feet,
(25) Still let me stretch my arms and cling to thee,
Meek nurse of souls through their long infancy!

—Samuel Taylor Coleridge

Infant Sorrow

My mother groaned, my father wept;
Into the dangerous world I leapt,
Helpless, naked, piping loud,
Like a fiend hid in a cloud.
Line
(5) Struggling in my father's hands,
Striving against my swaddling bands,
Bound and weary, I thought best
To sulk upon my mother's breast.

—William Blake

[handwritten annotations: "couplets", "Imagery", "Exciting Tone repeated use of exclamation mark"]

GO ON TO THE NEXT PAGE.

Question 2

(Suggested time—40 minutes. This question counts as one-third of the total essay score.)

The following excerpt is from Don DeLillo's novel *Libra* (1988). In this passage, we are given a fictional treatment of the young Lee Harvey Oswald, who, as an adult would assassinate President John F. Kennedy. Read the passage carefully. Then, in a well-written essay, analyze how DeLillo uses literary elements and techniques such as diction, imagery, and point of view to portray the subject and the substance of the portrait itself.

In your response you should do the following:

- Respond to the prompt with a thesis that presents a defensible interpretation.
- Provide evidence to support your line of reasoning.
- Explain how the evidence supports your line of reasoning.
- Use appropriate grammar and punctuation in communicating your argument.

He returned to the seventh grade until classes ended. In summer dusk the girls lingered near the benches on Bronx Park South. Jewish girls, Italian girls in tight skirts, girls with

Line ankle bracelets, their voices murmurous with the sound of
(5) boys' names, with song lyrics, little remarks he didn't always understand. They talked to him when he walked by making him smile in his secret way.

Oh a woman with beer on her breath, on the bus coming home from the beach. He feels the tired salty sting in his eyes
(10) of a day in the sun and water.

"The trouble leaving you with my sister," Marguerite said, "she had too many children of her own. Plus the normal disputes of family. That meant I had to employ Mrs. Roach, on Pauline Street, when you were two. But I came home one
(15) day and saw she whipped you, raising welts on your legs, and we moved to Sherwood Forest Drive."

Heat entered the flat through the walls and windows, seeped down from the tar roof. Men on Sundays carried pastry in white boxes. An Italian was murdered in a candy
(20) store, shot five times, his brains dashing the wall near the comic-book rack. Kids trooped to the store from all around to see the traces of grayish spatter. His mother sold stockings in Manhattan.

A woman on the street, completely ordinary, maybe fifty
(25) years old, wearing glasses and a dark dress, handed him a leaflet at the foot of the El steps. Save the Rosenbergs, it said. He tried to give it back thinking he would have to pay for it, but she'd already turned away. He walked home, hearing a lazy radio voice doing a ballgame. Plenty of room, folks.
(30) Come on out for the rest of this game and all of the second. It was Sunday, Mother's Day, and he folded the leaflet neatly and put it in his pocket to save for later.

There is a world inside the world.

He rode the subway up to Inwood, out to Sheepshead
(35) Bay. There were serious men down there, rocking in the copper light. He saw, beggars, men who talked to God, men who lived on the trains, day and night, bruised, with matted hair, asleep in patient bundles on the wicker seats. He jumped the turnstiles once. He rode between cars, gripping
(40) the heavy chain. He felt the friction of the ride in his teeth. They went so fast sometimes. He liked the feeling they were on the edge. How do we know the motorman's not insane? It gave him a funny thrill. The wheels touched off showers of blue-white sparks, tremendous hissing bursts, on the edge of
(45) no-control. People crowded in, every shape face in the book of faces. They pushed through the doors, they hung from the porcelain straps. He was riding just to ride. The noise had a power and a human force. The dark had a power. He stood at the front of the first car, hands flat against the glass. The
(50) view down the tracks was a form of power. It was a secret and a power. The beams picked out secret things. The noise was pitched to a fury he located in the mind, a satisfying wave of rage and pain.

GO ON TO THE NEXT PAGE.

Question 3

(Suggested time—40 minutes. This question counts as one-third of the total essay score.)

"When a true genius appears in the world, you may know him by this sign, that the dunces are all in confederacy against him."

—Jonathan Swift
"Thoughts on Various Subjects, Moral and Diverting"

Either from your own reading or from the list below, choose a work of fiction in which the main character finds himself in conflict with the social or moral values of his environment. Then, in a well-written essay, analyze how that tension contributes to an interpretation of the work as a whole. Do not merely summarize the plot.

In your response you should do the following:

- Respond to the prompt with a thesis that presents a defensible interpretation.
- Provide evidence to support your line of reasoning.
- Explain how the evidence supports your line of reasoning.
- Use appropriate grammar and punctuation in communicating your argument.

The Age of Innocence
Americanah
The Bell Jar
The Bonesetter's Daughter
Breath, Eyes, Memory
Brighton Beach Memoirs
Ceremony
Cold Mountain
Death of a Salesman
Exit West
Great Expectations
Gulliver's Travels
Home
Homegoing
The Hummingbird's Daughter
Kindred
The Kite Runner
Lonely Londoners
The Mambo Kings Play Songs of Love
Mansfield Park
The Mill on the Floss

Mrs. Dalloway
My Ántonia
The Namesake
Native Son
Paradise Lost
The Piano Lesson
The Poisonwood Bible
Pudd'nhead Wilson
Pygmalion
Quicksand
The Return of the Native
The Scarlet Letter
Song of Solomon
Sons and Other Flammable Objects
The Sound and the Fury
The Tempest
Their Eyes Were Watching God
Where the Dead Sit Talking
Wuthering Heights

STOP
END OF EXAM
IF YOU FINISH BEFORE TIME IS CALLED, YOU MAY CHECK YOUR WORK ON THIS SECTION.

Practice Test 3:
Answers and
Explanations

PRACTICE TEST 3 ANSWER KEY

1.	A	21.	C	41.	B
2.	B	22.	C	42.	D
3.	B	23.	D	43.	D
4.	B	24.	A	44.	C
5.	A	25.	C	45.	C
6.	A	26.	E	46.	D
7.	B	27.	D	47.	D
8.	E	28.	C	48.	E
9.	A	29.	D	49.	C
10.	B	30.	B	50.	B
11.	A	31.	C	51.	A
12.	A	32.	B	52.	E
13.	D	33.	C	53.	A
14.	C	34.	A	54.	D
15.	C	35.	C	55.	E
16.	E	36.	E		
17.	E	37.	D		
18.	A	38.	C		
19.	B	39.	A		
20.	C	40.	B		

PRACTICE TEST 3 EXPLANATIONS

Questions 1–12

This passage is from *The Awakening* by Kate Chopin, published in 1899. It is considered an early feminist novel and delves into the themes of gender roles and social constraint.

1. **A**   Like many questions on the exam, this question is essentially a sophisticated vocabulary question. The key to understanding it is to note the unpleasant noises made by the birds at the outset. There is no sense of the playfulness of whimsy, (B), and though it isn't a lighthearted start, it is too lively and raucous to be brooding, (C). There is no humor intended to be satirical, (D), and there is none of the idyllic romantic depiction of nature in pastoral imagery, (E). It's all about the noise.

2. **B**   Although the passage is written in third person, there is a clear sense of Mr. Pontellier's distaste for his environment. He doesn't know what he wants, but it's not this. We do see an "exclamation of disgust" in the text, which might suggest volatility, (C). Though he may share some of the pettiness of the truly officious, (A), we do not see him as being particularly tidy, organized, or neat, nor do we see any signs of a fiery temper, so you can eliminate (C). Choice (D) can also be eliminated because he is transparent almost to a fault, and there is no evidence that he has any passion for power, as suggested in (E). Phrases like "expression and exclamation of disgust," along with the tendency for people to "cease to be entertaining," show his judgmental and intolerant nature.

3. **B**   Though Mr. Pontellier does not seem particularly happy or comfortable in his environment, we have no reason to believe that this retreat at Grand Isle is anything but pleasant, so eliminate (A). At this point, we haven't been introduced to Robert or Mrs. Pontellier, which means neither (C) nor (D) can be correct. And while there is initial annoyance at the various birds mentioned, this is not a consistent nature motif that goes beyond the beginning of the passage. Therefore, eliminate (E). The passage does depict Mr. Pontellier as being restless, unsatisfied, and out of place throughout, as exemplified by such words as "maddening," "restlessly," and referring to his "disgust" at his lack of "any degree of comfort." Choice (B) is the correct answer.

4. **B**   The writers of the exam love to include words with many viable definitions and then ask the reader to choose the best one. This can be tricky if the word is used in an unconventional or dated manner as it is here. It is up to the reader to decipher the definition based on the context. In this situation, Mr. Pontellier is speaking about his time in New Orleans prior to arriving at Grand Isle. Choice (B) is the best option because it makes sense that he did not have time to read the paper prior to leaving the day before.

5. **A**   Mr. Pontellier appears completely devoid of any meaningful connection to humanity. He doesn't hate people, but he doesn't seem to like anyone, either. He shows no signs of curiosity, (B), warmth, (D), or antagonism, (E), toward others, and his ambivalence toward his wife's friendship with Robert does not connote mistrust, (C). Indeed, people often "cease to be entertaining" to him, and he easily walks away from them when they become tiresome, making (A) the best answer.

6. **A**   Though Mr. Pontellier doesn't seem to care much for humanity, he apparently takes pride in having robust children. We may hope that the children have the necessary thick skin to tolerate their father, but we do not know whether he is neglectful, so get rid of (B). We receive surprisingly little physical description of Mrs. Pontellier, so (C) is likely incorrect. Although Mr. Pontellier is portrayed as being of "medium height" and "slender build," we have no evidence that the children are not his, nor does he express any suspicion of this, so eliminate (D). We know almost nothing of the physical features of the island's inhabitants other than that there are "a good many persons of the *pension*" along with "young" Robert, "fresh, pretty" Mrs. Lebrun, two young twins, Mrs. Pontellier, and others; therefore, (E) is incorrect. To call his children "sturdy" is downright effusive coming from Mr. Pontellier, but it is the only possible answer. Choice (A) is correct.

7. **B**   If you are stumped by the wording or intent of this question, you might be able to use your sense of diction to figure out the answer. One of these words is not like the others. Choice (A), smoke, implies something noxious or implies the presence of fire—neither of which is evident in Pontellier's depiction. Choice (C), gaunt, may describe his appearance somewhat, but not his personality. Pontellier's use of "folly" gives us the impression that he wouldn't know a good time if it bit him, so eliminate (D). Choice (E), plunge, is far too active of a verb for this idle man. Choice (B) is correct.

8. **E**   If you are familiar with this work already, you may be inclined to think (A) is correct. But in this passage, there is no evidence of any animosity on Mr. Pontellier's behalf toward Robert, so (A) is not true. Similarly, there is no evidence of Mr. Pontellier's athleticism, so (B) is untrue as well. He mocks the two adults for committing the "folly [of bathing] at such an hour in this heat." Eliminate (C). Mr. Pontellier's scolding of his wife and his judgment of her looks as "property that had suffered some damage" shows a complete lack of concern for his wife's health, so eliminate (D). This statement does, however, clearly illustrate contempt, and furthermore, his pride in having gone swimming at dawn shows how much he likes himself and congratulates himself for his choices—in other words, his self-righteousness. Therefore, (E) is the answer.

9. **A**   Again, we have a literary term identification question. Onomatopoeia, (B), is a literary device in which a word imitates the sound it makes, like "crack" or "boom." Assonance, (C), uses vowel-sound repetition to create internal rhyme. Understatement, (D), occurs when a speaker uses less intensity or enthusiasm to express something than the occasion or feeling warrants. Mr. Pontellier's charged and scolding statements toward his wife are, essentially, the opposite of this. Apostrophe, (E), occurs when a speaker addresses a person or object in a rhetorical manner, not expecting an answer to their addressing of it, and though Robert and Mrs. Pontellier do not respond to Mr. Pontellier's braying, he was, likely, expecting a response from them. Hyperbole, (A) is exaggeration for effect, and, since Mr. Pontellier recognizes his wife and Robert, one can assume that they are not literally "burnt beyond recognition."

10. **B**   The description of Mrs. Pontellier's "strong, shapely hands" does not make her sound unattractive, eliminating (A). There is no suggestion that Robert is uncomfortable around Mr. Pontellier, (C). In fact, Robert seems oblivious to him, focusing only on Mrs. Pontellier. The characterization of Mrs. Pontellier as a "piece of personal property" (lines 68–69) in her husband's eyes does not support the idea that she is the dominant one in their relationship, so (D) is incorrect. Mr. Pontellier's "burnt

beyond recognition" comment (line 67) does not reflect concern or protectiveness when coupled with that same "personal property that has suffered some damage" attitude, which eliminates (E). A strained relationship (B) is supported throughout the selection: in Mr. Pontellier's criticism and way of looking at his wife, in her trip to the beach with Robert and in her exchange of laughter with him.

11. **A** Once again, if you have read the novel, you could get into trouble here. Later on in *The Awakening*, there is quite a bit of passion, conflict, and secrecy, but none of this is evident in the opening chapter, eliminating (B), (D), and (E). While the interactions between Mrs. Pontellier and Robert relegate Mr. Pontellier to awkward "third wheel" status, the slowness of their stroll from the water, the way they sit facing each other, and the "answering smile" she gives Robert all indicate a closeness that eliminates (C), leaving (A) as the answer.

12. **A** Though Mr. Pontellier seems to criticize nearly everyone and everything, he does not extend this attitude toward his children, so (B) cannot be true. On the contrary, though Mr. Pontellier does not allow his children to follow him to Klein's, he does "kiss them and promise to bring them back bonbons and peanuts." If Pontellier is concerned about his wife's friendship with Robert, he certainly doesn't show it. Instead, he encourages his wife to spend time with him until "he bores you." Therefore, (C) and (E) are also incorrect, as he neither fears nor desires to be rid of Robert. While loathing small talk might be in line with his character, there is no evidence that Mr. Pontellier does so in lines 86–90. Eliminate (D). When his wife asks him whether he'll be returning for dinner, his response is very indicative of his character and thus his attitude toward his marriage: he shrugs. This means that (A) is the answer.

Questions 13–23

The passage is by Christina Rossetti (1830–1894), and was written when she was in her early thirties. The poem's spiritual, death-haunted theme is typical of Rossetti, who was beset with ill health her entire, and relatively long, life.

The Rossettis, Christina and her brothers, William Michael and Dante Gabriel, were at the center of an influential mid-19th-century arts movement called the Pre-Raphaelite Brotherhood. Pre-Raphaelite painting and writing were concerned with medieval themes, romance (often tinged with self-destruction or death), nature, nostalgia, vivid imagery, and color.

Christina's brother Dante (arguably the leader of the Pre-Raphaelite movement) is guilty of one of the truly cheese-ball acts of narcissism in literary history. When Dante Gabriel Rossetti's wife died, the painter-poet buried the manuscripts of several of his poems in the casket with her. Ah, love. Seven years later he decided maybe it wasn't such a good idea and had the mess dug up so he could get his poems back. The last laugh, however, is on Dante, whose reputation is waning. His sister Christina, however, has acquired a growing respect from the literary world after many years spent in her brother's shadow.

The poem on the test (like almost everything Christina Rossetti wrote) is a meditation on the transience of life and the inevitability of death. When, in the third stanza, God promises to come for the poet when her hour arrives, the poem becomes an avowal of faith.

Although the bulk of the poem's meaning is accessible to most readers, the questions asked on the test lay several traps for the unwary. When reading and interpreting poetry, be on guard against making assumptions that can't be justified. Several questions have incorrect choices that suggest the principal narrator is on her deathbed. You should not reason that the poem's intense contemplation of death indicates the speaker is gravely ill or about to die; those are unwarranted assumptions. Do not assume or infer anything that is not very close to what is actually written in the passage. (And this goes for reading sections on any standardized test!)

Another difficulty you face when answering the questions on the Rossetti passage is that the questions ask about some of the poem's subtler points. There are several questions, for example, about the important shift in the recurrent nature imagery in the poem's final stanza. Complications also rise from the presence of multiple speakers in the poem.

This long-standing tradition of conversing with the spiritual forces of the cosmos may seem a hopelessly old-fashioned device, but poets up to the present day continue to create interesting and important works using this convention. The Rossetti poem, however, not only has the speaker in dialogue with the metaphysical world, but also takes matters a degree further in the second stanza by having the Soul speak with the voice of the past. Following the line "Hearken what the past doth witness and say:" the Soul presents what the past has to say about human mortality. You needed to understand that in this stanza the past is *not* being directly presented as a speaker. In fact, the past is probably not even being quoted; the Soul is interpreting the past for the benefit of the principal narrator. This is a tangled piece of rhetorical construction and causes most students some problems.

Overall, the passage, taken together with its questions, is at the difficult end of the spectrum of work you will see on the AP English Literature and Composition Exam.

13. **D**   As noted in the passage description, this is a tough question. Most students choose (E), five. But the past is not a speaker. The past is being interpreted for the principal narrator by the Soul. Another choice that sophisticated readers sometimes pick is (A), one. The reasoning behind choosing (A) is usually that only the poet is speaking; the Soul, World, and God represent elements and ideas within the poet. In this reading, the poem is a kind of internal monologue in which the poet sorts out her feelings about death and the afterlife. This interpretation is absolutely plausible. (Rossetti certainly did not intend for you to think she had actually held a conversation with the World or with God.) The problem is that it is an *interpretation*. The question asks, "How many speakers does the poem directly present?" The emphasis is on what the poem presents, not what the poem might suggest. The question is not asking for an interpretation but simply for what the poem presents. It presents four speakers, so (D) is the correct answer.

14. **C**   This is one of the relatively rare knowledge questions on the test. You either know it or you don't. Eighty to ninety percent of the test is about your ability to understand the material you read, both the details and the larger picture. But there are some facts that the test-writers feel they can expect you know. They expect you to know the basic terminology of literary criticism and form (for example: simile, metaphor, couplet), and they occasionally ask about those literary historical references a well-read individual should recognize. This question is an example of the latter.

In ancient Greek and Roman society, a garland of laurel and bay leaves was awarded in recognition of triumph in sports, war, or poetry. The original "gold medal" of the Olympics was a laurel wreath, as is that wreath you always see framing Julius Caesar's bald pate. The reason the answer specifically mentions poets is that laurel (bay is a variety of laurel) was the symbolic flower of Apollo, patron God of poetry. Even today, when people are honored as the national poet, their title is *poet laureate*. Speaking of honors, graduation from college with a bachelor's degree will mean that you have earned your bacca*laureate*, a term derived from the medieval university tradition of crowning graduates with laurel.

15. **C** The incorrect answers all make use of imagery that draws on living things, especially plants, and of the changing seasons. In line 13, the image of "Rust in thy gold" is the one image of the poem that draws neither on the seasons nor on living things.

16. **E** The key to answering this question correctly is Process of Elimination (POE). Be methodical by checking each of the answer choices' explanation with the first stanza. This should help you get rid of (B) and probably (D) as well, since a surprise does not seem to be found in the stanza. Choice (A)'s explanation of the second stanza doesn't fit, so you can eliminate it right there. Choice, (E), with its expression of happiness, fits the third stanza better than (C), in which "supplication for divine intervention" doesn't adequately convey the idea that the speaker in the stanza is actually God.

17. **E** The question shouldn't have given you too much trouble. Basically, you were asked what "a moth in thine array" is meant to signify metaphorically. The image is yet one more description of the natural aging process. The incorrect choices offer various misreadings, either seeing illness where none is present or spiritual anxieties that neither the line in question, nor the poem as a whole, is concerned with.

18. **A** Understanding the lines in question is not as much about the lines themselves as it is about letting them make sense in the overall context of the poem. If you understood the bulk of the poem, then this question shouldn't have been difficult. If the poem itself gave you trouble, this question might have as well. The incorrect choices offer various misreadings and overinterpretations. Don't get too bogged down. Try Process of Elimination, and if you're still stuck, take a guess and move on.

19. **B** Always return to the passage. The third stanza presents a dramatic reversal in the poem's meaning and direction by refiguring imagery from the previous stanzas with an antithetical meaning. In the first two stanzas, Spring and the imagery of spring are used to represent youth, energy, and life. You might easily think, then, that Winter, as Spring's opposite, represents aging and loss of vigor, (E), or perhaps the coldness of the grave, (C), that is, death itself. But the question asks for the meaning of Winter in the *third* stanza. In this stanza God says that now "Winter passeth after the long delay." What follows are images of spring now clearly tied to death and the afterlife. Spring in the final stanza is a metaphor for the joy of reunion with God. In the final stanza, God offers death as a joyous, spring-like occasion. It is earthly life, separate from the Maker, which is the long Winter (B).

20. **C** As with all questions with longer answers, you must read carefully and eliminate when an answer is partially correct. "Partially correct" is what we call "half wrong," and as you know, "half wrong = all wrong." Otherwise, the reasoning behind this question is fully covered in the explanation to question 19.

21. **C** This is another terminology question. If it gave you any trouble, refer to our glossary of literary terms (found on p. 335) for the AP English Literature and Composition Exam. Also, remember to use Process of Elimination to get rid of those answers you are sure are wrong and guess with what is left. No blanks!

22. **C** This is essentially a vocabulary question, but chances are you were unfamiliar with the passage's usage of the word "spray." Figure out the meaning from the context. None of the incorrect answer choices makes sense in context except possibly (A), and we hope that between (A) and (C), you chose (C).

23. **D** You are certain to see a question (or two or three) like this one on your test. If you got this question wrong, brush up on your skills with our section on grammar for the AP English Literature and Composition Exam (pages 83–84). As outlined in that section, the best way to figure out the construction of the kind of sentence the test-writers like to ask about is to rewrite the sentence (in your mind—you shouldn't need to actually write it down) into a more natural form. The sentences are never straightforward "subject, verb, direct-object, indirect object" sentences like "Jack threw the ball to me." The sentence that begins on line 24, "Arise, come away, night is past and lo it is day,/ My love, My sister, My spouse, thou shalt hear Me say," should be rewritten:

"Thou shalt hear me say, 'Arise, come away, night is past and lo it is day,

   My love, My sister, My spouse.'"

Notice we've put quotation marks around what God reports he will say. This is how the sentence would normally be punctuated. If you rewrite it in this manner, you should be able to see that "Thou" is the subject, so (D) is your answer.

Questions 24–36

This passage is from Anthony Trollope's novel *Barchester Towers*, the second of his Barsetshire novels. It was written in 1857 and, unlike many Victorian novels, was more concerned with the topics of the day than the recent past. However, like the Victorian prose you are apt to see on the test, the sentences can be somewhat convoluted, with multiple negations and other forms of twisted syntax. Tone isn't always easy to discern. Close reading is essential.

24. **A** The narrator states, "It is not my intention to breathe a word against Mrs Proudie," but then spends several paragraphs doing just that. Choice (B) is a colloquialism derived from figurative language describing a domineering wife. Because domineering is precisely what Mrs. Proudie is said to be, there is no irony here. Choice (C) is the juxtaposition of Mrs. Grantly, the archdeacon's wife, but there isn't enough said about her to know if this is ironic or not. Choice (D) might be construed as hyperbole, but it certainly is not the opposite of the author's intended meaning. Choice (E) is close; one might detect some sarcasm, also known as verbal irony, but the author doesn't mean the opposite of what he has stated, so (A) is the best answer.

25. **C** Although (C) describes Dr. Proudie, it does so in the context of how Mrs. Proudie's despotic behavior has cowed him. While tempting, (A) refers much more closely to Mrs. Proudie's ambitions and how they extend beyond the normal sphere of the wife of a bishop. Choice (B) refers to Mrs. Grantly, not Mrs. Proudie. Choice (D) refers to something Mrs. Proudie expects those under her roof to submit to, but it is not as pointed an example of her authoritarian nature as (C) is. Choice (E) uses a mythological allusion to a watchful, not authoritarian, character.

26. **E** Dr. Proudie is, in name, or title ("titular"), the lord of Mrs. Proudie but as the passage explains in great depth, it is Mrs. Proudie, in actuality, who lords over her husband. The situation is the opposite of what it is in name and that is a stellar example of irony (E). Choice (A) doesn't have much going for it, other than a big word that students who aren't adequately familiar with literary terms won't understand. Hyperbole is exaggeration, which does not apply here, so eliminate (A). Choices (B) and (D) do much the same thing, but with even fancier words. Choice (C) might appeal to a student who knows that onomatopoeia has something to do with how words sound, and "titular" does sound funny—but it's not a noun or verb, so it can't really sound like the noise made by the thing it describes.

27. **D** The phrase states that in domestic matters, he would not have offered the power to his wife but was happy to cede it. Choices (B) and (E) are based on careless reading of the phrases "domestic" or the vague memory that the passage was about his marriage. Choices (A) and (C) take deceptive language from elsewhere in the passage.

28. **C** In the context of the passage, which is devoted to describing Mrs. Proudie's character, the example of Mrs. Grantly, the archdeacon's wife, is used to describe Mrs. Proudie by contrast. Mrs. Grantly's virtues are laid out, and the transition into the subsequent paragraph, "Not so Mrs Proudie," makes the author's intention clear. Choice (A) is a trap answer designed to snare the careless reader who sees the words "the full privileges of her rank," which actually pertain to her role as a clergyman's wife. Choice (B) is another use of deceptive language. The transition into the paragraph, "In fact, the bishop is henpecked," refers to Dr. Proudie, not the archdeacon, Mrs. Grantly's husband. Choice (D) is probably the most evil of all trap answers, one designed to catch the rare student who may have read this novel or its sequels—in particular, *Framley Parsonage*, in which the rivalry of Mrs. Grantly and Mrs. Proudie is given substantial attention. It certainly is not the author's intention to suggest a rivalry, although he may have intended to foreshadow it. Choice (E) has some merit. From the description of Mrs. Grantly, it certainly seems as if the author favors women who exert their power domestically and privately. The passage states, "before the world she is a pattern of obedience; her voice is never loud… she knows what should be the limits of a woman's rule." Nevertheless, the language in the answer choice, "assert why women should be seen and not heard," suggests that the author provides evidence for a position stronger than the one he actually takes.

29. **D** Choice (A), pity, is best used to describe how the author feels toward Dr. Proudie, "her poor husband." Although the narrator may feign an appearance of objectivity, his opening comments make it clear that what he presents is his subjective opinion, so eliminate (B). Given that, (C), emotional judgment, might be tempting, but his language is strong enough to justify (D), sardonic condemnation. He is certainly mocking Mrs. Proudie, and his judgment of her does condemn her behavior. Choice (E) is too extreme for the passage.

30. **B** We do not get a sense of Dr. Proudie's devotion to his wife or of his moral compass, no matter what we might want to infer from knowing his profession, so (A) is out. Choice (B) is supported by the text of the third paragraph. Choices (C) and (D) suggest a happy and loving marriage, not the picture painted by this paragraph. Choice (E) might describe Mrs. Proudie's relationship to her husband, but not the reverse.

31.   **C**   He is described as "aware that submission produces the nearest approach to peace which his own house can ever attain." Choice (A) refers most nearly to a quality best attributed to Mrs. Proudie. Choices (B) and (E) are not supported by the text. Choice (D) is a trap answer for those who read quickly and saw that the passage was about the clergy and religious matters.

32.   **B**   Even if you weren't familiar with the Victorian use of "character" as shorthand for "character reference," you could derive the meaning from the context of the passage—the maid has been dismissed and because of this "character," she is unable to find decent employment. Choices (A), (C), and (D) all prey on a reader's familiarity with the dictionary definitions of the word, as opposed to the contextual meaning. Choice (E) is a trap for the reader who sees "character" and "foot" near each other in the passage and overinterprets—perhaps thinking that the footman is sent to escort the housemaid from the premises.

33.   **C**   The repetition of the phrase "Woe betide" accentuates the seriousness of the servants' situation. It neither slows down the prose, as in (A), nor satirizes or mocks the servants' fate, as in (B). The phrase is consistent with the narrator's attitude throughout the rest of the passage, so (D) is incorrect. Choice (E) is too extreme.

34.   **A**   The maid in question has been unfaithful to her duty. As is par for the course on a single phrase or word question, the primary dictionary definition, (D), is offered as an answer choice, as is a word it kind of sounds like, (B). The other choices have no merit whatsoever.

35.   **C**   The point of the paragraph is to illustrate Mrs. Proudie's hypocrisy. The paragraph does so by showing how strict she is in applying the rules to others when it comes to this single point of religious belief, although she is given to "[d]issipation and low dresses" the rest of the time. Choice (A) might be tempting because of the religious aspect, but in no place does this paragraph suggest a transformation for the domineering Mrs. Proudie. Choice (B) also has its merits, as this paragraph is where Mr. Slope is introduced, but no mention is made of him observing Mrs. Proudie (quite the contrary, one is expected to observe Mr. Slope). For similar reasons, the mention of religion, (D), might be attractive but as mentioned above, it doesn't counter speculation about her despotic reign. Rather, it extends it beyond her husband to her household staff—which she might have a hard time hiring, as (E) suggests, but that would not be the point of the paragraph.

36.   **E**   The author analyzes Mrs. Proudie in an amusing way, mocking her cleverly by first pointing out her flaws in contrast to a social equivalent, and then by exposing her hypocrisy. Most of the other answers fall into the half-right, half-wrong category, and using Process of Elimination will save the day here. Choice (A) is wrong on both counts—the passage is neither humorless nor pedantic. Although the passage is certainly subjective, it is hardly emotional, so as long as you know the definition of effusive, you can eliminate (B). Choice (C) starts out stronger; the passage is certainly descriptive. Alas, a few metaphors do not a metaphorical passage make. If you chose (C) or even kept it on your first pass through the answer choices, don't kick yourself. Close answer choices are one of the ways a question can be made more challenging. Lacking both terseness and epigrams, though, (D) should be an easy candidate for elimination for this particular passage.

Questions 37–46

This poem was written in 1922 by Amy Lowell, one of the leading female poets of her day, who was known for her frank and emotion-filled depictions of relationships and sensual love, and for being at the forefront of imagism, a literary movement of the early 20th century.

Amy Lowell has sparked recent critical interest because of her interesting use of language and sensual themes. The title ("In Excelsis") refers to the Latin exclamation of praise that is a part of the Catholic Mass. In this poem, the rejoicing is due to the speaker's lover, whom she talks about throughout. A challenging part of this poem is keeping track of what Lowell is referring to with each of her many uses of figurative language, particularly simile and metaphor. If you've done that successfully, you probably won't have too much trouble with most of the questions. Using Process of Elimination carefully will definitely help you spot the small differences between answer choices that are often key to picking the correct one.

37. **D** The interactions cannot be described as antagonistic, (A), and there's no contrast—figurative or otherwise—in this part of the poem, so you can also get rid of (E). The other three choices look temping because they all have to do with the physicality of the speaker's lover, who is the subject of the poem. However, you can't justify the idea that the relationship is more physical than emotional—that's too much reading into the lines. Eliminate (C). Choices (B) and (D) are similar, but the lines go beyond pointing out the beauty and, with their action verbs ("eat" and "drink"), imply that the speaker is having some interaction or feeling about the physicality of the person she's talking about. That makes (D) the better answer, but this is definitely a tough one!

38. **C** The meaning of the given phrase is actually fairly straightforward, so the key is to not read too much into it. Choice (A) is a bit too literal an interpretation, and we don't learn about the lover in these phrases, so (B) is out as well. Choice (E) is certainly a possible interpretation, but it strays a bit far from the words themselves—it might be appropriate to write in an essay, but not in a multiple-choice question. Choice (D), with its interest in the physical world (the sea and sky) is a bit too literal again, just like (A).

39. **A** The speaker repeats "you" with a dash like that almost as if she can't believe that her lover even exists, and this fits tonally as well as in terms of the content with the rest of the poem. (Remember to keep your answers consistent!) No difficulty, (B), or inability, (C), is expressed anywhere else, and while the use of the dashes might suggest (D), there's no evidence for that in the poem either. Choice (E) is also incorrect, as the speaker gives no indication that she is worrying about not being clear—or knows about anything else, for that matter!

40. **B** This question requires a bit of close reading. Choices (A), (D), and (E) were probably fairly easy for you to spot (and, therefore, to eliminate, since we're looking for the thing that is NOT supported by the passage here!). However, eliminating (C) requires an understanding of the last stanza, in which the comparison made is less obvious: The speaker draws that comparison to say that her lover is as necessary to her as those other things which one takes for granted. Choice (B), by the way, is a comparison drawn in the poem, but it's a comparison to the lover's "fancies," or ideas, not to a lover's personal characteristics, so it is the odd one out.

41. **B**   The speaker is comparing herself to a jar that will be filled, which fits with the language of (B). The same comparison is mentioned in (A), but that choice gets the point of the comparison wrong. Choices (C) and (E) are not supported by the passage. Choice (D) looks good, except that it's the subject of the poem, not the speaker, who is referred to with those comparisons. Make sure you read the answer choices as carefully as you do the poem!

42. **D**   All of the choices are metaphors used in the poem, but (A), (B), and (C) are all about either the speaker's lover or her relationship. Choice (E) is what the speaker compares her own voice to. Choice (D) gets at the thrust of that last stanza: it's the "things which [she] say[s]" that are compared to rubies—and the poem itself is what she's saying.

43. **D**   The use of the word "shrine," at which the speaker will kneel, is your major clue here (stanza 5). The other stanzas suggest devotion, certainly, but other than the title and maybe some coded references to Jesus imagery (which the test won't expect you to pick up on), there's nothing else here that's religious.

44. **C**   This question relies on your knowledge of the terms in the glossary, so study them if you had trouble. Since this is a comparison using the word "as," it is a simile, not any of the other terms listed. Choice (E), a metaphysical conceit, would be associated with John Donne and his era, and because this poem was written in the 20th century, it definitely doesn't apply.

45. **C**   Choice (A) is untrue: the speaker is actually using heaven as an example of something she takes for granted, rather than something she is thankful for. Rule out (A). Similarly, you can rule out (B) and (D), which recycle words like "earth" and "rubies" from the last stanza but do not match the theme. Choice (C) is correct in that neither the morning nor her lover is something that the author feels the need to thank the universe for: they're both simply things she needs to survive. Last, rule out (E), which is a logical conclusion but is not supported by the text. The correct answer is (C).

46. **D**   Consistency of Answers (see Chapter 4) should help you identify (D) as correct, especially at this point when you've done so many questions in this passage. Choice (B) looks tempting, but it mixes up parts of the passage: it's her lover that the speaker is reverential toward, not nature. Choice (A) might also look good, but it refers to a figurative, not literal, idea expressed in the poem. Her lover isn't really as far away as the high clouds. In fact, we don't know that the lover is actually any place in particular at all. Therefore, (D) is the answer.

Questions 47–55

This is a poem by Margaret Atwood, an award-winning Canadian poet, novelist, teacher, and environmentalist. She is wildly prolific and known in present times most famously for her book *The Handmaid's Tale*, which was made into a popular television show. This poem, "February" was published in her poetry collection *Morning in the Burned House* (1995). It is an exploration of sexual repression and the cold of winter months through the use of an annoying, needy, cat and the promise of Spring.

47. **D**   Based on the context of the last line of the poem, "increase" will be the opposite of "death" and result in something like "spring." Choice (D), growth, is the correct answer.

48. **E** Metonymy, (A), is a thing or concept that is not called by its own name, but by the name of something intimately associated with that thing or concept. This is often confused with synecdoche, (C), as they're both part/whole concepts, but the key here is common association. Humans are not commonly associated with sharks. Apostrophe, (B), is a literary device in which a speaker addresses a person or object in a rhetorical manner, not expecting an answer. In this case, the narrator was not addressing the sharks directly. Had the sharks been referred to as "doing" something human, then personification, (D), would be correct. As it is, "sharks" are used to refer to their practice of eating their young in a hyperbolic suggestion that humans also try it, an example of a simile. The correct answer is (E).

49. **C** "Houdini eyes" is a reference to Harry Houdini, an early 20th century magician known for his sensational escape acts. (A), (D), and (E) are each traps related to Houdini's "magic," but the phrase is simply a descriptor for the cat's appearance, or (C). Eliminate (B), as the description does not reference any "animosity" on the part of the cat. The correct answer is (C).

50. **B** The lines in question here, "February, month of despair, with a skewered heart in the centre," show the narrator's winter struggle punctuated by Valentine's Day. While (A) is tempting, it goes beyond the scope of the text. Choice (B) is an appropriate match, but (A), (C), (D), and (E) go beyond the scope of the text. The correct answer is (B).

51. **A** Whether the subject is February, dead of winter, or the kitty cat that the speaker addresses, the speaker pretty clearly demonstrates "pessimism and impatience." Some examples: interpreting the cat's motives to be as base as "telling whether or not [the narrator is] dead," directing the cat to "get going on a little optimism," or the claim the narrator "think[s] dire thoughts." Eliminate (B), (C), (D), and (E) for being too positive. The correct answer is (A).

52. **E** In lines 2–11, the narrator details how the cat "jumps up on the bed," "wants to be scratched," and "settles on [the narrator's] chest." While the narrator does include complaints about the cat, she ultimately allows all of the cat's attempts to be close to her, which matches (E). Eliminate (A) for miserable, (B) for one-sided, and (D) for evil. The correct answer is (E).

53. **A** In lines 27–28, the narrator's "dire thoughts" are much more significant than her food cravings are. To claim that she "loses herself" or is "driven solely" by food goes beyond the scope of the text, so eliminate (B) and (C). Similarly, there is no indication of how the narrator feels about the food, so eliminate (D) and (E). The correct answer is (A).

54. **D** While "off" usually functions as an adjective, adverb, or preposition, in this case, it takes the place of the verb in the implicit command for the cat to "[get] off my face!" Therefore, (D) is correct.

55. **E** Choice (C) is close to being correct, but "overwhelmed" is a little too strong to be adequately supported by the poem. The other answer choices are all based on various misreadings: Choice (A) makes too much of the poem's religious references, (D) may be true of some of the rhetorical devices but not all of them, and (B) is simply fancy-sounding language that doesn't fit with the meaning of the poem—there's no juxtaposition there. The correct answer is (E).

Practice Test 4

The Exam

AP® English Literature and Composition Exam

SECTION I: Multiple-Choice Questions

DO NOT OPEN THIS BOOKLET UNTIL YOU ARE TOLD TO DO SO.

At a Glance

Total Time
1 hour
Number of Questions
55
Percent of Total Grade
45%
Writing Instrument
Pencil required

Instructions

Section I of this examination contains 55 multiple-choice questions. Fill in only the ovals for numbers 1 through 55 on your answer sheet.

Indicate all of your answers to the multiple-choice questions on the answer sheet. No credit will be given for anything written in this exam booklet, but you may use the booklet for notes or scratch work. After you have decided which of the suggested answers is best, completely fill in the corresponding oval on the answer sheet. Give only one answer to each question. If you change an answer, be sure that the previous mark is erased completely. Here is a sample question and answer.

Sample Question

Chicago is a
(A) state
(B) city
(C) country
(D) continent
(E) village

Sample Answer

Ⓐ ● Ⓒ Ⓓ Ⓔ

Use your time effectively, working as quickly as you can without losing accuracy. Do not spend too much time on any one question. Go on to other questions and come back to the ones you have not answered if you have time. It is not expected that everyone will know the answers to all the multiple-choice questions.

About Guessing

Many candidates wonder whether or not to guess the answers to questions about which they are not certain. Multiple-choice scores are based on the number of questions answered correctly. Points are not deducted for incorrect answers, and no points are awarded for unanswered questions. Because points are not deducted for incorrect answers, you are encouraged to answer all multiple-choice questions. On any questions you do not know the answer to, you should eliminate as many choices as you can, and then select the best answer among the remaining choices.

GO ON TO THE NEXT PAGE.

ENGLISH LITERATURE AND COMPOSITION

SECTION I

Time—1 hour

Directions: This section consists of selections from literary works and questions on their content, form, and style. After reading each passage or poem, choose the best answer to each question and then completely fill in the corresponding oval on the answer sheet.

<u>Questions 1–11</u>. Choose your answers to questions 1–11 based on a careful reading of the following poem by Andrew Marvell.

The Mower's Song

My mind was once the true survey
    Of all these meadows fresh and gay,
    And in the greenness of the grass
Line   Did see its hopes as in a glass;
(5)   When Juliana came, and she
What I do to the grass, does to my thoughts and me.

    But these, while I with sorrow pine,
    Grew more luxuriant still and fine,
    That not one blade of grass you spied,
(10)   But had a flower on either side;
    When Juliana came, and she
What I do to the grass, does to my thoughts and me.

    Unthankful meadows, could you so
    A fellowship so true forgo,
(15)   And in your gaudy May-games meet,
    While I lay trodden under feet?
    When Juliana came, and she
What I do to the grass, does to my thoughts and me.

    But what you in compassion ought,
(20)   Shall now by my revenge be wrought:
    And flow'rs, and grass, and I and all,
    Will in one common ruin fall.
    For Juliana comes, and she
What I do to the grass, does to my thoughts and me.

(25)   And thus, ye meadows, which have been
    Companions of my thoughts more green,
    Shall now the heraldry become
    With which I will adorn my tomb;
    For Juliana comes, and she
(30) What I do to the grass, does to my thoughts and me.

1. What does "survey" in line 1 most nearly mean in context?

    (A) View
    (B) Mirror
    (C) Comprehension
    (D) Inspection
    (E) Audit

2. What activity is the speaker engaged in?

    (A) Cutting the grass
    (B) Pruning the grass
    (C) Ensuring the grass is kept green
    (D) Creating pictures of the grass
    (E) Mourning a lost love

3. What can readers infer that Juliana is doing to the speaker?

    (A) Jeering at his lowly status
    (B) Rejecting him
    (C) Ignoring him
    (D) Toying with his affections
    (E) Competing with him

4. What change occurs between stanza 3 and stanza 5?

    (A) The speaker moves from despairing to hopeful
    (B) The speaker is hopeful and then expresses despair
    (C) The speaker moves from feeling commonality with the renewal of spring grass to feeling that it is flourishing while he is downcast
    (D) The speaker moves from feeling cut down like the grass to lying dead in a tomb
    (E) The speaker moves from celebrating the hopeful revival of green grass to wanting to ruin it by cutting it down

5. What is NOT likely the intended effect of each stanza ending with the same refrain?

    (A) It mimics the swinging back and forth of a scythe
    (B) It is monotonous, like mowing
    (C) It implies consistent and repeated rejection
    (D) It casts the speaker as everyman
    (E) It unifies the poem

6. How does the speaker feel about his plight?

    (A) Vengeful and jealous
    (B) Steadfast and calm
    (C) Spontaneous and capricious
    (D) Obsessive and driven
    (E) Melancholy and despairing

GO ON TO THE NEXT PAGE.

7. The poem as a whole is best understood as a(n)

    (A) elegy for a young man
    (B) pastoral about a yeoman
    (C) ballad about rustic life
    (D) rhapsody about love's power
    (E) lament for unrequited love

8. Who is "you" in "what you in compassion ought/ Shall now by my revenge be wrought" (lines 19–20) and why?

    (A) Juliana, because she should have pity on the speaker
    (B) The grass, which should show common feeling with the mower
    (C) The audience, because they pity the speaker
    (D) The pastoral god Pan, who implicitly overhears the poem
    (E) Juliana, because she should fear revenge

9. The poem employs all of the following EXCEPT

    (A) personification
    (B) couplets
    (C) refrain
    (D) blank verse
    (E) simile

10. The speaker's primary purpose is most nearly to

    (A) declare love for Juliana
    (B) bid farewell to the world
    (C) vent his anguish
    (D) apostrophize the grass
    (E) express bitterness

11. In context, the change in tense between lines 5, 11, and 17 ("Juliana came") and lines 23 and 29 ("Juliana comes") implies that

    (A) Juliana will continue to come in the future, but the speaker has lost hope
    (B) Juliana's arrival is imminent
    (C) Juliana will continue to come by the field after he is dead
    (D) the speaker feels a spark of hope that she will eventually love him
    (E) Juliana will continue to live and he won't

GO ON TO THE NEXT PAGE.

Questions 12–23. Read the following passage carefully before choosing your answers. The selection is an excerpt from the short story "An Occurrence at Owl Creek Bridge," by Ambrose Bierce.

The preparations being complete, the two private soldiers stepped aside and each drew away the plank upon which he had been standing. The sergeant turned to the captain,
Line saluted and placed himself immediately behind that officer,
(5) who in turn moved apart one pace. These movements left the condemned man and the sergeant standing on the two ends of the same plank, which spanned three of the cross-ties of the bridge. The end upon which the civilian stood almost, but not quite, reached a fourth. This plank had been held in place
(10) by the weight of the captain; it was now held by that of the sergeant. At a signal from the former the latter would step aside, the plank would tilt and the condemned man go down between two ties. The arrangement commended itself to his judgment as simple and effective. His face had not been
(15) covered nor his eyes bandaged. He looked a moment at his "unsteadfast footing," then let his gaze wander to the swirling water of the stream racing madly beneath his feet. A piece of dancing driftwood caught his attention and his eyes followed it down the current. How slowly it appeared to move, What a
(20) sluggish stream!

He closed his eyes in order to fix his last thoughts upon his wife and children. The water, touched to gold by the early sun, the brooding mists under the banks at some distance down the stream, the fort, the soldiers, the piece of
(25) drift—all had distracted him. And now he became conscious of a new disturbance. Striking through the thought of his dear ones was a sound which he could neither ignore nor understand, a sharp, distinct, metallic percussion like the stroke of a blacksmith's hammer upon the anvil; it had
(30) the same ringing quality. He wondered what it was, and whether immeasurably distant or near by—it seemed both. Its recurrence was regular, but as slow as the tolling of a death knell. He awaited each stroke with impatience and—he knew not why—apprehension. The intervals of silence grew
(35) progressively longer, the delays became maddening. With their greater infrequency the sounds increased in strength and sharpness. They hurt his ear like the thrust of a knife; he feared he would shriek. What he heard was the ticking of his watch.

(40) He unclosed his eyes and saw again the water below him. "If I could free my hands," he thought, "I might throw off the noose and spring into the stream. By diving I could evade the bullets and, swimming vigorously, reach the bank, take to the woods and get away home. My home, thank God, is as yet
(45) outside their lines; my wife and little ones are still beyond the invader's farthest advance."

....

As Peyton Farquhar fell straight downward through the bridge he lost consciousness and was as one already dead. From this state he was awakened—ages later, it
(50) seemed to him—by the pain of a sharp pressure upon his throat, followed by a sense of suffocation. Keen, poignant agonies seemed to shoot from his neck downward through every fiber of his body and limbs. These pains appeared

to flash along well-defined lines of ramification and to
(55) beat with an inconceivably rapid periodicity. They seemed like streams of pulsating fire heating him to an intolerable temperature. As to his head, he was conscious of nothing but a feeling of fulness—of congestion. These sensations were unaccompanied by thought. The intellectual part of his nature
(60) was already effaced; he had power only to feel, and feeling was torment. He was conscious of motion. Encompassed in a luminous cloud, of which he was now merely the fiery heart, without material substance, he swung through unthinkable arcs of oscillation, like a vast pendulum. Then all at once,
(65) with terrible suddenness, the light about him shot upward with the noise of a loud splash; a frightful roaring was in his ears, and all was cold and dark. The power of thought was restored; he knew that the rope had broken and he had fallen into the stream. There was no additional strangulation; the
(70) noose about his neck was already suffocating him and kept the water from his lungs. To die of hanging at the bottom of a river!—the idea seemed to him ludicrous. He opened his eyes in the darkness and saw above him a gleam of light, but how distant, how inaccessible! He was still sinking, for the light
(75) became fainter and fainter until it was a mere glimmer. Then it began to grow and brighten, and he knew that he was rising toward the surface—knew it with reluctance, for he was now very comfortable. "To be hanged and drowned," he thought? "that is not so bad; but I do not wish to be shot. No; I will not be shot; that is not fair."

12. What is the reader to infer from lines 8–13 ("The end upon which....between two ties")?

   (A) The man is about to be hung
   (B) The man is about to be shot
   (C) The man is about to be bayonetted
   (D) The man is at risk of drowning
   (E) The man can escape by jumping into the water

13. What is the narrator conveying about the man's character in the lines "the arrangement commended itself to his judgment as simple and effective" (lines 13–14)?

   (A) He thinks only of escape
   (B) He faces death stolidly
   (C) He is passionately opposed to the soldiers
   (D) He respects the officers
   (E) He thinks of death with horror

14. In line 21, the words "to fix" most nearly mean

   (A) to repair
   (B) to seal
   (C) to finalize
   (D) to supply
   (E) to steady

GO ON TO THE NEXT PAGE.

15. The tone of the passage as a whole can best be described as

    (A) objective and distanced
    (B) tragic and resigned
    (C) hopeful and optimistic
    (D) ironic and facetious
    (E) pessimistic and despairing

16. How can the actions of the soldiers in lines 1–5 ("The preparations….one pace") best be described?

    (A) Vengeful and emotional
    (B) Stately and calm
    (C) Invasive and marauding
    (D) Improvised and haphazard
    (E) Unfair and disrespectful

17. What is the author most nearly conveying with the contrasting descriptions in "swirling water of the stream racing madly" (lines 16–17) and "what a sluggish stream!" (lines 19–20)

    (A) The stream's velocity changes with the passage of time.
    (B) Peyton Farquhar's sense of time is distorted.
    (C) The narrator is omniscient and Peyton Farquhar is not.
    (D) The soldiers chose a creek with alternating rapids and slow moving water.
    (E) The water illustrates how subjective the human experience of time is.

18. What does NOT occur in the actions between lines 26 ("Striking through") and 39 ("watch")?

    (A) The watch sounds a kind of death knell.
    (B) The man moves from calmness to terror.
    (C) The man loses touch with reality.
    (D) The character's sense of time becomes very elastic.
    (E) The man descends into madness.

19. The narrator's purpose in saying "there was no additional strangulation; the noose around his neck was already suffocating him and kept the water from his lungs" (lines 69–71) most nearly

    (A) keeps readers involved in the plot of Farquhar's escape
    (B) displays the narrator's omniscience, as this can only be occurring in Farquhar's mind
    (C) instills doubt about Farquhar's perception of reality, as a noose isn't likely to keep water fully out
    (D) exemplifies irony, as the noose meant to kill him turns out to save him
    (E) explains how Farquhar might swim underwater to evade the soldiers' bullets

20. What most closely represents the progression between the first paragraph (lines 1–20) and third paragraph (lines 40–46)?

    (A) Severity toward a condemned man to sympathy with his struggles.
    (B) Meditations on mortality to a sense of release.
    (C) Horror about imminent death to relief.
    (D) Oscillation between objective representation of both the scene and the character to the character's internal thoughts of a character.
    (E) Near-cinematic representation of a scene to the desperate mind of a character.

21. The metaphor of "Encompassed in a luminous cloud, of which he was now merely the fiery heart" (lines 61–62) chiefly

    (A) emphasizes Farquhar's insignificance
    (B) underscores the simile in "like streams of pulsating fire" (line 56)
    (C) unifies the paragraph with images of light and fire
    (D) indicates the strength of Farquhar's emotions
    (E) creates hyperbole

22. The phrase "heating him to an intolerable temperature" (lines 56–57) most clearly echoes which other part of the passage?

    (A) "like the thrust of a knife" (line 37)
    (B) "a feeling of fulness—of congestion" (line 58)
    (C) "unthinkable arcs of oscillation" (lines 63–64)
    (D) "a frightful roaring" (line 66)
    (E) "the stroke of a blacksmith's hammer" (line 29)

23. The function of the descriptors in "the water, touched to gold" (line 22) and "brooding mists" (line 23) primarily

    (A) introduces the beauty of a rural setting
    (B) discredits the story's historical accuracy
    (C) satirizes the soldiers' self-importance
    (D) injects a dose of irony into the scene
    (E) provokes sympathy for Farquhar

GO ON TO THE NEXT PAGE.

Questions 24–34. Choose your answers to each of the following questions based on careful reading of the following poem by Rita Dove.

Cozy Apologia

For Fred

I could pick anything and think of you—
This lamp, the wind-still rain, the glossy blue
My pen exudes, drying matte, upon the page.
Line I could choose any hero, any cause or age
(5) And, sure as shooting arrows to the heart,
Astride a dappled mare, legs braced as far apart
As standing in silver stirrups will allow—
There you'll be, with furrowed brow
And chain mail glinting, to set me free:
(10) One eye smiling, the other firm upon the enemy.

This post-postmodern age is all business: compact disks
And faxes, a do-it-now-and-take-no-risks
Event. Today a hurricane is nudging up the coast,
Oddly male: Big Bad Floyd, who brings a host
(15) Of daydreams: awkward reminiscences
Of teenage crushes on worthless boys
Whose only talent was to kiss you senseless.
They all had sissy names—Marcel, Percy, Dewey;
Were thin as licorice and as chewy,
(20) Sweet with a dark and hollow center. Floyd's

Cussing up a storm. You're bunkered in your
Aerie, I'm perched in mine
(Twin desks, computers, hardwood floors):
We're content, but fall short of the Divine.
(25) Still, it's embarrassing, this happiness—
Who's satisfied simply with what's good for us,
When has the ordinary ever been news?
And yet, because nothing else will do
To keep me from melancholy (call it blues),
(30) I fill this stolen time with you.

24. "Thin as licorice" (line 19) is an example of

(A) metaphor
(B) conceit
(C) simile
(D) personification
(E) metonym

25. The "you" in "whose only talent was to kiss you sense-less" (line 17) refers to

(A) Fred
(B) the subject of the poem
(C) the reader of the poem
(D) the narrator
(E) Big Bad Floyd

26. Lines 6–10 ("astride a dappled mare…firm upon the enemy") most likely are an allusion to

(A) a knight riding to the rescue
(B) an historic re-enactor
(C) a trainer of horses
(D) the love of the speaker's life
(E) the ideal of chivalry

27. What does "We're content, but fall short of the Divine" (line 24) imply in context?

(A) Castigation for the lack of god's love
(B) Sarcasm about the pettiness of home life
(C) Celebration of domesticity's happiness
(D) Anxiety about the emphasis on earthly joys
(E) Irony about overreliance on technology

28. What is implied by the contrast between the verbs "bunkered" (line 21) and "perched" (line 22)?

(A) The narrator plans to leave her partner.
(B) The narrator is less grounded than her partner.
(C) The narrator laments her partner's insular nature.
(D) The narrator and her partner occupy different floors.
(E) The narrator is flighty, but the partner is sensible.

29. The poem as a whole is best understood as

(A) a celebration of earthly bliss
(B) a jeremiad against the world's exigencies
(C) a defense of domestic happiness
(D) a confession of love
(E) a dirge for the modern world

30. All of the following poetic elements exist in the poem EXCEPT

(A) Conceit
(B) Couplets
(C) Off rhyme
(D) Colloquialism
(E) Enjambment

GO ON TO THE NEXT PAGE.

31. What does the personification of "Big Bad Floyd" most nearly convey (line 14)?

    (A) The speaker's partner has a potential rival
    (B) He's a memory trigger for the speaker
    (C) Unleashed nature threatens the home
    (D) Destructive impulses rage within and without
    (E) He's a disruptive force unlikely to succeed

32. What is the most likely reason the speaker feels embarrassed in lines 25–27 ("it's embarrassing…ever been news?")?

    (A) She's daydreaming of old loves.
    (B) The neighbors might be jealous of her domestic happiness.
    (C) She's not fulfilling the writer's mission of catching higher truths.
    (D) Her love is too much for the circumstances.
    (E) The modern age is outstripping the ability of poets to write about.

33. One effect of the shift in the speaker's focus between the first and second stanza is to

    (A) consider the future and the past rather than the present
    (B) imply a movement to a world bigger than domestic love
    (C) argue that technology intrudes on places dedicated to the life of the mind
    (D) emphasize the continuities between past, present, and future
    (E) lament that only through past dissatisfactions can she find happiness

34. The implied analogy of the narrator's past crushes and candy ("were thin…center"), lines 19–20, most nearly means

    (A) they were unhealthy
    (B) they were insubstantial
    (C) they left her hollow inside
    (D) they weren't engaging
    (E) they experienced gender conflicts

GO ON TO THE NEXT PAGE.

Questions 35–44. Choose your answers to each of the following questions based on careful reading of the following excerpt from a short story by Edgar Allan Poe.

I was not a little astonished to discover that the literary world has hitherto been strangely in error respecting the fate of the vizier's daughter, Scheherazade, as that fate is depicted
Line in the "Arabian Nights"; and that the dénouement there
(5) given, if not altogether inaccurate, as far as it goes, is at least to blame in not having gone very much farther.

....

It will be remembered, that, in the usual version of the tales, a certain monarch having good cause to be jealous of his queen, not only puts her to death, but makes a vow, by
(10) his beard and the prophet, to espouse each night the most beautiful maiden in his dominions, and the next morning to deliver her up to the executioner.

Having fulfilled this vow for many years to the letter, and with a religious punctuality and method that conferred great
(15) credit upon him as a man of devout feeling and excellent sense, he was interrupted one afternoon (no doubt at his prayers) by a visit from his grand vizier, to whose daughter, it appears, there had occurred an idea.

Her name was Scheherazade, and her idea was, that she
(20) would either redeem the land from the depopulating tax upon its beauty, or perish, after the approved fashion of all heroines, in the attempt.

Accordingly, and although we do not find it to be leap-year (which makes the sacrifice more meritorious), she
(25) deputes her father, the grand vizier, to make an offer to the king of her hand. This hand the king eagerly accepts—(he had intended to take it at all events, and had put off the matter from day to day, only through fear of the vizier),—but, in accepting it now, he gives all parties very distinctly to
(30) understand, that, grand vizier or no grand vizier, he has not the slightest design of giving up one iota of his vow or of his privileges. When, therefore, the fair Scheherazade insisted upon marrying the king, and did actually marry him despite her father's excellent advice not to do any thing of the kind—
(35) when she would and did marry him, I say, will I, nill I, it was with her beautiful black eyes as thoroughly open as the nature of the case would allow.

It seems, however, that this politic damsel (who had been reading Machiavelli, beyond doubt), had a very ingenious
(40) little plot in her mind. On the night of the wedding, she contrived, upon I forget what specious pretence, to have her sister occupy a couch sufficiently near that of the royal pair to admit of easy conversation from bed to bed; and, a little before cock-crowing, she took care to awaken
(45) the good monarch, her husband (who bore her none the worse will because he intended to wring her neck on the morrow),—she managed to awaken him, I say, (although on account of a capital conscience and an easy digestion, he slept well) by the profound interest of a story (about a rat
(50) and a black cat, I think) which she was narrating (all in an undertone, of course) to her sister. When the day broke, it so happened that this history was not altogether finished, and that Scheherazade, in the nature of things could not finish it just then, since it was high time for her to get up and be
(55) bowstrung—a thing very little more pleasant than hanging, only a trifle more genteel!

The king's curiosity, however, prevailing, I am sorry to say, even over his sound religious principles, induced him for this once to postpone the fulfilment of his vow until next
(60) morning, for the purpose and with the hope of hearing that night how it fared in the end with the black cat (a black cat, I think it was) and the rat.

The night having arrived, however, the lady Scheherazade not only put the finishing stroke to the black cat and the rat
(65) (the rat was blue) but before she well knew what she was about, found herself deep in the intricacies of a narration, having reference (if I am not altogether mistaken) to a pink horse (with green wings) that went, in a violent manner, by clockwork, and was wound up with an indigo key. With this
(70) history the king was even more profoundly interested than with the other—and, as the day broke before its conclusion (notwithstanding all the queen's endeavors to get through with it in time for the bowstringing), there was again no resource but to postpone that ceremony as before, for twenty-
(75) four hours. At all events, Scheherazade, who, being lineally descended from Eve, fell heir, perhaps, to the whole seven baskets of talk, which the latter lady, we all know, picked up from under the trees in the garden of Eden; Scheherazade, I say, finally triumphed, and the tariff upon beauty was
(80) repealed.

35. The "depopulating tax upon its beauty" (lines 20–21) refers to

(A) the murder of the monarch's brides
(B) the fleeing of beautiful women from the country
(C) the efforts of fathers to pay tariffs rather than surrender their daughters
(D) a tax levied upon notably beautiful women
(E) the winnowing of one out of every 10 women

36. The style of the passage as a whole can be described as

(A) distanced and measured
(B) horrified and fearful
(C) effusive and admiring
(D) sly and satiric
(E) witty and concise

GO ON TO THE NEXT PAGE.

37. The narrator's attitude toward Scheherazade can best be described as

    (A) duplicitous
    (B) arch
    (C) admiring
    (D) disgusted
    (E) pitying

38. What is the likely primary effect of the repetition of colors in the text?

    (A) To call into question Scheherazade's sanity
    (B) To highlight Scheherazade's creativity
    (C) To challenge the reader's suspension of belief
    (D) To portray her stories as a fevered dream
    (E) To clarify why the monarch wanted to hear the stories

39. What is "a man of devout feeling and excellent sense" an example of in context?

    (A) Hyperbole
    (B) Irony
    (C) Paradox
    (D) Oxymoron
    (E) Synecdoche

40. What can we infer about the grand vizier in paragraph 5 ("this hand....kind," lines 26–34)?

    (A) He's ineffectual
    (B) He fails to stop the murders
    (C) He's a good father
    (D) He's afraid of the monarch
    (E) He's resting on his laurels

41. Which statement best describes the relationship between Eve and Scheherazade in paragraph 8?

    (A) Both are victorious in their respective quests
    (B) They are united in story-telling capability
    (C) They are opposites though related by blood
    (D) They exemplify appropriate courses of action for their time
    (E) Both symbolize women as active agents

42. What does "no resource" mean in context (lines 73–74)?

    (A) No new wives
    (B) No time remaining before daybreak
    (C) No time remaining before the execution
    (D) No other plan of action
    (E) No naturally occurring resources

43. What does the passage "her idea...attempt" (lines 19 –22) indicate about Scheherazade's motivation?

    (A) She intends to make the king love her
    (B) She desires the overthrow of hackneyed plots
    (C) She wants to make her country better
    (D) The events incense her
    (E) The events terrify her

44. The echo of "depopulating tax" (line 20) and "tariff" (line 79) serves to

    (A) remind us of Scheherazade's patriotism
    (B) provide a clue that the narrator is uncaring
    (C) transition the story away from the realm of emotion
    (D) distance the reader from the fact of murder
    (E) question the narrator's veracity

GO ON TO THE NEXT PAGE.

Questions 45–55. Choose your answers to each of the following questions based on a careful reading of the following excerpt from a novel by British writer Arnold Bennett.

The peculiar angle of the earth's axis to the plane of the ecliptic--that angle which is chiefly responsible for our geography and therefore for our history--had caused the
Line phenomenon known in London as summer. The whizzing
(5) globe happened to have turned its most civilized face away from the sun, thus producing night in Selwood Terrace, South Kensington. In No. 91 Selwood Terrace two lights, on the ground-floor and on the first-floor, were silently proving that man's ingenuity can outwit nature's. No. 91
(10) was one of about ten thousand similar houses between South Kensington Station and North End Road. With its grimy stucco front, its cellar kitchen, its hundred stairs and steps, its perfect inconvenience, and its conscience heavy with the doing to death of sundry general servants, it uplifted tin
(15) chimney-cowls to heaven and gloomily awaited the day of judgment for London houses, sublimely ignoring the axial and orbital velocities of the earth and even the reckless flight of the whole solar system through space. You felt that No. 91 was unhappy, and that it could only be rendered happy by
(20) a 'To let' standard in its front patch and a 'No bottles' card in its cellar-windows. It possessed neither of these specifics. Though of late generally empty, it was never untenanted. In the entire course of its genteel and commodious career it had never once been to let.

(25) Go inside, and breathe its atmosphere of a bored house that is generally empty yet never untenanted. All its twelve rooms dark and forlorn, save two; its cellar kitchen dark and forlorn; just these two rooms, one on the top of the other like boxes, pitifully struggling against the inveterate gloom of the
(30) remaining ten! Stand in the dark hall and get this atmosphere into your lungs.

The principal, the startling thing in the illuminated room on the ground-floor was a dressing-gown, of the colour, between heliotrope and purple, known to a
(35) previous generation as puce; a quilted garment stuffed with swansdown, light as hydrogen--nearly, and warm as the smile of a kind heart; old, perhaps, possibly worn in its outlying regions and allowing fluffs of feathery white to escape through its satin pores; but a dressing-gown to dream of. It
(40) dominated the unkempt, naked apartment, its voluptuous folds glittering crudely under the sun-replacing oil lamp which was set on a cigar-box on the stained deal table. The oil lamp had a glass reservoir, a chipped chimney, and a cardboard shade, and had probably cost less than a florin;
(45) five florins would have purchased the table; and all the rest of the furniture, including the arm-chair in which the dressing-gown reclined, a stool, an easel, three packets of cigarettes and a trouser-stretcher, might have been replaced for another ten florins. Up in the corners of the ceiling, obscure in the
(50) eclipse of the cardboard shade, was a complicated system of cobwebs to match the dust on the bare floor.

Within the dressing-gown there was a man. This man had reached the interesting age. I mean the age when you think you have shed all the illusions of infancy, when you think
(55) you understand life, and when you are often occupied in speculating upon the delicious surprises which existence may hold for you; the age, in sum, that is the most romantic and tender of all ages--for a male. I mean the age of fifty. An age absurdly misunderstood by all those who have not reached it!
(60) A thrilling age! Appearances are tragically deceptive.

The inhabitant of the puce dressing-gown had a short greying beard and moustache; his plenteous hair was passing from pepper into salt; there were many minute wrinkles in the hollows between his eyes and the fresh crimson of his
(65) cheeks; and the eyes were sad; they were very sad. Had he stood erect and looked perpendicularly down, he would have perceived, not his slippers, but a protuberant button of the dressing-gown. Understand me: I conceal nothing; I admit the figures written in the measurement-book of his tailor. He
(70) was fifty. Yet, like most men of fifty, he was still very young, and, like most bachelors of fifty, he was rather helpless. He was quite sure that he had not had the best of luck.

45. In context, the word "inveterate" (line 29) most nearly means

(A) long-standing
(B) ineradicable
(C) entrenched
(D) settled
(E) universal

46. No. 91 Selwood Terrace is described as all of the following EXCEPT

(A) foul and pestilent
(B) drearily common
(C) multi-leveled
(D) dirty and uncared for
(E) mostly empty

47. The relationship of the first paragraph (lines 1–24) to the fourth paragraph (lines 52-60) represents a shift from

(A) objective description to subjective description
(B) an ironic narrative to a realistic portrayal
(C) an aristocratic point of view to democratic fellow-feeling
(D) an overview of the cosmos to a specific individual
(E) time-honored tradition to the modern world

GO ON TO THE NEXT PAGE.

48. What does the personification of the building in lines 18–21 ("felt that No. 91 was unhappy...windows") most convey?

    (A) It bears responsibility for servant deaths
    (B) It serves as a proxy for all houses in London
    (C) Its future would brighten with just a few signs
    (D) Its relationship to religion is uneasy
    (E) It wants more people to inhabit it

49. What most conveys the meaning of "whizzing globe... turned its most civilized face away from the sun" (lines 4–6) and the "sun-replacing oil lamp" (line 41)?

    (A) Man has outwitted nature
    (B) Both humans and nature abandon the sun
    (C) The modern world is far away from light and warmth
    (D) The universe, like the house, is dark and devoid of warmth
    (E) Earth turns away from the sun, but man attempts to supplant it

50. Which of the following statements best conveys the effect of the sentences in "the startling thing....deal table" (lines 32–42)?

    (A) The adjectives paint the dressing gown as a spot of color in a dark world.
    (B) The diction implies that the dressing gown is the stuff of which dreams are made.
    (C) The tone conveys how out of place the dressing gown is in the dingy room.
    (D) The narrator believes the dressing gown represents comfort in a harsh world.
    (E) The structure reveals that the once-glorious dressing gown is now falling apart.

51. What is closest to the narrator's view of the man in paragraphs 4 and 5 (lines 52–72)?

    (A) He's young
    (B) He's disillusioned
    (C) He's unhappy
    (D) He needs the dressing gown as a shield
    (E) He's down on his luck

52. What can we infer about the man from "Had he stood erect and looked....tailor" (lines 60–64)?

    (A) He is embarrassed about the size of his stomach
    (B) He is an artist
    (C) He is left behind by events
    (D) He doesn't know what to do
    (E) He is overweight

53. The purpose of the florins in paragraph 3 is most likely intended to

    (A) reveal that the furnishings are cheap
    (B) imbue the surroundings with exoticism
    (C) imply that the man is well-traveled
    (D) lament the lack of craftsmanship
    (E) castigate a society that doesn't remunerate artists

54. In lines 14–15, "uplifted tin chimney-cowls to heaven"

    (A) implies that spiritual appeals are flimsy
    (B) analogizes the building to a deeply spiritual person
    (C) condemns cheap building practices
    (D) compares chimneys to praying monks
    (E) portrays buildings as spiritual places

55. The main point of the first sentence (lines 1–4) can best be paraphrased as

    (A) human events grow out of region and climate
    (B) human events are influenced by planetary oddities
    (C) heavenly bodies influence geography, which in turn influences human events
    (D) the arc between the sun and the British capital encompasses the reader's universe
    (E) summer, light, and warmth are all passing phenomena

STOP

END OF SECTION I

IF YOU FINISH BEFORE TIME IS CALLED, YOU MAY CHECK YOUR WORK ON THIS SECTION.
DO NOT GO ON TO SECTION II UNTIL YOU ARE TOLD TO DO SO.

SECTION II

Total Time—2 hours

Question 1

(Suggested time—40 minutes. This question counts as one-third of the total essay score.)

In the following poem by Louise Glück (published in 1992), the speaker reflects on a relationship. Read the poem carefully. Then, in a well-written essay, analyze how Glück uses poetic elements and techniques to convey the speaker's complex perspective on the relationship.

In your response you should do the following:

- Respond to the prompt with a thesis that presents an interpretation and may establish a line of reasoning.
- Select and use evidence to develop and support your line of reasoning.
- Explain the relationship between the evidence and your thesis.
- Use appropriate grammar and punctuation in communicating your argument.

    The White Lilies

    As a man and woman make
    a garden between them like
    a bed of stars, here
Line they linger in the summer evening
 (5) and the evening turns
    cold with their terror: it
    could all end, it is capable
    of devastation. All, all
    can be lost, through scented air
(10) the narrow columns
    uselessly rising, and beyond,
    a churning sea of poppies--

    Hush, beloved. It doesn't matter to me
    how many summers I live to return:
(15) this one summer we have entered eternity.
    I felt your two hands
    bury me to release its splendor.

        From *The Wild Iris.*

GO ON TO THE NEXT PAGE.

Question 2

(Suggested time—40 minutes. This question counts as one-third of the total essay score.)

The following excerpt is from the short story "A Lodging for the Night: A Story of Francis Villon" (1877) by Robert Louis Stevenson. In this passage, we are introduced to a group of monks and scholars who, despite their learning, live as unrepentant thieves and murderers in medieval Paris. Read the passage carefully. Then, in a well-written essay, analyze how Stevenson uses literary elements and techniques such as imagery and point of view to portray the characters and their world.

In your response you should do the following:

- Respond to the prompt with a thesis that presents an interpretation and may establish a line of reasoning.
- Select and use evidence to develop and support your line of reasoning.
- Explain the relationship between the evidence and your thesis.
- Use appropriate grammar and punctuation in communicating your argument.

It was late in November 1456. The snow fell over Paris with rigorous, relentless persistence; sometimes the wind made a sally and scattered it in flying vortices; sometimes
Line there was a lull, and flake after flake descended out of the
(5) black night air, silent, circuitous, interminable. To poor people, looking up under moist eyebrows, it seemed a wonder where it all came from. Master Francis Villon had propounded an alternative that afternoon, at a tavern window: was it only Pagan Jupiter plucking geese upon Olympus, or
(10) were the holy angels moulting? He was only a poor Master of Arts, he went on; and as the question somewhat touched upon divinity, he durst not venture to conclude....

The air was raw and pointed, but not far below freezing; and the flakes were large, damp, and adhesive. The whole
(15) city was sheeted up. An army might have marched from end to end and not a footfall given the alarm. If there were any belated birds in heaven, they saw the island like a large white patch, and the bridges like slim white spars, on the black ground of the river. High up overhead the snow settled
(20) among the tracery of the cathedral towers. Many a niche was drifted full; many a statue wore a long white bonnet on its grotesque or sainted head. The gargoyles had been transformed into great false noses, drooping toward the point. The crockets were like upright pillows swollen on one
(25) side. In the intervals of the wind there was a dull sound of dripping about the precincts of the church....

Yet there was a small house, backed up against the cemetery wall, which was still awake, and awake to evil purpose, in that snoring district. There was not much to
(30) betray it from without; only a stream of warm vapor from the chimney-top, a patch where the snow melted on the roof, and a few half-obliterated footprints at the door. But within, behind the shuttered windows, Master Francis Villon, the poet, and some of the thievish crew with whom he consorted,
(35) were keeping the night alive and passing round the bottle.

A great pile of living embers diffused a strong and ruddy glow from the arched chimney. Before this straddled Dom Nicolas, the Picardy monk, with his skirts picked up and his fat legs bared to the comfortable warmth. His dilated shadow
(40) cut the room in half; and the firelight only escaped on either side of his broad person, and in a little pool between his outspread feet. His face had the beery, bruised appearance of the continual drinker's; it was covered with a network of congested veins, purple in ordinary circumstances, but now
(45) pale violet, for even with his back to the fire the cold pinched him on the other side. His cowl had half fallen back, and made a strange excrescence on either side of his bull neck. So he straddled, grumbling, and cut the room in half with the shadow of his portly frame.

(50) On the right, Villon and Guy Tabary were huddled together over a scrap of parchment; Villon making a ballade which he was to call the Ballade of Roast Fish, and Tabary spluttering admiration at his shoulder. The poet was a rag of a man, dark, little, and lean, with hollow cheeks and
(55) thin black locks. He carried his four-and-twenty years with feverish animation. Greed had made folds about his eyes, evil smiles had puckered his mouth. The wolf and pig struggled together in his face....

The wind was freshening without; it drove the snow
(60) before it, and sometimes raised its voice in a victorious whoop, and made sepulchral grumblings in the chimney. The cold was growing sharper as the night went on....

"Can't you hear it rattle in the gibbet?" said Villon. "They are all dancing the devil's jig on nothing, up there. You may
(65) dance, my gallants, you'll be none the warmer! Whew, what a gust! Down went somebody just now! A medlar the fewer on the three-legged medlar-tree.—I say, Dom Nicolas, it'll be cold to-night on the St. Denis Road?" he asked.

Dom Nicolas winked both his big eyes, and seemed to
(70) choke upon his Adam's apple. Montfaucon, the great grisly Paris gibbet, stood hard by the St. Denis Road, and the pleasantry touched him on the raw.

GO ON TO THE NEXT PAGE.

Question 3

(Suggested time—40 minutes. This question counts as one-third of the total essay score.)

Many works of literature are concerned with the passage of time, on environments, individuals, memory, or perceptions. These concerns can take many forms. Characters may be comparing past and present or meditating on how their perceptions transformed over time. Either from your own reading or from the list below, choose a work of fiction in which characters are affected by the passage of time. Then, in a well-written essay, analyze how the treatment of time contributes to an interpretation of the work as a whole. Do not merely summarize the plot.

In your response you should do the following:

- Respond to the prompt with a thesis that presents an interpretation and may establish a line of reasoning.
- Select and use evidence to develop and support your line of reasoning.
- Explain the relationship between the evidence and your thesis.
- Use appropriate grammar and punctuation in communicating your argument.

The Adventures of Huckleberry Finn
As I Lay Dying
The Autobiography of Miss Jane Pittman
Beloved
Breath, Eyes, Memory
The Bonesetter's Daughter
Ceremony
The Cherry Orchard
David Copperfield
East of Eden
Fences
Frankenstein
A Handmaid's Tale
Henry IV, Part 2
House of Mirth
House on Mango Street
House of Seven Gables
Jane Eyre
Jude the Obscure
The Kite Runner

The Last of the Mohicans
Long Day's Journey Into Night
Lord Jim
The Lowland
Macbeth
Middlemarch
The Mill on the Floss
The Odyssey
Passing
Persuasion
Portrait of a Lady
Remains of the Day
Richard II
Sula
The Scarlet Letter
The Sympathizer
To the Lighthouse
Tristram Shandy
War and Peace
Wide Sargasso Sea
Wuthering Heights

STOP
END OF EXAM
IF YOU FINISH BEFORE TIME IS CALLED, YOU MAY CHECK YOUR WORK ON THIS SECTION.

Practice Test 4:
Answers and
Explanations

PRACTICE TEST 4 ANSWER KEY

1.	B	21.	D	41.	E
2.	A	22.	E	42.	D
3.	B	23.	A	43.	C
4.	D	24.	C	44.	D
5.	D	25.	D	45.	C
6.	E	26.	A	46.	A
7.	E	27.	C	47.	D
8.	B	28.	B	48.	E
9.	D	29.	C	49.	E
10.	C	30.	A	50.	E
11.	A	31.	E	51.	C
12.	A	32.	C	52.	E
13.	B	33.	B	53.	A
14.	E	34.	B	54.	D
15.	A	35.	A	55.	C
16.	B	36.	D		
17.	C	37.	B		
18.	E	38.	B		
19.	C	39.	B		
20.	D	40.	A		

PRACTICE TEST 4 EXPLANATIONS

Questions 1–11

Andrew Marvell (1621–1678) was an English poet, and one of the prime representatives of Metaphysical poetry. "The Mower's Song," one of a group of related works known as the Mower poems, was published in 1680. In his lifetime, Marvell was better-known as a satirist and was also a politician. His lyric and Metaphysical poetry didn't achieve widespread acclaim until the 20th century.

1. **B** Several of these are definitions or synonyms of "survey." But what does the speaker mean by it? Choice (B) comes the closest. If you paraphrase the meaning of the poem (as you should always!), the speaker says that he once felt the hopeful spring grass reflected his hopes—but that it became verdant and flourishing ("Grew more luxuriant still and fine," line 8) just as he began to droop with sorrow. If this wasn't clear to you, remember that POE can ride to the rescue. Is it (A), view? No, because view doesn't get across the splendor of his happy mind and the grass. Is it (C), comprehension? That's a bit off as well. And both (D) and (E), "inspection" and "audit," are definitely not correct.

2. **A** Choice (A) is the clear answer. You can know this by the title—he is a mower, mowing the grass. But even if you missed the title (Don't! Every word counts!), you can determine it by using POE. The "ruin" discussed in line 22, in which "flowers and grass" fall, refers to cutting the grass and flowers, because cutting them means death. It isn't consistent with (B), pruning, so you can eliminate (B). Pruning is measured cutting to make growth flourish more, not ruin. Choice (C) is out because, although the grass is green in the first stanzas, the speaker isn't keeping it green. The season is. While grass adorning a tomb is mentioned in the poem, again, the speaker isn't doing it, so eliminate (D). And (E) is tricky for several reasons. It comes close, but not as close as (A). The speaker is distressed that Juliana doesn't love him, we can infer—but is the tone mournful, exactly? Also, there's no concrete evidence that Juliana is a lost love—only an unrequited one. They may never have connected at all, except in the speaker's mind. Choice (E) should be cast out because (A) is the more clearly correct answer.

3. **B** The poem never explicitly states what Juliana is doing. This poem uses an extended metaphor to tell you. Each stanza ends with the statement that Juliana is doing to the speaker what he is doing to the grass. "Mowing down" is symbolically most analogous to rejection. The answer is (B), rejecting him. You have no evidence that she's making fun of him, so (A) is definitely out. The textual support for (E), competing with him, is also zero. Because you know that he is experiencing some sort of emotional distress because of Juliana, either (C), ignoring him or (D), toying with his affections, might have seemed appealing as a correct answer. But remember a key test strategy: correct answers will be consistent with the overall meaning of the passage. To find the overall meaning of a poem, read it as if it were prose. Ignoring doesn't at all comport with mowing down, and it isn't analogous to toying with him, either, so both (C) and (D) are out. That leaves (B).

4. **D** The correct answer is (D), because stanza 3 shows the speaker "trodden under feet," like cut blades of grass, while stanza 5 envisions his tomb. If you were tempted to choose (C), look again. That progression does occur in the poem, but not between stanzas 3 and 5; it happens between stanzas

1 and 2. Similarly, (E) occurs in the poem, but between stanzas 1 and 4 rather than 3 and 5. Remember, *if one part of the answer is wrong, it all is.* Answer (A), on the other hand, should have gone by the wayside immediately, because it's all wrong (the speaker is never hopeful). Choice (B) is slightly tricky; he never expresses hope in the poem itself, but only mentions he at one point felt it. Also, the action in (B) doesn't happen between stanzas 3 and 5.

5. **D** This is an EXCEPT/LEAST/NOT question. Remember, in these you are looking for a potential opposite to a correct answer. Does (A) seem possibly correct? Yes. So do (B) and (C). Neither can be your answer here, then. How about (D)? Hmmm…the speaker isn't everyman. For one thing, the refrain brings in a very specific character as his love object, Juliana. For another, not everyone is engaged in cutting grass. Keep this in mind as you consider (E). Well, (E) is correct, as repeated lines are a unifying device. Choice (D) it is.

6. **E** In assessing how a speaker feels, look for both specific statements and connotations. The answer is (E), melancholy and despairing. If you're unsure, use POE. Were you tempted by (A), vengeful and jealous? His desire to mow down "flow'ers, and grass, and I and all" (line 21) in "common ruin" (line 22) could give support to vengeful—but jealousy is never mentioned. If one part of an answer is wrong, it nixes the whole thing. Is he steadfast and calm, (B)? Not really—and when you get to (E), it should be apparent that (E) fits better than (B), even if you are persuaded by calm in his acceptance of eventual death. Choice (C) seems tempting if his movement from seeing the spring grass as a mirror to wanting to ruin it seems capricious…but again, (E) fits better. Similarly, the repetition of the end line in each stanza contributes to (D) seeming like it fits. But you have no particular reason to believe he's driven—in fact, he's given up and envisions death. Choice (E) it is.

7. **E** The answer is (E), lament for unrequited love. You may have been tempted by (A), elegy for a young man, because elegies are meditations on death, and the poem discusses eventual death. But (E) is much closer. (Never make a choice without reading all the potential answers, because the right fit may be waiting at the end!) (B) may also have seemed slightly tempting, because pastorals are about rustic outdoor life—and here is our mower, outside. But again, when you get to (E), the fit is much closer, so you can then cast out (B). Choice (C) is another slim possibility, because ballads have a very regular meter and rhyme, as this poem does. Again, (E) fits the bill more—plus, ballads are usually longer. It definitely isn't (D), a rhapsody.

8. **B** The answer is (B), the grass. Always remember to read the specific lines and the lines immediately above and below. Choices (A) and (E) should be eliminated because the speaker never addresses Juliana directly. He is implicitly speaking to an audience, (C), but only to witness. There is no pastoral god, (D), in the poem at all, so have fun eliminating it immediately.

9. **D** The answer is (D), blank verse. This is an EXCEPT/LEAST/NOT question, so the answer can be arrived at with POE. Choose correct answers and eliminate them fearlessly. The poem clearly exhibits (B), (C), and (E), so those are out. And the speaker personifies the grass as an element that first does, and then should, reflect his feelings so (A) is out. Choice (D) is the last element standing, so it's the correct answer.

10. **C**   The answer is (C). All of these exist to some degree in the poem, but the question is asking for the primary purpose. That has to apply throughout all the stanzas. He is not bidding farewell to the world (B), throughout the entire piece, nor (D), apostrophizing the grass. (An apostrophe is a poetic address.) He has some bitterness that Spring doesn't reflect his mood, but (E) isn't overarching enough to be the primary purpose. While readers can infer that he loves Juliana, (A) isn't the primary purpose because his feelings never amount to a straightforward declaration.

11. **A**   The answer is (A). When in doubt, paraphrase the meaning of the poem and use POE. In the first three stanzas, Juliana's coming is in the past ("came"). But in the last two stanzas, it can be read as present or potential future ("comes"). We infer that Juliana has rejected the speaker at some point, but his meditations on death clearly indicate he has no hope that her continuing to arrive will change things for the better. There's no clear textual support for (B); her arrival could be immediate, but it could also be tomorrow or next month. It could also be (C) or (E), but (A) is more clearly true. It clearly isn't (D).

Questions 12–23

This passage is an excerpt from the short story "An Occurrence at Owl Creek Bridge," which takes place during the U.S. Civil War. The author, Ambrose Bierce, served in that conflict and published the short story collection *Tales of Soldiers and Civilians*, in which "An Occurrence at Owl Creek Bridge" appeared, in 1891

12. **A**   The answer is (A), about to be hung. This takes careful reading of the lines, since it is not explicitly stated in this section. You may be tempted by (B) and (D), as they seem like possibilities—but they aren't as close as (A). Choice (C) doesn't occur. Choice (E) is something the character believes at the end of the passage, but is not in the quoted lines.

13. **B**   In the relevant lines, the man faces death stolidly; the answer is (B). You may be tempted by (D), as "simple and effective" may imply respect. But it's not as close as (B). Choice (A) is partially true in other sections of the excerpt, but not here. Also, he doesn't think only of escape; that one word makes the answer untrue. You have no evidence in the cited lines of (E) and no evidence at all of (C).

14. **E**   That the answer is (E), to steady, ought to be clear if you read the relevant lines (which you always should; the test makers will always supply answers to mislead you if you don't!). The character is firmly steadying his mind on his wife and children after contemplating the scene around him. All the other choices aren't relevant in context, although many do refer to other uses of the word "fix."

15. **A**   Overall, the tone is (A), objective and distanced. While the character oscillates between resigned (B) and (C) hopeful, the tone itself is neither. (Nor is the tone particularly tragic or optimistic.) Both (B) and (C) can be eliminated. Choices (D) and (E) clearly don't match the passage's tone.

16. **B**   Always read the lines in context. The movements of the soldiers are stately and calm, (B). You might be drawn to (D) because setting up a hanging on a railroad bridge is somewhat improvised, but the context implies that it's well thought out for what they intend to do. One wrong word makes the answer all wrong. Did (C) seem possible? It may if you remember that soldiers

are referred to as "the invader," later in the passage, but that's not the tone of the cited lines here. While soldiers in general may display (A) and (E), that's not the case in the cited lines, so eliminate these.

17. **C** The answer is (C). Did (B) look tempting? We know from the character Peyton Farquhar's thoughts about his ticking watch that his sense of time has become distorted, but that occurs elsewhere in the passage, not here. Eliminate (B). Choice (E) may also appear attractive. Hmmm, how do you choose between (C) and (E)? If you're in a situation where two answers seem correct, you can choose between them by figuring out which one best answers the specific question. In this passage, the author is drawing a contrast between what the narrator tells readers (the stream is fast) and what a character thinks (the stream is sluggish). (Remember that narrators are not the same as authors.) The narrator is omniscient, capable of looking clearly at the actions and then following the mind of a character. Choice (E) is a less-good answer than (C), so (C) is your choice. You have no evidence that the narrator and Farquhar are looking at the stream either at different times (the passages are close together in time, seemingly) or at different areas of the water, so neither (A) nor (D) are correct choices.

18. **E** As ever, in EXCEPT/LEAST/NOT questions, your task is to be sure and choose an answer that's not an appropriate one, not pick (inadvertently) one that is. Eliminate the correct answers and the last one standing is your best bet. Choices (A) and (B) are clearly true, so you can eliminate them immediately. Time seems to slow down, so (D) is clearly also true; fearlessly strike it out. Because he no longer recognizes his watch (the ticking seems like an "anvil," line 29), he is losing touch with reality, so (C) is true—strike it out as well. Wait, is (E) a correct answer? You may initially jump to the conclusion that it's in the action as well, as the word "maddening" is used. But that doesn't mean he descends into madness, the sense of the word is closer to "infuriated." Choice (E) is the only answer remaining for the win.

19. **C** The lines quoted should provoke dissonance in the minds of an attentive reader, for several reasons. Would a noose keep water out, really? Wouldn't it go down his nose? And wouldn't it suffocate him anyway, if it's that tight? It's a big signal that the narrator doesn't fully intend us to trust the man's perceptions, a concept introduced in his understanding of the speed of both the river and his watch. But this passage is tricky, because several answers are tantalizingly close. As ever, you need to utilize POE like a shining sword. Choice (A) is likely on the narrator's mind, as the lines keep the plot moving. Hold (A) to one side as you read the other answers. Whoops, (B) also seems like a good choice; we are in Farquhar's mind. Hold that one too. Choice (D), irony, may be on display. The only one you can completely strike out on the first pass is (E), because the narrator describes him as already suffocating from the noose. He can't keep swimming under those conditions. Okay, how do you choose between the potentials of (A), (B), (C), and (D)? Well the question stem asks you to choose "most closely." (A) is a broader reason, so it's not as close as either (B) or (C). Strike it out. But if we accept (C), that we might not think the man's perception entirely trustworthy, can we know for a fact it is irony, (D)? He may not be ultimately saved if the noose is suffocating him. Choice (D) can fall by the wayside. So how to choose between the two final competing candidates, (B) and (C)? Well, the narrator is displaying omniscience, but that alone is not a purpose, as the question stem asks for. (B) is not

as close to the purpose, which is to throw some hints of shade on the man's perceptions. (B) falls and (C) stands as the winner.

20. **D** This is also a rather complex question, in which several answers may seem appealing right off the bat. Is "severity" what one feels in paragraph 1? It's not a good description of the tone, and that should lead you to strike out (A). There's no meditation on mortality in paragraph 1, either, so (B) falls to the wayside. While there's some relief in paragraph 3, readers' impressions of paragraph 1 isn't horror, so it's not (C). Choice (E) may seem tempting, but remember, part of paragraph 1 is also the man's thoughts. That makes paragraph 1 not solely representation, so (E) is not a correct answer. Choice (D) it is.

21. **D** Don't be fooled by the word "merely" into thinking it's about his insignificance and choose (A). A fiery heart isn't insignificant! It's also not (B), because the simile of "like…fire" refers to the pain he's feeling, while the quoted passage doesn't. It is (C)? These images do exist, so set (C) aside while you read the others. Does it indicate strong emotions? Set aside (D). Is it the last choice, (E)? No hyperbole is going on here, so you can eliminate (E). You need to choose between (C) and (D). While the images do unify the paragraph, the metaphor's more central role is indicating the strength of Farquhar's emotions, so the correct answer is (D).

22. **E** The answer is (E), because a blacksmith's hammer heats metal, just as the character feels he is being heated. While all the other choices are examples of pain and travail he is feeling, they don't echo the action of being heated to a high temperature.

23. **A** After the story surveys preparations for a hanging, these lines introduce the rural setting and its beauty. The only other answer that even comes close is (E)—but (A) is much closer than (E).

Questions 24–34

Rita Dove is an American poet, born in 1952. She was the first African-American poet named as the U.S. Poet Laureate, in 1993, and won the Pulitzer Prize for a verse-novel, *Thomas and Beulah*, in 1986. This poem is from the collection *American Smooth*, published in 2004.

24. **C** Similes are comparisons that usually use "as" or "like," of course, so (C) is the answer. If this gave you pause, review the glossary.

25. **D** You may be lead astray by assuming that all referents to "you" are the same throughout. Many are another person, who is the current love, and you could thus infer that it's (A), Fred—but a careful reading of the specific lines referenced should reveal that it's not. You also may be misled into thinking the subject of the poem is the more prevalent "you," but it's not that either—the subject is the relationship itself. (B) is not a correct choice. It's definitely not (C) or (E).

26. **A** The details in the passage describe a knight and "to set me free" implies he's coming to rescue the speaker, so (A) is the correct choice. It's clearly not (B) or (C). Choice (D) is close, but (A) is much closer. Choice (E) may come close, but it's too broad.

27.   **C**   By capitalizing "Divine," (line 24), the speaker seems to be pointing to god, and saying the couple fall short of it. But is the tone castigation, (A), (B), sarcasm, or (D), anxiety? No. So all of those bite the dust. The speaker is strongly implying that domesticity is comfortable and happy throughout, so falling short of the Divine is not that big a deal! Choice (C) comes the closest. Because of the closely adjacent mention of technology, such as "computers" (line 23) and "compact disk" (11), (E) may have seemed possible, but the tone is not ironic.

28.   **B**   Although "perched" is something a bird might do shortly before flying from a branch, you can't infer than the narrator plans to leave, (A). While "bunkered" can connote being walled off from the outside, the narrator is not lamenting, so (C) isn't a correct choice. (Of course you know that if part of an answer is wrong, it all is.) Because "bunkered" is sometimes associated with occupying a basement, you might have thought (D) was possible. But read closely; they're both in an "aerie"— an uppermost floor. In (E), there's no textual support for the negative connotations of "flighty." Choice (B) is the closest.

29.   **C**   You may be tempted by (A), a celebration. But look at the title—an "apologia" is an apology for something. Even if you didn't catch that, falling short of the Divine (line 24) and "stolen time" (line 30) indicate a slight issue with the happy scene on the narrator's part. It's enough to make (A) not the best choice. Although statements of love are made, it's not (D), a confession, because there's no indicator that the recipient didn't know it already. And it's definitely neither a jeremiad (B) nor a dirge (E), so you can wield a strike-out mark on those immediately!

30.   **A**   Examples of all these appear EXCEPT (A), so it's the proper answer to an EXCEPT/LEAST/NOT question. Remember that your strategy here is to tick off the correct answers as ones that can't fit the bill for this type of question.

31.   **E**   "Big Bad Floyd" may seem like (C) or (D), but in context, does the narrator appear truly threatened? No. In fact, a slight irony is implied—Big Bad Floyd's cusses are talking big, but not a real threat. The home is still portrayed as secure. The correct choice is (E). Did (B) tempt you? The hurricane itself serves as a memory trigger, but the personification itself is less central to that. Strike out (B). It's definitely not (A), a potential rival—not even the boys she's kissed in the past rival the narrator's current partner.

32.   **C**   Why does the speaker mention that the happiness is embarrassing (line 25)? Because it's "simply what's good for us" (line 26), yet falls "short of the Divine" (line 24). We can infer that (C), not fulfilling the writer's mission of catching higher truths, is the reason. None of the other choices exist in the poem except (A), and that isn't in these lines.

33.   **B**   The speaker shifts to considerations about the present world and past experiences in stanza 2, from a focus on her love object in stanza 1. Choice (B) is the correct answer. Choice (A) is definitely out, because the age that is "all business" is now—she is considering the present. The mention of technology doesn't cast it as an intrusion so much as a feature, so (C) isn't a good pick. In (D), the speaker is not focusing on the future—one word makes it all wrong. Choice (E) mentions past dissatisfactions, but the tone is not lamenting, nor does it imply that they were the road to her current happiness.

34. **B** Choice (D), engaging, doesn't use the analogy strongly enough, so although it conforms to the sense, it's not as close as (B). You may be slightly tempted by (A), as the descriptor "dark and hollow center" (line 20) is used—but it's more sweet than unhealthy. Also, since it's the crushes who are hollow, rather than the narrator, (C) isn't a correct choice. While their names are described as "sissy," (line 18) that has nothing to do with the analogy of candy (nor do you have any evidence that it was a conflict), so (E) is out.

Questions 35–44

Edgar Allan Poe (1809–1849), one of the best-known and most widely anthologized U.S. authors, wrote short stories, poetry, and criticism. His "The Murders in the Rue Morgue" is considered the first detective story, and short stories such as "The Masque of the Red Death" and "The Pit and the Pendulum" exemplify nineteenth-century horror and the macabre. The excerpt is from the short story "The Thousand-and-Second Tale of Scheherazade," originally published in 1845.

35. **A** The narrator is referring to the brides being delivered "up to the executioner," (line 12), so the correct choice is (A). While the word "tariff" appears later in the passage, neither (C) nor (D) is correct. It's clearly neither (B) nor (D).

36. **D** If you have any doubts, wield POE. It's floridly written, so it's definitely not measured, (A). The tone is neither horrified nor afraid, so it's not (B). (And, by the way, never let any outside knowledge of an author's works influence your choices. Your choices need to be based on only the lines you're analyzing. While Poe is known for horror and terror, that's not the overall tone here.) Is it (C)? Well, there are some indications that the narrator wants us to admire Scheherazade, but they're undercut by a sarcastic tone, so (D) is closer. You may think wit is involved, too—but the tone is anything but concise, so (E) is not a correct choice.

37. **B** Did (C), admiring, seem like a good idea? Some descriptions, such as her beautiful eyes, do seem admiring, but the overall tone is much more arch, (B), which means saucy and somewhat ironic. He's not (A) duplicitous; because he's less lying than being ironic. It's neither (D) nor (E) (even if the circumstances seem to call for the latter).

38. **B** Scheherazade's creatures become more and more fantastical—blue, pink, and green. The answer is (B). You may not have believed in animals of those hues, but story-tellers are allowed fantasy colors without making you disbelieve the entire story, so it's not (C). Does it question her sanity, (A)? No. The narrator's tone becomes a bit feverish, but not only because of the colors, so (D) is out. Choice (E) is not close enough to be a correct answer choice.

39. **B** Did (A) lead you astray? While "hyperbole" does mean exaggeration or overstatement, this phrase is less that than totally wrong given the context. It's the wrongness of the statement compared with the relative straight face of the delivery that makes it ironic. It's none of the others.

40. **A** The closest answer is (A), ineffectual. The fact that the monarch hadn't yet taken his daughter as his bride because of "fear of the vizier" (line 28) means that he may have had some power to stop

the murders—but (B) is only partially correct, because he stops neither them nor the marriage. Choice (C) may have also seemed possible, since he advises her not to marry the king—but his advice is disregarded; ineffectual, again. There's no textual support for (D). It's definitely not (E).

41. **E** The linkage between Eve and Scheherazade indicates both were active agents in their respective lives, so (E) it is. If in doubt, turn to POE. While you're told that Scheherazade "triumphed," (line 79), you have no textual information on whether Eve did, so (A) is out. While you know from the text that Scheherazade demonstrated capability to tell stories, you don't know whether Eve did—only that she picked up "baskets of talk" (line 77). Choice (B) is out. You know by "heir" (line 76) that they are related—but there's no sense of them being opposites, so (C) falls by the wayside. As for appropriate courses of action—nothing in the passage indicates that about Eve, and it's distanced about Scheherazade. Choice (D) is out.

42. **D** The sense of the line is they can't go through with the execution because the king wants to hear the rest of the story, so no other planned action (than the story) can occur. It's (D). It should be pretty clear that it's not (A), (B), or (C), and it's definitely not (E).

43. **C** Scheherazade's attempt to "redeem the land" (line 20) indicates that her motivation is her country; the answer is (C). There's no textual support for (A) or (D). Even though the text talks about her perishing, there's no indication that's she afraid at all, so (E) is out. "The approved fashion of all heroines" (lines 21–22) might have led you to consider (B), hackneyed plots—but it's much less close than (C).

44. **D** Casting a murder as a tax or a tariff distances the reader from the murders, (D). If in doubt, use POE. The lines do move the story from the realm of emotion, (C), so set (C) aside. They also remind us that Scheherazade's motive is freeing the country rather than the women, so (A) can also be left as you read through the others. When you get to (D), though, you should see that (D) is closer that the other two. Choice (B) might be tempting, but the narrator is more ironic than specifically uncaring. While the narrator's veracity might be questioned in other parts of the passage, it isn't here, so (E) is out.

Questions 45–55

Arnold Bennett (1867-1931) was a British novelist, playwright, and critic. He is credited with bringing elements of European realism to British letters. He is best known for the "Five Towns" novels, which portray the Potteries, the region of Staffordshire then best known for producing china and earthenware. The excerpt is from his 1908 novel *Buried Alive: A Tale of These Days*.

45. **C** There are fine shades of meaning here, as in all literary passages. If you were tempted by (B), ineradicable, consider the context. Yes, it's gloomy, but there's an implication that, if some dark rooms are lighted, the others theoretically could be as well—they're just not. Ineradicable refers to something that can't be rooted out at all, so (B) is not a correct answer choice. Both (A) and (D) may have seemed like possibilities, but they aren't as close as (C). It's definitely not (E).

46. **A** All the choices except for (A) are part of the description. Remember, the answer to an EXCEPT/ LEAST/NOT answer choice must be something it is not, and the best strategy is to tick off correct answers to find the appropriate choice for the type of question.

47. **D** The first and fourth paragraphs move from the cosmos of the earth's "axis" (line 1) to a specific individual, so the answer is (D). If this gave you pause, use POE. Certain elements in the first paragraph are objective, others are subjective, so (A) is out. Both paragraphs contain ironic and realistic elements, so it's not (B). Aristocracy and democracy are not part of the passage, so (C) can be quickly eliminated. Tradition and modernity are not an important part either, so (E) goes as well.

48. **E** The building is personified in several ways throughout, and all help you to understand the connotations of the setting. Choice (C) may draw your attention, because the house is portrayed as wanting a few signs. But is the overall sense that that's all the house needs? No, so (E) is much closer. (B) and (D) may seem tempting, but (E) is closer. Choice (A) is also mentioned, but in another set of lines (and even there, it's an ironic treatment of the difficulty of a servant's life).

49. **E** Choice (A) is a possible answer, but (E) is much closer, so when you get to see it, (A) bites the dust. Choice (D) is a possible inference of the meaning, but it is overly broad once you see (E). Choice (B) doesn't convey the right meaning, because the "whizzing globe" doesn't permanently abandon the sun. Choice (C) is rendered incorrect for the same reason; the earth only temporarily doesn't see the sun; and the answer is also too broad.

50. **E** This is a complicated question, in which you have to parse both meaning (in the latter part of the question stem) and literary choices (in the first part of the question stem). Choice (E) is the closest answer because the structure lets us know that the dressing gown is a beautiful color, light, and warm before letting us know that it's frayed and "worn" (line 37). The order in which details are revealed is very important. It's not (A), because the room is specifically "illuminated" (line 32), not dark. (The overall house is dark, but in this passage we're on to specifics; remember that the test makers will try to trick you by introducing something you've read, but not in the area covered by the question.) Choice (B) isn't the best choice because of the word "implies"; we are told outright that it's the stuff of dreams. (C) isn't the best choice because the details convey this rather than the tone. While the gown does represent comfort, (D), it also seems to represent dreams and kindness, so (D) is not as close as (E).

51. **C** The closest is (C), unhappy—which we know because his eyes are described as "sad…very sad" (line 60). Did you immediately choose (A)? While we're told he's young, other details contradict that, such as his greying hair and facial wrinkles (lines 57–58), and his age, 50. Oops, that means "young" is irony! Choice (E) may also have sung a siren song, because the narrator feels he hasn't had the best luck (line 67). But that's slightly different from being down on his luck, which means genuinely unfortunate, rather than simply not grabbing the brass ring. Strike out (E). Choice (B) may have drawn you in, because the narrator speaks of an age as having "shed all the illusions" (line 49). But that's operating without illusions rather than disillusioned; the latter strongly implies a lack of trust. A shield, (D), isn't what the narrator portrays it is, exactly—it's too far afield to be a correct answer.

52. **E** He's overweight because he can't see his slippers (and it's implied that the tailor's measurements are large). The narrator implies that people may be embarrassed about their tailor's measurements (line 69), but that's not how the character is described, so (A) doesn't answer the question. We can infer he's an artist by the presence of an easel (line 47), but that's not in the cited lines. Choice (B) is out. There is a sense of him being both left behind (C), and not knowing what to do (D), but not in the cited lines, so both those can be eliminated.

53. **A** If the answer wasn't immediately apparent, see what POE can do. Choices (B) and (C) both cleverly trade on the fact that the currency is a florin—not the currencies more commonly associated with the London setting, such as the pound sterling. Has the character been to exotic climes? You don't know that textually, so (B) can't be an answer, plus (A) is much closer. (Fun fact: florins were briefly a British coin during the time period—but the test will never expect you to know anything outside of the passage that's so obscure.) It clearly isn't (D) or (E).

54. **D** The use of "chimney-cowls" (line 15), chiefly compares the chimneys to monks, even if ironically, so (D) is the answer. (One definition of "cowl" is a chimney covering, but most people know it in the context of clothing, and the line plays on both meanings.) Several of these answers may have seemed appealing. Tin is a relatively flimsy metal, so (A) may have seemed possible. But it's much broader than (D). Choice (B) is also partially correct—but is the building like a deeply spiritual person? No, that's too far from the overall tone and sense of the passage. Correct answers must be consistent with those elements. Choice (B) is out. Choice (E) may seem possible, but the spiritual allusions are ironic given the tone about the building; plus, it's too broad. Choice (C) is clearly out.

55. **C** This should pretty clearly be (C). If it's not, use POE. Choice (A) is partially correct, but leaves out the reference to the planets, which is part of the main point. (B) is trying to trick you into assenting to "oddities" because of the use of "peculiar" (line 1) in the sentence—beware of falling for it! Remember, the question is asking you for the main point, which should cast out (B). While the first sentence does move between the sun and London, that's more of an inference than a main point, so it's not (D). The lines aren't really close to (E), and (C) beats it by a mile.

Part VII
Glossary

- Glossary of Basic Parts of Speech
- Glossary of Literary Terms for the AP English Literature and Composition Exam

**Become a
Grammar Guru**

Need to brush up on your
grammar before exam
day? Pick up a copy of
Grammar Smart, which
contains tons of grammar
guidance and practice.

GLOSSARY OF BASIC PARTS OF SPEECH

You need to know the basic parts of speech.

- **Noun:** A person, place, thing, or idea (or an abstraction—for example, *strength* and *determination* are nouns).
- **Verb:** An action word or a word that expresses a state of being.
- **Adjective:** A word that modifies, describes, or limits a noun or pronoun.
- **Adverb:** A word that modifies, describes, or limits a verb, an adjective, or another adverb. (In the phrase *the profoundly nasty little poodle, nasty* and *little* are adjectives, but *profoundly* is an adverb, as it modifies the adjective *nasty.*)
- **Preposition:** A word that shows the relationship between a noun or pronoun and some other word in the sentence. A preposition should not be the last word in a sentence in formal writing. A preposition is the first word of a prepositional phrase. The phrase will begin with a preposition and end with a noun or pronoun. (Take, for instance, the phrase *in the lake. In* is the preposition and *lake* is the noun that ends the phrase.)
- **Pronoun:** A word that replaces a noun. Words such as *he, she, it, they, them, who,* and *that* can replace a noun. The noun to which a pronoun refers is called the *antecedent.* You find the antecedent by looking back from the pronoun to the part of the passage immediately preceding the pronoun and looking at the nouns that are in those sentences. One of those nouns, either because it is the closest to the pronoun or because it makes the most sense in context, is the noun to which the pronoun refers.
- **Gerund:** A word that serves two functions. It acts like a noun and it acts like a verb. Look at the following sentence. *Swimming across the lake is fun. Swimming* is the gerund.
- **Participle:** A word that serves two functions. It acts like an adjective and it acts like a verb. Look how *swimming* is used in the following sentence. *The girl, swimming across the lake, reminds me of my sister.* In this case the word *swimming* is describing the girl and, therefore, is a participle.
- **Infinitive:** A phrase that begins with the word *to* and is followed by a verb form. *To swim* is an infinitive. In the following sentence, *to swim* is the infinitive: *To swim across the lake is fun.* Infinitives function as verbs, but they can also function as nouns, adjectives, or adverbs.

GLOSSARY OF LITERARY TERMS FOR THE AP ENGLISH LITERATURE AND COMPOSITION EXAM

abstract

An *abstract* style (in writing) is typically complex, discusses intangible qualities like good and evil, and seldom uses examples to support its points.

academic

As an adjective describing style, this word means dry and theoretical writing. When a piece of writing seems to be sucking all the life out of its subject with analysis, the writing is *academic*.

accent

In poetry, *accent* refers to the stressed portion of a word. In "To be, or not to be," accents fall on the first "be" and "not." It sounds silly any other way. But accent in poetry is also often a matter of opinion. Consider the rest of the first line of Hamlet's famous soliloquy, "That is the question." The stresses in that portion of the line are open to a variety of interpretations.

aesthetic, aesthetics

Aesthetic can be used as an adjective meaning "appealing to the senses." Aesthetic judgment is a phrase synonymous with artistic judgment. As a noun, an aesthetic is a coherent sense of taste. The kid whose room is painted black, who sleeps in a coffin, and listens only to funeral music, has an aesthetic. The kid whose room is filled with pictures of kittens and daisies but who sleeps in a coffin and listens to polka music has a contradictory aesthetic. The plural noun, *aesthetics*, is the study of beauty. Questions like *What is beauty?* or *Is the beautiful always good?* fall into the category of aesthetics.

allegory

An *allegory* is a story in which each aspect has a symbolic meaning outside the tale itself. Many fables have an allegorical quality. For example, Aesop's "The Ant and the Grasshopper" isn't merely the story of a hardworking ant and a carefree grasshopper, but is also a story about different approaches to living—thrifty and devil-may-care. It can also be read as a story about the seasons of summer and winter, which represent a time of prosperity and a time of hardship, or even as representing youth and age. Bunyan's epic poem, *Pilgrim's Progress,* is an allegory of the soul, in which each and every part of the tale represents some feature of the spiritual world and the struggles of an individual to lead a Christian life.

alliteration

The repetition of initial sounds is called *alliteration*. In other words, clusters coming closely cramped and compressed—no coincidence.

Want More Vocab Review?

Check out another book we wrote, *Word Smart, 6th Edition: 1400+ Words That Belong in Every Savvy Student's Vocabulary* for even more top notch vocab review.

allusion

A reference to another work or famous figure is an *allusion*. A classical allusion is a reference to Greek and Roman mythology or literature such as *The Iliad*. Allusions can be topical or popular as well. A topical allusion refers to a current event. A popular allusion refers to something from popular culture, such as a reference to a television show or a hit movie.

anachronism

The word *anachronism* is derived from Greek. It means "misplaced in time." If the actor playing Brutus in a production of *Julius Caesar* forgets to take off his wristwatch, the effect will be anachronistic (and probably comic).

analogy

An *analogy* is a comparison. Usually analogies involve two or more symbolic parts and are employed to clarify an action or a relationship. *Just as the mother eagle shelters her young from the storm by spreading her great wing above their heads, so does Acme Insurers of America spread an umbrella of coverage to protect its policyholders from the storms of life.*

anecdote

An *anecdote* is a short narrative.

antagonist

A character, group, characteristic, or entity that opposes the protagonist.

antecedent

The word, phrase, or clause that a pronoun refers to or replaces. In *The principal asked the children where they were going, they* is the pronoun and *children* is the *antecedent*.

anthropomorphism

In literature, when inanimate objects, animals, or natural phenomena are given human characteristics, behavior, or motivation, *anthropomorphism* is at work. For example, *In the forest, the darkness waited for me, I could hear its patient breathing....* Anthropomorphism is often confused with personification, which requires that the nonhuman quality or thing take on a human shape.

anticlimax

An *anticlimax* occurs when an action produces far smaller results than one had been led to expect. Anticlimax is frequently comic. *Sir, your snide manner and despicable arrogance have long been a source of disgust to me, but I've overlooked it until now. However, it has come to my attention that you have fallen so disgracefully deep into that mire of filth which is your mind as to attempt to besmirch my wife's honor and my good name. Sir, I challenge you to a game of badminton!*

aphorism

A short and usually witty saying, such as " 'Classic'? A book which people praise and don't read."—Mark Twain.

apostrophe

An address to someone not present or to a personified object or idea.

archaism

The use of deliberately old-fashioned language. Authors sometimes use *archaisms* to create a feeling of antiquity. Tourist traps use archaisms with a vengeance, as in "Ye Olde Candle Shoppe."

archetypes

Standard or clichéd character types, such as the drunk, the miser, and the foolish girl.

argumentation

The act or process of analyzing evidence, drawing conclusions, and developing claims. Literary argumentation applies this process to literature.

aside

A speech (usually just a short comment) made by an actor to the audience, as though momentarily stepping outside of the action on stage. (See *soliloquy*.)

aspect

A trait or characteristic, as in "an *aspect* of the dew drop."

atmosphere

The emotional tone or background that surrounds a scene.

attitude

A speaker's, author's, or character's nature toward or opinion of a subject. (See *tone*.)

ballad

A long, narrative poem usually in very regular meter and rhyme. A *ballad* typically has a naive folksy quality, a characteristic that distinguishes it from epic poetry.

bathos

When writing strains for grandeur it can't support and tries to elicit tears from every little hiccup, that's *bathos*.

black humor

This is the use of disturbing themes in comedy. In Samuel Beckett's *Waiting for Godot*, the two tramps, Didi and Gogo, comically debate over which should commit suicide first and whether the branches of the tree will support their weight. This is *black humor*.

bombast

This is pretentious, exaggeratedly learned language. When one tries to be eloquent by using the largest, most uncommon words, one falls into *bombast*.

burlesque

A *burlesque* is broad parody, one that takes a style or a form such as tragic drama and exaggerates it into ridiculousness. A parody usually takes on a specific work, such as *Hamlet*. For the purposes of the AP Exam, you can think of the terms *parody* and *burlesque* as interchangeable.

cacophony

In poetry, *cacophony* is using deliberately harsh, awkward sounds.

cadence

The beat or rhythm of poetry in a general sense. For example, *iambic pentameter* is the technical name for a rhythm. One sample of predominantly iambic pentameter verse could have a gentle, *pulsing* cadence, whereas another might have a *conversational* cadence, and still another might have a vigorous, *marching* cadence.

canto

The name for a section division in a long work of poetry, similar to the way chapters divide a novel.

caricature

A portrait (verbal or otherwise) that exaggerates a facet of personality.

catharsis

This is a term drawn from Aristotle's writings on tragedy. *Catharsis* refers to the "cleansing" of emotion an audience member experiences having lived (vicariously) through the experiences presented on stage.

character

In literary terms, description, representations, or discussions of the features that make up an individual and represent who they are. Character can also refer to an individual in a play.

chorus

In drama, a *chorus* is the group of people who stand outside the main action on stage and comment on it.

classic, classical

What a troublesome word! Don't confuse classic with classical. *Classic* can mean typical, as in *Oh, that was a classic blunder*. It can also mean an accepted masterpiece, for example, *Death of a Salesman*. But, *classical* refers to the arts of ancient Greece and Rome and the qualities of those arts.

coinage (neologism)

A *coinage* is a new word, usually one invented on the spot. People's names often become grist for coinages, as in, *Oh, man, you just pulled a major Wilson*. Of course, you'd have to know Wilson to know what that means, but you can tell it isn't a good thing. The technical term for coinage is *neologism*.

colloquialism

This is a word or phrase used in everyday conversational English that isn't a part of accepted "schoolbook" English. For example, *I'm toast. I'm a crispy-critter man, and now I've got this wicked headache.*

complex, dense

These two terms carry the similar meaning of suggesting that there is more than one possibility in the meaning of words (image, idea, opposition); there are subtleties and variations; there are multiple layers of interpretation; the meaning is both explicit and implicit.

conceit, controlling image, extended metaphor

In poetry, *conceit* doesn't mean stuck-up. It refers to a startling or unusual metaphor, or one developed and expanded upon over several lines. When the image dominates and shapes the entire work, it's called a *controlling image*. A metaphysical conceit is reserved for metaphysical poems only.

connotation, denotation

The *denotation* of a word is its literal meaning. The *connotations* are everything else that the word suggests or implies. For example, in the phrase *the dark forest*, *dark* denotes a relative lack of light. The connotation is of danger, or perhaps mystery or quiet; we'd need more information to know for sure, and if we did know with complete certainty that wouldn't be connotation, but denotation. In many cases, connotation eventually so overwhelms a word that it takes over the denotation. For example, *livid* is supposed to denote a dark purple-red color like that of a bruise, but it has been used so often in the context of extreme anger that many people have come to use *livid* as a synonym for enraged, rather than a connotative description of it.

consonance

The repetition of consonant sounds within words (rather than at their beginnings, which is alliteration). A flo*ck* of si*ck*, bla*ck*-che*ck*ered du*cks*.

couplet

A pair of lines that end in rhyme:

> But at my back I always *hear*
> Time's winged chariot hurrying *near*.
> —from "To His Coy Mistress" by Andrew Marvell

decorum

In order to observe *decorum*, a character's speech must be styled according to social station and in accordance with the occasion. A tool of storytelling can be flipping expectations about decorum, for example, showing an elderly women dressed in fine clothing, cruising down the street on a skateboard. In Neoclassical and Victorian literature, the authors observed decorum, meaning they did not write about the indecorous.

details, choice of details

The items or parts that make up a larger picture or story. Writers can use *details* to bring their characters to life. Chaucer's "Prologue" to *The Canterbury Tales* is one example of how an author can use *details* to develop a character.

devices of sound

Various techniques used by poets to create sound imagery through specific word choice (e.g., rhyme, alliteration, assonance, consonance, and onomatopoeia) to evoke an emotional response, clarify meaning, enhance the reader's experience, and so on.

diction

Word choice.

dirge

A song for the dead. Its tone is typically slow, heavy, and melancholy.

dissonance

The grating of incompatible sounds.

doggerel

Crude, simplistic verse, often in sing-song rhyme. Limericks are a kind of *doggerel*.

dramatic irony

When the audience knows something that the characters in the drama do not.

dramatic monologue

When a single speaker in literature says something to a silent audience.

dystopia

A seemingly ideal world where the actual implementation of perfection is unsuccessful and destructive; opposite of utopia (see definition).

elegy

A type of poem that meditates on death or mortality in a serious, thoughtful manner. *Elegies* often use the recent death of a noted person or loved one as a starting point. They also memorialize specific dead people.

elements

This word is used constantly and with the assumption that you know exactly what it means—that is, the basic techniques of each genre of literature. For a quick refresher, here's a short and sweet list for each genre:

> **elements of fiction**
> Exposition, conflict, rising action, climax, falling action, resolution, denouement

> **rhetorical elements**
> Argument (Ethos, Logos, Pathos), evidence/examples, reason/explanation

enjambment

The continuation of a syntactic unit from one line or couplet of a poem to the next with no pause.

epic

In a broad sense, an *epic* is simply a very long narrative poem on a serious theme and in a dignified style. *Epics* typically deal with glorious or profound subject matter: a great war, a heroic journey, the Fall from Eden, a battle with supernatural forces, a trip into the underworld, and so on. The mock-epic is a parody form that deals with mundane events and ironically treats them as being worthy of epic poetry.

epitaph

Lines that commemorate the dead at their burial place. An *epitaph* is usually a line or handful of lines, often serious or religious but sometimes witty and even irreverent.

ethos

The appeal to credibility; establishing common ground and trust with an audience.

euphemism

A word or phrase that takes the place of a harsh, unpleasant, or impolite reality. The use of *passed away* for *died*, and *let go* for *fired* are two examples of *euphemisms*.

euphony

When sounds blend harmoniously, the result is *euphony*.

explicit

Something said or written directly and clearly (this is a rare happening in literature because the whole game is to be "implicit"—that is, to suggest and imply).

farce

Today we use this word to refer to extremely broad humor. Writers in earlier times used *farce* as a more neutral term, meaning simply a funny play; a comedy. (And you should know that for writers of centuries past, *comedy* was the generic term for any play; it did not imply humor.)

feminine rhyme

Lines rhymed by their final two syllables. A pair of lines ending with *running* and *gunning* would be an example of *feminine rhyme*. Properly, in a *feminine rhyme* (and not simply a double rhyme) the penultimate syllables are stressed and the final syllables are unstressed.

figurative language

Writing that uses words to mean something other than their literal meaning. Examples of *figurative language* include metaphor, simile, and irony.

first-person narrator

See *point of view*.

foil

A secondary character whose purpose is to highlight the characteristics of a main character, usually by contrast. For example, an author will often give a cynical, quick-witted character a docile, naive, sweet-tempered friend to serve as a *foil*. Some classic examples include Benvolio and Tybalt or Gatsby and Tom.

foot

The basic rhythmic unit of a line of poetry. A *foot* is formed by a combination of two or three syllables, either stressed or unstressed.

foreshadowing

An event or statement in a narrative that suggests a larger event that comes later.

free verse

Poetry written without a regular rhyme scheme or metrical pattern.

genre

A subcategory of literature. Science fiction and detective stories are *genres* of fiction.

gothic, gothic novel

Gothic is the sensibility derived from dark novels. This form first showed up in the mid-18th century and has continued to woo audiences ever since. Think in terms of Poe, Shelley, and even Stephen King. The dark and twisty stories are considered gothic in nature.

hubris

The excessive pride or ambition that leads to the main character's downfall (another term from Aristotle's discussion of tragedy).

hyperbole

Exaggeration or deliberate overstatement.

imagery

An author's use of figurative language, images, or sensory details that appeal to the reader's senses (e.g., sight, sound, or touch). *Imagery* coupled with figures of speech (such as similes, metaphors, personification, and onomatopoeia) creates a vivid depiction of a scene that strikes as many of the reader's senses as possible.

implicit

Something said or written that suggests and implies but never says it directly or clearly. "Meaning" is definitely present but it's in the imagery, or "between the lines."

in medias res

Latin for "in the midst of things." One of the conventions of epic poetry is that the action begins *in medias res*. For example, when *The Iliad* begins, the Trojan war has already been going on for seven years.

inversion

Switching the customary order of elements in a sentence or phrase. When done badly it can give a stilted, artificial, look-at-me-I'm-poetry feel to the verse, but poets do it all the time. This type of messing with syntax is called *poetic license. I'll have one large pizza with all the fixins*—presto chango instant poetry: *A pizza large I'll have, one with the fixins all.* If you are a fan of STAR WARS films, you might recognize this type of phrasing as the style of Yoda.

irony

Three types of irony can be found in literature:

> **situational irony**
> The contradiction between what is expected and what actually occurs

> **dramatic irony**
> The contradiction between what we as readers know to be true and what characters have yet to discover

> **verbal irony**
> The contradiction between what is said and what is meant; sarcasm

juxtaposition

Placing two or more concepts, places, characters, or their actions together for the purpose of comparison or contrast.

lament

A poem of sadness or grief over the death of a loved one or other intense loss.

logos

An appeal to logic.

loose and periodic sentences

A *loose* sentence is complete before its end. A *periodic* sentence is not grammatically complete until it has reached its final phrase. (The term *loose* does not in any way imply that the sentences are slack or shoddy.)

> Loose sentence: *Jack loved Barbara despite her irritating snorting laugh, her complaining, and her terrible taste in shoes.*

> Periodic sentence: *Despite Barbara's irritation at Jack's peculiar habit of picking between his toes while watching MTV and his terrible haircut, she loved him.*

lyric

A type of poetry that explores the poet's personal interpretation of and feelings about the world (or the part that his poem is about). When the word *lyric* is used to describe a tone, it refers to a sweet, emotional melodiousness.

masculine rhyme

A rhyme ending on the final stressed syllable (aka, regular old rhyme).

means, meaning

This is the big one, the one task you have to do all the time. You are discovering what makes sense, what's important. There is *literal* meaning which is concrete and explicit, and there is *metaphorical* or *abstract* meaning.

melodrama

A form of cheesy theater in which the hero is very, very good, the villain mean and rotten, and the heroine oh-so-pure. (It sounds dumb, but *melodramatic* movies make tons of money every year.)

metaphor

A comparison between two relatively unlike ideas in which you call one thing something it's not (e.g., *the pond was his watery tomb*—he died in the pond, but the pond itself isn't actually a burial place).

metonym

A word that is used to stand for something else that it has attributes of or is associated with. For example, a herd of 50 cows could be called 50 *head* of cattle.

monologue

A speech given by one character alone on stage.

motif

A recurring symbol.

narrative techniques

The methods employed in the telling of a story or an account. Examples of *narrative techniques* include point of view, manipulation of time, dialogue, and internal monologue.

neologism

See *coinage*.

objectivity

An *objective* treatment of subject matter is an impersonal or outside view of events.

omniscient narrator

See *point of view*.

onomatopoeia

Words that imitate sounds (e.g., boom, pow, buzz, gargle, babble, splat).

opposition

One of the most useful concepts in analyzing literature. It means that you have a pair of elements that contrast sharply. It is not necessarily "conflict" but rather a pairing of images (or settings or appeals, for example) whereby each becomes more striking and informative because it's placed in contrast to the other one. This kind of *opposition* creates mystery and tension. Oppositions can be obvious. Oppositions can also lead to irony, but not necessarily so.

oxymoron

A phrase composed of opposites; a contradiction. *Bright black. A calm frenzy. Jumbo shrimp. Dark light. A truthful lie.*

parable

Like a fable or an allegory, a *parable* is a story that instructs.

paradox

A situation or statement that seems to contradict itself but on closer inspection does not.

parallelism

Repeated syntactical similarities used for effect. For example: I love fishing, swimming, and hiking. All parts of the list are grammatically sound, as opposed to the unparallel version: I love fishing, to swim, and a hike.

paraphrase

To restate phrases and sentences in your own words; to rephrase. Paraphrase is not analysis or interpretation, so don't fall into the thinking that traps so many students. *Paraphrasing* is just a way of showing that you comprehend what you've just read—that you can now put it in your own words. No more, no less.

parenthetical phrase

A phrase set off by commas that interrupts the flow of a sentence with some commentary or added detail. *Jack's three dogs, <u>including that miserable little spaniel</u>, were with him that day.*

parody

A work that makes fun of another work by exaggerating many of its qualities to ridiculousness.

pastoral

A poem set in tranquil nature, or even more specifically, one about shepherds.

pathos

An appeal to emotions.

periodic sentence

See *loose sentence*.

persona

A created personality, reflective of the author; provides insight from a third person, not a first person, point of view.

personification

Giving an inanimate object human qualities or form. *The darkness of the forest became the figure of a beautiful, pale-skinned woman in night-black clothes.*

plaint

A poem or speech expressing sorrow.

point of view

The perspective from which the action of a novel (or narrative poem) is presented, whether the action is presented by one character or from different vantage points over the course of the novel. Be sensitive to *point of view*, because the AP Exam writers like to ask questions about it and also like you to mention point of view in your essays.

Related to *point of view* is the narrative form that a novel or story takes. There are a few common narrative positions:

- **Third-person omniscient narrator:** This is a third-person narrator who sees, like God, into each character's mind and understands all the action going on.
- **Third-person limited omniscient narrator:** This is a third-person narrator who generally reports what only one character (usually the main character) sees, and who reports the thoughts of only that one privileged character.
- **Third-person narrator:** This is a third-person narrator who reports only what would be visible to a camera. The objective narrator does not know what the character is thinking unless the character speaks of it.
- **First-person narrator:** This is a narrator who is a character in the story and tells the tale from his or her point of view. When the first-person narrator is crazy, a liar, very young, or for some other reason not entirely credible, the narrator is *unreliable*.
- **Stream of consciousness:** This method is like first-person narration but instead of the character telling the story, the author places the reader inside the main character's head and makes the reader privy to all of the character's thoughts as they scroll through her consciousness.

prelude

An introductory poem to a longer work of verse.

protagonist

The main character of a novel or play.

pun

The usually humorous use of a word in such a way to suggest two or more meanings.

refrain

A line or set of lines repeated several times over the course of a poem.

requiem

A song of prayer for the dead.

rhapsody

An intensely passionate verse or section of verse, usually of love or praise.

rhetorical question

A question that suggests an answer. In theory, the effect of a rhetorical question is that it causes the listener to feel she has come up with the answer herself. For example, if someone is eating with their mouth open, smacking loudly, you might ask, "is it good?" You don't actually expect an answer, but you convey your point that the smacking is annoying.

rhetorical techniques

The devices used to create effective or persuasive language. Common examples of these techniques include contrast, repetition, paradox, understatement, sarcasm, and rhetorical questions.

satire

A form of humor that focuses on making fun of society through witty, sometimes dark social commentary; taking things that should be funny and picking on them in a way that raises awareness to ridiculousness and societal frustrations (think *SNL, Family Guy,* or movies such as *Get Out* or *Don't Look Up*).

setting

The physical location of a play, story, or novel, which often includes information about time and place. The *setting* can also provide background information to a story.

simile

A comparison between two relatively unlike ideas using *like* or *as* (e.g., *her hair is as bright as the sun*—we all know that the sun is yellow; therefore, we can deduce that her hair is blonde).

soliloquy

A speech given by one character alone on stage in which the character expresses his/her thoughts or feelings.

stanza

A group of lines in verse, roughly analogous in function to the paragraph in prose.

stream of consciousness

See *point of view*.

structure

The way in which a work is arranged or divided. *Structure* can also refer to the relationship between the parts of a work and the work as a whole. The most common principles of structure are series (A, B, C, D, E), contrast (A versus B, C versus D, E versus A), and repetition (AA, BB, AB). The most common units of structure in plays are scene and act; in novels, chapter; and in poems, line and stanza.

style

The manner in which an author writes, which can distinguish him or her from another writer. Examples of *style* include expository, argumentative, descriptive, persuasive, and narrative. *Style* also refers to the technique(s) writers employ as their mode of expression. Examples of these techniques include diction, syntax, figurative language, imagery, selection of detail, sound effects, tone, and voice.

subjective

A subjective treatment uses the interior or personal view of a single observer and is typically colored with that observer's emotional responses.

subjunctive mood

If I were you, I'd learn this one! That's a small joke because the grammatical situation involves the words "if" and "were." What you do is set up a hypothetical situation, a kind of wishful thinking: *if I were you, if he were honest, if she were rich.* You can also get away from the person and into the "it": *I wish it were true, would it were so* (that even sounds like Shakespeare and poetry). Go to line 111 on page 160 for the example: "Were one not already the Duke…."

suggest

To imply, entail, and/or indicate. This is another one of those basic tools of literature. It goes along with the concept of *implicit*. As the reader, you have to do all the work to pull out the meaning.

summary

A simple retelling of what you've just read. It's mechanical, superficial, and a step beyond the paraphrase in that it covers much more material and is more general. You can summarize a whole chapter or a whole story, whereas you paraphrase word-by-word and line-by-line. *Summary* hits the highlights of a piece without revealing all of the facts.

suspension of disbelief

The demand made of a theater audience to accept the limitations of staging and supply the details with imagination. Also, the acceptance on an audience's or reader's part of the incidents of plot in a play or story. If there are too many coincidences or improbable occurrences, the viewer/reader can no longer suspend disbelief and subsequently loses interest.

symbol/symbolism

Anything that stands for or represents something beyond itself.

syncope

Contracting, or shortening, a word by removing internal sounds, syllables, or letters and inserting an apostrophe; or by dropping unstressed vowels, letters, syllables, or consonants from the middle of a word and replacing with an apostrophe. Examples include "heav'n," "ev'ry," and "fail'd" in Phillis Wheatley's poem "On the Death of J.C. an Infant" (see page 143).

synecdoche

Figure of speech in which a part represents the whole.

syntax
Sentence structure; the way in which words and phrases are structured to create meaning.

technique
The methods, the tools, the "how-she-does-it" ways of the author. The elements are not techniques. In poetry, *onomatopoeia* is a technique within the element of rhythm. In drama, *blocking* is a technique, as is *lighting*. Concrete details are not techniques, but *tone* is. Main idea is not a technique, but *opposition* is.

theme
The main idea or central insight into life or human nature revealed through a literary work.

thesis
The main position of an argument. The central contention that will be supported. The guiding statement that reveals an argument's purpose/goal; essentially a contract with a reader that lets him/her know exactly what you plan to discuss or prove in an essay.

tone
The manner in which an author expresses his or her attitude about a subject. Writers convey *tone* through the use of many devices, such as word choice/diction. (See *attitude*.)

tragic flaw (hamartia)
In a tragedy, this is the weakness of character in an otherwise good (or even great) individual that ultimately leads to his demise.

travesty
The distortion, corruption, or terribly false representation of something.

truism
A way-too-obvious truth.

unreliable narrator
See *point of view*.

utopia
An idealized place. Imaginary communities in which people are able to live in happiness, prosperity, and peace. Several works of fiction have been written about *utopias*.

verisimilitude
The appearance of being real or true.

zeugma
The use of a word to modify two or more words but used for different meanings. *He closed the door and his heart on his lost love.*

The Princeton Review®

Completely darken bubbles with a No. 2 pencil. If you make a mistake, be sure to erase mark completely. Erase all stray marks.

1. YOUR NAME:
(Print)　　　Last　　　First　　　M.I.

SIGNATURE:　　　DATE:　　/　　/

HOME ADDRESS:
(Print)　　　Number and Street

City　　　State　　　Zip Code

PHONE NO. :
(Print)

5. YOUR NAME

First 4 letters of last name				FIRST INIT	MID INIT

IMPORTANT: Please fill in these boxes exactly as shown on the back cover of your test book.

2. TEST FORM

3. TEST CODE

4. REGISTRATION NUMBER

6. DATE OF BIRTH

Month	Day	Year
JAN		
FEB		
MAR		
APR		
MAY		
JUN		
JUL		
AUG		
SEP		
OCT		
NOV		
DEC		

7. SEX
MALE
FEMALE

The Princeton Review®
© TPR Education IP Holdings, LLC
FORM NO. 00001-PR

Practice Test 1   If a section has fewer questions than answer spaces, leave the extra answer spaces blank.

1. A B C D E
2. A B C D E
3. A B C D E
4. A B C D E
5. A B C D E
6. A B C D E
7. A B C D E
8. A B C D E
9. A B C D E
10. A B C D E
11. A B C D E
12. A B C D E
13. A B C D E
14. A B C D E
15. A B C D E

16. A B C D E
17. A B C D E
18. A B C D E
19. A B C D E
20. A B C D E
21. A B C D E
22. A B C D E
23. A B C D E
24. A B C D E
25. A B C D E
26. A B C D E
27. A B C D E
28. A B C D E
29. A B C D E
30. A B C D E

31. A B C D E
32. A B C D E
33. A B C D E
34. A B C D E
35. A B C D E
36. A B C D E
37. A B C D E
38. A B C D E
39. A B C D E
40. A B C D E
41. A B C D E
42. A B C D E
43. A B C D E
44. A B C D E
45. A B C D E

46. A B C D E
47. A B C D E
48. A B C D E
49. A B C D E
50. A B C D E
51. A B C D E
52. A B C D E
53. A B C D E
54. A B C D E
55. A B C D E

The Princeton Review®

Completely darken bubbles with a No. 2 pencil. If you make a mistake, be sure to erase mark completely. Erase all stray marks.

1. YOUR NAME:
(Print)   Last   First   M.I.

SIGNATURE: _____ DATE: _____ / _____ / _____

HOME ADDRESS: _____
(Print)   Number and Street

_____
City   State   Zip Code

PHONE NO. : _____
(Print)

5. YOUR NAME

First 4 letters of last name				FIRST INIT	MID INIT
A	A	A	A	A	A
B	B	B	B	B	B
C	C	C	C	C	C
D	D	D	D	D	D
E	E	E	E	E	E
F	F	F	F	F	F
G	G	G	G	G	G
H	H	H	H	H	H
I	I	I	I	I	I
J	J	J	J	J	J
K	K	K	K	K	K
L	L	L	L	L	L
M	M	M	M	M	M
N	N	N	N	N	N
O	O	O	O	O	O
P	P	P	P	P	P
Q	Q	Q	Q	Q	Q
R	R	R	R	R	R
S	S	S	S	S	S
T	T	T	T	T	T
U	U	U	U	U	U
V	V	V	V	V	V
W	W	W	W	W	W
X	X	X	X	X	X
Y	Y	Y	Y	Y	Y
Z	Z	Z	Z	Z	Z

IMPORTANT: Please fill in these boxes exactly as shown on the back cover of your test book.

2. TEST FORM

3. TEST CODE

4. REGISTRATION NUMBER

6. DATE OF BIRTH

Month	Day	Year
JAN		
FEB		
MAR	0	0 0 0 0
APR	1	1 1 1 1
MAY	2	2 2 2 2
JUN	3	3 3 3 3
JUL	4	4 4 4
AUG	5	5 5 5
SEP	6	6 6 6
OCT	7	7 7 7
NOV	8	8 8 8
DEC	9	9 9 9

7. SEX
- MALE
- FEMALE

The Princeton Review®
© TPR Education IP Holdings, LLC
FORM NO. 00001-PR

Practice Test 2
If a section has fewer questions than answer spaces, leave the extra answer spaces blank.

1. A B C D E
2. A B C D E
3. A B C D E
4. A B C D E
5. A B C D E
6. A B C D E
7. A B C D E
8. A B C D E
9. A B C D E
10. A B C D E
11. A B C D E
12. A B C D E
13. A B C D E
14. A B C D E
15. A B C D E

16. A B C D E
17. A B C D E
18. A B C D E
19. A B C D E
20. A B C D E
21. A B C D E
22. A B C D E
23. A B C D E
24. A B C D E
25. A B C D E
26. A B C D E
27. A B C D E
28. A B C D E
29. A B C D E
30. A B C D E

31. A B C D E
32. A B C D E
33. A B C D E
34. A B C D E
35. A B C D E
36. A B C D E
37. A B C D E
38. A B C D E
39. A B C D E
40. A B C D E
41. A B C D E
42. A B C D E
43. A B C D E
44. A B C D E
45. A B C D E

46. A B C D E
47. A B C D E
48. A B C D E
49. A B C D E
50. A B C D E
51. A B C D E
52. A B C D E
53. A B C D E
54. A B C D E
55. A B C D E

Completely darken bubbles with a No. 2 pencil. If you make a mistake, be sure to erase mark completely. Erase all stray marks.

The Princeton Review®

1. YOUR NAME:
(Print)　　　　Last　　　　First　　　　M.I.

SIGNATURE: 　　　　　　　DATE: ____ / ____ / ____

HOME ADDRESS:
(Print)　　　　Number and Street

　　　　City　　　　State　　　　Zip Code

PHONE NO. :
(Print)

IMPORTANT: Please fill in these boxes exactly as shown on the back cover of your test book.

2. TEST FORM

6. DATE OF BIRTH

Month	Day		Year	
○ JAN				
○ FEB				
○ MAR	⓪	⓪	⓪	⓪
○ APR	①	①	①	①
○ MAY	②	②	②	②
○ JUN	③	③	③	③
○ JUL	④	④		④
○ AUG		⑤		⑤
○ SEP		⑥		⑥
○ OCT		⑦		⑦
○ NOV		⑧		⑧
○ DEC		⑨		⑨

3. TEST CODE

4. REGISTRATION NUMBER

7. SEX
○ MALE
○ FEMALE

The Princeton Review®
© TPR Education IP Holdings, LLC
FORM NO. 00001-PR

5. YOUR NAME

First 4 letters of last name				FIRST INIT	MID INIT

Practice Test 3　If a section has fewer questions than answer spaces, leave the extra answer spaces blank.

1. Ⓐ Ⓑ Ⓒ Ⓓ Ⓔ
2. Ⓐ Ⓑ Ⓒ Ⓓ Ⓔ
3. Ⓐ Ⓑ Ⓒ Ⓓ Ⓔ
4. Ⓐ Ⓑ Ⓒ Ⓓ Ⓔ
5. Ⓐ Ⓑ Ⓒ Ⓓ Ⓔ
6. Ⓐ Ⓑ Ⓒ Ⓓ Ⓔ
7. Ⓐ Ⓑ Ⓒ Ⓓ Ⓔ
8. Ⓐ Ⓑ Ⓒ Ⓓ Ⓔ
9. Ⓐ Ⓑ Ⓒ Ⓓ Ⓔ
10. Ⓐ Ⓑ Ⓒ Ⓓ Ⓔ
11. Ⓐ Ⓑ Ⓒ Ⓓ Ⓔ
12. Ⓐ Ⓑ Ⓒ Ⓓ Ⓔ
13. Ⓐ Ⓑ Ⓒ Ⓓ Ⓔ
14. Ⓐ Ⓑ Ⓒ Ⓓ Ⓔ
15. Ⓐ Ⓑ Ⓒ Ⓓ Ⓔ

16. Ⓐ Ⓑ Ⓒ Ⓓ Ⓔ
17. Ⓐ Ⓑ Ⓒ Ⓓ Ⓔ
18. Ⓐ Ⓑ Ⓒ Ⓓ Ⓔ
19. Ⓐ Ⓑ Ⓒ Ⓓ Ⓔ
20. Ⓐ Ⓑ Ⓒ Ⓓ Ⓔ
21. Ⓐ Ⓑ Ⓒ Ⓓ Ⓔ
22. Ⓐ Ⓑ Ⓒ Ⓓ Ⓔ
23. Ⓐ Ⓑ Ⓒ Ⓓ Ⓔ
24. Ⓐ Ⓑ Ⓒ Ⓓ Ⓔ
25. Ⓐ Ⓑ Ⓒ Ⓓ Ⓔ
26. Ⓐ Ⓑ Ⓒ Ⓓ Ⓔ
27. Ⓐ Ⓑ Ⓒ Ⓓ Ⓔ
28. Ⓐ Ⓑ Ⓒ Ⓓ Ⓔ
29. Ⓐ Ⓑ Ⓒ Ⓓ Ⓔ
30. Ⓐ Ⓑ Ⓒ Ⓓ Ⓔ

31. Ⓐ Ⓑ Ⓒ Ⓓ Ⓔ
32. Ⓐ Ⓑ Ⓒ Ⓓ Ⓔ
33. Ⓐ Ⓑ Ⓒ Ⓓ Ⓔ
34. Ⓐ Ⓑ Ⓒ Ⓓ Ⓔ
35. Ⓐ Ⓑ Ⓒ Ⓓ Ⓔ
36. Ⓐ Ⓑ Ⓒ Ⓓ Ⓔ
37. Ⓐ Ⓑ Ⓒ Ⓓ Ⓔ
38. Ⓐ Ⓑ Ⓒ Ⓓ Ⓔ
39. Ⓐ Ⓑ Ⓒ Ⓓ Ⓔ
40. Ⓐ Ⓑ Ⓒ Ⓓ Ⓔ
41. Ⓐ Ⓑ Ⓒ Ⓓ Ⓔ
42. Ⓐ Ⓑ Ⓒ Ⓓ Ⓔ
43. Ⓐ Ⓑ Ⓒ Ⓓ Ⓔ
44. Ⓐ Ⓑ Ⓒ Ⓓ Ⓔ
45. Ⓐ Ⓑ Ⓒ Ⓓ Ⓔ

46. Ⓐ Ⓑ Ⓒ Ⓓ Ⓔ
47. Ⓐ Ⓑ Ⓒ Ⓓ Ⓔ
48. Ⓐ Ⓑ Ⓒ Ⓓ Ⓔ
49. Ⓐ Ⓑ Ⓒ Ⓓ Ⓔ
50. Ⓐ Ⓑ Ⓒ Ⓓ Ⓔ
51. Ⓐ Ⓑ Ⓒ Ⓓ Ⓔ
52. Ⓐ Ⓑ Ⓒ Ⓓ Ⓔ
53. Ⓐ Ⓑ Ⓒ Ⓓ Ⓔ
54. Ⓐ Ⓑ Ⓒ Ⓓ Ⓔ
55. Ⓐ Ⓑ Ⓒ Ⓓ Ⓔ

The Princeton Review®

Completely darken bubbles with a No. 2 pencil. If you make a mistake, be sure to erase mark completely. Erase all stray marks.

1. YOUR NAME:
(Print)   Last   First   M.I.

SIGNATURE: _____ DATE: ___/___/___

HOME ADDRESS: _____
(Print)   Number and Street

City   State   Zip Code

PHONE NO. : _____
(Print)

5. YOUR NAME

First 4 letters of last name				FIRST INIT	MID INIT
A	A	A	A	A	A
B	B	B	B	B	B
C	C	C	C	C	C
D	D	D	D	D	D
E	E	E	E	E	E
F	F	F	F	F	F
G	G	G	G	G	G
H	H	H	H	H	H
I	I	I	I	I	I
J	J	J	J	J	J
K	K	K	K	K	K
L	L	L	L	L	L
M	M	M	M	M	M
N	N	N	N	N	N
O	O	O	O	O	O
P	P	P	P	P	P
Q	Q	Q	Q	Q	Q
R	R	R	R	R	R
S	S	S	S	S	S
T	T	T	T	T	T
U	U	U	U	U	U
V	V	V	V	V	V
W	W	W	W	W	W
X	X	X	X	X	X
Y	Y	Y	Y	Y	Y
Z	Z	Z	Z	Z	Z

IMPORTANT: Please fill in these boxes exactly as shown on the back cover of your test book.

2. TEST FORM

3. TEST CODE

0	A	0	0	0	0	0	0	0	0	0	0
1	B	1	1	1	1	1	1	1	1	1	1
2	C	2	2	2	2	2	2	2	2	2	2
3	D	3	3	3	3	3	3	3	3	3	3
4	E	4	4	4	4	4	4	4	4	4	4
5	F	5	5	5	5	5	5	5	5	5	5
6	G	6	6	6	6	6	6	6	6	6	6
7		7	7	7	7	7	7	7	7	7	7
8		8	8	8	8	8	8	8	8	8	8
9		9	9	9	9	9	9	9	9	9	9

4. REGISTRATION NUMBER

6. DATE OF BIRTH

Month	Day		Year	
JAN				
FEB				
MAR	0	0	0	0
APR	1	1	1	1
MAY	2	2	2	2
JUN	3	3	3	3
JUL		4	4	4
AUG		5	5	5
SEP		6	6	6
OCT		7	7	7
NOV		8	8	8
DEC		9	9	9

7. SEX
MALE
FEMALE

The Princeton Review®

© TPR Education IP Holdings, LLC
FORM NO. 00001-PR

Practice Test 4
If a section has fewer questions than answer spaces, leave the extra answer spaces blank.

1. A B C D E
2. A B C D E
3. A B C D E
4. A B C D E
5. A B C D E
6. A B C D E
7. A B C D E
8. A B C D E
9. A B C D E
10. A B C D E
11. A B C D E
12. A B C D E
13. A B C D E
14. A B C D E
15. A B C D E

16. A B C D E
17. A B C D E
18. A B C D E
19. A B C D E
20. A B C D E
21. A B C D E
22. A B C D E
23. A B C D E
24. A B C D E
25. A B C D E
26. A B C D E
27. A B C D E
28. A B C D E
29. A B C D E
30. A B C D E

31. A B C D E
32. A B C D E
33. A B C D E
34. A B C D E
35. A B C D E
36. A B C D E
37. A B C D E
38. A B C D E
39. A B C D E
40. A B C D E
41. A B C D E
42. A B C D E
43. A B C D E
44. A B C D E
45. A B C D E

46. A B C D E
47. A B C D E
48. A B C D E
49. A B C D E
50. A B C D E
51. A B C D E
52. A B C D E
53. A B C D E
54. A B C D E
55. A B C D E

NOTES

TURN YOUR COLLEGE DREAMS INTO REALITY!

From acing tests to picking the perfect school, The Princeton Review has proven resources to help students like you navigate the college admissions process.

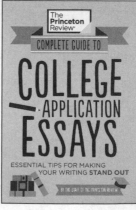

Visit PrincetonReviewBooks.com to browse all of our products!

1534c

The Princeton Review is not affiliated with Princeton University. Test names are the registered trademarks of their respective owners, who are not affiliated with The Princeton Review.